CALVIN COOLIDGE

and the Coolidge Era

CALVIN COOLIDGE

and the Coolidge Era

Essays on the History of the 1920s

Edited by John Earl Haynes

Published by the Library of Congress

WASHINGTON, D.C.

Distributed by University Press of New England

HANOVER AND LONDON

Published by the Library of Congress, Washington, D.C.

Distributed by University Press of New England, Hanover, NH 03755

Contents

Contents

Preface

JAMES H. BILLINGTON, Librarian of Congress

The historian John Braeman begins his essay in this volume with the comment that "the appearance in recent years of a large body of new scholarship on the 1920s makes timely a reassessment of the current state of our knowledge." This statement catches the chief purpose of the Library of Congress's 1995 symposium, "Calvin Coolidge and the Coolidge Era," and of this volume, which publishes essays first presented at that symposium. As the essays in this book show, the 1920s were years rich in cultural, social, and economic growth and change. Yet until recently, scholarship tended to neglect the era. While an impressive body of research has permitted us better to understand the complexities of that time, a simpler, shallow image of that era has lingered in many texts.

The essayists in this volume are not of one mind; readers will notice a number of well-argued disagreements; and many areas and issues are not addressed here. But the range of coverage is impressive—complex reconsiderations of income statistics, the rise and import of motion pictures, the interaction of new immigrant populations with established American society, the dilemmas women faced in the political arena once they gained the vote, American policymakers dealing with world power in the wake of World War I, and, of course, Calvin Coolidge himself, that unusual personality who held the presidency during most of that era and has too often been a subject of caricature rather than serious study. Both scholars and general readers stand to gain a fuller picture of America in this still too-little-understood decade.

The Library of Congress is glad to have brought these scholars together and expresses its gratitude to Mr. Laurance S. Rockefeller and his late wife, Mary. Their generosity and infectious interest made both the conference and this volume possible.

Introduction

JOHN EARL HAYNES

When plans for a Library of Congress symposium on Calvin Coolidge and the Coolidge era reached my desk, I could not but reflect on my views of President Coolidge and the 1920s. I remember well as a graduate student in history chuckling at the witty ridicule depicting Coolidge as a simple-minded fool in books that were required reading in my graduate seminars. Many were from writers who sketched Coolidge as a blind follower of an intellectually bankrupt ideology of laissez-faire, portraying him as one who led, or, rather, by his lack of leadership, allowed the nation to drift into a false prosperity, a sort of decadent and greedy debauch that inevitably resulted in the catastrophe of the Great Depression.

It took several decades, but my understanding of both Coolidge and the 1920s changed. The Manuscript Division of the Library of Congress maintains Coolidge's presidential papers, and some years ago I had occasion to examine file #111 in the collection.[1] This file dealt with thirty-one federal prisoners who had been convicted under wartime statutes covering crimes based on interference with the war-effort in 1917 and 1918. By 1923, most persons convicted for such crimes had served their sentences or been released early by amnesties proclaimed by President Harding. Most of those who remained were members of the Industrial Workers of the World (IWW), an anarcho-syndicalist labor union that advocated resistance to military conscription, industrial sabotage, and the eventual overthrow of the government through a general strike.

File #111 contains letters from clergymen and civil liberties groups urging full pardons on free-speech grounds for those still imprisoned, arguing that they had been convicted for their beliefs rather than for overt acts. The file also contains a letter from Senator William Borah (Republican, Idaho) urging that the prisoners be pardoned on the grounds that their trials had been legally flawed. A statement by U.S. Judge Frank Rudkin, who had presided at some of the IWW trials, took a similar position. He felt that decisions later reached by U.S. appeals courts rendered the convictions of these prisoners on several counts inappropriate and that on those counts where conviction could still be sustained, the prisoners had served sufficient time.

Present as well were letters from those hostile to releasing the IWW militants. The presiding judge in Los Angeles' Superior Court advised Coolidge that releasing the prisoners would make enforcement of the prohibition law difficult because the crimes of the IWW prisoners made violations of the Volstead Act seem trivial. Letters and statements from the American Legion, the Sons of the American Revolution, and a variety of individuals also opposed amnesty.

Coolidge appointed a committee to advise him on the matter: Newton D. Baker (President Wilson's secretary of war), Episcopal Bishop Charles H. Brent (former chief of chaplains for the American Expeditionary Force), and General James G. Harbord (former chief of staff of the AEF). The committee recommended that the prisoners be released but not pardoned; Coolidge then commuted the sentences of all thirty-one to the time already served and released them.

What is striking about the file is that it provides ample information about what various people thought and advised Coolidge to do, and it documents what Coolidge did, but there is nothing that tells one *why* Coolidge decided to commute the sentences. Did he think the prisoners improperly convicted as did Senator Borah and various civil liberties groups? Did he regard it as an act of charity for misguided and essentially harmless men who had been punished enough as did Bishop Brent? Did he think it was time to put the controversies of the war behind as did Newton Baker? In the file, a copy of the White House announcement of Coolidge's commutation order only announces the decision and is devoid of explanation.

File #111 is typical of many of those in the Coolidge papers and of much of Coolidge's correspondence. Edward Clark, Coolidge's presidential secretary, later wrote to a colleague about Coolidge's correspondence files. He noted that "Mr. Coolidge did not follow the practice of other Presidents in trying to explain his administration through letters to friends." Clark contrasted this with President Hoover, for whom Clark also worked. "Mr. Hoover, for instance, has tried to dictate a memorandum after every important conference giving his recollection of the event and I have no doubt that he also followed Wilson's practice in embodying the same history information in letters. Mr. Coolidge, however, strictly avoided this and the file, therefore consisted of the huge number of letters to him which might be of interest but with replies which reveal little or nothing."[2]

Coolidge, I came to realize, was not silent because he was inarticulate or had nothing to say. Rather, Coolidge believed that a person, particularly someone exercising governmental power, should be judged by their acts and the consequences of their acts. He did not much care for those who thought intentions more important than consequences; in his view, focusing on motives was a sort of moral evasion of responsibility for one's acts. Few people, and particularly few politicians, ever own up to ill intentions and most can come up with well-intentioned reasons for doing whatever they did. In this century when we have seen tens of millions of humans shot, starved, impoverished, and imprisoned in the name of ideologies and by persons that evade responsibility for the disastrous consequences of their acts by citing humanitarian intentions, Coolidge's focus on effects rather than motives has much to recommend it.

Not only did my view of Coolidge change, my view of the 1920s shifted as well. The prosperity of the 1920s had its problems, but falsity was not one of them. Paul Johnson, in the keynote address to the symposium, included in this volume under the title "Calvin Coolidge and the Last Arcadia," remarked that "Coolidge Prosperity was huge, real, widespread though not ubiquitous, and unprecedented. It was not permanent—what prosperity ever is? But it is foolish and unhistorical to judge it unsubstantial because of what we now know followed later. At the time it was as solid as houses built, meals eaten, automobiles driven, cash spent and property acquired. Prosperity was more widely distributed in the America of the 1920s than had been possible in any community of this size before, and it involved the acquisition, by tens of millions of ordinary families, of the elements of economic security which had hitherto been denied them throughout the whole of history."

The astounding growth of the American economy in the 1920s along with the development of structural weaknesses are well surveyed in Michael Bernstein's essay, "The American Economy of the Interwar Era: Growth and Transformation from the Great War to the Great Depression." Economist Gene Smiley's essay, "New Estimates of Income Shares During the 1920s," addresses a topic that may seem of interest chiefly to those of an econometric bent. And, indeed, only skilled economists are likely to follow the mathematics Smiley used to derive his data. The issue, however, is data that premises many judgments about the 1920s by non-economists. To simplify a complex matter, the data relied on by most scholars held that economic growth in the 1920s was badly skewed, with a narrow elite not only absorbing the increase in national income, but in real terms the income of the bulk of the population actually fell. Smiley argues that this data was flawed by a technical error. And when the data is reestimated with the error removed, it shows that while relative inequality increased in the 1920s, in real terms both upper- and low-income groups gained.

Three essays directly address the tremendous cultural changes in America in the 1920s. Lynn Dumenil's "Re-Shifting Perspectives on the 1920s: Recent Trends in Social and Cultural History" evaluates the remarkable volume of scholarly studies in recent years that examine the extraordinary changes during that era in American attitudes and practices toward gender relationships, racial attitudes, youth culture, ethnicity, and sexual ethics. Ronald Edsforth's essay, "Made in the U.S.A.: Mass Culture and the Americanization of Working-Class Ethnics in the Coolidge Era" focuses on one aspect of the era's social history with an examination of the complex inter-action of the newly emerging consumer culture with the ethnic identities of first and second generation immigrant workers. Daniel Leab's essay, "Coolidge, Hays, and 1920s Movies: Some Aspects of Image and Reality," discusses the motion picture industry that established its central role in the emerging mass-consumption culture in the 1920s. Along the way, he also gives an unexpected view of Calvin Coolidge himself, a man he judges to be one of the first modern politicians to achieve an "understanding and intelli-gent use of the mass media."

Among the other misleading images of the 1920s that have come down is that of the era as one of isolationism. Warren Cohen's survey, "America and the World in the 1920s," takes the issue on directly and concludes that "indeed the era marked the greatest peacetime involvement in world affairs in American history." While Cohen looks broadly at America's place in world affairs, Stephen Schuker's "American Foreign Policy: The European Dimension, 1921–1929" focuses on what still remained the central concern of American foreign policy. As Schuker shows, the United States was a cen-tral player in the process of Europe's economic recovery from World War I, a recovery that involved the complex issue of war debts and reparations.

As is only appropriate for a symposium entitled "Calvin Coolidge and the Coolidge Era," two of the essays concentrate on Coolidge the man and the politician. Robert Ferrell in his "Calvin Coolidge, the Man and the President" writes that "the Coolidge personality, let us face it, was not easy." Indeed, it is not easy to understand this very shy and laconic man who nonetheless was a popular president and who won reelection with an impressive majority in 1924. Ferrell gives a striking portrait of this "Dick-ensian character." George Nash offers another way of looking at Coolidge in his "The 'Great Enigma' and the 'Great Engineer': The Political Rela-tionship of Calvin Coolidge and Herbert Hoover." The two served to-gether in the government for eight years and, of course, Hoover succeeded Coolidge as president. Yet their personalities and their style of politics and government were not merely different but even clashed. Nash presents the convoluted Coolidge-Hoover relationship as one in which we can see in "microcosm some of the political fault lines of a decade far more intriguing than is usually perceived."

Elisabeth Perry's essay also deals with a political topic that has long been a bit of a puzzle. The campaign for votes for women was one of the most successful reform movements of the early twentieth century. Advocates for votes for women can be found voicing their cause, with limited success, for decades before 1900. But this movement gathered power and strength early in the century and overwhelmed resistance to carry the day in 1920. Yet once women had the vote, the clarity and focus that had characterized the suffrage movement gave way to a path, as Perry puts it, "strewn with perilous traps and agonizing choices." In " 'Now At Last We Can Begin!': The Impact of Woman Suffrage in New York," Perry offers a case study of the pitfalls and dilemmas that awaited women once the vote was theirs.

The view of the 1920s as a simple and shallow era with an easily under-stood history faces a stern attack in John Braeman's "The American Polity in the Age of Normalcy: A Reappraisal." This most formidable biblio-graphic essay surveys and evaluates the impressive accumulation of schol-arly research on political, governmental, economic, and organizational as-pects of the 1920s era. As he concludes, "the picture that emerges is in sharp contrast with the dominant image that has so long prevailed of a decade of stagnation, even reaction. On the contrary, the 1920s was a time when Americans and their leaders grappled with the problems of managing an ever-more complex and pluralist socio-economic order. To many, the transformation of the United States into a modern urban-industrial nation was a shock and threat; for others, a challenge and opportunity. The ten-sion between those conflicting impulses was responsible for the mixed, oft-times contradictory, responses that gave the era its distinctive character." While Braeman concentrates his attention on issues linked to the role of the state, Lynn Dumenil's bibliographic study looks at social history. (Any student of history seeking a comprehensive bibliographic guide to the 1920s would be well advised to consult the Braeman and Dumenil essays.) Her perspective differs markedly from Braeman's, but her conclusion is not dissimilar when she writes that "the decade embodies so much of what was making America modern: the growth of cities and the tensions implicit in their racial and ethnic pluralism; the social and cultural meanings of chang-ing roles for women; the significance of mass media in helping to construct a consumer culture; the implications of increasing corporate power; and the ramifications of transformations in the workplace."

As several of the contributors to this volume have noted, for many years mainstream historical understanding of the 1920s has tended to understate the tremendous economic, technological, and cultural dynamism of this decade; leaving the 1920s in the shadows as attention has been focused ei-ther earlier on the calamity of World War I or later on the travail of the Great Depression of the 1930s. There is, of course, some artifice in the habit of thinking of history in distinctive periods, particularly in the prac-tice of allowing our base-ten numbering system to frame a view of history moving in convenient decades. And the Coolidge era was not, strictly speaking, coterminous with the 1920s. Yet World War I and the Great De-pression do provide real, not artificial, boundaries to this era which, by its end, had witnessed the transformation of American culture and come to look and feel "modern" in a way familiar to contemporary Americans. To be sure, there is not some discrete turning point in time to which one can point. The America that looked and felt like the nineteenth century seamlessly blended into the modern. But while one cannot pinpoint the seam, that the crossover from the old to the new took place in the 1920s is manifest.

The Library of Congress's symposium on Calvin Coolidge and the Coolidge era brought together an impressive array of scholars: established veterans and bright new stars, broad synthesizers and dedicated archival researchers. The essays included in this volume were improved from those presented at the conference as their authors adjusted their text to take into account the comments, suggestions, criticisms, and additions made by the commentators and chairs of the panels at which the papers were originally presented. Many of the commentators' remarks were in themselves worthy of publication. It is therefore most regrettable that the practicalities of publishing precluded using the entire proceedings of the conference; none of the commentaries and not all of the papers could be included. Therefore, I would like to note with special thanks the contributions to the conference and to scholarship made by the other members of the scholastic panels:

KATHLEEN M. BLEE, director, Women's Studies Program, University of Pittsburgh, and author of *Women of the Klan: Racism and Gender in the 1920s* (1991) and *No Middle Ground: Women and Radical Protest* (1997).

THOMAS H. BUCKLEY, professor of history at the University of Tulsa and author of *The United States and the Washington Conference, 1921–1922* (1970) and *American Foreign and National Security Policies, 1914–1945* (1987, with Edwin B. Strong).

PAULA S. FASS, professor of history at the University of California at Berkeley and author of *The Damned and the Beautiful: American Youth in the 1920s* (1977), *Outside In: Minorities and the Transformation of American Education* (1989), and *Kidnapped: Child Abduction in America* (1997).

BURTON FOLSOM, Senior Fellow at the Mackinac Center for Public Policy in Michigan, editor of *Continuity: A Journal of History*, and author of *Urban Capitalists: Entrepreneurs and City Growth in Pennsylvania's Lackawana and Lehigh Regions* (1981) and *The Myth of the Robber Barons* (1991).

MICHAEL J. HOGAN, professor of history at Ohio State University, editor of *Diplomatic History* and author or editor of *Informal Entente: The Private Structure of Cooperation in Anglo-American Economic Diplomacy, 1918–1928* (1977), *The Marshall Plan: America, Britain, and the Reconstruction of Western Europe, 1947–1952* (1987), *Explaining the History of American Foreign Relations* (1991, with Thomas Paterson), *The End of the Cold War: Its Meaning and Implications* (1992), *America in the World: The Historiography of American Foreign Policy since 1941* (1995), and *Hiroshima in History and Memory* (1996).

JOHN KAROL, of Apertura, a firm producing documentary films for foundations and nonprofit organizations, is preparing a major film of the life of Calvin Coolidge.

NANCY MACLEAN, associate professor of history at Northwestern University, and author of *Behind the Mask of Chivalry: The Making of the Second Ku Klux Klan* (1994).

LARY MAY, associate professor of American studies and history at the University of Minnesota and author of *Screening Out the Past: The Birth of Mass Culture and the Motion Picture Industry* (1980) and *Recasting America: Culture and Politics in the Age of Cold War* (1989).

LEONARD J. MOORE, associate professor of history at McGill University in Montreal and author of *Citizen Klansmen: The Ku Klux Klan in Indiana, 1921–1928* (1991).

MICHAEL PARRISH, professor of history at the University of California, San Diego, and author of *Anxious Decades: America in Prosperity and Depression, 1920–1941* (1992), *Felix Frankfurter and His Times* (1982), *Securities Regulation and the New Deal* (1970), and *Power and Responsibility: Leadership in Modern America* (1986).

MICHAEL PLATT, author of *Rome and Romans According to Shakespeare* (1976), "Calvin Coolidge's Teacher, Throughout Life, Charles Garman of Amherst" (*Continuity*, 1994), and "The Life of Calvin Coolidge" (*Modern Age*, 1994).

THOMAS SILVER, chief deputy to Michael D. Antonovich of the Board of Supervisors of the County of Los Angeles, author of *Coolidge and the Historians* (1982) and editor of *Natural Right and Political Right: Essays in Honor of Harry V. Jaffa* (1984).

PETER TEMIN, Elisha Gray II Professor of Economics at the Massachusetts Institute of Technology and author of *Did Monetary Forces Cause the Great Depression?* (1976), *Lessons from the Great Depression* (1989), *Taking Your Medicine: Drug Regulation in the United States* (1980), *The Fall of the Bell System: A Study in Prices and Politics* (1987, with Louis Galambos).

ROBERT ZIEGER, professor of history at the University of Florida and author or editor of *The CIO: 1935–1955* (1995), *Republicans and Labor, 1919–1929* (1969), *Madison's Battery Workers, 1934–1952: A History of Federal Labor Union 19587* (1977), *Rebuilding the Pulp and Paper Workers' Union, 1933–1941* (1984), *American Workers, American Unions, 1920–1985* (1986), *Organized Labor in the Twentieth-Century South* (1991), and *John L. Lewis: Labor Leader* (1988).

Special thanks for the success of the symposium are also due to Carren Kaston, whose diligence and thoroughness as coordinator insured that the myriad details incident to a scholarly conference of this sort were accomplished.

Nor would the conference or this volume have been possible without the gift of Mr. Laurance S. Rockefeller and his late wife, Mary. We are deeply grateful for their generosity.

NOTES

1. Case file #111, box 111, Calvin Coolidge Papers, Manuscript Division, Library of Congress.

2. Edward Clark to Harry Ross, January 28, 1933, Edward Clark Papers, Manuscript Division, Library of Congress.

CALVIN COOLIDGE

and the Coolidge Era

1

Calvin Coolidge and the Last Arcadia

PAUL JOHNSON

When President Warren Harding died at the beginning of August 1923, his country, the United States, was by far the richest and most powerful in the world. To give only one example of its material and industrial supremacy: the four leading European car producers produced only 11 percent of the cars manufactured in the United States, where five out of every six cars registered all over the earth were to be found. Yet America was still in many ways an old-fashioned and unsophisticated country, true to its rural, earnest, and libertarian origins.

In those days there were still nearly two hundred working farms within the city limits of Washington, D.C., the nation's capital. When Harding campaigned for the presidency in 1920, he did not exactly "run" in the American sense, or "stand" in the British sense, he sat—on his front porch in Marion, Ohio. He stuck old President McKinley's flagpole in front of his house and invited the people to come and see him under it, ask questions, tell him their views, and hear what he had to say in reply. Over six hundred thousand people took advantage of his invitation. They included famous showbiz folk such as Al Jolson, Ethel Barrymore, and Lillian Gish, and the popular novelist Pearl White, but most of them were just ordinary people, including many thousands of blacks, taking advantage of the fact that over eight million American families now owned a car.

Harding came from a lower-middle-class background and had risen by his own efforts to become a successful small-town American businessman. He bought a failing local newspaper, the *Marion Star*, and made it into a success. He also sat on the boards of the local bank, building society, lumber firm, and phone company. He believed, and he said so often, that politics were not very important. People should not get excited about them or allow them to penetrate too far into their everyday lives. He regarded America's participation in the Great War, and the discontinuities and disruption it had brought, as a huge aberration from the great stabilities of the life of the Republic, the last refuge—in a distracted world—of decency, Christian values and honest toil honestly rewarded. To him, America was a working Arcadia, protected by two great oceans and the benevolent oversight of almighty God, where the state stood back and allowed hard-working men and women to better themselves. His campaign message was simple: "America's present need," he said in May 1920, "is not heroics but healing, not nostrums but normalcy, not revolution but restoration . . . not surgery but serenity." In effect, he said, "Forget foreign affairs, reject politics and change, and concentrate on earning a decent living." The voters responded, giving him 60.2 percent of the total, the largest popular majority yet recorded—16,152,000 votes to 9,147,000—and enabling him to carry every state except the Solid South. Harding endeavored, in his own way, to carry out his self-imposed minimalist mandate as president. He did nothing on the economic front except reduce the budget by a massive 40 percent of genuine savings. He allowed the postwar slump to cure itself, as by July 1921 it had. He released virtually all the political extremists who had been jailed by President Wilson's ferocious attorney general Mitchell Palmer. On Sundays in Washington, he attended church, then took a slow horse-ride through the city, raising his hat when people saluted him in the streets. He was not above answering the White House front door in person. He chewed tobacco, a curious American habit which British visitors from Mrs. Trollope and Dickens onward found mighty offensive but which was viewed by many American males as a symptom of social health. As the inventor Thomas Edison, then the greatest living American, put it: "Harding is all right—any man who chews tobacco is all right."

Unfortunately, some of Harding's friends, as he ruefully came to admit himself, were not all right. This is not the time to demolish the misleading historiography of the Harding presidency, which presents him as the front man of a long-term master conspiracy to loot America, conducted by the Ohio Gang. On the whole, the evidence we now have, especially of the Harding Papers, shows him not as corrupt or dishonest but as gullible. In general he was a shrewd and honorable president, but he trusted too much. The man he trusted most was Albert Fall, senator for New Mexico, whom he made secretary of the interior. Fall received a bribe of $400,000 for granting favorable oil leases in California and at Teapot Dome in Wyoming, and he eventually went to jail for a year. But it is worth pointing out that Harding was not the only one to be duped by Fall. When he appeared after his nomination before the Senate, he was confirmed by immediate acclamation, the only time in American history, I think, that a cabinet member has been accorded such a vote of confidence.

However, Harding's administration was besmirched by scandal, and he died before he could deal with it or defend his own record or put his case to the American people. His memory may well be one of those historical lost causes it is useless to expend precious time and energy on resurrecting. However that may be, though Harding died, the American Arcadia continued and in some ways intensified. His successor, Vice President Calvin Coolidge, came not from a small town of the old Midwest but from rustic Vermont, a district even more closely associated with the pristine values of the American utopia. Vermont was the only New England state without a coastline and therefore largely untouched by the moral infiltration of commerce. It was the first state to join the original thirteen, in 1791, and it was by no means unprogressive; in fact its state constitution was the first to abolish slavery and provide for universal manhood suffrage. But it was, and is, rural conservative. In Coolidge's day it lived chiefly by dairy farming, and he was brought up on a farm near the little town of Plymouth which his father, Colonel Coolidge of the Vermont state militia, worked himself. Indeed, when Vice President Coolidge was summoned to the White House in August 1923, he was at his father's farm, spending two weeks of his vacation helping to get in the hay, swinging a scythe, handling a pitchfork, and driving a two-horse hitch. This was not done for a photo opportunity either, for no photos were taken. Coolidge never had a press secretary in his life. He would not have dreamt of calling a newspaperman by his first name, as Harding constantly did, and no reporter, as far as I know, was ever welcomed at the Coolidge farm until after the presidency descended on him.

The scene when the news penetrated to Plymouth, Vermont, during the night of 2 August 1923, that Harding was dead and that the local boy, Coolidge, was now the thirtieth president, is worth recalling. The only communication between the outside world and the Coolidge family farm was by hilly track and post. There was no phone at the farm, the nearest being two miles away down the hill. The Coolidge family was awakened a few minutes after midnight by a post office messenger pounding on the door. He had two telegrams. One from Harding's secretary was the official notification of the president's death, another from the attorney general advised Coolidge to qualify for the presidency immediately by taking the oath. So the oath was copied out, and Coolidge's father, being a notary public, administered it by the light of a kerosene lamp, for there was no electricity at the house. It was just a tiny farmhouse sitting room, with an airtight wood stove, an old-fashioned walnut desk, a few chairs, and a marble-topped table on which stood the old family Bible, open. As he read the last words of the oath, the younger Coolidge placed his hand on the book and said, with great solemnity, "So help me God."

Coolidge was not all that remote from our times. He was born in July 1872, a few weeks after Bertrand Russell, whom I used to know well. The Brooklyn Bridge was opened the same month, and that summer Verdi's

Aida was the hit opera and George Eliot's *Middlemarch* was the most talked-about novel. Coolidge saw himself as go-ahead in his own way. He liked to quote Sydney Smith: "It is a grand thing for a man to find his own line and keep to it—you go so much faster on your own rail." He declined to follow his father into farming and chose his own line of law and public service—nor did he seek a partnership in an established firm but put out his own sign in Northampton, Massachusetts, at the age of twenty-five, "Calvin Coolidge, Attorney and Counsellor-at-Law." Two years later he took his first step on the political ladder, as a Republican city councilman, followed by election as city solicitor, two terms in the state legislature, a spell as mayor of Northampton, followed by service in the state senate as president, and then as lieutenant governor and governor.

Like his predecessor Harding, only more systematically and of set purpose and belief, Coolidge was a minimalist politician. He thought the essence of the Republic was not so much democracy itself as the rule of law, and that the prime function of government was to enforce it. Of course government had an enabling function, too. As a city administrator, he took steps to enable local farmers to provide citizens with an adequate supply of fresh milk at competitive prices. He took enormous trouble in supervising railroad bills to enable the companies to provide reliable and cheap public transport in Massachusetts. He was a wizard at both city and state finance, paying off debt, accumulating surpluses, and so, as a result, raising the salaries of state teachers and attracting the best. Examination of his record in Massachusetts both as legislator and as governor shows in detail that he was not a "property-is-always-right" man. Quite the contrary. He loathed the pressure-group and lobby system of powerful property interests. He was a "the-law-is-always-right" man. As governor he made an important statement of the freedom of the elected individual to ignore bullying by the interests and the media. He said, "We have too much legislating by clamor, by tumult, by pressure. Representative government ceases when outside influence of any kind is substituted for the judgment of the representative." Voters have the right to vote, but a representative, having been voted into office, must use his judgment. "This does not mean that the opinion of constituents is to be ignored. It is to be weighed most carefully, for the representative must represent, but his oath provides that it must be 'faithfully and agreeably to the rules and regulations of the Constitution and laws.' Opinions and instructions do not outmatch the Constitution. Against it they are void." For a state like Massachusetts to pass a law providing for the manufacture of light beer and wines, the so-called Two-and-a-Half-Per-Cent Beer Bill, in defiance of federal prohibition, was an insult to law. He called it indeed "nullification," the unlawful course of the rebellious South, in defiance of the Constitution, and as governor he had no alternative but to veto. "The binding obligation of obedience [to the law] against personal desire," he said, was the essence of civilized, constitutional government, without which "all liberty, all security is at an end, and force alone will prevail." "Can those entrusted with the gravest authority," he continued, "set any example save that of the sternest obedience to law?"

An absolute adherence to the principle of the rule of law, and a meticulous attention to its details, distinguished Coolidge's successful handling of the 1919 Boston Police Strike, an event that brought him to the attention of the entire nation. Coolidge's conduct was marked by a willingness to take on any group in society, however powerful—in this case the American Federation of Labor—in defense of the law, by an insistence that the duly constituted authority—in this case the Boston Police Commissioner—be left to exercise his judgment and powers until such time as he publicly confessed that the situation was beyond his control, and then by an equal willingness to exercise the full constitutional powers of the governorship, including his rights as the commander in chief of the State Guard, which was called out in its entirety. The policy was minimalist until both the facts of the case and the state of public opinion demanded maximalist measures, which had been carefully and secretly prepared before and were then put into action immediately and in full. It was also backed by a well-formulated and easily grasped expression of political philosophy: "There is no right to strike against the public safety by anybody, anywhere, any time." Coolidge's handling of this dangerous strike, at a time when public order was under threat virtually all over the world, is a model for any chief executive to follow at either the state or federal level. It was evidently seen as such by both the political class and the whole nation at the time and prepared the way for Coolidge's nomination as vice presidential candidate the following year.

However, though propelled to national attention by the vigorous and unhesitating exercise of gubernatorial authority, Coolidge was anxious to reassure the nation that such state intervention was for extreme emergencies only and that in normal times minimal government must be the norm. In his acceptance speech, indeed, he spoke of "restoring the Lincoln principles" by insisting on "a government of the people, for the people and by the people." He made it absolutely clear what he meant by this: "The chief task which lies before us is to repossess the people of their government and their property."

Coolidge's minimalism was not just an expression of a political philosophy, though it was certainly that. As a prosperous nation with a largely self-regulating economy and protected by great natural defenses, America was in a position to follow the advice of Lord Salisbury, who had governed Britain when Coolidge was a young man—"The country is carried comfortably down the river by the current, and the function of government is merely to put out an oar when there is any danger of its drifting into the bank." That was the Coolidge philosophy, too, but it was more than a philosophy, it was a state of mind, almost a physical compulsion. Coolidge, like the great Queen Elizabeth I of England, was a supreme exponent of masterly inactivity. But he was also, unlike that queen, who could be talkative at times, a person who devoted much thought and a lifetime of experience to strategies of silence. He got this from his father, but whereas the Colonel was silent by instinct, Coolidge turned it into a political virtue. He rejoiced in his nickname, "Silent Cal"—it often saved him from taking steps or making statements that might prove counterproductive. A reputation for silence was itself a form of authority. As president of the state senate in 1914, he delivered the shortest inaugural on record. It is worth recalling. Here it is, in its entirety.

> Do the day's work. If it be to protect the rights of the weak, whoever objects, do it. If it be to help a powerful corporation better to serve the people, whatever the opposition, do that. Expect to be called a standpatter, but don't be a standpatter. Expect to be called demagogue, but don't be a demagogue. Don't hesitate to be as revolutionary as science. Don't hesitate to be as reactionary as the multiplication table. Don't expect to build up the weak by pulling down the strong. Don't hurry to legislate. Give administration a chance to catch up with legislation.

Good points, well noted. Reelected without opposition, he made his second inaugural even shorter—a mere four sentences.

> Conserve the firm foundations of our institutions. Do your work with the spirit of a soldier in the public service. Be loyal to the Commonwealth, and to yourselves. And be brief—above all things, be brief.

He practiced this brevity. Often he said nothing whatever. Campaigning in 1924, he noted: "I don't recall any candidate for president that ever injured himself very much by not talking." Or again: "The things I never say never get me into trouble." When he finally retired, he confessed that his most important rule "consists in never doing anything that someone else can do for you." He added: "Nine-tenths of a president's callers at the White House want something they ought not to have. If you keep dead still they will run out in three or four minutes." Coolidge was usually silent but slight twitches in his facial muscles spoke for him. He was described as "an eloquent listener."

Yet when he did speak, what he said was always worth hearing. It was direct, pithy, disillusioned, unromantic, and usually true. No one in the twentieth century defined more elegantly the limitations of government and the need for individual endeavor, which necessarily involves inequalities, to advance human happiness. Thus: "Government cannot relieve from toil. The normal must take care of themselves. Self-government means self-support. . . . Ultimately, property rights and personal rights are the same thing. . . . History reveals no civilized people among whom there was not a highly educated class and large aggregations of wealth. Large profits mean large payrolls. Inspiration has always come from above." It was essential, he argued, to judge political morality not by its intentions, but by its effects. Thus, in his 1925 Inaugural, the key sentence was "Economy is idealism in its more practical form." Later that year, in an address to the New York Chamber of Commerce, he produced a classic and lapidary statement of his laissez-faire philosophy. Government and business, he said, should remain independent and separate, one directed from Washington, the other from New York. Wise and prudent men should always prevent the mutual usurpations "which foolish men sought on either side. Business was the pursuit of gain but it also had a moral purpose: the mutual organized effort of society to minister to the economic requirement of civilization. . . . It rests squarely on the law of service. It has for its main reliance truth and faith and justice. In its larger sense it is one of the greatest contributing forces to the moral and spiritual advancement of the race." That was why government had a warrant to promote its success by providing the conditions of competition within a framework of security. The job of government and law was to suppress privilege wherever it manifested itself and uphold lawful possession by providing legal remedies for all wrongs: "The prime element in the value of all property is the knowledge that its peaceful enjoyment will be publicly defended." Without this legal and public defense, "the value of your tall buildings would shrink to the price of the waterfront of old Carthage or corner-lots in ancient Babylon." The more business regulated itself, he concluded, the less need there would be for government to act to ensure competition. It could therefore concentrate on its twin tasks of economy and of improving the national structure within which business could increase profits and investment, raise wages, and provide better goods and services at the lowest possible prices.

It was one of the characteristics of America as the Last Arcadia that its chief executive for much of the 1920s preached and practiced this public philosophy. Virtually everywhere else, the trend was toward the expansion of government, greater intervention, and more power to the center. Of those who came to power at the same time as Coolidge, all the most notable were dedicated to expanding the role of the state. Mussolini, supreme in Italy from 1922, put it bluntly: "Everything within the state, nothing outside the state, nothing against the state." Stalin, in power from 1923, began his great series of five-year plans for the entire country. The new nation-creators of the 1920s, Kemal Attaturk, president of Turkey from 1923, Chiang Kai-shek, ruler of China from 1925, Ibn Saud of Saudi Arabia

(1926), and Reza Shah of Persia (1925) all took government into corners of their countries it had never before penetrated. Even Poincaré of France and Baldwin of Britain were, by Coolidge's standards, rampant interventionists. Coolidge took the same view of his masterful cabinet colleague Herbert Hoover, who was by training a mechanical engineer and by political instinct a social engineer. Coolidge felt that Hoover was itching to get his hands on the levers of power at the White House so that he could set the state to work to hasten the millennium. He referred to Hoover with derision as "the Wonder Boy" and, after he had left office, said of his successor, "That man has offered me unsolicited advice for six years, all of it bad." It is possible, though I think it unlikely, that if Coolidge had known in advance that the interventionist Hoover was sure to take over the leadership of the Republican Party, he would have run for another term.

All that we can now say is that, on the facts, Coolidge's minimalism was justified by events. Coolidge prosperity was huge, real, widespread though not ubiquitous, and unprecedented. It was not permanent—what prosperity ever is? But it is foolish and unhistorical to judge it unsubstantial because of what we now know followed later. At the time it was as solid as houses built, meals eaten, automobiles driven, cash spent, and property acquired. Prosperity was more widely distributed in the America of the 1920s than had been possible in any community of this size before, and it involved the acquisition, by tens of millions of ordinary families, of the elements of economic security that had hitherto been denied them throughout the whole of history. The twenties were characterized by the longest housing boom recorded. As early as 1924, some 11 million families had acquired their own homes, and the process was only just beginning. Automobiles gave farmers and industrial workers a mobility never enjoyed before outside the affluent classes. For the first time, many millions of working people acquired assurance—life and industrial insurance passed the 100 million mark in the 1920s—savings, which quadrupled during the decade, and a stake in the economy. An analysis of those buying fifty or more shares in one of the biggest public utility stock issues of the 1920s shows that the largest groups were, in order: housekeepers, clerks, factory workers, merchants, chauffeurs and drivers, electricians, mechanics, and foremen. Coolidge prosperity showed that the concept of a property-owning democracy could be realized.

Nor was this new material advance essentially gross and philistine, as the popular historiography of the 1920s has it, "a drunken fiesta" to use Edmund Wilson's phrase, or as Scott Fitzgerald put it, "the greatest, gaudiest spree in history." Middle-class intellectuals are a little too inclined to resent poorer people acquiring for the first time material possessions and luxuries, of a kind they themselves have always taken for granted. Experience shows that in a democratic and self-improving society like the United States, when more money becomes available, the first priority for both local governments and for families is to spend it on more and better education. That is certainly what happened in the 1920s. Between 1910 and 1930, but especially in the second half of the period, total education spending in the United States rose fourfold, from $425.25 million to 2.3 billion. Spending on higher education rose fourfold too, to nearly a billion a year. Illiteracy fell 7.7 percent to 4.3 percent. The 1920s was the age of the Book of the Month Club and the Literary Guild, of booming publishing houses and bookshops, and especially a popular devotion to the classics. Throughout the 1920s, *David Copperfield* was rated "America's favorite novel," and those voted by Americans as "the ten greatest men in history" included Shakespeare, Longfellow, Dickens, and Tennyson.

It is hard to point to any aspect of culture in which the 1920s did not mark spectacular advances. By the end of it, there were over thirty thousand youth orchestras in the United States. In February 1924, when Coolidge first began campaigning for election in his own right, Gershwin's *Rhapsody in Blue* had its first performance by the Paul Whiteman band at the Aeolian Hall, and by the time he was elected in November, perhaps the greatest season in Broadway's history had opened. The season included Gershwin's *Lady, Be Good!*, the first mature American musical, and more than forty others by Irving Berlin, Jerome Kern and others, as well as Aaron Copland's First Symphony and the arrival of Serge Koussevitsky at the Boston Symphony Orchestra. In the theater, Eugene O'Neill, Thornton Wilder, Cole Porter, Richard Rodgers, Oscar Hammerstein, and Lorenz Hart were hard at work, and the novels of the period included Scott Fitzgerald's *This Side of Paradise* (1920), Sinclair Lewis's *Main Street* (1920), John Dos Passos's *Three Soldiers* (1921), Theodore Dreiser's *An American Tragedy* and William Faulkner's *Soldier's Pay* (1926), Upton Sinclair's *Boston* (1928), and, in 1929, Hemingway's *A Farewell to Arms* and Thomas Wolfe's *Look Homeward, Angel*. That is, by any standard, a brilliant decade. During the 1920s, in fact, America began suddenly to acquire a cultural density, or what Lionel Trilling called "a thickening of life," which it had never before possessed and whose absence Henry James had plaintively deplored a generation before. It was also learning, like more mature European societies, to cherish its past. It was during the 1920s that the national conservation movement really got under way and restored colonial Williamsburg, for example, while at the same time contemporary paintings were brought together in the new Museum of Modern Art, which opened in 1929. A sharp French observer, André Siegfried, following a hundred years later in the steps of De Tocqueville, produced an aperçu of the nation in 1927 whose message was presented by its title, *America Comes of Age*. The American people, he declared, "as a result of the revolutionary changes brought about by modern methods of production . . . are now creating on a vast scale an entirely original social structure."

This was the blossoming scene Calvin Coolidge chose to leave as abruptly as he had entered it. It was an aspect of his minimalist approach to life and office that he not only refrained from doing whatever was not strictly necessary but also believed it right to stop doing anything at all as soon as he felt he had performed his dutiful service. He was widely read in history, like Woodrow Wilson, but he was much more conscious than Wilson of Lord Acton's warning about the tendency of power to corrupt. He liked the idea of an America in which a man of ability and righteousness emerged from the backwoods to take his place as first citizen and chief executive of the Republic and then, his term of office completed, retired, if not exactly with relief, then with no regrets, to the backwoods again. In one sense Coolidge was a professional politician, in that he had ascended the ladder of office, step-by-step, for over thirty years. But he was sufficiently old-fashioned to find the concept of a professional political, making a career of office-seeking and hanging on to the bitter end, profoundly distasteful and demeaning. He had a strong, if unarticulated, sense of honor, and it was offended by the prospect that some people, even in his own party let alone outside it, might accuse him of "clinging" to power. He had a genuine respect for the American tradition of the maximum two-term presidency. That would not have been infringed, of course, by his offering himself a second time, but he had served two years of Harding's mandate, making six in all, and he felt that was enough. Coolidge was never exactly popular—he lacked both personal charm and the slightest desire to develop winning ways—but he was hugely respected. The Republican nomination was his for the asking, and he would have had no difficulty in carrying the country in 1928, probably with a greater plurality than Hoover. He was only fifty-six. But as he told Supreme Court Justice Harlan Stone, "It is a pretty good idea to get out when they still want you." As a historian, I have come to the conclusion that it is indeed a pretty good idea, and valid for all times and places, and an idea that the vast majority of successful politicians find almost impossible to accept. But Coolidge had the sense to follow his own advice. He was not without humor, albeit of a very dry kind, and he liked to surprise. In the Oval Office he would sometimes call in his staff by bell, then hide under his desk, observing their mystification with wry pleasure. On August 2, 1927, he summoned some thirty journalists and, when they arrived, told them: "The line forms on the left." He then handed each a two-by-nine-inch sheet of paper on which he himself had typed, "I do not choose to run for president in 1928." That was it: no questions were allowed. It may be that the following year, seeing Hoover's triumph, he regretted this decision, but he never made the slightest move to reverse it. At the time, he gave no explanation for it either. Indeed, his last words to the press at the White House were characteristically negative, snapping at them: "Perhaps one of the most important characteristics of my administration has been minding my own business."

When he ventured to explain himself, in the final chapter of his *Autobiography*, published in 1929, he contented himself with saying that eight years in the White House was enough, perhaps more than enough: "An examination of the records of those Presidents who have served eight years will disclose that in almost every instance the latter parts of their term have shown very little in the way of constructive accomplishment. They have often been clouded with grave disappointments." That is true enough. Coolidge had served only six years in the White House. But a second term would have kept him for ten, and he thought that much too much. There may have been a personal reason, too. Coolidge was the reverse of a demonstrative man, but there were powerful emotions operating under the surface of his laced-in exterior, and the evidence is strong that he was deeply attached to his immediate family. While he was in office as president, he lost both his son Calvin, in 1924, and his beloved father, the Colonel, in 1926. There is no evidence that Coolidge was particularly superstitious, but he seems to have got it into his head that neither death would have occurred had he not occupied the White House. The death of his father he felt deeply and believed that it had come prematurely because the consequences of his own eminence had, as he put it, "overtaxed his strength." The loss of Calvin was shattering. "When he went," Coolidge wrote, "the power and the glory of the presidency went with him." He mused sadly, "The ways of Providence are often beyond our understanding. . . . I do not know why such a price was exacted for occupying the White House." That last is a curious remark. But Coolidge was not a New England Puritan for nothing, and it may be that he felt, in retrospect, that his son was taken from him as punishment for his own sins of pride in the exercise of power. There was a particular incident that later haunted him— his firing of a long-serving Secret Service agent, Jim Haley, in a fit of petulance. Haley was blameless, but Coolidge thought he had exposed Mrs. Coolidge, his much-adored Grace, to needless danger. Such an episode would never have given a second's concern to a Franklin Roosevelt or a Winston Churchill who, amid their grander moments, regularly abused power, and in a far more shameless fashion. But it worried Coolidge, and he may have come to the conclusion, by August 2, 1927, the fifth anniversary of his accession to power, that his son's death had been a warning. So he slipped away, almost without a word, pulling down the curtain on Arcadia.

There is, of course, another explanation: that Coolidge felt in his bones that the good times were coming to an end, and he did not want to be in charge when the bottom fell out of the bull market. I am sure this was a fac-

tor. By Coolidge's day, the history of the trade cycle was fairly well understood, and Coolidge—by nature a pessimist rather than an optimist—knew
perfectly well that the boom would not last. All that was uncertain was
when it would end and how dramatically. His closest adviser, Stone, who
studied the markets, warned him of trouble ahead. He himself was certain
the market would break, probably sooner rather than later. That was his
private sentiment, reflected in his wife Grace's remark, "Poppa says there's
a depression coming." But Coolidge did not feel it was his duty or in America's interests to talk the boom down publicly, to hasten the downturn, or to
take steps to limit its severity. Among his other lapidary phrases, he might
easily have coined the maxim, "If it works, don't fix it." That is certainly
what he believed. That a depression would come was certain, but Coolidge
probably assumed it would be on the scale of 1920, to be cured by a similar
phase of masterly inactivity. If, however, something more was required, he
felt he was not the man to do it. Grace Coolidge said he told a member of
his cabinet: "I know how to save money. All my training has been in that direction. The country is in a sound financial condition. Perhaps the time has
come when we ought to spend money. I do not feel I am qualified to do that."

It is hard to resist asking the question: if Coolidge had indeed served another term, would he have been able to preserve the Last Arcadia a little
longer? Would he have handled the break in the market and the subsequent depression better than Hoover? That question is more easily asked
than answered. I do not know the answer. The older I get, the more I study
and the more I think about these years, the more convinced I become that
the Great Depression is one of the major mysteries of history. I have never
read to this day why the market crash, albeit severe, had such a huge impact
on the real economy. Earlier market breaks had been just as panicky but
had had no such tremendous consequences. Nor is it easy to understand
why the depression was so protracted and why the efforts to alleviate it
were so ineffectual. It may be that government intervention, as Coolidge
would certainly have argued, was counterproductive. Neither the irresolute
tinkering of Hoover, the nemesis of his social engineering, nor the more
noisy pump-priming of Franklin Roosevelt had any real effect. Indeed, the
Great Depression was never cured at all, until the coming of the Second
World War, by one of those horrific paradoxes of history, made Americans
really believe, this time, that "Happy days are here again." As those terrible
years gradually fall into the long perspective of economic history, I expect
we will be able to provide a confident answer to this whole conundrum at
last. But those days are not yet, and in the meantime we must retain a large
question-mark over the public wisdom of Calvin Coolidge and his true
place in the pantheon of American presidents. But I already feel it will be a
high one. And of one thing I am quite sure. In the present conjunction of
American politics, with the nation finally aroused to the urgent need to

bring the budget into balance, to reduce the terrifying deficit and the still more alarming national debt, to question the purpose and functioning and indeed the necessity of the welfare state and the whole degree to which government supplements the efforts of individuals, Calvin Coolidge is a highly relevant and indeed bang-up-to-date figure. He stated, with complete conviction and admirable pith, certain truths about human government which need restating periodically, and never more so than today at the end of the millennium. So the man is well worth studying now.

NOTES

This essay was the keynote address to the Library of Congress symposium on "Calvin Coolidge and the Coolidge Era," delivered on October 5, 1995.

2

The American Polity in the Age of Normalcy

A Reappraisal

JOHN BRAEMAN

The appearance in recent years of a large body of new scholarship on the 1920s makes timely a reassessment of the current state of our knowledge.[1]

The dominant image of the 1920s that has prevailed—not simply among the public, but among historians—was fixed by journalist Frederick Lewis Allen's 1931 bestseller, *Only Yesterday: An Informal History of the Nineteen-Twenties*. In highly readable fashion, Allen portrayed the 1920s as "a distinct era in American history" marked off by the cataclysmic turning points of World War I and the stock market crash. A "political liberal by conviction, a Puritan by inheritance," Allen saw the depression as the punishment for the decade's sins. His major focus was upon the breakdown of traditional moral and sexual standards, the frenetic pursuit of novelty, and the ascendancy of the hedonist impulse. But he included in his indictment xenophobic politics, corruption in high places, and the irresponsibility of the country's political leadership. Allen was largely responsible for propagating the story about Republican bosses at the 1920 GOP convention meeting secretly "in a smoke-filled room" to put Warren G. Harding over as the presidential nominee. He dismissed the Ohioan as "the majestic Doric false front" behind which "[b]lowsy gentlemen with cigars stuck in their cheeks and rolls of very useful hundred-dollar bills in their pockets" wheeled and dealed. He was even more scathing about Harding's "meager-looking" successor. "The great god business was supreme in the land, and Calvin Coolidge was fortunate enough to become almost a demi-god by doing discreet obeisance before the altar."[2]

Much of the reason for the continuing appeal of *Only Yesterday* is its affinity with the "progressive history" vision of American history as an ongoing struggle of the people versus the interests. Perhaps most important, its portrayal of the decade made a wonderful straw man for the cosmopolitan liberalism that came to dominate the post–World War II academy. The leading historians of the 1920s—William E. Leuchtenburg, Arthur M. Schlesinger, Jr., and John D. Hicks—joined in picturing the decade as riven by conflicts pitting the older America of small towns and farms populated by native stock, white Protestants in what Leuchtenburg's *The Perils of Prosperity* called "a last stand in a lost cause against the legions of the city." And as legatees of the New Deal, they had a political motivation to paint as darkly as possible FDR's Republican predecessors. Leuchtenburg's account of Harding dealt exclusively with the corruption—"the worst in at least half a century"—marring his administration, while he pictured Coolidge as the willing servitor of big business and its Old Guard allies. For Coolidge, Schlesinger accused in *The Crisis of the Old Order*, "business was more than business; it was a religion; and to it he committed all the passion of his arid nature." With Coolidge's triumph in 1924, Hicks echoed in his *Republican Ascendancy*, "the spirit of governmental favoritism toward business, so earnestly cultivated during the preceding four years, began to achieve really spectacular results."[3]

In contrast to the "progressive" interpretation, contributors to the "organizational synthesis" have developed a more sophisticated treatment of the government-business relationship. More than any other single work, Robert H. Wiebe's *The Search for Order, 1877–1920* supplied the intellectual underpinnings for this approach. Those who followed along the lines that he pioneered did not simply abandon the people-versus-interests dichotomy of "progressive history" but denied that World War I represented a watershed in American development. Participation by the United States in the conflict accelerated the long-term movement underway from the late nineteenth century toward (in Louis Galambos's words) "organization building, both public and private, and the creation of new and elaborate networks of formal, hierarchical structures of authority." What was distinctive about the 1920s was its experimenting "with associative, noncoercive techniques for guiding business behavior in constructive directions." Ellis W. Hawley has focused upon Herbert Hoover as the driving force behind the search for a middle way between laissez-faire with its waste and inefficiency and statist regimentation. That middle ground—which Hawley has labeled the "associative state"—involved voluntary cooperation among organized interests under governmental aegis to advance the public good. More broadly, Hawley made the central theme of his survey of American history from 1917 to 1933 "the development of managerial institutions and values."[4]

This approach can be appropriated by the political right, as Albro Martin has done in his attack upon the shortsightedness of government regulation for denying the railroads the benefits that private organizational innovation could have brought. But most of those with a political ax to grind attracted by the organizational revolution theme have belonged to or had a strong intellectual kinship with the New Left. For New Left historians such as William Appleman Williams and Gabriel Kolko, big business was the most powerful among the organized interests emerging out of the post–Civil War economic transformation. The government-business relationship was thus inevitably skewed in its favor. In the foreign policy area, the New Left position is that corporate leaders, caught in a squeeze between expanding productive capacity and lagging consumer purchasing power, looked for salvation to markets and investment opportunities abroad in an "open door" world. In dealing with the domestic side, New Left historians divided into a moderate and radical camp. The first viewed government action, at least up to the Great Depression, as directed to smoothing the way for business self-government. The second saw the state as actively intervening to bring about the market stability desired by the corporate elite.[5]

In an important first step toward a more balanced appraisal of the decade, Arthur S. Link showed that, although progressivism "declined" in the 1920s, it was far from "defunct." Brandeis University historian Morton Keller has gone even farther in denying that World War I marked a break between the Progressive Era and a reactionary 1920s. There were differences. The twenties were more resistant to new regulatory initiatives in the economic realm. And the progressives' ambition to shape individual and group behavior via law took on a more "repressive" cast. Notwithstanding such differing emphases, Keller sees the years 1900–33 as a single period in which continuity is more the rule than change. He accepts that an organizational revolution—most strikingly exemplified in the rise of big business —occurred. But he underlines how the "polity's response was deeply, inexorably conditioned by preexisting values, interests, procedural and structural arrangements." Most important, he finds that the result was a heightened pluralism because of the multiplication of voices that had to be taken into account when making policy rather than domination by an all-powerful corporate elite. "[M]odern American economic regulation emerged from an expanding, roiling aggregate of interests, issues, institutions, ideas: in sum, an increasingly pluralist American polity." He similarly warns against exaggerating the success of native-stock Fundamentalist Protestants in imposing their sway in the realm of social policy. "Old individualism and a new pluralism," Keller concludes, "conjoined to check the outward reach of the state."[6]

Evidence of continuity is most visible in the area of electoral behavior. The sharp swing to the Republicans, first in 1918 and more fully in 1920, was part of the long period of Republican predominance dating from the 1890s that Paul Kleppner has labeled the "fourth electoral system," and that Walter Dean Burnham called the "system of 1896." The Democratic resurgence from 1910 to 1916 was a temporary deviation, owing more to a split in GOP ranks than any significant increase in Democratic support. Republican hegemony was stronger in the 1918–28 subperiod than during the first phase of the system. The Republicans appear to have retained the loyalty of the bulk of native-stock voters outside of the South, made substantial inroads among such former Democratic supporters as Germans, Catholics, and Confessional Lutherans, and attracted a surprisingly high degree of support from newer-stock, blue-collar workers. The German-Catholic-Confessional Lutheran switch to the Republicans probably reflected anti-Wilson sentiment from the war and the Versailles peace treaty. The support of such newer-stock, blue-collar voters as Italians and French Canadians was partly because of the continuing appeal of Republican high-tariff policies as the protector of higher wages, partly because local Republican parties were more willing than their largely Irish-dominated Democratic counterparts to grant "recognition" in the form of lower-level offices to members of such groups. Despite growing restiveness at the failure of the GOP to act more forcefully in support of African-American interests, most of the black vote remained loyal to the party of Lincoln.[7]

A major architect of the Republican success was Will H. Hays of Indiana, the GOP national chairman from 1918 to 1921. Hays not only smoothed over the old guard–progressive divisions but played a key role in preventing a party split over the League of Nations. Of longer-term institutional significance, he transformed the managerial functions of the national chairman. His innovations included opening a permanent national party headquarters, expanding the national committee's publicity activities, and instituting nationwide popular fund-raising campaigns to free the party from dependence upon a narrow group of wealthy contributors. One of the secrets of Hays's success was his policy of strict neutrality in factional battles and nominations.[8]

And the Republican presidential nominating process was remarkably open. Wesley Bagby has demolished the myth that Warren G. Harding's nomination in 1920 was the handiwork of a smoke-filled room of party bosses. Harding's success was due partly to the deadlock that developed among the front runners, partly to his availability as a man not identified with controversial and divisive issues. Calvin Coolidge's nomination for the vice presidency was even more the product of an upsurge of support among the rank-and-file of the delegates against the would-be party managers. Another rank-and-file revolt gave the 1924 vice presidential nomination to the erratic Charles G. Dawes. Perhaps the most striking illustration of the influence of popular sentiment was Herbert Hoover's nomination in 1928 with no more than token opposition despite the lack of enthusiasm for him among old-line party war horses or President Coolidge.[9]

In one sense, the election results of the 1920s were not so much a vote for the Republicans as a vote against the Democrats. In 1920, Harding's 60 percent of the vote amounted to less than 30 percent of the potential electorate as the turnout plunged to under 50 percent. The turnout fell even more in 1924. The Democrats appear to have been the harder hit by this downturn in voter participation. Because of the decline of party loyalties and accompanying growth in independent voting, the Democrats made a stronger showing in off-year elections and in state, congressional, and gubernatorial than presidential races. At the presidential level, however, the party's situation was gloomy. In 1924, the lackluster John W. Davis won barely over one-fourth of the total vote. Outside the South, the one solid Democratic constituency remaining was the Irish. The Republicans had come to outpoll the Democrats even in the border states in presidential years. Nationally, the Democrats lagged behind the Republicans in their organizational machinery. Even more damaging was the gap in financial resources. But analysts have placed major blame for the party's weakness upon the conflict that pitted native-stock western and southern Democrats against their largely Irish big-city counterparts. The most spectacular example of this division was the 1924 Democratic national convention, where the party split down the middle over the Ku Klux Klan and took 103 ballots to pick its presidential nominee.[10]

The standard interpretation—given its fullest explication in David Burner's *The Politics of Provincialism*—pictures the split as ethno-culturally based, with prohibition the symbolic issue around which conflict raged. Douglas B. Craig, in his *After Wilson*, has challenged this view, holding that the prohibitionist-"wet" split reflected a larger ideological division of Bryan-Wilson progressives favoring an activist government to regulate private enterprise and redistribute income versus conservatives standing for states' rights and minimal government. The most controversial aspect of this challenge is its treatment of Al Smith. Most writers about Smith have portrayed his governorship of New York as foreshadowing the New Deal despite his own later hostility to FDR. By contrast, Craig finds Smith at most an "enlightened conservative." Smith's support for labor legislation "was confined to the protection of women and children, since he believed that men were able to look after their own interests." Because of his own personal experience as a self-made man, he shared an "old-fashioned individualism" that made him "the darling of the northeastern conservatives." Whatever the limits of Smith's reformism—and Craig is guilty of judging him by latter-day standards of what constitutes liberalism—his western and southern rivals lacked his appeal to the city dwellers who would become the backbone of the Roosevelt coalition. Not simply did their prohibitionism alienate such voters, but their focus upon such time-worn issues as monopoly and the tariff did not speak to the needs of the urban working and lower-middle classes.[11]

A distinguishing hallmark of the "system of 1896" was the existence of two regionally based one-party systems—a solidly Democratic South and most states outside the South safely Republican. The result in the South was a personality-centered style of politics. The major exception to the "disorganization" of southern politics was Virginia, where Harry F. Byrd built a formidable machine that would dominate the Old Dominion for many years. One of the major themes in the decade's politics in the South was the crusade to uphold traditional moral values through the enforcement of prohibition, the adoption of laws against the teaching of evolution in the public schools, and antivice campaigns. The second, perhaps even more powerful, was the push led by business and professional leaders for economic development. Although demagogic spellbinders such as Coleman L. Blease in South Carolina, Eugene Talmadge in Georgia, Theodore G. Bilbo in Mississippi, and "Farmer Jim" Ferguson in Texas continued to find a receptive audience, the more typical successful southern politician of the twenties was the promoter of what George B. Tindall has aptly termed "business progressivism." Byrd, Austin M. Peay in Tennessee, Bibb Graves in Georgia, Cameron Morrison in North Carolina, and John M. Parker in Louisiana were champions of economy and efficiency who reorganized and modernized the structure of state government, introduced new administrative and tax systems, and expanded public services such as highways and education. The limits of such good-government reformism were most strikingly revealed in Louisiana. Parker's failure to break the grip of the planter-business–New Orleans political machine alliance that ran the Pelican State opened the way for Huey Long to come to power in 1928 as the spokesman for the resentments of Louisiana's workers and poorer farmers.[12]

Apart from Virginia, only Connecticut still had in the 1920s a traditional-style party organization that dominated state politics. Factional conflict was the rule throughout most of the rest of the country. In Wisconsin and California, the divisions within the GOP were a continuation of the prewar conflict between insurgents and old guard. In Wisconsin, Senator Robert M. La Follette, and after his death in 1925, his son and successor in the Senate, Robert, Jr., headed the progressive wing, while Senator Irvine Lenroot headed the Stalwarts. The progressives retained the upper hand, with John J. Blaine holding the governorship for three two-year terms before winning Lenroot's Senate seat in 1926. In California, the progressive faction came back after its defeat in the 1922 Republican primary to put C. C. Young in the governor's mansion four years later. In Iowa, Albert B. Cummins—who had risen to power in the Progressive Era as the champion of the farmer against the railroads—found himself outflanked on the left by the self-proclaimed populist Smith W. Brookhart. On the other hand, former Progressive Party leaders Albert J. Beveridge in Indiana and Miles

Poindexter in Washington moved so far to the right that past divisions lost any meaning.[13]

Insurgency remained a force west of the Mississippi because over-extended farmers were hard hit by the postwar fall in agricultural prices. But what was decisive for the future of the GOP was the eclipse of its re-form wing in the nation's "industrial-commercial core"—the Northeast and the belt of industrialized states along the Great Lakes. The reasons for the waning of Republican progressivism in this area included the wounds left by the 1912 split, disillusionment with American involvement in World War I and its aftermath, and worsening social, ethnic, and rural-urban divi-sions. Although more research is required on state developments, there are indications that as the GOP moved to the right the Democrats began to take over the mantle of reform. Heightened labor militancy alienated the independent businessmen and professionals who had constituted the back-bone of Republican progressivism. Further dampening the reform impulse among this group was how progressivism had become more and more identified with an attack by the West and South upon the core's favored po-sition in the American economy. The continuing growth in the size of the white-collar class—with an accompanying rapid increase in the number of professional, technical, and managerial positions—worked politically in the same direction. White-collar workers appear to have done well financially in the 1920s and thus were not likely recruits for protest movements.[14]

The most radical protest flared in the belt of states running from Min-nesota across to the Pacific and in the southwest. Aggrieved farmers joined with militant local labor groups to organize the Washington Farmer-Labor Party, the Idaho Progressive Party, and the Oklahoma Farmer-Labor Re-construction League. The impulse behind such movements was not simply bread-and-butter issues, but resentments arising out of the wartime repres-sion of Germans, Scandinavians, and political dissenters. The most suc-cessful were in North Dakota and Minnesota. During its heyday from 1915 to 1921, the farmers' Nonpartisan League dominated the North Dakota Republican Party and thereby the state government. Although factionalism coupled with a financial crisis resulting from the boycott of North Dakota bonds by the national capital market led to its loss of control over state gov-ernment in 1921, the League was the driving force behind the election of Lynn Frazier to the United States Senate the following year. After the de-feat of its bid to take over the Minnesota Republican Party in 1918, the farmers' Nonpartisan League joined with Socialist-influenced elements of organized labor in the Twin Cities to form a "Farmer-Labor" electoral ticket that came in a respectable second to the Republicans. By 1922 this ad hoc coalition evolved into a formal political party and successfully ran Henrik Shipstead for the U.S. Senate and proceeded to build a tightly knit, centralized organizational structure. This avowedly left-of-center Farmer-

Labor Party attracted national attention by electing Magnus Johnson to the Senate in a 1923 special election. Although Johnson was defeated by a Republican the following year for the full term, Shipstead won reelection in 1928. By the end of the decade, the Farmer-Labor Party strongly threatened the dominant Republicans and left the Democratic Party in a distant third place.[15]

Insurgency had much less impact at the national level. After his death, Theodore Roosevelt's followers went off on different paths. Even those who had returned with him to the GOP were so divided that their influence was fatally undermined. In 1920, the rivalry between Leonard Wood and Hiram Johnson to assume the Roosevelt mantle contributed to opening the way for Harding. The hope of Republican progressives led by Harold L. Ickes to win the 1924 presidential nomination for Johnson was stillborn. The ambition of T.R.'s eldest son, Theodore Roosevelt, Jr., to follow in his father's footsteps was dashed by his defeat by Al Smith in the 1924 New York gubernatorial race. A more radical group of ex–Bull Moosers, whose leading figures were George L. Record and Amos Pinchot—whom Eugene Tobin has labeled "independent progressives"—dreamed of leading a new movement for nationalization of the railroads, destruction of monopolies, and elimination of economic inequality. But these middle-class do-gooders, while appearing on the letterheads of one after another cause, had no mass following. A group of largely New York–based intellectuals set up in 1919 the Committee of Forty-Eight as the nucleus of a hoped-for third party. After months of friction and squabbling, the more socialist-leaning Committee members joined with the tiny National Labor Party to form the Farmer-Labor Party with an unknown Utah lawyer named Parley P. Christensen as its presidential nominee. Without the backing of any significant farmer organization or union, the Farmer-Labor Party passed swiftly into historical oblivion.[16]

Robert M. La Follette's 1924 presidential bid as the standard bearer of a reborn Progressive Party looked to be a more formidable undertaking. He had the support of the railroad brotherhoods and even gained the endorsement of American Federation of Labor (AFL) president Samuel Gompers. The Socialist Party of America added its backing. La Follette was a name candidate with a large personal following. But the campaign dashed the expectations that had attended the party's launching. Money was short; the national campaign staff was geographically fragmented and inexperienced; and local organization was almost nonexistent. Most progressive-minded officeholders running for reelection refused to bolt the old parties. There was continuing friction between the Socialists and the La Follette group over the movement's future direction. As the campaign faltered, the railroad brotherhoods and the AFL backed away from active support. And La Follette's emphasis upon the antimonopoly theme failed to strike a responsive chord with the voters. His 4.8 million votes, 16.5 percent of the total, left him a distant third.[17] "The idea of a third party," California's Hiram Johnson lamented, "has gone glimmering."[18]

The far left presented no threat except in the overheated imaginations of xenophobic superpatriots. The Socialist Party of America, whose rapid growth in the early years of the century had so alarmed T.R. and did much to spur reforms aimed at undercutting radicalism, ceased to be a significant force. Eugene V. Debs's near–one million votes in 1920 was more a testimonial to him personally than an indicator of Socialist Party strength. The party was reduced to an empty shell partly because of the splits in its ranks over United States involvement in World War I and then the Bolshevik Revolution, partly because of government repression and private vigilantism during the war and the Red Scare. The ambition of Socialists and radicals to turn the Conference for Progressive Political Action into the nucleus for an American counterpart of the British Labour Party was frustrated. The final blow was the ineffectual leadership of former Presbyterian minister Norman Thomas, who became the Socialist Party's perennial standard bearer for the presidency starting in 1928. The Bolshevik Revolution led to the formation of two rival groups, the Communist Party and the Communist Labor Party. Even after the two joined in 1923, the American Communist Party remained a pariah on the margins of politics, rent by factional strife, and under Moscow's thumb, with a membership (approximately 9,300 in 1929) drawn predominantly from recent immigrants. Its time of influence would come in the next decade.[19]

The question that has most fascinated students of American politics is the extent to which forces were at work beneath the surface foreshadowing the realignment that occurred during the New Deal. There are those who see a long-term trend toward increased Democratic support among ethnic voters that was first temporarily disrupted by the reaction against Wilson in 1920 and then disguised by the three-party race in 1924. Others find the Progressive Party of 1924 a "halfway house" for a substantial number of Republicans on the way to the Democratic column. But the most favored candidate for realigning force has been the election of 1928. Contemporary political scientists Roy V. Peel and Thomas C. Donnelly thought Herbert Hoover's impressive showing in the border states and the South the harbinger of a more lasting switch to the Republicans in "those southern centers which are rapidly being industrialized." They simultaneously underlined the potential significance of the Democratic gains in the large urban centers of the northeast and middle west—"the Slavic-Latin-Celtic-German areas." And in their account of the 1932 campaign, Peel and Donnelly recognized how "Roosevelt more than held the magnificent accession of strength which Smith obtained in the cities in 1928." Samuel Lubell was the most influential popularizer of the view that 1928 was a "critical election" responsible for breaking the GOP's grip upon the nation's cities. "Before the Roosevelt Revolution," Lubell held, "there was an Al Smith Revolution. . . . What Smith really embodied was the revolt of the under-dog, urban immigrant against the top dog of 'old American' stock."[20]

John F. Kennedy's race for the presidency spurred new interest in the election of 1928. New scholarship more fully explored the Democratic nominating process; the roles of the religious issue, prohibition, and eth-nicity; the reactions of Protestant churches and churchmen; the parties' campaign tactics; the influence of farm issues and organized labor; and the strains upon southern Democrats' party loyalty. Events swiftly revealed that 1928 in the South was a "deviating" election. The leading Democratic defectors to Hoover suffered from a voter backlash for their desertion of the white man's party. Analysts are divided over the impact outside of the South. One group holds that Al Smith's candidacy resulted in a massive surge of newer ethnic votes to the Democrats. But the preponderance of case studies is more deflationary about the election's significance, finding 1928 at most a phase in a longer realigning sequence in which the depres-sion and New Deal were the decisive influences. The most thorough analy-sis of the 1928 vote finds that urban versus rural, class, and even ethnicity were not significant variables. Voting polarized sharply along religious lines —Roman Catholic versus Protestant. While Smith ran strongly in cities with a large Roman Catholic population, Hoover captured those with a Protestant majority. And how much of even the increased Catholic vote the Democrats would have retained if not for the Great Depression and New Deal is questionable. In Philadelphia, for example, the Italians who rallied to Smith returned to their Republican loyalties until 1934.[21]

Although winning the electoral battles of the 1920s, the GOP lost the historical war. Repeated polls of historians rate Warren G. Harding as the worst of the nation's presidents. That negative image was largely fixed by liberal-minded journalists who found that accounts of scandals such as Teapot Dome made excellent copy and that sensationalism about his sex life a still surer route to sales. The resulting portrait was not without basis. There is no question of Harding's personal frailties and intellectual limita-tions. The corruption that scarred his presidency has been thoroughly doc-umented. Many of his top appointees were mistakes. Even if he had not been purchasable, Albert Fall was not the man for secretary of the interior given his publicly expressed commitment to rapid and unfettered private development of the public domain. Attorney General Harry Daugherty's biographer cannot find much favorable to say beyond that Daugherty was "outgoing and friendly," "a skillful manager and organizer," "fiercely loyal" to his friends, and devoted to his wife. In their volume on Harding for the American Presidency series, Eugene P. Trani and David L. Wilson exoner-ate Harding from the worst accusations of his journalist detractors. "[H]e was a shrewd politician who communicated effectively if not articulately; he was not the captive of Daugherty or his wife, or the Senate's Old Guard; he was not involved in the scandals that shook his administration." But their over-all appraisal remains negative. While "there were some accomplishments in the administration," most were "short-term" and "temporizing." "[L]ittle was done between 1921 and 1923 to bring long-range, large-scale solutions to problems."[22]

At his death, Harding was highly popular. That popularity owed much to the straits in which Woodrow Wilson had left the country. Because of the Wilson administration's abdication of responsibility for directing the country's reconversion from wartime, the economy went through a roller coaster of ups and downs that climaxed in a severe recession starting mid-1920. When business began to pick up in the latter part of 1922, the incumbent administration—rightly or wrongly—received the credit. But more than sheer luck was involved. While Harding had his defenders even at the nadir of his reputation, the major stimulus to a reconsideration was the long-delayed opening of his papers in the 1960s. If many of his appointees were blunders, others were of high quality. Charles Evans Hughes at State, Andrew Mellon at Treasury, Herbert Hoover at Commerce, and Henry C. Wallace at Agriculture rank among the ablest individuals to have held those positions. The case has been made that even Fall's leasing of Teapot Dome —whatever his motives—represented sound economic policy, and Fall's successor at Interior, Dr. Hubert Work, not only did much to improve departmental efficiency but also did much to promote new conservation initiatives. Harding himself was not the nonentity that he typically has been portrayed as. Given his newspaper background, he had an astute grasp of how the press worked. And he made significant contributions to the presidential techniques for the management of public opinion. One was adding to the White House staff a formally designated "speech writer." Even more important was his revival of regularly scheduled news conferences. As a former senator, he started out inclined to accept legislative primacy in policy making. As time went on, however, he assumed an increasingly active leadership role.[23]

Calvin Coolidge ranks no more than marginally higher than Harding in the historians' ratings of the presidents. Furthermore, Coolidge has not been fortunate in his biographers. William Allen White's *A Puritan in Babylon*, published in 1938, was most responsible for shaping Coolidge's historical reputation. The theme of White's account is that Coolidge had a sincere—but misguided—"faith that 'the rich' are indeed the 'wise and good.'" White's influence was due partly to his writing style, partly to how the work fitted in with the dominant attitude among contemporary enlightened opinion that the excesses of business in the 1920s were to blame for the Great Depression. Claude Fuess's treatment was more sympathetic, even defensive, but simply lacked the stylistic verve of *A Puritan in Babylon* and, unfortunately for Coolidge, appeared in the heyday of Franklin D. Roosevelt. What appeared to confirm Coolidge's low standing was Donald McCoy's self-styled "new look." In his introduction, McCoy called Coolidge "a President who deserves some praise and much understanding along with criticism." But the praise was handed out sparingly. McCoy's Coolidge remained the Coolidge of the New Deal historians. "In reputation as well as in fact," McCoy summed up, "Coolidge has been a victim of his reserve and of his popularity, for together they restrained him from serious involvement in most of the great problems of the 1920s. . . . Coolidge's failure was the failure of a President who does not look ahead and does not fight to head off the problems of the future."[24]

One is tempted to ask what political leaders have such a gift of prophecy. More to the immediate point, new evidence makes possible a more positive appraisal. Fortune did play a large part in Coolidge's rise, perhaps more than for many successful persons. But he had important positive qualities. Hendrik Booraem's perceptive account of his psychological development through his graduation from Amherst College showed how the painfully shy and insecure Vermonter acquired the traits that would serve him well in later years: "disciplined routine effort, mastery of rhetoric, keen observation, and emotional control." He had a deserved reputation for personal honesty. While admiring the successful businessman, he was not the loyal tool of big business. Although a devotee of self-reliance, he had a genuine feeling for the less fortunate members of society. His success in separating himself from, and defusing, the Harding administration scandals when they began coming to light showed political skill of a high level. The discovery by Howard Quint and Robert H. Ferrell of a typescript of his presidential press conferences has revealed a different Coolidge than the dour, silent, passive, even indolent, chief executive of legend. Coolidge consciously used his off-the-record talks with newspapermen to shape public opinion along the lines he wished. And he—as Quint and Ferrell point out —"ranged over a wide variety of subjects with a degree of expertise that historians of a later generation not always have appreciated." Not simply did he show the "mastery over detail that every truly successful politician must possess," but "his analysis of the issues could be penetrating." And, as John L. Blair noted, he "was a wise enough politician to know when to pick up his chips and leave."[25]

In most accounts of the 1920s, Secretary of Commerce Herbert Hoover looms larger than his titular chiefs. He transformed his department into a powerhouse government agency offering businessmen a wide range of services—statistical data, improved measuring devices from the Bureau of Standards, assistance in the simplification and standardization of products. He intruded into what had been the State Department preserve of foreign economic policy by promoting markets abroad for American exports, re-sisting foreign raw materials cartels, and trying to regulate the flow of private loans abroad. He involved himself in a wide range of policy issues not before (or since) regarded as within the province of the Commerce Department: unemployment, labor-management relations, agricultural policy, child health, natural resource conservation and environmental protection, control of radio broadcasting, and expansion of outdoor recreational opportunities. But Hoover was more than simply one of the most forceful bureaucratic empire builders in American history. His larger aim was to make the Commerce Department into an instrument for cooperative relations between business and government. And he had a fully articulated philosophy that envisaged a basic reshaping of American political economy. The keystone of that vision was the development of "a nonstatist system of countercyclical planning." His goal, as Guy Alchon has detailed, was the institution of "a three-legged apparatus" linking philanthropic foundations, the National Bureau of Economic Research, and the Commerce Department in educating individual businessmen to act in ways that would "enhance the stability of the economy as a whole."[26]

Hoover built up a formidable public relations machine that kept him in the limelight. At a personal level, his relations with Harding were warmer than with Coolidge. Coolidge appears to have been jealous of what he regarded as Hoover's self-promotion. And he distrusted Hoover's activist impulses. On his side, Hoover worried lest Coolidge prove a roadblock to his own presidential ambitions. Even under Coolidge, however, Hoover was second only to the president in shaping domestic policies. He won his running battle with the Justice Department over the legality of trade association information-sharing practices when the Supreme Court ruled in the 1925 Maple Flooring and Cement Institute decisions that such information-sharing—absent explicit price-fixing—did not violate the antitrust laws. From the start, the conciliatory and amiable secretary of labor, James J. Davis, was inclined to follow Hoover's lead in labor matters. By contrast, Hoover was at odds with Secretary of Agriculture Henry C. Wallace. The dispute did not simply involve bureaucratic rivalries over which department would have responsibility for dealing with the marketing of farm products but expanded to include policy issues when Wallace became a supporter of the McNary-Haugen plan. Under Harding, Wallace appears to have retained the upper hand. But Coolidge shared Hoover's hostility to government price-fixing. After Wallace's death in 1924, Hoover found his successor, William M. Jardine, more to his way of thinking. The most spectacular triumph of Hoover's voluntarist philosophy was his response to the devastating Mississippi River flood in 1927, which left over a million people homeless and destitute and did untold property damage. Hoover's masterful performance as chairman of the Special Mississippi River Flood

Committee in raising funds and arranging cooperation by governmental and private agencies for relief and rehabilitation reinforced his image as the "Great Humanitarian."[27]

Any assessment of presidential performance must take into account the contextual limits of what could be done. At the top of the list is the institutional fragmentation that has been so distinctive a feature of the American state. Aggravating the situation was the late development of a federal government bureaucracy capable of initiating and implementing complex programs. Another limitation was that typically regulatory initiatives dealing with the problems growing out of economic and technological changes came first at the state level. The result was the growth of entrenched interests resisting national government intrusion. By 1920, forty-two states and the District of Columbia were regulating telephones. State regulation of public utilities was an obstacle to responding effectively to the rise of giant holding companies in the electric power industry. Perhaps the most striking example of state regulation as a bar against federal control was insurance. Many of the larger firms had come by the turn of the century to favor national government supervision as preferable to the maze of often stringent state regulations. But resistance by state insurance commissioners, opposition from smaller firms in the South and West, and doubts about the constitutionality of federal regulation given the Supreme Court's 1868 ruling in *Virginia v. Paul* that an insurance contract was not a transaction in interstate commerce blocked congressional action. Support for federal regulation rapidly waned in the aftermath of the 1905 Armstrong investigation of the life insurance industry, and state regulation settled down as a matured and accepted institution.[28]

The prevailing narrow view of the scope of national government power also limited presidential initiative. Although the Supreme Court had upheld federal regulation of trusts, railroads, and the meat, food, and drug industries, the five-to-four ruling in *Hammer v. Dagenhart* (1918) striking down the national child labor act of 1916 signaled a stiffening attitude toward any further expansion of national authority vis-à-vis the states. Perhaps most important, there was a deeply rooted tradition of popular suspicion of centralized power. The experience of World War I, the postwar "Red Scare," and the resentments fanned by prohibition reinforced this hostility. As Lynn Dumenil notes, the defeat of the proposed federal department of education reveals the decade's "pervasive suspicion of encroaching federal power." Much the same coalition—leading Roman Catholic spokesmen, states' rights politicians, and patriotic groups such as the Sentinels of the Republic alarmed at the "red" threat—joined with business and agricultural interest groups to block ratification of the national child labor amendment. "Before the depression," William R. Brock reminds us, "no one talked seriously of federal relief, and it is difficult to imagine that anything short of this catastrophe would have made it politically feasible. Some professional experts believed that the states should organize social insurance, but few had a good word to say for the various forms of compulsory insurance run by European governments. No one suggested that the federal government might organize and help to pay for a national program of old-age pensions or unemployment insurance."[29]

Given these circumstances, the continued growth of the national government in the 1920s appears the more striking. The Republican talk about governmental economy was not empty rhetoric. Over the decade, the federal government ran a surplus that allowed a reduction in the national debt by a third. But federal spending—even when adjusted in real terms—was still between two and three times higher than before World War I. Federal expenditures, which were at most 2.4 percent of GNP before the war, averaged 3.1 percent of a much larger GNP in 1929. Although much of the increased spending was war-related—current defense spending, debt service, and veterans' benefits—there were substantial increases in expenditures for the promotion and regulation of commerce, transportation, and communication; science, education, and research; and public welfare. The most important development in the social services area was the expansion of traditional payments to Indians and veterans to include matching funds to the states for "new welfare clienteles." The Smith-Hughes Act of 1917 instituted federal support for vocational education. In 1920, Congress approved federal grants-in-aid to state bureaus of vocational education to establish vocational rehabilitation programs for the industrially disabled. The following year, the Children's Bureau orchestrated passage of the Sheppard-Towner Act providing federal grants-in-aid to the states for maternal and infant health. Although the dollar amounts remained "modest," per capita federal civilian welfare expenditures nearly tripled between 1913 and 1928. Despite their limitations, Edward Berkowitz and Kim McQuaid conclude, "the new programs did escalate the level of Washington's social welfare responsibility. . . . Beginning in the 1920s, Washington began to become a source of funds to states to initiate new welfare activities."[30]

From a long-term perspective, perhaps the Harding administration's most significant contribution was its strengthening of the institutional capacities of the presidency through the adoption of the Budget and Accounting Act of 1921. Under the old system, each department submitted its funding requests independently, with the president's role limited to approving the revenue bills passed by Congress. The sharp rise in spending and the national debt during World War I made putting the federal government's fiscal management in order appear imperative. Accordingly, President Harding successfully called upon Congress to approve the machinery for an executive budget. The legislation required the chief executive to give Congress each January annual estimates of how much money would be required to run the government, how much funding each federal program should receive, and how much tax revenues would be. To assist the president in preparing the budget, the 1921 act established the Bureau of the Budget as an agency within the Treasury Department. Its first director, Chicago banker Charles G. Dawes, moved vigorously with Harding's backing to expand the Bureau's role to include overall supervision of the different agencies within the federal government. A December 1921 directive required that all recommendations for legislation that would involve a charge upon the Treasury—which would include nearly all legislation—should be given to the Bureau of the Budget for its review to see if the proposal was in accord with the administration's financial program. And the Bureau was given the power to reduce agency funding requests. Most important, Congress largely followed the Bureau's recommendations.

At the same time, Hoover took the lead in pushing a far-reaching plan for reorganization of the executive branch. The most controversial proposals involved a large-scale shifting of agencies to the Commerce Department to make that department the center of governmental activities dealing with industry, trade, and transportation, merging the War and Navy Departments into a Department of National Defense, transferring the Forest Service from Agriculture to Interior, and creating a Department of Education and Welfare. Even more alarming to Congress were the proposals to strengthen the White House's managerial capabilities. These involved shifting the Bureau of the Budget directly under the chief executive, transferring the General Accounting Office (which Congress had made its watchdog over the executive) to presidential control, and giving the president continuing reorganization authority. Although Harding gave the plan his strong backing, Coolidge's lukewarmness doomed its adoption. Lawmakers' reluctance to give the president a free hand when adopting the Classification Act of 1923 similarly impeded progress toward a more rational career and salary structure for the federal service. Despite the lack of much immediate payoff, the Harding administration's initiatives were a landmark in American state-building. Its reorganization plan became the model for later more successful efforts. And Paul Van Riper, the leading historian of the federal service, finds that the Classification Act "marked a major milestone in the development of federal public personnel administration."[31]

Just as Hoover was the driving force behind proposals to rationalize the administration of the executive branch, he labored to overcome the diffusion of authority resulting from the federal system. When a problem appeared to require regional coordination—such as the integration and interconnection of the electric utility industry in the northeast or the control of oil overproduction—Hoover worked to promote voluntary agreement among the states involved. His most successful initiative along that line was his role in arranging the Colorado River Compact of 1922 for allocating the Colorado's water among the states through which the river passed. Another favorite Hoover tactic was to hold a high-profile national conference to focus public attention upon an issue that he thought important—such as unemployment, the future of radio, or child welfare—and to recommend follow-up action by state and local governments and the private sector. But the single most powerful weapon in extending the reach of the national government was the expansion of the conditional grant-in-aid. The controlling influence exercised by the Bureau of Public Roads over state highway construction was due not simply to its technical expertise, but its distributing approximately one hundred million dollars annually for highway construction. The lure of grants-in-aid under the Sheppard-Towner Act led all but three states to set up maternal and infant health programs. While historians have largely ignored this development, contemporary political scientists were aware of its importance. "The most significant expansion of federal power as against the states in recent years," the 1933 report of the President's Research Committee on Social Trends concluded, "has come in connection with the policy of conditioned grants in aid." [32]

Another development of major long-term importance was the emergence within the executive branch of centers of activist policy innovation. The women reformers in the Children's Bureau aspired to become the guiding directorate and coordinator of a broad-gauged movement for social welfare reforms based upon the strategy of building a network of contacts with women's groups throughout the country. A group of ambitious and energetic bureaucrats in the conservation field—William B. Greeley of the Forest Service, Elwood Mead of the Bureau of Reclamation, Stephen T. Mather and Horace M. Albright of the National Park Service, and Hugh Bennett in soil erosion—succeeded in gaining increased funding, in expanding their agencies' responsibilities, and in building supporting constituencies. Within the Justice Department, J. Edgar Hoover at the Federal Bureau of Investigation was laying the foundations for his future empire. The agency that had most successfully built up an independent power base was the Department of Agriculture. By the 1920s, the Department of Agriculture had a staff of nearly 20,000 employees, an annual budget of almost $47 million, a corps of scientific research and regulatory bureaus, and had forged links with a broad range of professional associations, research institutions, and state agencies. Its network of field offices and Extension Service county agents gave the Department a presence in local communities across the country. Secretary Henry C. Wallace's support for the McNary-Haugen plan brought the Department into an alliance with the mass-membership Farm Bureau Federation at the grass roots and with middle western rural lawmakers—a preview of the later iron triangle solidified under the New Deal. And its Bureau of Agricultural Economics gave the Department its own planning and policy-formation apparatus. [33]

One of the worst flaws in liberal historians' treatment of the 1920s is their exaggeration of the extent to which the Republican administrations represented a break with the Progressive Era. The switch from confrontation to cooperation with the more responsible industry elements in enforcing the Pure Food and Drug Act of 1906 antedated Harding's coming to the White House. The Wilson administration first began in a large way the practice in antitrust cases of consent decrees—informal agreements whereby offending companies were saved from prosecution in return for changes in their practices. Wilson's Secretary of Commerce William C. Redfield anticipated Hoover's encouragement of trade associations. The Wilson administration's promotion of business-government cooperation to boost exports included a provision in the Federal Reserve Act allowing national banks to open foreign branches, the Webb-Pomerene Act of 1918 exempting export combinations from the antitrust laws, and the Edge Act of 1919 permitting American banks to establish foreign banking and investment subsidiaries under federal charter. Despite growing support for nationalization (or "postalization") of the telephone industry culminating in a favorable report by Postmaster-General Albert Burleson in 1913, Wilson did not follow through. When the federal government did take over the telephones and telegraph after United States entry into the war, the experiment proved a failure. In response to the loud public complaints about the post office's inefficient, "grasping," and "domineering" management, Congress voted to return the wires to private ownership at the war's end. Although the Waterpower Act of 1920 affirmed the principle of federal government regulation of hydroelectric power development on navigable streams, the new Federal Power Commission lacked the resources for exercising effective supervision. And the legislation's abandonment of the concept of multipurpose river development, Samuel Hays writes, "marked the end of a conservation era."[34]

Decisions made in Wilson's last days foreshadowed, and shaped, future policy in other areas. Because of the threatened breakdown of the nation's railroads under wartime strains, the government took over their operation. The United States Railroad Administration under Secretary of the Treasury William G. McAdoo did more than buy labor peace by generous treatment of the workers; it also improved operating efficiency through unification and rationalization. Despite the support of the railroad brotherhoods, the American Federation of Labor, and liberal intellectuals for the so-called Plumb Plan for government ownership, Wilson was determined to return the railroads to private hands. But he offered no leadership about the terms except to set a deadline for congressional action. Unwilling—or unable—to resolve the cross pressures from rival interests, the lawmakers in the Transportation Act of 1920 handed over final decision-making authority to the Interstate Commerce Commission (ICC) without meaningful guidelines about how to apply its powers. The same conflicts that led Congress to shift to the ICC responsibility for making the hard choices about the future of the nation's railroads paralyzed the commission. The result was to leave the industry dangerously vulnerable when the stock market crashed.[35]

By the war's end, the United States Shipping Board had acquired a massive fleet that was already built or under construction. Neither the White House nor the Republican Congress wished to continue government ownership and operation. The Jones Act of 1920 was the product of collaboration between Admiral William S. Benson, Wilson's appointee as chair of the Shipping Board, and the Senate Committee on Commerce. While authorizing the Shipping Board to operate vessels on essential routes for developmental purposes, the measure envisaged the sale of the Board-owned fleet to private operators as soon as practicable. The act made explicit what had emerged as a consensus in government circles—that the federal government must act to maintain a strong merchant marine for national security reasons. When the sharp postwar fall in freight rates not only frightened off purchasers but resulted in mounting losses for the United States Treasury, Harding saw no alternative except to offer private operators more generous inducements. Although stiff opposition from farm-belt lawmakers and the Democrats blocked action until after Harding's death, Congress in 1924 gave private shipping interests most of their wishes—sale by the Shipping Board of its best ships at bargain prices, low-interest government-loans for new ship construction, and operating subsidies in the form of mail contracts. Despite the resulting abuses, the New Deal's Merchant Marine Act of 1936 continued offering operating and construction subsidies to keep American merchant marine financially afloat.[36]

No aspect of the Harding-Coolidge years has been more sharply indicted—or worse misrepresented—than tax policy. Wilson administration officials favored much the same cuts in the wartime rates that Republicans would propose. Second, Mellon anticipated Keynesianism in regarding investment as the key determinant of economic growth. He reasoned that lower marginal tax rates would lead the wealthy to shift their investments from tax-exempt securities to more productive investments. Third, the tax reductions of the 1920s did not shift the burden of federal taxation from the rich to those in the lower-income brackets. In 1920, people who earned less than $10,000 per year paid almost as much in total income taxes as did those who earned over $100,000 a year. In 1929, those in the over $100,000 bracket paid 65.2 percent of the total federal personal income tax bill while those under $10,000 paid only 1.3 percent. Because of increased exemptions, most Americans paid no income tax. Although cutting personal income rates, Mellon kept corporate rates high. He personally even favored taxing "unearned" income from investments at a higher rate than "earned" income from salaries and wages on ability-to-pay grounds. Last, federal taxes in the twenties averaged over 3 percent of the GNP contrasted with roughly 1 percent before the war. Thus, even the reduced tax of the Coolidge administration still imposed a burden which was three times higher than that of the pre–World War I era.[37]

The accusation that the Republican administrations of the 1920s gutted the antitrust laws similarly demands revision. By the 1920s, dominant public opinion had come to accept the giant corporation not simply as here to stay but as a positive good. Still, the continuing symbolic appeal of antitrust made GOP leaders shy away from any major revision of the antitrust laws. When petroleum company executives appealed to President Coolidge to sanction their joining to restrict production to deal with the price-depressing oil surplus, Coolidge rebuffed their plea. And Hoover thought that William J. Donovan, the head of the Justice Department's antitrust division under Coolidge, was too tolerant of cartelization. Although wishing to gain what he saw as the efficiencies resulting from business cooperation, Hoover accepted the existing antitrust framework except for special cases such as export associations and natural resources. Accordingly, after Hoover came to the White House, the Justice Department initiated prosecutions of a number of arrangements that Donovan had approved, and pressured the Federal Trade Commission into scrapping its program of approving codes of fair competition formulated by industry. Most important, the Supreme Court retained final say on what was or was not lawful. In its 1920 United States Steel decision, the Court held that bigness was not itself illegal so long as there was "no adventitious interference . . . to either fix or maintain prices." But the Court remained hostile to collusive pricing arrangements. Despite the decisions in the Maple Flooring and Cement Institute cases approving trade association information-sharing, the Court in *United States v. Trenton Pottery Company* (1927) held that price-fixing—in this case, the prices of vitreous pottery for bathrooms and lavatories by the Sanitary Potters' Association—was illegal per se.[38]

Even in the heyday of the reform movement, progressives hewed to what Stanford University law professor Robert Rabin has termed a "policing model" of regulation. That model was premised upon "an autonomous market-controlled economy," government intervention limited to special circumstances of what is today called market failure. The Republican administrations of the 1920s took this same pragmatic approach. Thus, for example, Harding acceded to the demand by the so-called farm bloc in Congress for action to deal with the postwar farm crisis. New technology was another catalyst for the expansion of federal regulatory power. After a special presidential investigating board blamed the lagging development of American commercial aviation upon the lack of a national policy in the area, the Aviation Act of 1926 was adopted imposing federal sovereignty over air space and authorizing a Bureau of Aeronautics in the Commerce

Department to regulate the industry. Radio broadcasting was another example. The failure of the attempt by Secretary of the Navy Josephus
Daniels in 1918 and 1919 to nationalize the industry settled that broadcasting would not be government owned. After the naval monopoly of broadcasting was replaced at the war's end by privately owned and operated stations, Secretary of Commerce Hoover assumed regulation of the industry
by issuing licenses and assigning wave lengths under the questionable legal
authority of the Radio Act of 1912. After the Supreme Court ruled against
his doing so, Congress approved the Radio Act of 1927 to bring order out
of the resulting chaos by establishing a five-member Federal Radio Commission to assign broadcast frequencies.[39]

Most contemporary liberal historians automatically look upon institution of government regulation as a positive advance. But fuller scrutiny
shows that bigger government had its darker side. Those who regard as inevitable the capture of the regulatory agencies by the industries regulated
can find ample support in the 1920s. The new Federal Radio Commission
immediately became the handmaiden of the emerging broadcasting networks. Government regulation of commercial aviation brought cartelization of the industry. In 1921, Congress adopted at the behest of the independent telephone companies the Willis-Graham Act of 1921 giving the
Interstate Commerce Commission power to oversee mergers and acquisitions of telephone companies. From 1921 to 1934, the ICC approved 271
of the 274 acquisitions of competing exchanges proposed by American
Telephone and Telegraph. The regulatory agency that probably most disappointed the expectations of those favoring stricter government regulation was the Federal Trade Commission. Although many historians have
blamed Coolidge's appointment of former Washington state Republican
congressman William E. Humphrey for pulling the teeth of the FTC, Wilson's appointees were hardly an impressive lot. The Commission's close
ties with business groups went back to Edward N. Hurley, a former president of the Illinois Manufacturers' Association, who became FTC chair in
1916. And the FTC's concentration upon fraudulent and deceptive practices rather than larger issues of corporate power antedated Humphrey's
coming on the Commission.[40]

The post–New Deal focus upon the president as the driving force in the
American political system has led historians to skimp on their attention to
Congress. The GOP grip was not as firm on Congress in the 1920s as it was
on the White House. Although the Republicans ran up solid majorities in
presidential years, the Democrats narrowed the gap in the off-year elections. At the same time, members of Congress, regardless of party affiliation or even political ideology, had their own institutional interests to defend vis-à-vis the executive.[41]

There is no more than a handful of studies of individual members of the

House of Representatives. Most are of insurgent Republicans (or at least those involved in farm protest) or of Democrats who would go on to hold influential positions during the 1930s. Nicholas Longworth of Ohio has received far more attention as the husband of Alice Roosevelt than for his speakership of the House from 1925 to 1931. Even specialists in twentieth-century American political history would be hard-pressed to name his predecessor as Speaker or the numbers two and three men in the Republican House leadership during the 1920s (Frederick H. Gillett of Massachusetts was Speaker, 1919–25. The majority leadership was held by Franklin W. Mondell of Wyoming, 1919–23; Longworth, 1923–25; and John Q. Tilson of Connecticut, 1925–31. The majority whips were Harold Knutson of Minnesota, 1919–23; and Albert Vestal of Indiana, 1923–31). By contrast, there are two first-rate in-depth accounts of probably the most atypical House member, New York City's maverick Republican Fiorello La Guardia.

The bulk of the research upon the House has been by political scientists interested in long-term institutional development. Their major theme has been the decreasing ability of the party leadership to control the House after the successful revolt in 1910–11 against the iron-handed rule of Speaker Joseph G. Cannon. How far this process had proceeded by the twenties is difficult to answer. Nelson Polsby and his collaborators conclude that the Republican takeover of the House in 1919 resulted in a "major leap forward" in the decentralization of power in the House. And there was a significant fall-off in the cohesiveness of party voting in the 1920s compared with the late nineteenth century and the first decade of the twentieth. On the other hand, GOP leaders took advantage of their large majority after the 1924 election to punish those Republicans who had supported Robert M. La Follette's presidential bid by demoting them in committee rank or removing them from committees. Ronald M. Peters, the leading student of the speakership, finds Longworth "a powerful and effective speaker, the first assertive speaker since Cannon."[42]

Formal leadership of the Senate was firmly in regular hands. The GOP floor leaders were Henry Cabot Lodge of Massachusetts up to 1924, Charles Curtis of Kansas until his election as vice president in 1928, and James E. Watson of Indiana. But the balance of power in the upper chamber during much of the decade lay with a group of insurgent or progressive Republicans—mostly from west of the Mississippi—that were known as the "Sons of the Wild Jackass." The Senate insurgents have received extensive, and largely favorable, attention from historians. But there are grounds for skepticism about whether their reform commitments went much beyond tapping the treasury for the benefit of their farmer constituents. William Borah of Idaho appears to have been involved in play acting—talking the reform line, but doing no more than talking. Hiram Johnson of California was on his way to a crabbed irascibility that involved negativism for negativism's sake. Arthur J. Capper of Kansas and Charles L. McNary of Oregon were regular Republicans except on farm issues. Few of the Senate progressives of the 1920s would support the New Deal after the immediate crisis of the first hundred days. Nor did the insurgents achieve much in the way of legislation. Rarely did they have sufficient votes to pass their own measures. And when they did—as with the McNary-Haugen plan—they faced a presidential veto. For the most part—as with Mellon's tax proposals—they accomplished no more than to fight a rear guard, delaying action against administration initiatives.[43]

One reason for their lack of accomplishment was that most of these Republican progressives were temperamentally not team players and thus the group rarely could present a solid front. A second reason was their Jeffersonian-Jacksonian heritage with its deep-rooted suspicion of governmental favoritism to special interests. Few had a vision of a positive role for government. A third reason was the unreliability of their Democratic allies. The ranks of northern and western Democrats included such dependable supporters as Robert F. Wagner of New York, Burton K. Wheeler of Montana, and Thomas J. Walsh of Montana. But southerners dominated the Democratic Senate contingent—and they had their own agenda. Many were as committed as any Old Guard Republican to states' rights, limited government, and keeping spending down where no direct benefit for the southern interests was at stake. The growth of manufacturing below the Mason-Dixon line was beginning to undermine even traditional Democratic hostility to the protective tariff. Although a majority of southern congressmen still opposed the increased rates of the Fordney-McCumber tariff of 1922, there was a marked increase in the southern backing for protectionism. The insurgents' major victory—the fight by George W. Norris of Nebraska for continued government ownership of the hydroelectric- and nitrate-producing facilities at Muscle Shoals, Alabama—was because the majority of southern Democrats came to support that policy as promoting the region's economic development.[44]

The declining role of party as the coordinating force in the shaping of public policy heightened the leverage of organized pressure groups. The prime example of interest-group politics—even in the days when party discipline was stronger—was tariff-making. From the perspective of Republican politicians, tariff-making in the twenties was a success. The judicious inclusion of payoffs to farm interests in the Emergency Tariff of 1921 and the Fordney-McCumber Act of 1922 averted the split between the northeast and middle west that had proved so damaging to the GOP in the fight over the Payne-Aldrich Tariff of 1909. And GOP lawmakers read the results of the 1928 election when the party had taken a strongly protectionist line as a mandate for another boost in tariff rates in the Smoot-Hawley tariff. Many—then and since—have questioned the economic soundness of

American tariff policy. Critics have accused American high tariffs of aggravating the war debt-reparations tangle by preventing European nations
from earning the dollars needed to pay their debts by selling their goods to
the United States. The Smoot-Hawley tariff has been blamed for worsening the depression by provoking foreign retaliation that had a disastrous
impact upon foreign trade. But the tariff appears to have played at most a
secondary part in Europe's financial difficulties given the advantage American producers had over their foreign counterparts in most lines. The impact of even Smoot-Hawley upon world trade appears similarly to have
been exaggerated.[45]

Economic interest groups were a familiar phenomenon. Newer was the
emergence in the early twentieth century of what may be termed "ideological" interest groups. One of the most vocal included champions of
woman suffrage. The suffragettes were confident—and their opponents
were fearful—that votes for women would have a revolutionary impact
upon American politics. These expectations proved false. Contemporary
analysts blamed women's apathy for the sharp drop in voter turnout during
the 1920s. More recent studies have revised upward the percentage of
women who took advantage of the ballot. And the figures cast doubt upon
the familiar bromide that women voted as their husbands did. Still the results were far removed from the hopes of most suffragists. There were accompanying gains in women's legal status. Congress approved in 1922 the
Cable Act providing that a woman should have citizenship independently
of her husband. Twenty states admitted women to jury service. But the network of discriminations from which women suffered remained largely intact. Although the Classification Act of 1923 stipulated the principle of
equal pay for equal work in the federal civil service, bureau chiefs continued
to be permitted to exclude women from their domains. A 1928 survey
found that the majority of school districts did not permit a married woman
to teach. As late as 1940, a quarter of the states did not permit a wife to
make a contract. To the extent that woman suffrage made a difference, the
impact may have been the reverse of what its champions had anticipated.
Allan Lichtman finds that "women were more inclined than men to support presidential candidates who seemed less likely than their opponents to
tamper with the status quo."[46]

One fact is indisputable: women did not vote as a bloc. Nor was there
much effort made to organize such a bloc except for the feminists belonging to Alice Paul's National Woman's Party. For the NWP, suffrage was
no more than the first step. Its larger goal was to "remove all remaining
forms of subjection of women"; its major plank was adoption of a federal
constitutional amendment stating, "Men and Women shall have equal
rights throughout the United States." The NWP leadership made support
for that amendment the sole criterion for its backing of political candidates.

But the NWP was a tiny minority—numbering probably fewer than ten thousand members—even among women activists in the twenties. When Carrie Chapman Catt took the lead in launching the League of Women Voters as the successor to the National American Woman Suffrage Association, she stood firm against the League's focusing exclusively upon women's issues or supporting a candidate simply because she was a woman. Its image of women as good citizens rather than as a special interest group led the League to balk at the proposed equal rights amendment. As time passed, the League became more and more identified with mugwumpish-type governmental reform. The League, Eleanor Flexner has suggested, may "have short-circuited the political strength of the most gifted suffragist women. Certainly it planted firmly in the minds of a goodly number of politicians the idea that 'the ladies' were not really interested in politics—as politicians understood the term—but rather in 'reform,' which was quite another matter."[47]

Each of the national parties gave women representation on party committees and set up special women's divisions. Whatever the benefits that individuals gained from participation in these activities, women for the most part remained more window dressing than significant actors in party affairs. One of the few exceptions was Mark Hanna's daughter, Ruth Hanna McCormick, who became head of the GOP's woman's division before going on to win election in 1928 to Congress as representative-at-large from Illinois. A handful of women won election as state legislators, mayors, and members of the United States House of Representatives. Two women were elected governors in 1924—"Ma" Ferguson in Texas, when legal difficulties prevented "Pa" Ferguson from running, and Nellie Tayloe Ross in Wyoming, who won a special election to fill the last two years of her husband's term after his death. Women social workers had gained an influential position in federal, state, and local welfare bureaucracies. Outside this realm, however, women were rare in the higher administrative ranks. The highest ranking woman federal government official was Assistant Attorney General Mabel Brown Willebrandt. Probably the most politically influential woman of the decade was Al Smith's adviser Belle Moskowitz, whom many see as the brains behind Smith. What is most revealing about her role is the pains that she took to keep a low profile so as not to appear threatening to her male associates.[48]

Future research will no doubt fill in many details, thus more fully illuminating areas that still remain shadowy. But given the formidable body of scholarship presently on the books, the broad lineaments of development in the political realm during the twenties can be discerned. And the picture that emerges is in sharp contrast with the dominant image that has so long prevailed of a decade of stagnation, even reaction. On the contrary, the 1920s was a time when Americans and their leaders grappled with the prob-

lems of managing an ever more complex and pluralist socio-economic order. To many, the transformation of the United States into a modern urban-
industrial nation was a shock and threat; for others, a challenge and opportunity. The tension between those conflicting impulses was responsible for
the mixed, oft-times contradictory, responses that gave the era its distinctive character.

NOTES

The work on this paper was finished while I was a fellow at the Social Philosophy
and Policy Center, Bowling Green State University. I wish to thank the Center and
its staff for providing an ideal environment for scholarship.

1. Previous surveys include Richard Lowitt, "Prosperity Decade, 1917–1928,"
in William H. Cartwright and Richard L. Watson, Jr., eds., *Interpreting and Teach-
ing American History* (Washington, D.C., 1961), 231–61; John D. Hicks, "Research
Opportunities in the 1920's," *The Historian* 25 (November 1962): 1–13; Merle
Curti, *The 1920's in Historical Perspective* [Cotton Memorial Papers, Texas Western
College, No. 2] (El Paso, 1966); Burl Noggle, "The Twenties: A New Historio-
graphical Frontier," *Journal of American History* 53 (September 1966): 299–314;
Noggle, "Configurations of the Twenties," in Cartwright and Watson, eds., *The
Reinterpretation of American History and Culture* (Washington, D.C., 1973), 465–
90; Alan Brinkley, *Prosperity, Depression, and War, 1920–1945* (Washington, D.C.,
1990); and Henry F. May, "Shifting Perspectives on the 1920's," *Mississippi Valley
Historical Review* 43 (December 1956): 405–26. On American foreign policy, see
John Braeman, "American Foreign Policy in the Age of Normalcy: Three Historiographical Traditions," *Amerikastudien/American Studies* 26, no. 2 (1981): 125–58;
"Power and Diplomacy: The 1920s Reappraised," *Review of Politics* 44 (July 1982):
342–69; and "The New Left and American Foreign Policy During the Age of Normalcy: A Re-examination," *Business History Review* 57 (Spring 1983): 73–104.

2. Frederick Lewis Allen, *Only Yesterday: An Informal History of the Nineteen-
Twenties* (New York, 1931), xiii, 40–42, 126–29, 181–85.

3. William E. Leuchtenburg, *The Perils of Prosperity, 1914–32* (Chicago, 1958),
84–103, 224; Arthur M. Schlesinger, Jr., *The Crisis of the Old Order, 1919–1933*
(Boston, 1957), 57; John D. Hicks, *Republican Ascendancy, 1921–1933* (New York,
1960), 106. On their reform sympathies, see Stephen F. Depoe, *Arthur M.
Schlesinger, Jr., and the Ideological History of American Liberalism* (Tuscaloosa, Ala.,
1994); William E. Leuchtenburg, *In the Shadow of FDR: From Harry Truman to
Ronald Reagan*, rev. ed. (Ithaca, N.Y., 1985), vii–xi; John D. Hicks, *My Life with History: An Autobiography* (Lincoln, Nebr., 1968), 145–47, 163, 230; Thomas B. Silver,
Coolidge and the Historians (Durham, N.C., 1982).

4. Louis Galambos, "The Emerging Organizational Synthesis in Modern
American History," *Business History Review* 44 (Autumn 1970): 279–90; Robert D.
Cuff, "American Historians and the 'Organizational Factor,'" *Canadian Review of*

American Studies 4 (Spring 1973): 19–31; Ellis W. Hawley, "The Discovery and Study of a Corporate Liberalism," *Business History Review* 52 (Autumn 1978): 309–20; Robert F. Berkhofer, Jr., "The Organizational Interpretation of American History: A New Synthesis," *Prospects* 4 (1979): 611–29; Robert H. Wiebe, *The Search for Order, 1877–1920* (New York, 1967), 286–302; Galambos, "Technology, Political Economy, and Professionalization: Central Themes of the Organizational Synthesis," *Business History Review* 57 (Autumn 1978): 471; Louis Galambos and Joseph Pratt, *The Rise of the Corporate Commonwealth: United States Business and Public Policy in the Twentieth Century* (New York, 1988), 41; Hawley, "Secretary Hoover and the Bituminous Coal Problem, 1921–1928," *Business History Review* 42 (Autumn 1968): 247–70; Hawley, "Herbert Hoover, the Commerce Secretariat, and the Vision of an Associative State," *Journal of American History* 61 (June 1974): 116–40; Hawley, "Secretary Hoover and the Changing Framework of New Era Historiography" and "Herbert Hoover and Economic Stabilization, 1921–22," both in Hawley, ed., *Herbert Hoover as Secretary of Commerce: Studies in New Era Thought and Practice* (Iowa City, 1981), 11–16, 43–79; Hawley, "Three Facets of Hoover Associationalism: Lumber, Aviation, and Movies, 1921–1930," in Thomas K. McCraw, ed., *Regulation in Perspective: Historical Essays* (Cambridge, Mass., 1981), 95–123; "Industrial Policy in the 1920s and 1930s," in Claude E. Barfield and William E. Schambra, eds., *The Politics of Industrial Policy* (Washington, D.C., 1986), 63–86; and "Neo-Institutional History and the Understanding of Herbert Hoover," in Lee Nash, ed., *Understanding Herbert Hoover: Ten Perspectives* (Stanford, 1987), 65–84; Hawley, *The Great War and the Search for a Modern Order: A History of the American People and Their Institutions, 1917–1933* (New York, 1979), vi.

5. Albro Martin, *Enterprise Denied: Origins of the Decline of American Railroads, 1897–1917* (New York, 1971); Irwin Unger, "The 'New Left' and American History," *American Historical Review* 72 (July 1967): 1237–63; Joseph Siracusa, *New Left Diplomatic Histories and Historians* (Port Washington, N.Y., 1973); William Appleman Williams, *The Tragedy of American Diplomacy* (Cleveland, 1959), 118; Williams, "The Legend of Isolationism in the 1920's," *Science & Society* 18 (Winter 1954): 1–20; James Weinstein, *The Corporate Ideal in the Liberal State, 1900–1916* (Boston, 1968); Martin J. Sklar, *The Corporate Reconstruction of American Capitalism, 1890–1916: The Market, Law, and Politics* (Cambridge, U.K., 1988); and R. Jeffrey Lustig, *Corporate Liberalism: The Origins of Modern American Political Theory, 1890–1920* (Berkeley, 1982); Gabriel Kolko, *Main Currents in Modern American History* (New York, 1976), especially 1–33, 107–53.

6. Arthur S. Link, "What Happened to the Progressive Movement in the 1920's?" *American Historical Review* 64 (July 1959): 833–51; Morton Keller, *Regulating a New Economy: Public Policy and Economic Change in America, 1900–1933* (Cambridge, Mass., 1990), 3; Keller, *Regulating a New Society: Public Policy and Social Change in America, 1900–1933* (Cambridge, Mass., 1994), 5–7.

7. Walter Dean Burnham, "The System of 1896," in Paul L. Kleppner et al., *The Evolution of American Electoral Systems* (Westport, Conn., 1981), 147–202; Kleppner, *Continuity and Change in Electoral Politics, 1893–1928* (New York, 1987). Arthur M. Schlesinger, Jr., and Fred L. Israel, eds., *History of American Presidential Elections, 1789–1968*, 4 vols. (New York, 1971), includes Donald R. McCoy, "Election of 1920" (3: 2349–85), David M. Burner, "Election of 1924" (3: 2459–90), and

Lawrence H. Fuchs, "Election of 1928" (3:2585–609). More specialized studies are Clifford Nelson, *German-American Political Behavior in Nebraska and Wisconsin 1916–1920*, University of Nebraska-Lincoln Publications, no. 217 (Lincoln, Nebr., 1972); John M. Allswang, *A House for All Peoples: Ethnic Politics in Chicago, 1890–1936* (Lexington, Ky., 1971), 40–47, 49, 51, 77, 79; R. A. Burchell, "Did the Irish and German Voters Desert the Democrats in 1920? A Tentative Statistical Answer," *Journal of American Studies* 6 (August 1972): 153–64; John W. Jeffries, *Testing the Roosevelt Coalition: Connecticut Society and Politics in the Era of World War II* (Knoxville, 1979), 1–20; Richard A. Varbero, "The Politics of Ethnicity: Philadelphia's Italians in the 1920's," in Francesco Coradasco, ed., *Studies in Italian American Social History: Essays in Honor of Leonard Covallo* (Totowa, N.J., 1975), 164–81; Stefano Luconi, "The New Deal Realignment and the Italian-American Community of Philadelphia," *Journal of American Studies* 28 (December 1994): 405–9; Gerald M. Gramm, *The Making of New Deal Democrats: Voting Behavior and Realignment in Boston, 1920–1940* (Chicago, 1989), 45–58, 75–86, 100; Richard B. Sherman, "The Harding Administration and the Negro: An Opportunity Lost," *Journal of Negro History* 49 (July 1964): 151–68; Allswang, "The Chicago Negro Voter and the Democratic Consensus: A Case Study, 1918–1936," *Journal of the Illinois State Historical Society* 60 (Summer 1967): 145–75; John C. Blair, "A Time for Parting: The Negro During the Coolidge Years," *Journal of American Studies* 3 (December 1969): 177–99; William Giffin, "Black Insurgency in the Republican Party of Ohio, 1920–1932," *Ohio History* 82 (Spring 1973): 25–45; Marsha Hurst, "Structures of Inequality: Two Decades of New York Black Republican Politics," in Louis Maisel and Joseph Cooper, eds., *Political Parties: Development and Decay* (Beverly Hills, 1978): 99–143; Allan J. Lichtman, *Prejudice and the Old Politics: The Presidential Election of 1928* (Chapel Hill, 1979): 144–59.

8. Daniel Leab, "Coolidge, Hays, and 1920s Movies: Some Aspects of Image and Reality," paper presented at the Library of Congress "Calvin Coolidge and the Coolidge Era" conference, October 5–7, 1995, published herein, chap. 4; Ralph M. Goldman, *The National Party Chairmen and Committees: Factionalism at the Top* (Armonk, N.Y., 1990), 274–303; and Will Hays, *The Memoirs of Will H. Hays* (Garden City, N.Y., 1955).

9. Wesley M. Bagby, "The 'Smoked-Filled Room' and the Nomination of Warren G. Harding," *Mississippi Valley Historical Review* 41 (March 1955): 657–74; Bagby, *The Road to Normalcy: The Presidential Campaign and Election of 1920* (Baltimore, 1962); Donald E. Williams, "Dawes and the 1924 Republican Vice Presidential Nomination," *Mid-America* 44 (January 1962): 3–18; Donald R. McCoy, "To the White House: Herbert Hoover, August 1927–March 1929," in Martin L. Fausold and George T. Mazuzan, *The Hoover Presidency: A Reappraisal,* (Albany, N.Y., 1974), 29–36; Robert Skowronek, *The Politics Presidents Make: Leadership from John Adams to George Bush* (Cambridge, Mass., 1993), 268–69.

10. William Dean Burnham, "The United States: The Politics of Heterogeneity," in Richard Rose, ed., *Electoral Behavior: A Comparative Handbook* (New York, 1974), 662–80; Paul Kleppner, *Who Voted? The Dynamics of Electoral Turnout, 1870–1980* (New York, 1982), 55–82; Michael E. McGerr, *The Decline of Popular Politics: The American North, 1865–1928* (New York, 1986), 184–210; Jerome M. Clubb, William H. Flanigan, and Nancy H. Zingale, *Partisan Realignment: Voters, Parties,*

and Government in American History (Beverly Hills, 1980), 137–38, 168–69, 195, 207–8; William Claggett and John Van Wingen, "The 'Onward March of Party Decomposition' in the American Electorate: An Empirical Examination, 1876–1924," *Social Science History* 17 (Spring 1993): 37–70. In 1920, Harding even carried Tennessee: Gary Reichard, "The Aberration of 1920: An Analysis of Harding's Victory in Tennessee," *Journal of Southern History* 36 (February 1970): 33–49. Regarding the Democratic plight: Allan J. Lichtman, "They Endured: Democrats Between World War I and the Depression," in Peter B. Kovler, ed., *Democrats and the American Idea: A Bicentennial Appraisal* (Washington, D.C., 1992), 229–46; Judith M. Stanley, "Cordell Hull and Democratic Party Unity," *Tennessee Historical Quarterly* 32 (Summer 1973): 169–87; James E. Cebula, *James M. Cox: Journalist and Politician* (New York, 1985); C. H. Cramer, *Newton D. Baker: A Biography* (Cleveland, 1961); William H. Harbaugh, *Lawyer's Lawyer: The Life of John W. Davis* (New York, 1973); Frank Freidel, *Franklin D. Roosevelt*, vol. 2, *The Ordeal* (Boston, 1954); Robert K. Murray, *The 103rd Ballot: Democrats and the Disaster in Madison Square Garden* (New York, 1976); Lee Allen, "The McAdoo Campaign for the Presidential Nomination in 1924," *Journal of Southern History* 29 (May 1963): 211–28; Allen, "The Underwood Movement of 1924," *Alabama Review* 15 (April 1962): 83–99; David H. Stratton, "Splattered with Oil: William G. McAdoo and the 1924 Democratic Presidential Nomination," *Southwestern Social Science Quarterly* 44 (January 1963): 62–75; David M. Burner, "The Democratic Party in the Election of 1924," *Mid-America* 45 (January 1963): 18–35.

11. David M. Burner, *The Politics of Provincialism: The Democratic Party in Transition, 1918–1932* (New York, 1968). Re: Al Smith's progressivism: Oscar Handlin, *Al Smith and His America* (Boston, 1958); Matthew Josephson and Hannah Josephson, *Al Smith: Hero of the Cities: A Portrait Drawn from the Papers of Frances Perkins* (Boston, 1969); Richard O'Connor, *The First Hurrah: A Biography of Al Smith* (New York, 1970); Paula Eldot, *Governor Al Smith: The Politician as Reformer* (New York, 1983); Don C. Neal, *The World Beyond the Hudson: Alfred E. Smith and National Politics, 1918–1928* (New York, 1983); Douglas B. Craig, *After Wilson: The Struggle for the Democratic Party, 1920–1934* (Chapel Hill, 1992), especially 112–30.

12. James C. Garand and Donald A. Gross, "Changes in the Vote Margins for Congressional Candidates: A Specification of Historical Trends," *American Political Science Review* 78 (March 1984): 17–30; Gross and Garand, "The Vanishing Marginals, 1824–1980," *Journal of Politics* 46 (February 1984): 224–37; Gross and Donald Breaux, "Historical Trends in U.S. Senate Elections, 1912–1988," *American Politics Quarterly* 19 (July 1991): 284–309. The classic description of southern politics under the one-party system by V. O. Key, Jr., with Alexander Heard, *Southern Politics in State and Nation* (New York, 1949), 16, applies as much to the 1920s as to the later period upon which the work focuses. Allen W. Moger, *Bourbonism to Byrd, 1870–1925* (Charlottesville, 1968); Raymond A. Pulley, *Old Virginia Restored: An Interpretation of the Progressive Impulse, 1870–1930* (Charlottesville, 1968); Joseph A. Fry and Bent Tarter, "The Redemption of the Fighting Ninth: The 1922 Congressional Election in the Ninth District of Virginia and the Origins of the Byrd Organization," *South Atlantic Quarterly* 77 (Summer 1978): 352–70; Fry, "Senior Adviser to the Democratic 'Organization': William Thomas Reed and Virginia Politics, 1925–1935," *Virginia Magazine of History and Biography* 85 (October 1977): 445–69;

Edward Younger and James Tice Moore, eds., *The Governors of Virginia, 1860–1978* (Charlottesville, 1982); Ronald L. Heinemann, *Harry Byrd of Virginia* (Charlottesville, 1996); George B. Tindall, *The Emergence of the New South, 1913–1945* (Baton Rouge, 1967), 184–284; Dewey W. Grantham, *The Life and Death of the Solid South* (Lexington, Ky., 1988), 78–101; Grantham, *The South in Modern America: A Region at Odds* (New York, 1994), 88–115; Blaine A. Brownell, *The Urban Ethos in the South, 1920–1930* (Baton Rouge, 1975); David R. Colburn and Richard K. Scher, *Florida's Gubernatorial Politics in the Twentieth Century* (Tallahassee, 1980); James R. Scales and Danney Goble, *Oklahoma Politics: A History* (Norman, Okla., 1982); Numan V. Bartley, *The Creation of Modern Georgia* (Athens, Ga., 1982); James F. Cook, *The Governors of Georgia, 1754–1995* (Macon, Ga., 1995); William R. Majors, *Change and Continuity: Tennessee Politics since the Civil War* (Macon, Ga., 1986); David D. Lee, *Tennessee in Turmoil: Politics in the Volunteer State, 1920–1932* (Memphis, 1979); Timothy P. Donovan and Willard B. Gatewood, Jr., eds., *The Governors of Arkansas: Essays in Political Biography* (Fayetteville, Ark., 1981); Lowell D. Harrison, ed., *Kentucky's Governors, 1792–1985* (Lexington, Ky., 1985); Albert D. Kirwan, *Revolt of the Rednecks: Mississippi Politics, 1876–1925* (Lexington, Ky., 1951); Norman D. Brown, *Hood, Bonnet, and Little Brown Jug: Texas Politics, 1921–1928* (College Station, Tex., 1984); George B. Tindall, "Business Progressivism: Southern Politics in the Twenties," *South Atlantic Quarterly* 62 (Winter 1963): 92–106; Alan P. Sindler, *Huey Long's Louisiana: State Politics, 1920–1952* (Baltimore, 1956); T. Harry Williams, *Huey Long* (New York, 1972); Perry H. Howard, *Political Tendencies in Louisiana*, rev. ed. (Baton Rouge, 1971); William I. Hair, *The Kingfish and His Realm: The Life and Times of Huey Long* (Baton Rouge, 1991); Daniel W. Hollis, "Cole Blease: The Years Between the Governorship and the Senate, 1915–1924," *South Carolina Historical Magazine* 80 (January 1979): 1–17 and "Cole L. Blease and the Senatorial Campaign of 1924," *Proceedings of the South Carolina Historical Association* (1978), 53–68; Bryant Simon, "The Appeal of Cole Blease of South Carolina: Race, Class, and Sex in the New South," *Journal of Southern History* 62 (February 1996): 57–86; Reinhard Luthin, *American Demagogues: Twentieth Century* (Boston, 1954), 153–81; William Anderson, *The Wild Man from Sugar Creek: The Political Career of Eugene Talmadge* (Baton Rouge, 1975); A. Wigfall Green, *The Man Bilbo* (Baton Rouge, 1963); and Chester W. Morgan, *Redneck Liberal: Theodore G. Bilbo and the New Deal* (Baton Rouge, 1985).

13. David R. Mayhew, *Placing Parties in American Politics: Organization, Electoral Settings, and Government Activity in the Twentieth Century* (Princeton, 1986), 224–25; Herbert F. Janick, Jr., *A Diverse People: Connecticut 1914 to the Present* (Chester, Conn., 1975), 24–37; Herbert F. Margulies, "The Election of 1920 in Wisconsin: The Return to 'Normalcy' Reappraised," *Wisconsin Magazine of History* 41 (Autumn 1957): 15–22; Paul W. Glad, *The History of Wisconsin*, vol. 5, *War, a New Era, and Depression, 1914–1940* (Madison, 1990), 266–345; Herbert Margulies, *Senator Lenroot of Wisconsin: A Political Biography 1900–1929* (Columbia, Mo., 1977); Jackson K. Putnam, "The Persistence of Progressivism in the 1920s: The Case of California," *Pacific Historical Review* 35 (November 1966): 395–411; Michael P. Rogin and John L. Shover, *Political Change in California: Critical Elections and Social Movements, 1890–1966* (Westport, Conn., 1970), 51–52; Tom Sitton, *John Randolph Haynes: California Progressive* (Stanford, 1992); Jerry Nepresh, *The Brookhart Campaigns in*

Iowa, 1920–1926: A Study in the Motivation of Political Attitudes (New York, 1932); George W. McDaniel, "New Era Radicalism: Smith W. Brookhart and the Radical Critique," *Annals of Iowa* 49 (Winter/Spring 1988): 208–20; McDaniel, *Smith Wildman Brookhart: Iowa's Renegade Republican* (Ames, Iowa, 1995); John Braeman, *Albert J. Beveridge: American Nationalist* (Chicago, 1970); Howard W. Allen, *Poindexter of Washington: A Study in Progressive Politics* (Carbondale, Ill., 1981).

14. Ron Briley, "Insurgency and Political Realignment: Regionalism and the Senatorial Elections of 1922 in Iowa, Nebraska, North Dakota, and Minnesota," *Mid-America* 72 (January 1990): 49–69; Frederick C. Luebke, "Political Response to Agricultural Depression in Nebraska, 1922," *Nebraska History* 47 (March 1966): 15–55. Regarding the "industrial-commercial core": Richard F. Bensel, *Sectionalism in American Political Development, 1880–1980* (Madison, 1984), 22–128; Elizabeth Sanders, "Farmers and the State in the Progressive Era," in Edward S. Greenberg and Thomas F. Mayer, eds., *Changes in the State: Causes and Consequences* (Newbury Park, Calif., 1990), 183–205; James Wright, *The Progressive Yankees: Republican Reformers in New Hampshire, 1906–1919* (Hanover, N.H., 1987), 142–85; J. Joseph Hutchmacher, *Massachusetts People and Politics, 1919–1933* (Cambridge, Mass., 1959), 45–76; Robert F. Wesser, *A Response to Progressivism: The Democratic Party and New York Politics, 1902–1918* (New York, 1986), 74–98, 161–66, 194–217; Paula Baker, *The Moral Frameworks of Public Life: Gender, Politics, and the State in Rural New York, 1870–1930* (New York, 1991), 155–77; John F. Reynolds, *Testing Democracy: Electoral Behavior and Progressive Reform in New Jersey, 1880–1920* (Chapel Hill, 1988), 145–67; Hoyt Landon Warner, *Progressivism in Ohio, 1897–1917* (Columbus, Ohio, 1964), 467–95; Thomas R. Pegram, *Partisans and Progressives: Private Interest and Public Policy in Illinois, 1870–1922* (Urbana, 1992), 151–223. For the impact of the war: Stuart I. Rochester, *American Liberal Disillusionment in the Wake of World War I* (University Park, Penn., 1976); the growth in the white collar class: Jürgen Kocka, *White Collar Workers in America, 1890–1940: A Social-Political History in International Perspective* (London, 1980), 165–91; Frank Stricker, "Affluence for Whom? Another Look at Prosperity and the Working Classes in the 1920s," *Labor History* 24 (Winter 1983): 13–14.

The one apparent exception to the waning of Republican progressivism in this area was Gifford Pinchot's success in Pennsylvania: M. Nelson McGeary, *Gifford Pinchot: Forester-Politician* (Princeton, 1960), 272–358; Samuel J. Astorino, "The Contested Senate Election of William Scott Vare," *Pennsylvania History* 28 (April 1961): 187–201; James A. Kehl and Astorino, "A Bull Moose Responds to the New Deal: Pennsylvania's Gifford Pinchot," *Pennsylvania Magazine of History and Biography* 88 (January 1964): 37–51; Lawrence L. Murray, "The Mellons, Their Money, and the Mythical Machine: Organizational Politics in the Republican Twenties," *Pennsylvania History* 42 (July 1975): 221–41.

15. Hamilton Cravens, "The Emergence of the Farmer-Labor Party in Washington Politics, 1919–20," *Pacific Northwest Quarterly* 57 (October 1966): 148–57; Jonathan Dembo, *Unions and Politics in Washington State, 1885–1935* (New York, 1983); Merle W. Wells, "Fred T. DuBois and the Nonpartisan League in the Idaho Election of 1918," *Pacific Northwest Quarterly* 56 (January 1965): 17–29; Hugh T. Lovin, "The Farmer Revolt in Idaho, 1914–1922," *Idaho Yesterdays* 20 (Fall 1976): 2–15; Lovin, "The Nonpartisan League and Progressive Renaissance in Idaho,

1919–1924," *Idaho Yesterdays* 32 (Fall 1988): 2–15; Gilbert C. Fite, "The Nonpartisan League in Oklahoma," *Chronicles of Oklahoma* 24 (Summer 1946): 146–57; Garin Burbank, "Agrarian Radicals and Their Opponents in Southern Oklahoma, 1910–1924," *Journal of American History* 58 (June 1971): 5–23; James R. Green, *Radical Movements in the Southwest, 1895–1943* (Baton Rouge, 1978); John Thompson, *Closing the Frontier: Radical Response in Oklahoma, 1889–1923* (Norman, Okla., 1986); Michael P. Rogin, *The Intellectuals and McCarthy: The Radical Specter* (Cambridge, Mass., 1967), 72–75, 120–24, 144–51; Carl H. Chrislock, *Ethnicity Challenged: The Upper Midwest Norwegian-American Experience in World War I* (Northfield, Minn., 1987), 122–44; Albert F. Gunns, *Civil Liberties in Crisis: The Pacific Northwest, 1917–1940* (New York, 1983); Carlos Schwantes, "The Ordeal of William Morley Bouck, 1918–1919: Limits to Federal Suppression of Agrarian Dissidents," *Agricultural History* 59 (July 1985): 417–28; Theodore Saloutos, "The Rise of the Nonpartisan League in North Dakota, 1915–1917," *Agricultural History* 20 (January 1946): 43–61; Saloutos, "The Expansion and Decline of the Nonpartisan League in the Western Middle West, 1917–1921," *Agricultural History* 20 (October 1946): 235–52; Robert Morlan, *Political Prairie Fire: The Nonpartisan League, 1915–1922* (Minneapolis, 1955); Dale Baum, "The New Day in North Dakota: The Nonpartisan League and the Politics of Negative Revolution," *North Dakota History* 40 (Spring 1973): 5–18; Edward Blackorby, *Prairie Rebel: The Public Life of William Lemke* (Lincoln, Nebr., 1963); Patrick McGuire, "The Nonpartisan League and Social Democracy in the United States: Social Networks, Class Power, State Occupancy, and Embedded Class Biases," *Political Power and Social Theory* 9 (1995): 61–87; Charles R. Lamb, "The Nonpartisan League and Its Expansion into Minnesota," *North Dakota Quarterly* 49 (Summer 1981): 108–43; Carl Chrislock, *The Progressive Era in Minnesota, 1898–1918* (St. Paul, Minn., 1971); Bruce Larson, *Lindbergh of Minnesota: A Political Biography* (New York, 1971); Millard Gieske, *Minnesota Farmer-Laborism: The Third Party Alternative* (Minneapolis, 1979); George Mayer, *The Political Career of Floyd B. Olson* (Minneapolis, 1951); Paul S. Holbo, "The Farmer-Labor Association: Minnesota's Party *within* a Party," *Minnesota History* 42 (Spring 1970): 301–9; David P. Nord, "Hothouse Socialism: Minneapolis, 1910–1925," in Donald T. Critchlow, ed., *Socialism in the Heartland: The Midwestern Experience, 1900–1925* (Notre Dame, Ind., 1986), 133–66; Nord, "Minneapolis and the Pragmatic Socialism of Thomas Van Lear," *Minnesota History* 45 (Spring 1976): 3–10; Donald G. Sofchalk, "Organized Labor and the Iron Miners of Northern Minnesota, 1907–1936," *Labor History* 12 (Spring 1971): 214–42; Richard M. Vallely, *Radicalism in the States: The Minnesota Farmer-Labor Party and the American Political Economy* (Chicago, 1989).

16. Paul Glad, "Progressives and the Business Culture of the 1920s," *Journal of American History* 53 (June 1966): 75–89; Jack C. Lane, *Armed Progressive: General Leonard Wood* (San Rafael, Calif.: 1978); Richard C. Lower, *A Bloc of One: The Political Career of Hiram Johnson* (Stanford, 1993); Robert E. Hennings, "Harold Ickes and Hiram Johnson in the Presidential Primary of 1924," in Donald F. Tingley, ed., *Essays in Illinois History in Honor of Glen Huron Seymour* (Carbondale, 1968), 101–19, 150–55; Linda Lear, *Harold Ickes: The Aggressive Progressive, 1874–1933* (New York, 1981); Larry Madaras, "Theodore Roosevelt, Jr., Versus Al Smith: The New York Gubernatorial Election of 1924," *New York History* 47 (October 1966): 372–90; Eu-

gene M. Tobin, *Organize or Perish: America's Independent Progressives, 1913–1933* (New York, 1986); Stanley Shapiro: "The Twilight of Reform: Advanced Progressives after the Armistice," *The Historian* 33 (May 1971): 349–64, "'Hand and Brain': The Farmer Labor Party of 1920," *Labor History* 26 (Summer 1985): 405–22, and "The Passage of Power: Labor and the New Social Order," *Proceedings of the American Philosophical Society* 120 (December 1976): 464–74; John R. Sillito, "The Making of an Insurgent: Parley P. Christensen and Utah Republicanism, 1900–1912," *Utah Historical Quarterly* 60 (Fall 1992): 319–34.

17. Kenneth C. MacKay, *The Progressive Movement of 1924* (New York, 1947); James H. Shideler, "The Progressive Party Campaign of 1924," *Wisconsin Magazine of History* 33 (June 1953): 444–57; Shideler, "The Disintegration of the Progressive Party Movement of 1924," *The Historian* 13 (Spring 1951): 189–201; Alan R. Havig, "A Disputed Legacy: Roosevelt Progressives and the La Follette Campaign of 1924," *Mid-America* 53 (January 1971): 44–64; Scott D. Johnston, "Wisconsin Socialists and the Conference for Progressive Political Action," *Wisconsin Magazine of History* 37 (Winter 1953–1954): 96–100; Johnston, "Robert M. La Follete and the Socialists: Aspects of the 1924 Presidential Campaign Re-examined," *Social Science* 50 (Spring 1975): 69–77; and John L. Shover, "The California Progressives and the 1924 Campaign," *California Historical Quarterly* 51 (Spring 1972): 59–74.

18. Tobin, *Organize or Perish*, 158.

19. Bernard K. Johnpoll, with Lillian Johnpoll, *The Impossible Dream: The Rise and Demise of the American Left* (Westport, Conn., 1981), 297–325; Werner Sombart, *Why Is There No Socialism in the United States?* (White Plains, N.Y., 1976); Daniel Bell, *Marxian Socialism in America* (Princeton, 1967); Bryan Sharp, "Historians and American Socialism, 1900–1920," *Science and Society* 34 (Winter 1971): 387–97; John H. M. Laslett and Seymour M. Lipset, eds., *Failure of a Dream? Essays in the History of American Socialism* (Garden City, N.Y., 1974); David A. Shannon, *The Socialist Party of America: A History* (New York, 1955); James Weinstein, *The Decline of Socialism in America, 1912–1925* (New York, 1975); Henry G. Stetler, *The Socialist Movement in Reading, Pennsylvania, 1896–1936: A Study in Social Change* (Philadelphia, 1974); Critchlow, *Socialism in the Heartland*; Bruce M. Stave, ed., *Socialism and the Cities* (Port Washington, N.Y., 1975); John T. Walker, "Socialism in Dayton, Ohio, 1912 to 1925: Its Membership, Organization, and Demise," *Labor History* 26 (Summer 1985): 384–404; Elmer A. Beck, *The Sewer Socialists: A History of the Socialist Party of Wisconsin, 1897–1940*, 2 vols. (Fennimore, Wis., 1982); Douglas E. Booth, "Municipal Socialism and City Government Reform: The Milwaukee Experience, 1910–1940," *Journal of Urban History* 12 (November 1985): 51–74; James Weinstein, "Radicalism in the Midst of Normalcy," *Journal of American History* 52 (March 1966): 773–90; Bernard K. Johnpoll, *Pacifist's Progress: Norman Thomas and the Decline of American Socialism* (Chicago, 1970); Harry Fleischman, *Norman Thomas: A Biography* (New York, 1964); Murray B. Seidler, *Norman Thomas: Respectable Rebel* (Syracuse, N.Y., 1961): W. A. Swanberg, *Norman Thomas: The Last Idealist* (New York, 1976); Theodore Draper, *American Communism and Soviet Russia* (New York, 1960); Harvey Klehr and John Earl Haynes, *The American Communist Movement: Storming Heaven Itself* (New York, 1992), 8–58; Harvey Klehr, John Earl Haynes, and Fridrikh I. Firsov, *The Secret World of American Communism* (New Haven, 1995), 20–30; Eldridge F. Dowell, *A History of Criminal Syn-*

dicalism Legislation in the United States (Baltimore, 1939); Carol Jenson, *Network of Control: State Supreme Courts and State Security Statutes, 1920–1970* (Westport, Conn., 1982); Woodrow C. Whitten, "Criminal Syndicalism and the Law in California: 1919–1927," *Transactions of the American Philosophical Society*, No. 59, Part 2 (1969); Stephen F. Rohde, "Criminal Syndicalism: The Repression of Radical Political Speech in California," *Western Legal History* 3 (Summer/Fall 1990): 309–39.

20. Kenneth Allen, *Components of Electoral Evolution: Realignment in the United States, 1912–1940* (New York, 1988), 119–21; V. O. Key, Jr., "Secular Realignment and the Party System," *Journal of Politics* 21 (May 1958): 198–210; Burner, *Politics of Provincialism*, 207–53; Samuel J. Eldersveld, "The Influence of Metropolitan Party Pluralities in Presidential Elections since 1920: A Study of Twelve Key Cities," *American Political Science Review* 43 (December 1949): 1194–95; Duncan MacRae, Jr., and James Meldrum, "Critical Elections in Illinois, 1888–1958," *American Political Science Review* 54 (September 1960): 677; Bruce M. Stave, "The 'La Follette Revolution' and the Pittsburgh Vote, 1932," *Mid-America* 49 (October 1967): 244–51; Roy V. Peel and Thomas C. Donnelly, *The 1928 Campaign: An Analysis* (New York, 1931), 123–24; Peel and Donnelly, *The 1932 Campaign: An Analysis* (New York, 1935), 220; Samuel Lubell, *The Future of American Politics* (New York, 1952), 36, 41.

21. Richard Hofstadter, "Could a Protestant Have Defeated Hoover in 1928?" *The Reporter*, 17 March 1960, 31–33; Paul A. Carter, "The Other Catholic Candidate: The 1928 Presidential Bid of Thomas J. Walsh," *Pacific Northwest Quarterly* 35 (January 1964): 1–8; Peter L. Peterson, "Stopping Al Smith: The 1928 Democratic Primary in South Dakota," *South Dakota History* 4 (Fall 1974): 439–54; William G. Carleton, "The Popish Plot of 1928: Smith-Hoover Presidential Campaign," *Forum* 112 (September 1949): 141–47; Edmund A. Moore, *A Catholic Runs for President: The Campaign of 1928* (New York, 1958); Paul Carter, "The Campaign of 1928 Re-examined: A Study in Political Folklore," *Wisconsin Magazine of History* 46 (Summer 1963): 263–72; James H. Smylie, "The Roman Catholic Church, the State, and Al Smith," *Church History* 29 (September 1960): 321–43; Andrew R. Baggeley, "Religious Influence in Wisconsin Voting, 1928–1960," *American Political Science Review* 56 (March 1962): 66–70; William Ogburn and Nell S. Talbot, "A Measurement of the Factors in the Presidential Election of 1928," *Social Forces* 8 (December 1929): 175–83; Richard A. Watson, "Religion and Politics in Mid-America: Presidential Voting in Missouri, 1928 and 1960," *Midcontinent American Studies Journal* 5 (Spring 1964): 33–55; Ruth Silva, *Rum, Religion, and Votes: 1928 Re-examined* (University Park, Penn., 1962), especialy 43–50; Robert M. Miller, "A Footnote to the Role of the Protestant Churches in the Election of 1928," *Church History* 25 (June 1956): 154–59; Douglas C. Stange, "Al Smith and the Republican Party at Prayer: The Lutheran Vote—1928," *Review of Politics* 32 (July 1970): 347–64; Hilyer H. Straton and Ferenc M. Szaz, "The Reverend John Roach Straton and the Presidential Campaign of 1928," *New York History* 49 (April 1968): 200–17; Virginius Dabney, *Dry Messiah: The Life of Bishop Cannon* (New York, 1949); Kenneth K. Bailey, *Southern White Protestantism in the Twentieth Century* (New York, 1964), 92–110; David Burner, "The Brown Derby Campaign," *New York History* 46 (October 1965): 356–80; McCoy, "To the White House"; Kent Schofield, "The Public Image of Herbert Hoover in the 1928 Campaign," *Mid-America* 51 (October 1969):

278–93; Gilbert C. Fite, "The Agricultural Issue in the Presidential Campaign of 1928," *Mississippi Valley Historical Review* 37 (March 1951): 653–72; Vaughn D. Bornet, *Labor Politics in a Democratic Republic: Moderation, Division, and Disruption in the Presidential Election of 1928* (Washington, D.C., 1964); Key, *Southern Politics*, 318–29; Hugh D. Reagan, "Race as a Factor in the Presidential Election of 1928 in Alabama," *Alabama Review* 19 (January 1966): 5–19; Richard A. Bradford, "Religion and Politics: Alfred E. Smith and the Election of 1928 in West Virginia," *West Virginia History* 36 (April 1975): 213–21; Herbert J. Doherty, Jr., "Florida and the Presidential Election of 1928," *Florida Historical Quarterly* 26 (October 1977): 174–86; Donald B. Kelley, "Deep South Dilemma: The Mississippi Press in the Presidential Election of 1928," *Journal of Mississippi History* 25 (April 1963): 63–93; Ben G. Edmunson, "Pat Harrison and Mississippi in the Presidential Elections of 1924 and 1928," *Journal of Mississippi History* 33 (November 1971): 333–50; G. Michael McCarthy, "The Brown Derby Campaign in West Tennessee: Smith, Hoover, and the Politics of Race," *West Tennessee Historical Society Papers* 27 (1973): 81–98; Nevin E. Neal, "The Smith-Robinson Campaign of 1928," *Arkansas Historical Quarterly* 19 (Spring 1960): 3–11; Richard L. Watson, Jr., "A Political Leader Bolts—F. M. Simmons in the Presidential Election of 1928," *North Carolina Historical Review* 37 (October 1966): 516–43; Stephen D. Zink, "Cultural Conflict and the 1928 Presidential Campaign in Louisiana," *Southern Studies* 17 (Summer 1978): 175–97; J. Mills Thornton III, "Alabama Politics, J. Thomas Heflin, and the Expulsion Movement of 1929," *Alabama Review* 22 (April 1968): 83–112; Glen T. Harper, "'Cotton Tom' Heflin and the Election of 1930: The Price of Party Disloyalty," *The Historian* 30 (May 1968): 389–401; Richard L. Watson, Jr., "A Southern Democratic Primary: Simmons vs. Bailey in 1930," *North Carolina Historical Review* 42 (Winter 1965): 21–46; Michael S. Patterson, "The Fall of a Bishop: James Cannon, Jr., *Versus* Carter Glass, 1909–1934," *Journal of Southern History* 39 (November 1973): 493–518; Grantham, *Life and Death of the Solid South*, 77; V. O. Key, "A Theory of Critical Elections," *Journal of Politics* 17 (February 1955): 3–18; Carl N. Degler, "American Political Parties and the Rise of the City: An Interpretation," *Journal of American History* 51 (June 1964): 51; Gerald M. Pomper, "Classification of Presidential Elections," *Journal of Politics* 29 (August 1967): 554; Allswang, *A House for All Peoples*, 54–56, 75–80; William J. Magavern, "Buffalo, New York: Political Realignments in the 1928 Presidential Election," *Clio: A Journal of History* 72 (Summer 1986): 25–40; Jerome M. Clubb and Howard W. Allen, "The Cities and the Election of 1928: Partisan Realignment?" *American Historical Review* 74 (April 1969): 1205–20; John L. Shover, "Was 1928 a Critical Election in California?" *Pacific Northwest Quarterly* 58 (October 1967): 196–204; Charles M. Dollar, "Innovation in Historical Research: A Computer Approach," *Computers and the Humanities* 3, no. 2 (1969): 139–51; Donald J. Alvarez and Edmund J. True, "Critical Elections and Political Realignment: An Urban Test Case," *Polity* 5 (Summer 1973): 563–76; Rogin, *The Intellectuals and McCarthy*, 80–81, 126–28, 151–54; W. Phillips Shively, "A Reinterpretation of the New Deal Alignment," *Public Opinion Quarterly* 35 (Winter 1971–1972): 621–24; Marc V. Levine, "Standing Political Decisions and Critical Realignment: The Pattern of Maryland Politics, 1872–1948," *Journal of Politics* 38 (May 1976): 292–325; Walter Dean Burnham, *Critical Elections and the Mainsprings of American Politics* (New York, 1970), 34–70; John L. Shover, "The Emergence of a Two-Party

System in Republican Philadelphia, 1924–1936," *Journal of American History* 60 (March 1974): 985–1002; Lawrence G. McMichael and Richard J. Trilling, "The Structure and Meaning of Critical Realignment: The Case of Pennsylvania, 1928–1932," in Bruce A. Campbell and Trilling, eds., *Realignment in American Politics: Toward a Theory* (Austin, 1980), 21–51; David Brady, "A Reevaluation of Realignments in American Politics: Evidence from the House of Representatives," *American Political Science Review* 79 (March 1985): 28–49; Lichtman, *Prejudice and the Old Politics*, 194–246; Luconi, "The New Deal Realignment," 407–14.

22. Gary M. Mancell, "The Evaluation of the Presidents: An Extension of the Schlesinger Poll," *Journal of American History* 57 (June 1970): 104–13; Robert K. Murray and Tim H. Blessing, "The Presidential Performance Study: A Progress Report," *Journal of American History* 70 (December 1983): 535–55; Murray and Blessing, *Greatness in the White House: Rating the Presidents*, 2d ed. (University Park, Penn., 1994), 16–17. Critical accounts include William Allen White, *Masks in a Pageant* (New York, 1928); M. R. Werner, *Privileged Characters* (New York, 1931); Samuel Hopkins Adams, *Incredible Era: The Life and Times of Warren Gamaliel Harding* (Boston, 1939); Karl Schriftgiesser, *This Was Normalcy: An Account of Party Politics During Twelve Republican Years, 1920–1932* (New York, 1948); Francis Russell, *The Shadow of Blooming Grove: Warren G. Harding and His Times* (New York, 1968); Stanley J. Underdal, "Warren G. Harding, the Politics of Normalcy, and the West," *Journal of the West* 34 (April 1995): 24–35; Eugene P. Trani and David L. Wilson, *The Presidency of Warren G. Harding* (Lawrence, Kans., 1977), 190–91. In regard to the scandals and poor appointments afflicting Harding's administration: Burl Noggle, "The Origins of the Teapot Dome Investigation," *Mississippi Valley Historical Review* 44 (September 1975): 237–66; Noggle, *Teapot Dome: Oil and Politics in the 1920's* (Baton Rouge, 1962); Noggle, "Oil and Politics," in John Braeman, Robert H. Bremner, and David Brody, eds., *Change and Continuity: The 1920's* (Columbus, Ohio, 1968), 33–65; Robert A. Waller, "Business and the Initiation of the Teapot Dome Investigation," *Business History Review* 36 (Autumn 1962): 334–53; J. Leonard Bates, "Watergate and Teapot Dome," *South Atlantic Quarterly* 73 (Spring 1974): 145–59; Bates, *The Origins of Teapot Dome: Progressives, Parties, and Petroleum, 1909–1921* (Urbana, 1963); David H. Stratton, "Behind Teapot Dome: Some Personal Insights," *Business History Review* 31 (Winter 1957): 393; Stratton, "New Mexico Machiavellian? The Story of Albert B. Fall," *Montana: The Magazine of Western History* 7 (October 1957): 2–14; Stratton, ed., *The Memoirs of Albert B. Fall* (El Paso, 1966); Davis D. Joyce, "Before Teapot Dome: Senator Albert B. Fall and Conservation," *Red River Valley Historical Review* 4 (Fall 1979): 44–51; James N. Giglio, *H. M. Daugherty and the Politics of Expediency* (Kent, Ohio, 1978), especially 201–3.

23. The fluctuations of the economy are treated in Frederic L. Paxson, "The Great Demobilization," *American Historical Review* 54 (January 1939): 237–51; John D. Hicks, *Rehearsal for Disaster: The Boom and Collapse of 1919–1920* (Gainesville, Fla., 1961); Arthur S. Link, "The Federal Reserve Policy and the Agricultural Depression of 1920–1921," *Agricultural History* 20 (July 1946): 166–75; Kenneth D. Roose, "The Production Ceiling and the Turning-Point of 1920," *American Economic Review* 48 (June 1958): 348–56; John D. Pilgrim, "The Upper Turning Point of 1920: A Reappraisal," *Explorations in Economic History* 11 (Spring 1974): 271–98;

Christina D. Romer, "World War I and the Postwar Depression: A Reinterpretation Based on Alternative Estimates of GNP," *Journal of Monetary Economics* 22 (July 1988): 91–115; J. R. Vernon, "The 1920–21 Deflation: The Role of Aggregate Supply," *Economic Inquiry* 29 (July 1991): 572–80. More favorable appraisals of Harding and his administration include Mark Sullivan, *Our Times: The United States 1900–1925*, vol. 6, *The Twenties* (New York, 1935), 138–264; Frederic L. Paxson, *American Democracy and the World War*, vol. 3, *Postwar Years: Normalcy, 1918–1923* (Berkeley, 1948); Laurin L. Henry, *Presidential Transitions* (Washington, D.C., 1960), 139–270; Donald E. Pitzer, "An Introduction to the Harding Papers," *Ohio History* 75 (Spring-Summer 1966): 76–84, and Kenneth W. Duckett, "The Harding Papers: How Some Were Burned . . . ," *American Heritage* 16 (February 1965): 24–31, 102–9; Eric F. Goldman, "A Sort of Rehabilitation for Warren G. Harding," *New York Times Magazine*, 26 March 1972, 42–43, 80–88; Burl Noggle, "The New Harding," *Reviews in American History* 1 (March 1973): 126–32; Louis W. Potts, "Who Was Warren G. Harding?" *The Historian* 36 (August 1974): 621–45; G. D. Libecap, "The Political Allocation of Mineral Rights: A Re-Evaluation of Teapot Dome," *Journal of Economic History* 44 (June 1984): 381–91; Eugene P. Trani, "Hubert Work and the Department of Interior, 1923–28," *Pacific Northwest Quarterly* 61 (January 1970): 31–40; Elmer E. Cornwell, Jr., *Presidential Leadership of Public Opinion* (Bloomington, Ind., 1965), 61–73; Andrew Sinclair, *The Available Man: The Life Behind the Masks of Warren Gamaliel Harding* (New York, 1965); Randolph C. Downes, "The Harding Muckfest: Warren G. Harding—Chief Victim of the Muck-for-Muck's Sake Writers and Readers," *Northwest Ohio Quarterly* 39 (Summer 1967): 5–37; Downes, *The Rise of Warren Gamaliel Harding, 1865–1920* (Columbus, Ohio, 1970); Robert K. Murray, "President Harding and His Cabinet," *Ohio History* 75 (Spring-Summer 1966): 108–25; Murray, *The Harding Era: Warren G. Harding and His Administration* (Minneapolis, 1969); Murray, *The Politics of Normalcy: Governmental Theory and Practice in the Harding-Coolidge Era* (New York, 1973); Murray, "The Twenties," in John A. Garraty, ed., *Interpreting American History: Conversations with Historians* (New York, 1970), 2:145–68.

24. William Allen White, *A Puritan in Babylon: The Story of Calvin Coolidge* (New York, 1938), 224; Claude M. Fuess, *Calvin Coolidge: The Man from Vermont* (Boston, 1939); Donald R. McCoy, *Calvin Coolidge: The Quiet President* (New York, 1967), viii, 421–22.

25. Hendrik Booraem V, *The Provincial: Calvin Coolidge and His World, 1885–1895* (Lewisburg, Penn., 1994), 188; J. Leonard Bates, "The Teapot Dome Scandal and the Election of 1924," *American Historical Review* 60 (January 1955): 303–22; Robert J. Maddox, "Keeping Cool with Coolidge," *Journal of American History* 53 (March 1967): 772–80; Howard H. Quint and Robert H. Ferrell, eds., *The Talkative President: The Off-the Record Press Conferences of Calvin Coolidge* (Amherst, Mass., 1964), 2, 53–54; Elmer E. Cornwell, Jr., "Coolidge and Presidential Leadership," *Public Opinion Quarterly* 21 (Summer 1957): 265–78; Cornwell, *Presidential Leadership of Public Opinion*, 73–98; John L. Blair, "Coolidge the Image-Maker: The President and the Press, 1923–1929," *New England Quarterly* 46 (December 1973): 499–522; John L. Blair, ed., "The Clark-Coolidge Correspondence and the Election of 1932," *Vermont History* 34 (April 1966): 84.

26. David Burner, *Herbert Hoover: A Public Life* (New York, 1979); Joseph S.

Davis, "Herbert Hoover, 1874–1964: Another Appraisal," *South Atlantic Quarterly* 68 (Summer 1969): 295–318; George H. Nash, *The Life of Herbert Hoover: The Engineer, 1874–1914* (New York, 1983), and *The Life of Herbert Hoover: The Humanitarian, 1914–1917* (New York, 1988); Richard Hofstadter, *The American Political Tradition and the Men Who Made It* (New York, 1948), 279–310; Carl Degler, "The Ordeal of Herbert Hoover," *Yale Review* 52 (Summer 1963): 563–83; Peri E. Arnold, "Herbert Hoover and the Continuity of American Public Policy," *Public Policy* 20 (Fall 1972): 525–44; Arnold, "Hoover as Administrator," *Review of Politics* 42 (July 1980): 329–48; Joan Hoff Wilson, *Herbert Hoover: Forgotten Progressive* (Boston 1975); Murray N. Rothbard, "Herbert Hoover and the Myth of Laissez-Faire," in Ronald Radosh and Rothbard, eds., *A New History of Leviathan: Essays on the Rise of the American Corporate State* (New York, 1972), 111–45; Gary D. Best, *The Politics of American Individualism: Herbert Hoover in Transition, 1918–1921* (Westport, Conn., 1975); Hawley, *Herbert Hoover as Secretary of Commerce*; Lawrence E. Gelfand, ed., *Herbert Hoover: The Great War and Its Aftermath, 1914–1922* (Iowa City, 1979); Carl E. Krog and William Tanner, eds., *Herbert Hoover and the Republican Era: A Reconsideration* (Washington, D.C., 1984); Herbert Hoover, *The Memoirs of Herbert Hoover: The Cabinet and the Presidency, 1920–1933* (New York, 1952); J. Joseph Huthmacher and Warren I. Susman, eds., *Herbert Hoover and the Crisis of American Capitalism* (Cambridge, Mass., 1973); *Herbert Hoover Reassessed: Essays Commemorating the Fiftieth Anniversary of the Inauguration of Our Thirty-First President*, Sen. Doc. 96-631, 96th Congress, 2d sess. (Washington, D.C., 1981); Nash, *Understanding Herbert Hoover*; Mark M. Dodge, ed., *Herbert Hoover and the Historians* (West Branch, Iowa, 1989); Joseph Brandes, *Herbert Hoover and Economic Diplomacy: Department of Commerce Policy, 1921–1928* (Pittsburgh, 1962); Carolyn Grin, "The Unemployment Conference of 1921: An Experiment in National Cooperative Planning," *Mid-America* 55 (April 1973): 83–107; Vaughn D. Bornet, "Herbert Hoover's Planning for Unemployment and Old Age Insurance Coverage, 1921 to 1933," in John W. Schacht, ed., *The Quest for Security: Papers on the Origins of the American Social Insurance System* (Iowa City, 1982), 36–59; Robert Zieger, "Herbert Hoover, the Wage-Earner, and the 'New Economic System,' 1919–1929," *Business History Review* 51 (Summer 1977): 161–89; Zieger, "Labor, Progressivism, and Herbert Hoover in the 1920's," *Wisconsin Magazine of History* 58 (Spring 1975): 196–208; James H. Shideler, "Herbert Hoover and the Federal Farm Board Project, 1921–1925," *Mississippi Valley Historical Review* 42 (March 1956): 710–29; Joan Hoff Wilson, "Hoover's Agricultural Policies, 1921–1928," *Agricultural History* 51 (April 1977): 355–61; Gary H. Koerselman, "Secretary Hoover and National Farm Policy: Problems of Leadership," *Agricultural History* 51 (April 1977): 378–95; William R. Johnson, "Herbert Hoover and the Regulation of Grain Futures," *Mid-America* 51 (July 1969): 155–74; James N. Giglio, "Voluntarism and Public Policy Between World War I and the New Deal: Herbert Hoover and the American Child Health Association," *Presidential Studies Quarterly* 13 (Summer 1983): 430–52; James P. Johnson, "Herbert Hoover: The Orphan as Children's Friend," *Prologue* 12 (Winter 1980): 193–206; Kendricks A. Clements, "Herbert Hoover and Conservation, 1921–1933," *American Historical Review* 89 (February 1984): 67–88; Douglas C. Drake, "Herbert Hoover, Ecologist: The Politics of Oil Pollution Control, 1921–1926," *Mid-America* 55 (July 1973): 207–28; Daniel E. Garvey, "Secretary Hoover and the

Quest for Broadcast Regulation," *Journalism History* 3 (Autumn 1976): 60–70, 85; Carl E. Krog, "'Organizing the Production of Leisure': Herbert Hoover, Fishing, and Outdoor Recreation in the 1920s," *Wisconsin Magazine of History* 67 (Spring 1984): 199–218; Evan Metcalf, "Secretary Hoover and the Emergence of Macroeconomic Management," *Business History Review* 49 (Spring 1975): 60–80; William J. Barber, *From the New Era to the New Deal: Herbert Hoover, the Economists, and American Economic Policy, 1921–1933* (Cambridge, U.K., 1985), 1–78; and Patrick D. Reagan, "From Depression to Depression: Hooverian National Planning, 1921–1933," *Mid-America* 70 (January 1988): 35–60; Guy Alchon, *The Invisible Hand of Planning: Capitalism, Social Science, and the State in the 1920s* (Princeton, 1985), 3–7, 73–76.

    27. Craig Lloyd, *Aggressive Introvert: A Study of Herbert Hoover and Public Relations Management, 1921–32* (Columbus, 1972); Louis W. Liebovich, *Bylines in Despair: Herbert Hoover, the Great Depression, and the U. S. News Media* (Westport, Conn., 1994), 1–81; M. Browning Carrott, "The Supreme Court and American Trade Associations, 1921–1925," *Business History Review* 44 (Autumn 1970): 320–38; Robert F. Himmelberg, *The Origins of the National Recovery Administration: Business, Government, and the Trade Association Issue, 1921–1933* (New York, 1976), 4–53; Robert H. Zieger, "The Career of James J. Davis," *Pennsylvania Magazine of History and Biography* 98 (January 1974): 67–89; Edward L. Schapsmeier and Frederick H. Schapsmeier, "Disharmony in the Harding Cabinet: Hoover-Wallace Conflict," *Ohio History* 75 (Spring/Summer 1966): 126–36, 188–90; David E. Hamilton, *From New Day to New Deal: American Farm Policy from Hoover to Roosevelt, 1928–1933* (Chapel Hill, 1991), 26–41; Bruce A. Lohoff, "Herbert Hoover, Spokesman of Humane Efficiency: The Mississippi Flood of 1927," *American Quarterly* 22 (Fall 1970): 690–700; Lohoff, *Herbert Hoover and the Mississippi Flood of 1927* (Syracuse, N.Y., 1968).

    28. Stephen Skowronek, *Building a New American State: The Expansion of National Administrative Capacities, 1877–1920* (Cambridge, U.K., 1982), 3–46; Margaret Weir and Theda Skocpol, "State Structures and the Possibilities for 'Keynesian' Responses to the Great Depression in Sweden, Britain, and the United States," in Peter B. Evans, ed., *Bringing the State Back In* (Cambridge, U.K., 1985), 134–36; Jeffrey E. Cohen, "The Telephone Problem and the Road to Telephone Regulation in the United States, 1876–1917," *Journal of Policy History* 3, no. 1 (1991): 32–51; Alan Stone, *Wrong Number: The Breakup of AT&T* (New York, 1989), 24–48; James C. Bonbright, *Public Utilities and the National Power Policies* (New York, 1940), 22–28; Morton Keller, *The Life Insurance Enterprise, 1885–1910: A Study in the Limits of Corporate Power* (Cambridge, Mass., 1963), 235–42, 288–89; H. Roger Grant, *Insurance Reform: Consumer Action in the Progressive Era* (Ames, Iowa, 1979); Karen Orren, *Corporate Power and Social Change: The Politics of the Life Insurance Industry* (Baltimore, 1974), 18–33.

    29. Stephen B. Wood, *Constitutional Politics in the Progressive Era: Child Labor and the Law* (Chicago, 1968), 111–303; Huthmacher, *Massachusetts People and Politics*, 64–71; Lynn Dumenil, "'The Insatiable Maw of Bureaucracy': Antistatism and Education Reform in the 1920s," *Journal of American History* 77 (September 1990): 499–524; Richard B. Sherman, "The Rejection of the Child Labor Amendment," *Mid-America* 45 (January 1963): 7–17; Clarke A. Chambers, *Seedtime of Reform:*

American Social Service and Social Action, 1920–1933 (Minneapolis, 1963), 38–42; Walter Trattner, *Crusade for the Children: A History of the National Child Labor Committee and Child Labor Reform in America* (Chicago, 1970), 163–86; Bill Kauffman, "The Child Labor Amendment Debate of the 1920s; or, Catholics and Mugwumps and Farmers," *Journal of Libertarian Studies* 10 (Fall 1992): 139–69; William R. Brock, *Welfare, Democracy, and the New Deal* (Cambridge, U.K., 1988), 44.

30. E. Cary Brown, "Episodes in the Public Debt History of the United States," in Rudiger Dornbusch and Mario Draghi, eds., *Public Debt Management: Theory and History* (Cambridge, U.K., 1990), 237–38; Carroll H. Woody, *The Growth of the Federal Government, 1915–1932* (New York, 1934), 1–3; Thomas E. Borcherding, "One Hundred Years of Public Spending, 1870–1970," in Borcherding, ed., *Budgets and Bureaucrats: The Sources of Government Growth* (Durham, N.C., 1977), 19–44; Roger L. Ransom, "In Search of Security: The Growth of Government Spending in the U.S., 1902–1970," in Ransom, Richard Sutch, and Gary M. Walton, eds., *Explorations in the New Economic History: Essays in Honor of Douglass C. North* (New York, 1982), 125–48; Robert Higgs, *Crisis and Leviathan: Critical Episodes in the Growth of the American Government* (New York, 1987), 150–51; Jacob Metzer, "How New Was the New Era? The Public Sector in the 1920s," *Journal of Economic History* 45 (March 1985): 119–26; Ballard C. Campbell, "Federalism, State Action, and 'Critical Episodes' in the Growth of American Government," *Social Science History* 16 (Winter 1992): 561–77; Edward D. Berkowitz and Kim McQuaid, "Bureaucrats as 'Social Engineers': Federal Welfare Programs in Herbert Hoover's America," *American Journal of Economics and Sociology* 39 (October 1980): 321–35; Berkowitz and McQuaid, *Creating the Welfare State: The Political Economy of Twentieth-Century Reform* (New York, 1980): 59–77. Studies of the individual programs include those on vocational education: Charles A. Prosser, *The Development of Vocational Education* (Chicago, 1951), and Bernice M. Fisher, *Industrial Education: American Ideals and Institutions* (Madison, 1967); and vocational rehabilitation: Mary E. Macdonald, *Federal Grants for Vocational Rehabilitation* (Chicago, 1944), and Edward D. Berkowitz, *Disabled Policy: American Programs for the Handicapped* (Cambridge, U.K., 1987).

31. Fritz M. Marx, "The Bureau of the Budget: Its Evolution and Present Role," *American Political Science Review* 39 (August 1945): 653–84; Edward Goedeken, "Charles G. Dawes Establishes the Bureau of the Budget," *The Historian* 50 (November 1987): 40–53; Frederick Mosher, *A Tale of Two Agencies: A Comparative Analysis of the General Accounting Office and the Office of Management and Budget* (Baton Rouge, 1984), 1–47; Charles G. Dawes, *The First Year of the Budget of the United States* (New York, 1923); Bascom N. Timmons, *Portrait of an American: Charles Gates Dawes* (New York, 1953); Peri E. Arnold, *Making the Managerial Presidency: Comprehensive Reorganization Planning, 1905–1980* (Princeton, 1986), 52–80; Paul V. Betters, *The Personnel Classification Board* (Washington, D.C., 1931); Ismar Baruch, *History of Position-Classification and Salary Standardization in the Federal Service, 1789–1941* (Washington, D.C., 1941); Paul P. Van Riper, *History of the United States Civil Service* (Evanston, Ill., 1958), 277–79, 296–314.

32. Leonard DeGraff, "Corporate Liberalism and Electric Power System Planning in the 1920s," *Business History Review* 64 (Spring 1990): 1–31; Clements, "Herbert Hoover and Conservation," 77–78; Norris Hundley, Jr., *Water and the West: The Colorado Compact and the Politics of Water in the American West* (Berkeley, 1975);

Grin, "Unemployment Conference of 1921"; Edward F. Sarno, "The National Radio Conferences," *Journal of Broadcasting* 13 (Spring 1969): 189–202; Costin, "Women and Physicians"; Bruce E. Seely, "Engineers and Government-Business Cooperation: Highway Standards and the Bureau of Public Roads, 1900–1940," *Business History Review* 58 (Spring 1984): 51–77; Seely, "The Diffusion of Science into Engineering: Highway Research at the Bureau of Public Roads, 1900–1940," in Peter J. Hugill and D. Bruce Dickson, eds., *The Transfer and Transformation of Ideas and Material Culture* (College Station, Tex., 1988), 143–62; Seely, *Building the American Highway System: Engineers as Policy Makers* (Philadelphia, 1987), chaps. 3–6; Austin F. Macdonald, *Federal Subsidies to the States: A Study in American Administration* (Philadelphia, 1923); Macdonald, *Federal Aid: A Study of the American Subsidy System* (New York, 1928); Macdonald, "Recent Trends in Federal Aid to the States," *American Political Science Review* 25 (August 1931): 628–34; V. O. Key, Jr., *The Administration of Federal Grants to the States* (Chicago, 1937); President's Research Committee on Social Trends, *Recent Social Trends in the United States*, 2 vols. (New York, 1933), 2:1395.

33. James Johnson, "The Role of Women in the Founding of the United States Children's Bureau," in Carol V. R. George, ed., *"Remember the Ladies": New Perspectives on Women in American History, Essays in Honor of Nelson Manfred Blake* (Syracuse, N.Y., 1975), 179–96; Jacqueline Parker and Edward M. Carpenter, "Julia Lathrop and the Children's Bureau: The Emergence of an Institution," *Social Service Review* 55 (March 1981): 60–77; Robyn Muncy, *Creating a Female Dominion in American Reform, 1890–1935* (New York, 1991); Molly Ladd-Taylor, "Hull House Goes to Washington: Women and the Children's Bureau," in Nora Lee Frankel and Nancy S. Dye, eds., *Gender, Class, Race, and Reform in the Progressive Era* (Lexington, Ky., 1991), 110–26; Ladd-Taylor, *Raising a Baby the Government Way: Mothers' Letters to the Children's Bureau, 1915–1932* (New Brunswick, N.J., 1986), 1–46; Donald C. Swain, *Federal Conservation Policy, 1921–1933* (Berkeley, 1963); George Morgan, *William B. Greeley: A Practical Forester, 1879–1955* (St. Paul, Minn., 1960); Robert Shankmen, *Steve Mather of the National Parks*, 3d ed. (New York, 1951); Swain, *Wilderness Defender: Horace M. Albright and Conservation* (Chicago, 1970); James R. Kluger, *Turning on Water with a Shovel: The Career of Elwood Mead* (Albuquerque, 1992); Richard G. Powers, *Secrecy and Power: The Life of J. Edgar Hoover* (New York, 1987), 130–78; Michal R. Belknap, "The Mechanics of Repression: J. Edgar Hoover, the Bureau of Investigation and the Radicals, 1917–1925," *Crime and Social Justice* 7 (Spring-Summer 1977): 49–58; David Williams, "The Bureau of Investigation and Its Critics, 1919–1921: The Origins of Federal Political Surveillance," *Journal of American History* 68 (December 1981): 560–79; Williams, "'They Never Stopped Watching Us': FBI Surveillance, 1924–1936," *UCLA Historical Journal* 2 (1981): 5–28; Athan G. Theoharis and John S. Cox, *The Boss: J. Edgar Hoover and the Great American Inquisition* (Philadelphia, 1988), 71–116; Theda Skocpol and Kenneth Finegold, "State Capacity and Economic Intervention in the Early New Deal," *Political Science Quarterly* 97 (Summer 1982): 255–78; David E. Hamilton, "Building the Associative State: The Department of Agriculture and American State-Building," *Agricultural History* 64 (Spring 1990): 207–18; Louis Ferleger and William Lazonick, "The Managerial Revolution and the Developmental State: The Case of U.S. Agriculture," *Business and Economic History*

22 (Winter 1993): 67–98; Gladys L. Baker, *The County Agent* (Chicago, 1939), and William J. Block, *The Separation of the Farm Bureau and the Extension Service: Political Issue in the Federal System* (Urbana, 1960); Russell Lord, *The Wallaces of Iowa* (Boston, 1947); Donald L. Winters, *Henry Cantwell Wallace as Secretary of Agriculture, 1921–1924* (Urbana, 1970); Winters, "Ambiguity and Agricultural Policy: Henry Cantwell Wallace as Secretary of Agriculture," *Agricultural History* 64 (Spring 1990): 91–98; John M. Hansen, "Choosing Sides: The Creation of an Agricultural Policy Network in Congress, 1919–1932," *Studies in American Political Development* 2 (1987): 183–229, Hansen, *Gaining Access: Congress and the Farm Lobby, 1919–1981* (Chicago, 1991), 26–77; Lloyd S. Tenny, "The Bureau of Agricultural Economics in the Early Years," and John D. Black, "The Bureau of Agricultural Economics—The Years in Between," *Journal of Farm Economics* 29 (November 1947): 1017–42; Harry C. McDean, "Professionalism, Policy, and Farm Economists in the Early Bureau of Agricultural Economics," *Agricultural History* 57 (January 1983): 64–82; McDean, "'Reform' Social Darwinists and Measuring Levels of Living on American Farms, 1920–1926," *Journal of Economic History* 43 (March 1983): 79–85; Richard S. Kirkendall, "L. C. Gray and the Supply of Agricultural Land," *Agricultural History* 37 (October 1963): 206–16; Ellis W. Hawley, "Economic Inquiry and the State in New Era America: Antistatist Corporatism and Positive Statism in Uneasy Coexistence," in Mary O. Furner and Barry Supple, eds., *The State and Economic Knowledge: The American and British Experiences* (Cambridge, U.K., 1990), 287–324; Joel Kunze, "The Bureau of Agricultural Economics' Outlook Program in the 1920s as a Pedagogical Device," *Agricultural History* 54 (Spring 1990): 252–61; Richard N. Lowitt, ed., *Journal of a Tamed Bureaucrat: Nils A. Olsen and the BAE, 1925–1935* (Ames, Iowa, 1980).

34. James Harvey Young, "Food and Drug Enforcement in the 1920s: Restraining and Educating Business," *Business and Economic History*, 2d ser., vol. 21 (1992), 119–28; Arthur S. Link, *Woodrow Wilson and the Progressive Era, 1914–1917* (New York, 1954), 76; Martin J. Sklar, "Woodrow Wilson and the Political Economy of Modern United States Liberalism," *Studies on the Left* 1 (Fall 1960): 17–47; Robert H. Wiebe, *Businessmen and Reform* (Cambridge, Mass., 1962), 147–48; Burton I. Kaufman, *Efficiency and Expansion: Foreign Trade Organization in the Wilson Administration, 1913–1921* (Westport, Conn., 1974), 63–90, 260–95; Cohen, "The Telephone Problem," 45–46, 58; John Brooks, *Telephone: The First Hundred Years* (New York, 1976), 147–53, 157–59; Alan Stone, *Public Service Liberalism: Telecommunications and Transitions in Public Policy* (Princeton, 1991), especially 195–204; Samuel P. Hays, *Conservation and the Gospel of Efficiency: The Progressive Conservation Movement, 1890–1920* (Cambridge, Mass., 1959), 198–240; Harold L. Platt, "World War I and the Birth of American Regionalism," *Journal of Policy History* 5, no. 1 (1993): 141–42.

35. David Burner, "1919: Prelude to Normalcy," in Braeman, *Change and Continuity: The 1920's*, 3–32; Burl Noggle, *Into the Twenties: The United States from Armistice to Normalcy* (Urbana, 1974); K. Austin Kerr, *American Railroad Politics, 1914–1920: Rates, Wages, and Efficiency* (Pittsburgh, 1968), 128–231; Skowronek, *Building a New American State*, 274–84; Robert L. Rabin, "Federal Regulation in Historical Perspective," *Stanford Law Review* 38 (May 1986): 1239–41; Ari and Olive Hoogenboom, *A History of the ICC: From Panacea to Palliative* (New York, 1976), 90–118; Robert B. Carson, *Main Line to Oblivion: The Disintegration of New*

York Railroads in the Twentieth Century (Port Washington, N.Y., 1971); Albro Martin, "The Self-Inflicted Wound: Government and the Destruction of the American Railroad System," in Joseph R. Frese, S. J., and Jacob Judd, eds., *Business & Government: Essays in Twentieth-Century Cooperation and Confrontation* (Tarrytown, N.Y., 1985, 53–83.

36. Paul M. Zeis, *American Shipping Policy* (Princeton, 1938), 81–236; John G. B. Hutchins, "The American Shipping Industry since 1914," *Business History Review* 18 (June 1954): 105–27; Jeffrey Safford, *Wilsonian Maritime Diplomacy, 1913–1921* (New Brunswick, N.J., 1978), 221–53; Safford, "World War I Maritime Policy and the National Security: 1914–1919," and John H. Kemble and Lane C. Kendall, "The Years Between the Wars: 1919–1939," in Robert A. Kilmarx, ed., *America's Maritime Legacy: A History of the U.S. Merchant Marine and Shipbuilding Industry Since Colonial Times* (Boulder, Col., 1979), 111–74.

37. Sidney Ratner, *American Taxation: Its History as a Social Force in Democracy* (New York, 1942), 425–26 and Ronald F. King, "From Redistribution to Hegemonic Logic: The Transformation of American Tax Politics, 1894–1963," *Politics and Society* 12 (1983): 1–52 indict 1920s tax policies as skewed in favor of the wealthy. Those policies are placed in fairer perspective by: Lawrence L. Murray, "Bureaucracy and Bi-Partisanship in Taxation: The Mellon Plan Revisted," *Business History Review* 52 (Summer 1978): 200–25; Benjamin Rader, "Federal Taxation in the 1920s: A Re-examination," *The Historian* 33 (May 1971): 415–35. Silver, *Coolidge and the Historians*, 101–27; Burton W. Folsom, Jr., *The Myth of the Robber Barons: A New Look at the Robber Barons* (Herndon, Va., 1991), 103–20, 156–60; W. Elliott Brownlee, "Economists and the Formation of the Modern Tax System in the United States: The World War I Crisis," in Furner and Supple, *State and Economic Knowledge*, 401–35; Gene Smiley and Richard H. Keehn, "Federal Personal Income Tax Policy in the 1920s," *Journal of Economic History* 55 (June 1995): 285–303; John F. Witte, *The Politics and Development of the Federal Income Tax* (Madison, 1985), 88–94; Carolyn Webber and Aaron Wildavsky, *A History of Taxation and Expenditures in the Western World* (New York, 1986), 421–27, 451–52; Robert E. Keleher and William P. Orzechowski, "Supply-Side Fiscal Policy: An Historical Analysis of a Rejuvenated Idea," in Richard H. Fink, ed., *Supply-Side Economics: A Critical Appraisal* (Frederick, Md., 1982), 145–47; Robert R. Keller, "Supply-Side Economic Policies During the Coolidge-Mellon Era," *Journal of Economic Issues* 16 (September 1982): 773–90; Metzer, "How New Was the New Era?" 120–21. Mellon still awaits a thoroughly researched scholarly biography. Harvey O'Connor's *Mellon's Millions: The Life and Times of Andrew Mellon* (New York, 1933) is a hostile polemic; Burton Hersh, *The Mellon Family* (New York, 1978), is gossipy and skeptical; David E. Koskoff, *The Mellons* (New York, 1970), is the most solid account available but is far from definitive. Whether the Mellon tax cuts were responsible for the prosperity of the 1920s is debated in Keller, "A Microeconomic History of Supply-Side Fiscal Policies in the 1920s," *Review of Social Economy* 42 (October 1984): 130–42 and Christopher Frenze, "Introduction to the Mellon Tax Cuts," *The Mellon and Kennedy Tax Cuts: A Review and Analysis* [A Staff Study Prepared for the Subcommittee on Monetary and Fiscal Policy of the Joint Economic Committee, Congress of the United States, 97th Congress, 2d Session] (Washington, D.C., 1982), 1–17.

38. Louis Galambos, *The Public Image of Big Business in America, 1880–1940: A Quantitative Study of Social Change* (Baltimore, 1975), 157–221; Gerald D. Nash, *United States Oil Policy, 1890–1964: Business and Government in Twentieth Century America* (Pittsburgh, 1968), 91–95; Himmmelberg, *Origins of the National Recovery Administration*; Ellis W. Hawley, "Antitrust and the Association Movement, 1920–1940," in *National Competition Policy: Historians' Perspectives on Antitrust and Government-Business Relations in the United States* (Washington, D.C., 1981), 104–13; Hawley, "Herbert Hoover and the Sherman Act, 1921–1933: An Early Phase of Continuing Issue," *Iowa Law Review* 74 (July 1989): 1067–103; Martin J. Sklar, *The Corporate Reconstruction of American Capitalism, 1890–1916: The Market, the Law, and Politics* (Cambridge, U.K., 1988), 86–175; Tony Freyer, *Regulating Big Business: Antitrust in Great Britain and America, 1880–1990* (Cambridge, U.K., 1992), 189–94; A. D. Neale, *The Antitrust Laws of the United States of America: A Study of Competition Enforced by Law*, 2d ed. (Cambridge, U.K., 1970), 32–50.

39. Rabin, "Federal Regulation in Historical Perspective," 1191–93; A. B. Genung, *The Agricultural Depression Following World War I and Its Political Consequences* (Ithaca, N.Y., 1954); James H. Shideler, *Farm Crisis, 1919–1923* (Berkeley, 1957); Nick A. Komons, *Bonfires to Beacons: Federal Civil Aviation Policy under the Air Commerce Act, 1926–1938* (Washington, D.C., 1978); Norris S. Hetherington, "The National Advisory Committee for Aeronautics: A Forerunner of Federal Government Support for Scientific Research," *Minerva* 28 (Spring 1990): 59–80; Roger E. Bilstein, *Flight Patterns: Trends of Aeronautical Development in the United States, 1918–1929* (Athens, Ga., 1983); David D. Lee, "Herbert Hoover and the Development of Commercial Aviation, 1921–1926," *Business History Review* 58 (Spring 1984): 78–102; Komons, "William P. McCracken, Jr., and the Regulation of Civil Aviation," and Lee, "Herbert Hoover and the Golden Age of Aviation," in William M. Leary, ed., *Aviation's Golden Age: Portraits from the 1920s and 1930s* (Iowa City, 1989), 35–59, 127–47, 155–60, 173–77; Murray Edelman, *The Licensing of Radio Services in the United States, 1927 to 1947* (Urbana, 1950); Walter B. Emery, *Broadcasting and Government: Responsibility and Regulation* (East Lansing, Mich., 1969); Susan Douglas, *Inventing American Broadcasting, 1899–1922* (Baltimore, 1987); Philip T. Rosen, "Broadcasting: The Politics of Innovation," *Continuity*, no. 3 (Fall 1981): 51–61, and *The Modern Stentors: Radio Broadcasting and the Federal Government, 1920–1934* (Westport, Conn., 1980); Hugh G. H. Aitken, *The Continuous Wave: Technology and American Radio, 1900–1932* (Princeton, 1985) and "Allocating the Spectrum: The Origins of Radio Regulation," *Technology and Culture* 35 (October 1994): 686–716; Garvey, "Hoover and the Quest for Broadcast Regulation"; Mary S. Mander, "The Public Debate about Broadcasting in the 1920s: An Interpretive History," *Journal of Broadcasting* 25 (Spring 1984): 167–85; Marvin R. Bensman, "The Zenith-WJAZ Case and the Chaos of 1926–27," *Journal of Broadcasting* 14 (Fall 1970): 423–40; Donald G. Godfrey, "Senator Dill and the 1927 Radio Act," *Journal of Broadcasting* 23 (Fall 1979): 477–89; Godfrey, "The 1927 Radio Act: People and Politics," *Journalism History* 4 (Autumn 1977): 74–78.

40. George J. Stigler, "The Theory of Economic Regulation," *Bell Journal of Economics and Management Science* 2 (Spring 1971): 3–21; Robert McChesney, *Telecommunications, the Mass Media, and Democracy: The Battle for Control of U. S. Broadcasting, 1928–1935* (New York, 1993), 16–37; Richard H. K. Vietor, "The Hubris of

Regulated Competition: Airlines, 1925–88," in Jack High, ed., *Regulation: Economic Theory and History* (Ann Arbor, Mich., 1991), 21–24; Cohen, "Telephone Problem," 63–64; G. Cullom Davis, "The Transformation of the Federal Trade Commission, 1914–1929," *Mississippi Valley Historical Review* 49 (December 1962): 437–55; Arthur M. Johnson, "The Federal Trade Commission: The Early Years, 1915–1935," in Frese and Judd, *Business & Government*, 163–70; Robert Wiebe, *Businessmen and Reform: A Study of the Progressive Movement* (Cambridge, Mass., 1962), 147–48; Keller, *Regulating a New Economy*, 39–40.

41. Frank Freidel, "Party or President? Historians View Twentieth-Century Politics," *Prologue* 19 (Summer 1979): 107–19; Skowronek, *Building a New American State*, 177–211.

42. Gilbert C. Fite, "Gilbert M. Haugen," in John N. Schacht, ed., *Three Progressives from Iowa* (Iowa City, 1980), 1–14; Peter T. Harstad and Bonnie Lindemann, *Gilbert N. Haugen: Norwegian-American Farm Politician* (Iowa City, 1992); Howard Zinn, *LaGuardia in Congress* (Ithaca, N.Y., 1959); Arthur Mann, *La Guardia: A Fighter Against His Times, 1882–1933* (Philadelphia, 1959); Philip A. Grant, Jr., "'Save the Farmer': Oklahoma Congressmen and Farm Relief Legislation, 1924–1928," *Chronicles of Oklahoma* 64 (Summer 1986): 75–87; Grant, "Southern Congressmen and Agriculture, 1921–1932," *Agricultural History* 53 (January 1979): 338–51; Irwin M. May, Jr., *Marvin Jones: The Public Life of an Agrarian Advocate* (College Station, Tex., 1980); Robert A. Waller, *Rainey of Illinois: A Political Biography, 1903–34* (Urbana, 1977); Bascom Timmons, *Garner of Texas* (New York, 1948); Anthony Champagne, *Congressman Sam Rayburn* (New Brunswick, N.J., 1984); D. B. Hardeman and Donald C. Bacon, *Rayburn: A Biography* (Austin, Tex., 1987); Robert P. Browder and Thomas C. Smith, *Independent: A Biography of Lewis W. Douglas* (New York, 1986); David Robertson, *Sly and Able: A Political Biography of James F. Byrnes* (New York, 1994); James Brough, *Princess Alice: A Biography of Alice Roosevelt Longworth* (Boston, 1975); Howard Teichman, *The Life and Times of Alice Roosevelt Longworth* (Englewood Cliffs, N.J., 1979); Carol Felsenthal, *Alice Roosevelt Longworth* (New York, 1988); Garrison Nelson, "Leadership Position-Holding in the United States House of Representatives," *Capitol Studies* 4 (Fall 1976): 11–36; Nelson W. Polsby, "The Institutionalization of the U.S. House of Representatives," *American Political Science Review* 62 (March 1968): 144–68; George B. Galloway, "Development of the Committee System in the House of Representatives," *American Historical Review* 65 (October 1959): 17–30; Galloway, "Leadership in the House of Representatives," *Western Political Quarterly* 12 (June 1959): 417–41; Allan G. Bogue et al., "Members of the House of Representatives and the Processes of Modernization, 1789–1960," *Journal of American History* 63 (September 1976): 275–302; Joseph Cooper and David W. Brady, "Institutional Context and Leadership Style: The House from Cannon to Rayburn," *American Political Science Review* 75 (June 1981): 411–25; Polsby, Miriam Gallaher, and Barry S. Rundquist, "The Growth of the Seniority System in the U.S. House of Representatives," *American Political Science Review* 63 (September 1969): 787–807; Jerome Clubb and Santa A. Traugott, "Partisan Cleavage and Cohesion in the House of Representatives, 1861–1974," *Journal of Interdisciplinary History* 7 (Winter 1977): 375–401; Barbara Sinclair, *Congressional Realignment, 1925–1978* (Austin, Tex., 1982), 20–28; Brady and John Ettling, "The Party System in the United States House of Repre-

sentatives," in L. Sandy Maisel and William G. Shade, eds., *Parties and Politics in American History: A Reader* (New York, 1994), 182–83, 196; Michael Abram and Joseph Cooper, "The Rise of Seniority in the House of Representatives," *Polity* 1 (Fall 1968): 75; Ronald M. Peters, Jr., *The American Speakership: The Office in Historical Perspective* (Baltimore, 1990), 98–106.

43. Margaret Munk, "Origin and Development of the Party Floor Leadership in the United States Senate," *Capitol Studies* 2 (Winter 1974): 36–38. Regarding the GOP regulars: John A. Garraty, *Henry Cabot Lodge: A Biography* (New York, 1953); Marvin Ewy, "Charles Curtis of Kansas: Vice President of the United States, 1929–1933," *Emporia State Research Studies* 10 (December 1961)· 3–58; John L. Nethers, "'Driest of the Dries': Simeon D. Fess," *Ohio History* 79 (Summer-Autumn 1970): 178–92, and *Simeon D. Fess: Educator and Politician* (Brooklyn, N.Y., 1973); Margulies, *Senator Lenroot of Wisconsin*; Thomas G. Alexander, "Reed Smoot, the L.D.S. Church and Progressive Legislation, 1903–1933," *Dialogue: A Journal of Mormon Thought* 7 (Spring 1972): 47–56, plus four articles in the *Utah Historical Quarterly* 45 (Fall 1977) as follows: James B. Allen, "The Great Protectionist: Sen. Reed Smoot of Utah," 325–45; Alexander, "Teapot Dome Revisited: Reed Smoot and Conservation in the 1920s," 352–68; Jeffrey L. Swanson, "That Smoke-Filled Room: A Utahn's Role in the 1920 GOP Convention," 369–79; and Jan Shipps, "The Public Image of Sen. Reed Smoot, 1903–32," 380–400. For the insurgents: Ray Tucker and Frederick R. Bartley, *Sons of the Wild Jackass* (1932; reprint ed., Seattle, 1970); Patrick G. O'Brien, "A Reexamination of the Senate Farm Bloc, 1921–1933," *Agricultural History* 47 (July 1973): 248–63; Erik Olssen, "The Progressive Group in Congress, 1922–1928," *The Historian* 42 (February 1980): 244–63; Cedric B. Cowing, "Sons of the Wild Jackass and the Stock Market," *Business History Review* 33 (Summer 1959): 138–55; Rader, "Federal Taxation in the 1920s," 431–32; Darrel L. Ashby, "Progressivism Against Itself: The Senate Western Bloc in the 1920's," *Mid-America* 50 (October 1968): 291–304; Patrick G. O'Brien, "Senator John J. Blaine: An Independent Progressive During 'Normalcy,'" *Wisconsin Magazine of History* 60 (Autumn 1975): 25–41 and "Senator Robert B. Howell: A Midwestern Progressive and Insurgent During 'Normalcy,'" *Emporia State Research Studies* 19 (December 1970); Reinhard H. Luthin, "Smith Wildman Brookhart of Iowa," *Agricultural History* 25 (October 1951): 87–97; McDaniel, *Smith Wildman Brookhart*; Belle Case La Follette and Fola La Follette, *Robert M. La Follette*, 2 vols. (New York, 1953); David P. Thelen, *Robert M. La Follette and the Insurgent Spirit* (Boston, 1976); Patrick J. Maney, *"Young Bob" La Follette: A Biography of Robert M. La Follette, Jr., 1895–1953* (Columbia, Mo., 1973); Patrick G. O'Brien, "William H. McMaster: An Agrarian Dissenter During 'Normalcy,'" *Emporia State Research Studies* 20 (June 1972): 24–39; Gilbert C. Fite, *Peter Norbeck: Prairie Statesman* (Columbia, Mo., 1948); Norman L. Zucker, *George W. Norris: Gentle Knight of American Democracy* (Urbana, 1966); Richard Lowitt, *George W. Norris: The Persistence of a Progressive, 1913–1933* (Urbana, 1971); Claudius O. Johnson, *Borah of Idaho* (1936; reprint ed., Seattle, 1967); Marian C. McKenna, *Borah* (Ann Arbor, Mich., 1961); John Milton Cooper, Jr., "William Borah, Political Thespian," *Pacific Northwest Quarterly* 56 (October 1965): 145–58 (with pro-Borah rebuttals by Claudius O. Johnson and Merle W. Wells); Leroy Ashby, *The Spearless Leader: Senator Borah and the Progressive Movement in the 1920's* (Urbana, Ill., 1972); Lower, *A Bloc of One*; Robert E.

Burke, "Hiram Johnson Looks at Herbert Hoover," in Nash, *Herbert Hoover: Ten Perspectives*, 141–63; Michael A. Weatherson and Hal W. Bochin, *Hiram Johnson: Political Revivalist* (Lanham, Md., 1995); Homer Socolofsky, *Arthur Capper: Publisher, Politician, and Philanthropist* (Lawrence, Kans., 1962); Roger T. Johnson, "Part-Time Leader: Charles L. McNary and the McNary-Haugen Bill," *Agricultural History* 54 (October 1980): 527–41; Steve Neal, *McNary of Oregon: A Political Biography* (Portland, Ore., 1985); Otis Graham, Jr., *An Encore for Reform: The Old Progressives and the New Deal* (New York, 1967); Ronald L. Feinman, *Twilight of Progressivism: The Western Republican Senators and the New Deal* (Baltimore, 1981).

44. George C. Osborn, *John Sharp Williams: Planter-Statesman of the Deep South* (Baton Rouge, 1943); Wayne Flynt, *Duncan Upshaw Fletcher: Dixie's Reluctant Progressive* (Tallahassee, Fla., 1971); Evans C. Johnson, *Oscar W. Underwood: A Political Biography* (Baton Rouge, 1980); Martha H. Swain, *Pat Harrison: The New Deal Years* (Jackson, Miss., 1978); Monroe L. Billington, *Thomas P. Gore: The Blind Senator from Oklahoma* (Lawrence, Kans., 1967); Henry C. Ferrell, Jr., *Claude A. Swanson of Virginia: A Political Biography* (Lexington, Ky., 1985); Caroline H. Keith, *"For Hell and a Brown Mule": The Biography of Senator Millard Tydings* (Lanham, Md., 1991); Daniel W. Hollis, "'Cotton Ed Smith'—Showman or Statesman?" *South Carolina Historical Magazine* 71 (October 1970): 235–56; Richard L. Watson, Jr., "Furnifold M. Simmons: 'Jehova of the Tarheels'?" *North Carolina Historical Review* 44 (Spring 1967): 166–87; Richard Bailey, "Harris Sheppard," in Kenneth E. Hendrickson, Jr., and Michael L. Collins, eds., *Profiles in Power: Twentieth-Century Texans in Washington* (Arlington Heights, Ill., 1993); J. Joseph Huthmacher, *Senator Robert F. Wagner and the Rise of Urban Liberalism* (New York, 1978); Richard Ruetten, "Senator Burton K. Wheeler and Insurgency in the 1920's," in Gene M. Gressley, ed., *The American West: A Reorientation* (Laramie, Wy., 1966), 111–31, 164–72; and "Burton K. Wheeler and the Montana Connection," *Montana: The Magazine of Western History* 27 (Summer 1977): 2–19; David H. Stratton, "Two Western Senators and Teapot Dome: Thomas J. Walsh and Albert Fall," *Pacific Northwest Quarterly* 65 (April 1974): 57–65; Carter, "The Other Catholic Candidate"; Bensel, *Sectionalism and American Political Development*, 128–47; Charles M. Dollar, "The South and the Fordney-McCumber Tariff of 1922: A Study in Regional Politics," *Journal of Southern History* 39 (February 1973): 45–66; Erik Olssen, "Southern Senators and Reform Issues in the 1920s" in Bruce Clayton and John A. Salmond, eds., *The South Is Another Land: Essays on the Twentieth-Century South* (New York, 1987), 49–66; Preston J. Hubbard, *Origins of the TVA: The Muscle Shoals Controversy, 1920–1932* (Nashville, 1968).

45. E. Pendleton Herring, *Group Representation Before Congress* (Baltimore, 1929); William B. Kelly, Jr., "Antecedents of Present Commercial Policy, 1922–1934," in Kelly, *Studies in United States Commercial Policy* (Chapel Hill, 1963), 6–20; Marc Hayford and Carl A. Pasurka, Jr., "The Political Economy of the Fordney-McCumber and Smoot-Hawley Tariff Acts," *Explorations in Economic History* 29 (January 1992): 30–50; J. Richard Snyder, "Coolidge, Costigan, and the Tariff Commission," *Mid-America* 50 (April 1968): 131–48; Snyder, "William S. Culbertson and the Making of Modern American Commercial Policy, 1917–1925," *Kansas Historical Quarterly* 35 (Winter 1969): 396–410; E. E. Schattschneider, *Politics, Pressure, and the Tariff: A Study in Free Private Enterprise in Pressure Politics, As Shown in*

the 1929–1930 Revision of the Tariff (New York, 1935); Barry Eichengreen, "The Political Economy of the Smoot-Hawley Tariff," *Research in Economic History* 12 (1989), 1–43; Robert Pastor, *Congress and the Politics of U.S. Foreign Economic Policy, 1929–1976* (Berkeley, 1980), 73–83; Colleen M. Callahan, Judith A. McDonald, and Anthony P. O'Brien, "Who Voted for Smoot-Hawley?" *Journal of Economic History* 54 (September 1994): 683–90; Carl-Ludwig Holtfrerich, "The Grown-up in Infant's Clothing: The U.S. Protectionist Relapse in the Interwar Period," John F. Kennedy-Institut fur Nordamerikastudien, Abteilung fur Wirtschaft, Freie Universitat Berlin, Working Paper No. 19 (1989); Joseph M. Jones, Jr., *Tariff Retaliation: Repercussions of the Hawley-Smoot Bill* (Philadelphia, 1934); John Conybeare, "Trade Wars: A Comparative History of Anglo-Hanse, Franco-Italian, and Hawley-Smoot Conflicts," *World Politics* 37 (October 1985): 147–72; M. E. Falkus, "United States Economic Policy and the 'Dollar Gap' of the 1920's," *Economic History Review*, 2d ser., 24 (November 1971): 599–623; Stephen A. Schuker, *American "Reparations" to Germany, 1919–33: Implications for the Third World Debt Crisis* (Princeton, 1988), 97–102; Alfred E. Eckes, Jr., "Revisiting Smoot-Hawley," *Journal of Policy History* 7, no. 3 (1995): 295–310, and *Opening America's Market: U.S. Foreign Trade Policy Since 1776* (Chapel Hill, 1995), 100–39.

46. Aileen S. Kraditor, *The Ideas of the Women's Suffrage Movement, 1890–1920* (New York, 1965); Ross Evans Paulson, *Women's Suffrage and Prohibition: A Comparative Study of Equality and Social Control* (Glenview, Ill., 1973); Ann Firor Scott, *The Southern Lady from Pedestal to Politics, 1830–1930* (Chicago, 1970); Steven M. Buechler, *The Transformation of the Woman Suffrage Movement* (New Brunswick, N.J., 1986); Buechler, *Women's Movements in the United States: Woman Suffrage, Equal Rights, and Beyond* (New Brunswick, N.J., 1990); Stuart D. Rice and Malcolm M. Willey, "American Women's Ineffective Use of the Vote," *Current History* 20 (1924): 641–47; Paul Kleppner, "Were Women to Blame?: Female Suffrage and Voter Turnout," *Journal of Interdisciplinary History* 12 (Spring 1982): 621–43; Sara Alpern and Dale Baum, "Female Ballots: The Impact of the Nineteenth Amendment," ibid., 16 (Summer 1985): 43–67; Dorothy M. Brown, *Setting a Course: American Women in the 1920s* (Boston, 1987); Felice D. Gordon, *After Winning: The Legacy of the New Jersey Suffragists, 1920–1947* (New Brunswick, N.J., 1986); Carol Nichols, *Votes and More for Women: Suffrage and After in Connecticut* [Women & History, no. 5, Spring 1983] (New York, 1983); Christine Bolt, *The Women's Movements in the United States and Britain from the 1790s to the 1920s* (Amherst, Mass., 1993), 249–67; Anne Firor Scott, "After Suffrage: Southern Women in the Twenties," *Journal of Southern History* 30 (August 1964): 298–318; Elisabeth I. Perry, "'Now at Last We Can Begin!' The Impact of Woman Suffrage in New York," paper presented at the Library of Congress "Calvin Coolidge and the Coolidge Era" conference, October 5–7, 1995 and published herein; Linda K. Kerber, "A Constitutional Right to Be Treated like American Ladies: Women and the Obligations of Citizenship," in Kerber, Alice Kessler-Harris, and Kathryn K. Sklar, eds., *U.S. History as Women's History: New Feminist Essays* (Chapel Hill, 1995), 28; Jean Christie, "After Suffrage: Women in the 1920's," in Christie and Leonard Dinnerstein, eds., *Divisions and Revisions: Interpretations of Twentieth-Century American History* (New York, 1975), 91–105; Lichtman, *Prejudice and the Old Politics*, 59–65.

47. Michael McGerr, "Political Style and Women's Power, 1830–1930," *Jour-*

nal of American History 77 (December 1990): 880–85; Nancy Cott, *The Grounding of Modern Feminism* (New Haven, 1987); Peter Geidel, "The National Woman's Party and the Origins of the Equal Rights Amendment, 1920–1923," *The Historian* 42 (August 1980): 557–82; Judith Sealander, "Feminist Against Feminist: The First Phase of the Equal Rights Amendment Debate, 1923–1963," *South Atlantic Quarterly* 81 (Spring 1982): 147–61; Cott, "Feminist Politics in the 1920s: The National Woman's Party," *Journal of American History* 71 (June 1984): 43–68; Susan Becker, *The Origins of the Equal Rights Amendment: American Feminism Between the Wars* (Westport, Conn., 1985); Christine A. Lunardini, *From Equal Suffrage to Equal Rights: Alice Paul and the National Woman's Party, 1910–1928* (New York, 1986); Louise M. Young, assisted by Ralph A. Young, Jr., *In the Public Interest: The League of Women Voters, 1920–1970* (New York, 1989); Robert B. Fowler, *Carrie Catt: Feminist Politician* (Boston, 1986), 98–103; Estelle Freedman, "Separatism as Strategy: Female Institution Building and American Feminism, 1870–1930," *Feminist Studies* 5 (Fall 1979): 512–29; Susan Becker, "International Feminism Between the Wars: The National Woman's Party Versus the League of Women Voters," in Lois Scharf and Joan Jensen, eds., *Decades of Discontent: The Women's Movement, 1920–1940* (Westport, Conn., 1983), 223–42; Eleanor Flexner, *Century of Struggle: The Woman's Rights Movement in the United States*, rev. ed. (Cambridge, Mass., 1975), 340.

48. Kristie Miller, *Ruth Hanna McCormick: A Life in Politics, 1880–1944* (Albuquerque, 1992); Emily Stier Adler and J. Stanley Lemons, "The Independent Woman: Rhode Island's First Woman Legislator," *Rhode Island History* 49 (February 1991), 3–11; Maitreyi Mazumdar, "The Alice's Restaurant: Expanding a Woman's Sphere," *Chronicles of Oklahoma* 70 (Fall 1992): 302–25; Office of the Historian, U. S. House of Representatives, *Women in Congress, 1917–1990* (Washington, D.C., 1991); Sandra Haarsage, *Bertha Knight Landes of Seattle: Big-City Mayor* (Norman, Okla., 1994); Elizabeth Taylor on Ferguson in Barbara Sicherman and Carol H. Green, eds., *Notable American Women: The Modern Record* (Cambridge, Mass., 1980), 230–32; T. A. Larson, *History of Wyoming* (Lincoln, Nebr., 1965), 457–60; George Martin, *Madam Secretary: Frances Perkins* (Boston, 1976); Lela B. Costin, *Two Sisters for Social Justice: A Biography of Grace and Edith Abbott* (Urbana, 1983); Mary Anderson, *Woman at Work: The Autobiography of Mary Anderson As Told to Mary N. Winslow* (Minneapolis, 1951); Dorothy M. Brown, *Mabel Walker Willebrandt: A Study of Power, Loyalty, and Law* (Knoxville, 1984); Elisabeth I. Perry, *Belle Moskowitz: Feminine Politics and the Exercise of Power in the Age of Al Smith* (New York, 1987).

3

Re-Shifting Perspectives on the 1920s

Recent Trends in Social and Cultural History

LYNN DUMENIL

Introduction

When Henry May wrote his seminal essay, "Shifting Perspectives on the 1920s" (1956), few professional historians had yet tackled the era of Calvin Coolidge. Much of May's discussion by default revolved around memoirs and journalistic accounts. Since then, of course, the historical literature on the twenties has multiplied dramatically, including several major syntheses. Much of it has aspired to dislodge the popular stereotypes of the decade, of jazzhounds and flappers, of fanatics and flagpole sitters, of dubious get-rich-quick schemes and speakeasies trafficking in bootleg liquor. This image has been remarkably resilient in popular culture and popular memory, despite scholars' efforts to challenge it. This essay leaves to others the impressive body of work on political, diplomatic, intellectual, and economic topics and instead focuses on social and cultural history written in the last twenty years.[1]

The thrust of social history has been to challenge conventional periodization and to emphasize both the unevenness of social change and the continuities that characterize the private world of individuals. Nonetheless, as I have argued in *The Modern Temper* (1995), we can view the twenties as a period of transition, as a time when Americans were acutely conscious of the emergence of a complex, pluralistic, bureaucratic, "modern society." This essay focuses on two major themes that allow us to see the modern quality of the 1920s. One involves the emergence of the consumer culture and the transformations in work, leisure, the mass media, and values. The other involves an examination of those groups traditionally outside the center of power: racial and ethnic minorities, the working class, and women. Studies of these previously neglected groups do more than round out the picture. By exploring challenges to traditional morality and gender roles, the position of workers in the corporate order, and the growing militancy of African Americans and ethnic minorities, these historians have deepened our understanding of the contours of our modern, pluralistic culture.[2]

Consumer Culture

In probing what could be called the modern side of the 1920s, one of the richest areas of scholarship focuses on the development of a consumer culture. Historians have examined not only the ways in which people turned to leisure and consumption to find satisfaction in life, but also the important causal factors: the degradation of work and the erosion of individual autonomy in a mass, corporate culture. The twenties were critical to these transformations, for the decade embodies much of what constitutes consumer culture: the cornucopia of material goods; an occupational and corporate structure that limits individual autonomy; and a shift in behavior and values away from the Victorian "production" ethos of work, restraint, and order, toward one that embraces leisure, consumption, and self-expression as vehicles for individual satisfaction. For many of the new middle class and some of the working class (especially men, because they were the ones who expected to remain in the work force permanently), work was becoming intrinsically less meaningful, while at the same time rising prosperity, consumer goods, and increased leisure time offered new venues for meaning: one could seek satisfaction and definition in the personal realm of leisure and consumption.

Other factors influenced both men and women. The increasing pluralism of American cities helped to challenge Victorian cultural hegemony and promote alternative visions of leisure and sociability. The expansion of the corporate national economy eroded local ties and propagated bureaucracy, specialization, and routinization, helping to undermine the individual's sense of community, continuity, and autonomy. Similarly, urban mass society underlined the individual's fragile status in an anonymous society and compounded a sense of fragmentation. Although many Americans sought to root themselves in religion, mounting secularization further contributed to a search for other forms of salvation. A decline in voting and an increasing indifference to reform signaled a rejection of civic responsibility and a shift to the private and the personal. Although prosperity was not universal, the flood of consumer goods, most spectacularly the omnipresent automobile, made more accessible by installment buying, did bring more Americans than ever into the delights and perils of conspicuous consumption. Moreover, the continued expansion of mass media and commercial entertainment, most notably the increased importance of advertising, professional sports, and movies, reflected and reinforced the thrust of the consumer culture toward leisure and consumption.

In examining these transformations, scholars have identified a behavioral and value shift reflected in the emergence of a new social type. In *The Lonely Crowd* (1950), David Riesman contrasted the nineteenth-century middle-class character type, "inner-directed," with the twentieth-century "other-directed" individual whose life was organized by keeping tuned into the impressions and opinions of others. Leo Lowenthal posited a shift from individuals geared to the production, "Horatio Alger" values of the nineteenth century to the consumer values of the twentieth. Warren Susman characterized the shift as linked to changing perceptions of the self, with the nineteenth-century emphasis on character giving way to a twentieth-century obsession with personality: "The vision of self-sacrifice began to yield to that of self-realization." T. Jackson Lears has identified this concern with personality as part of a therapeutic ethos, a ubiquitous trend in twentieth-century middle-class culture that pervaded religion, social sciences, success ideology, and advertising and concentrated on self-expression and self-realization through consumption and leisure.[3]

This reorientation of culture has been the focus of some of the most exciting work on the 1920s.[4] One of the first monographs to deal concretely with the emergence of the "modern" was Paula Fass's *The Damned and the Beautiful* (1977), a study of white, middle-class fraternities and sororities. "Flaming youth" represented a particularly potent symbol of "the upheaval in social relationships and the destruction of definitions and limitations" that agitated the traditionalists who were worried about the erosion of Victorian values. In addition to examining the demographic shifts that presaged the emergence of both a more affectionate family and the modern youth peer group, Fass explores the fads, courtship, leisure, and values of college men and women. She argues that indeed youth did represent the emergence of a new culture that "set the stage for a new pluralism in behavior and the rhythm for rapid change in cultural forms," but at the same time she notes that in contrast to contemporaries' sense of valueless youth in wild rebellion, these young collegians had created their own set of values, especially in matters of personal style. Using the peer group to validate new norms, they kept their rebellion within specific limits. The college flapper might engage in more sexual activity than her mother, but her goals hardly challenged the status quo, for new courtship patterns retained the traditional goal of marriage and family and remained subject to the sexual double standard. For men, the glorification of teamwork, competition within conformity, and an emphasis on consumption and style were perfect accouterments for success in the modern corporate order. Youth challenged old 'village' morality, but not the political or economic structures of their parents.[5]

As trendsetters, college youth were exemplars of the consumer culture, but the most important vehicle for disseminating new values was the mass media. Movies helped transform a national culture, a process richly explored by numerous scholars. Robert Sklar, in *Movie-Made America* (1975), traces the evolution of movies from a working-class venue for entertainment to a broad-based mass media. He notes how the extraordinary influence of movies became a source of tremendous concern especially to elite Americans who viewed themselves as custodians of culture. Anxiety about movies originating among the working class, the role of Jewish entrepreneurs in the industry, and the deleterious effect of movies on the moral fiber of the nation led to a drive for censorship that resulted in the industry's turn to self-regulation in the form of the Hays Office. In addition to noting the class and ethnic tensions embodied in the contemporary assessment of the movies, Sklar examines the messages of the movies and suggests that despite the emergence of new norms, especially in the arena of sexuality, movies tended to reinforce traditional, popular values. Thus, although there was much sexual titillation, movies invariably had moral endings, and, moreover, producers cast Europeans in "passionate" roles because "they could do so many things forbidden to Americans."[6]

A key work on the importance of movies to the "re-orientation of culture" is Lary May's *Screening Out the Past* (1980). The content of the films, according to May, reflects the efforts of filmmakers to grapple with and interpret the emergence of a more organized, bureaucratic society. Thus, before the war, the early films of D. W. Griffith reverberate with the desire to offer older virtues—of traditional womanhood, family, and social order—as antidotes to the disruptions of modern industrial society. By the late teens, however, modern messages emerge. In contrast to D. W. Griffith, Cecil B. De Mille embraced new values. Many of his characters remake themselves into more modern individuals in order to find ultimate happiness in updated marriages.

May also explores films that directly addressed the issue of the degradation of work. Many Douglas Fairbanks films of the late teens, for example, featured a white-collar worker frustrated by the confines of meaningless work: "he is trapped in an urban civilization where he is faced with office routine and no challenges." The solution to the dilemma was never to change work itself—but to find meaning in leisure. "The heroes in Fairbanks' films," May argues, "discover new energy through boxing, tumbling, fencing, or gymnastics." Like Sklar, May recognizes the persistence of traditional values, especially as films reinforced ideas of family and corporate order, but far more than Sklar, he emphasizes movies' role in forging a modern culture that focused on personal and privatized satisfactions.[7]

Other forms of mass media also reveal the complex emergence of a consumer culture. As Joan Shelley Rubin argues in *The Making of Middle/Brow*

Culture (1992), the managers and editors of the Book-of-the-Month-Club, founded in 1926, sent out mixed messages. On the one hand, the books the editors chose to feature were often those in keeping with the traditional genteel culture's emphasis on "character," such as Marjorie Kinnan Rawling's *The Yearling* or Clarence Day's *Life with Father*. But on the other, the Book-of-the-Month-Club's promotion techniques—its advertisements and newsletters—decidedly reflected the newer emphasis on the self and personality. In assuring the book buyer that he could be "completely informed about *all the interesting new books*"—that he "could know and talk about them,"—the Book-of-the-Month-Club, in Rubin's words, "promised to cure the floundering self's social distress by enabling subscribers to convey the instant and favorable impression required for success in a bureaucratic, anonymous society."[8]

The message that one could purchase what one needed for personal growth and success permeated the advertising industry, as numerous scholars have pointed out. Advertising itself mushroomed in the twenties. In 1914, estimates are that the volume of advertising stood at $682 million; by 1929, it had grown to $2,987 million. Even the most cursory examination reveals the consumer culture orientation of magazine advertising. With large, and as the decade progressed, colorful photographs of products and of individuals enjoying the products, advertisements repeatedly depicted the satisfactions of leisure and the products that created or enhanced leisure.

In addition to glorifying consumption and leisure, advertising reinforced consumers' anxieties. As Vincent Vinikas in *Soft Soap, Hard Sell* (1992) has noted, advertising for toiletries provides a particularly potent example of the other-directedness that Riesman analyzed. Mouthwash, deodorants, cosmetics, and perfumes were scarce products at the turn of the century, but by the 1920s, they had become a major industry with large advertising campaigns that made them the second most advertised range of products, next to food. Cosmetic manufacturers surrounded women with mirrors and underlined the centrality of fashionable and youthful appearance to personal fulfillment. Listerine publicized, and more or less invented, the fear of halitosis, "the unforgivable social offense," and promised to keep its users on "the safe and polite side." The Listerine campaign was especially revealing of the other-directed sense of the self conveyed in advertising, because the users of mouthwash "had to be so attuned to appeasing others that they would routinely engage in a practice, the results of which were, from the user's perspective, virtually imperceptible." Certainly not all ads played on consumers' anxieties and insecurities or promised antidotes to the various ills of modern society, but these themes were pervasive and point to the importance of advertising in shaping the contours of the personality-oriented consumer culture.[9]

In *Advertising the American Dream* (1985), Roland Marchand offered particularly valuable insights into this process when he argued that advertising agents were often self-consciously "apostles of modernism." In hawking their various products, they sought to associate their clients' goods with the modern era, with fashion, style, and progress. But on a different level, admen—and most were men—revealed a darker side of modernity and sought to sell their products by addressing those consumers' anxieties occasioned by the modern world and, in particular, sought to soothe the embattled self: "Adopting a therapeutic mission, advertising provided comforting reassurances to those who anxiously watched the institutions of their society assume a larger, more complex, and more impersonal scale."

Another advertising theme that seemed directed at the plight of the individual in modern mass society was the personal approach, the tendency to include "you" in the text. Advertisements, copying from tabloid journalism's and movie matinee's phenomenal success, created mini-dramas of the consumer's life and used products ranging from face creams to batteries to solve consumer problems. Other techniques of personalizing consumption included the celebrity endorsement, which linked movie stars and sports stars to ordinary Americans in shared consumption, and the advent of company spokespersons such as Betty Crocker, who humanized the corporate image. All of these techniques were aimed at reassuring consumers that they had connections to their purchases, that they could exercise some control even in a mass society.[10]

This quest for control in a mass society is a key theme in Jackson Lears's comprehensive study of advertising during the nineteenth and twentieth centuries, *Fables of Abundance* (1994). Although Lears was among the most prominent of the scholars who elaborated on the idea of new consumer culture built around a therapeutic ethos that emphasized leisure and consumption, in this new work he notes that he has reversed himself somewhat. The thrust of modern advertisements, he argues, embodies an emphasis on "personal efficiency." This trend has much of the Puritan past embedded within it, but it also serves modern managerial ends of keeping Americans hard at work to sustain the necessary consumption to maintain the economic order. Thus, the liberation from Victorian norms was within narrow bounds.

In the 1920s, Lears argues, advertising agencies evinced a clear sense of their audience as malleable and easily led, "For most agency executives, the notion of consumer sovereignty was a veneer over a deeper structure of belief that equated the consumer audience with a mass of doltish dupes." They self-consciously viewed Americans as victims of boring work and humdrum lives and pitched advertisements as alternative visions. This viewpoint was not as cynical as it might seem, according to Lears, since they believed in "the redemptive powers of corporate-sponsored technology" and saw themselves as social engineers who could assist consumers in making sense of the "complexity of modern life."[11]

The study of popular consumer culture raised the vexing question of audience. We now have a better sense of the messages that admen, movie makers, and other purveyors of mass culture projected; but how were they received? Although works like Sklar's tended to emphasize the power of the public to shape the movie's content, many others, while noting the dialectic process involved, pointed to the extraordinary power of mass media to shape belief. For example, Lears acknowledges that "the success of the managerial drive for domination remains an open question" and that "advertisers' reconstitution of personal well-being probably worked most effectively among would-be professionals like themselves,"[12] but the overall thrust of his work is to stress advertising's role in maintaining the power of corporate, managerial hegemony. That this will continue to be a key issue for interpreting the culture of both the 1920s and of the twentieth century is indicated by the prominence given it in an *American Historical Review* forum (December 1992). In the lead-off article, Lawrence W. Levine takes exception to the emphasis on hegemony when he excludes the possibility for audiences and consumers to produce culture themselves. He argues that the "process of popular culture" was not "the imposition of texts on passive people who constitute a tabula rasa but as a process of interaction between complex texts that harbor more than monolithic meanings and audiences who embody more than monolithic assemblies of compliant people."[13]

Scholars who have moved beyond the mainstream middle class provide especially strong evidence for Levine's argument. Labor historians have offered valuable insights by studying the way in which the working class, especially immigrants, challenged prevailing Victorian notions of restraint, sobriety, and morality. Although they do not deal specifically with the 1920s, Kathy Peiss's *Cheap Amusements* (1986) and Roy Rosenzweig's *Eight Hours for What We Will* (1983) have been especially influential in reminding us that cultural change can be pushed from the bottom up.[14] Similarly, Lawrence W. Levine, in *Black Culture, Black Consciousness* (1977), a book that spans the nineteenth and twentieth centuries, not only traces the development of African American culture—of folklore, music, humor—but also explores the complex cultural interaction between blacks and whites. Ann Douglas focuses specifically on the 1920s in *Terrible Honesty* (1995). Particularly persuasive is her treatment of the confluence of black and white culture in New York in the postwar decade. In her examination of the artists of the Harlem Renaissance and the performers and creators of jazz and the blues, she stresses that African Americans should be given "credit for shaping America's expression." The pluralism embodied in the New York cultural scene, she argues, was the essence of modernity; although in her concentration on blacks and whites, she ignored for the most part the rest of "mongrel" Manhattan that immigration and labor historians have recognized as a key part of modern pluralism.[15]

In addition to arguing that immigrants and African Americans have contributed to the shaping of mainstream culture, historians have also explored the way in which they resisted the homogenizing trends of mass, commercialized culture and pursued their leisure within an ethnic or racial context during the 1920s. Sports was an important leisure arena in which class and ethnicity mattered, as both Elliott Gorn in "The Manassa Mauler and the Fighting Marine" and Steven A. Ricss in *City Games* (1989) have argued. Many scholars have focused on the emergence of commercialized sports as a prime example of the mainstream consumer culture. But while major league baseball was a major forum for sports enthusiasts in the 1920s, working-class Americans were perhaps more likely to attend sandlot games, which were less expensive and more community oriented. This was especially evident among African Americans who were excluded from playing major league baseball. Negro professional leagues, which multiplied in the twenties, offered one arena for African Americans to enjoy baseball. Also common were the black sandlot, semiprofessional, semicommercialized teams that flourished in most American cities such as Pittsburgh, where Rob Ruck has described black-controlled teams as an important part of the African American community.[16]

Other leisure time activities revealed an alternative to mainstream consumer culture as well. In many urban neighborhoods, working-class people experienced a vibrant street life of visiting and ethnic food and music. African Americans, many of them new migrants to the cities, flocked to jazz clubs and rent parties. Chicanos in Los Angeles, George Sánchez reveals in *Becoming Mexican American* (1993), sustained Chicano theater, the *corridos* musical form, and numerous Spanish-language radio programs in the 1920s that helped to forge a new Mexican American culture.[17] Lizabeth Cohen's *Making a New Deal* (1990) provides particularly compelling evidence that some immigrant and African American communities maintained their distinctiveness even as vehicles of mass culture invaded them. In the early days of radio, most programs originated locally and offered ethnic, nationality hours or were produced by ethnic stations. Church, labor unions, and fraternal orders were among the most common broadcasters. Homes or shops with a radio became the gathering place for neighbors and friends who shared their entertainment. This local flavor was to change with the rise of national corporations by the end of the decade, but for a brief period, radio helped to promote "ethnic, religious, and working-class affiliations."

By the 1920s movies were already part of national corporations, but here, too, there was room for the neighborhood to influence how residents experienced mass culture. Cohen notes that in Chicago ethnic working-class neighborhoods, movie houses were not the sumptuous palaces that have attracted historians' attention, but rather modest, locally owned enterprises. Films might be interspersed with ethnic entertainments and perhaps even transformed by them.[18] By the 1930s, much of the distinctive ethnic components of popular culture had been muted in Chicago, but Cohen's work on the 1920s highlights the complex process by which the consumer culture forged by the mass media, chain stores, and other national corporations shaped modern America.

An Inclusive Pluralism

The second major thrust of recent scholarship that gives us a much richer sense of the pluralism and complexity of American society in the 1920s emerges in the growing body of literature on the experiences of racial and ethnic minorities and workers. For the most part, immigration scholars have concentrated on the prewar period, limiting their focus to the era before immigration restriction began to limit new infusion into ethnic communities. They concentrated on the first generation and the interplay between old-world life and new-world adjustments. But some historians have explored the later generations and their experiences in the 1920s. Thus, in *A House for All Peoples* (1971), John M. Allswang has traced the political coming of age of ethnic groups in Chicago and the growing importance they had in shaping the urban liberalism that was to typify the democratic party. Similarly, works on Alfred E. Smith and Fiorello La Guardia point out the important role ethnic voters had in supporting liberal reforms in the postwar generation that would eventually feed into the New Deal.[19] Another important body of work treats the pervasive nativism of the period, represented by the Red Scare, the Klan, and the drive for immigration restriction. John Higham's *Strangers in the Land* (1955) remains the classic text, but it is supplemented by Roger Daniels's and Yuji Ichioka's explorations of the extensive hostility to Japanese on the west coast and by Rodolfo Acuña, David Montejano, and George Sánchez on the discrimination experienced by people of Mexican descent.[20] Works on anti-Semitism and anti-Catholicism include Leonard Dinnerstein, *Anti-Semitism in America*; Leo P. Ribuffo, "Henry Ford and the International Jew"; and Lynn Dumenil, "The Tribal Twenties."[21]

There is, in addition, a growing scholarship on the question of ethnic community and identity. In addition to Lizabeth Cohen's book, another valuable study is Deborah Dash Moore's *At Home in America* (1981), which explores the emergence of a second generation of Eastern European Jews in New York City. By the 1920s, the Jewish population of the Lower East Side had been diminished as Jews migrated to the outer boroughs of the Bronx and Brooklyn. This dispersal did not mean a merging with mainstream America. In part because of residential discrimination, in part out of choice, Jews congregated in new communities, where leaders helped to create Americanized forms of Jewish institutions. The second generation created a distinct culture that merged their Jewish past with their American present.[22]

George Sánchez arrives at similar conclusions about first generation immigrants in *Becoming Mexican American*. Mexican immigrant communities are particularly interesting because, unlike Europeans and Asians, Mexicans were not proscribed by the immigration acts of the 1920s and over a half million entered the United States during the decade, creating large communities in California, the Southwest, and to a lesser extent in the Midwest. Examining popular culture, work, religion, the family, and demographic trends, Sánchez demonstrates the complexity of the Los Angeles Mexican community. He contrasts the efforts by the Mexican government to promote nationalistic sentiment among Mexicans living in Los Angeles with the efforts of Anglo leaders to Americanize the immigrants into obedient, productive workers but suggests that the immigrants themselves remained largely immune from the efforts of both. Individual immigrants, he argues, "learned to balance nationalistic sentiment with a new ethnic identity."[23]

This balancing act is a theme that emerges repeatedly in studies dealing with ethnic communities in the 1920s. While some, like Elizabeth Ewen's *Immigrant Women in the Land of Dollars* (1985), emphasize the Americanization process, most stress the combining of cultures and the emergence of a distinct ethnic identity. Ethnic leaders, as John Bodnar and John Higham argue, played a significant role in this process. Officials of voluntary associations, politicians, and entrepreneurs had a vested interest in promoting strong group identity; their success and status depended on it. At the same time, these leaders often served as bridges to Americanization by interpreting mainstream society and institutions. Many who achieved middle-class status assiduously promoted 'respectable behavior' that they felt would help win the group's legitimacy. Another tactic was to refute vigorously the assumptions of the nativists about who could properly be considered "real" Americans. Catholic and Jewish leaders in particular were active in anti-defamation campaigns. Although they did not use the term "cultural pluralism," which Horace Kallen coined in 1924, as they gave speeches, wrote editorials, and stumped for votes, they articulated an identity that was generally within the American mainstream. As I have argued in *The Modern Temper*, the spokespersons of disparate groups of minority outsiders constructed a vision of pluralism that made them representatives of a modern society in the process of sorting out the implications of religious, ethnic, and racial diversity.[24]

Compared to the material on ethnic groups, the work on African Americans is quite extensive. There are numerous biographies of men and women who were key figures in the 1920s: Paul Robeson, W. E. B. Du Bois, Marcus Garvey, Josephine Baker, and A. Philip Randolph have all received scholarly attention. And, although compared to works on white intellectuals of the "Lost Generation," relatively few biographies on Harlem Renaissance luminaries exist, there are some noteworthy ones, including Arnold Rampersad, *The Life of Langston Hughes* (1986) and Eugene Levy, *James Weldon Johnson* (1973).[25] The Harlem Renaissance itself has captured the attention of numerous scholars. The still classic work is Nathan Huggins, *Harlem Renaissance* (1971), which analyzes the works of major artists such as Langston Hughes, Jean Toomer, Alain Locke, Nora Zeal Hurston, and Claude McKay. As Huggins put it, "They saw art and letters as a bridge across the chasm between the races," which often led to a delicate balancing act as they sought to construct an identity that was both black and American. They struggled to define the distinctive quality of black culture, to locate an essential spirit that would be a source of pride and evidence of the contributions blacks had made to American culture. This theme was reflected in a fascination with Africa, evident in the poems of Hughes or the sculpture of Aaron Douglas. The search for black contributions to American culture also emerged in the interest in southern folk culture and spirituals, most notably in the work of Hurston. Huggins argues, however, that despite this eagerness to find distinctive contributions, Harlem Renaissance authors, with the exception of Hughes, were not willing to explore jazz and blues as examples of indigenous culture. Huggins suggests that they were wedded to western European cultural canons and hampered by the demands of their white publishers and patrons, factors that limited their artistic achievement.[26]

Writing since Huggins, other scholars have offered new insights. David Levering Lewis has explored the context of the Harlem Renaissance by charting the emergence of Harlem as the "race capital."[27] Paula Giddings, Maureen Honey, Barbara Christian, Cheryl A. Wall, among others, have examined the women of this male-dominated renaissance and have found challenges to the racial and gender hierarchies in prose and poems that superficially seem conventional and even conservative.[28] Other works have questioned Huggins's notion that most Harlem intellectuals rejected jazz and blues as not being sufficiently cultured. The younger generation behind the short-lived journal *Fire*, for example, called for more innovative approaches to African American art that would incorporate urban idioms. Many writers, as Kathy Ogren points out in *The Jazz Revolution* (1989), featured jazz performances in their works, as "evocative of both the modern sensibility generally and the black experience in particular."[29]

A number of scholars address the issue of the Harlem Renaissance, African American popular culture, and modernity. Rampersad argues that

Langston Hughes recognized that the expression of urban culture was central to interpreting the modern black experience and that he found in the blues "the tone, the texture, the basic language of true black modernism."[30] Most recently, Ann Douglas has contrasted the Harlem Renaissance with the Lost Generation and argues that the themes of despair and alienation so typical of white artists were largely absent among blacks, who reveal a sense of optimism and expectation for social change: "This sense of black opportunity," she writes, "was short-lived and never without doubts and conflicts, but in the early years of the modern era, New York's Talented Tenth felt themselves to be not lost but found: the description and reification of a modern world."[31] While it is true that for the most part these artists did not center their energies on the themes that their white counterparts classified as modernism, in the long view, as they focused on the issues of racial identity and community, their concerns were quintessentially "modern." As W. E. B. Du Bois said in 1903: "The problem of the twentieth century is the problem of the color-line," and it was this problem that preoccupied the majority of African American intellectuals in the 1920s.[32]

The attention that scholars such as Ogren, Douglas, and Rampersad have given African American popular culture reflect the trend to view the Harlem Renaissance as broader than the one fashioned by intellectuals and to recognize the multiple forms of the "New Negro." In many ways, the quintessential New Negro was Marcus Garvey, the controversial and charismatic founder of the Universal Negro Improvement Association (UNIA). Preaching black pride and self-help with Africa as a central motif in his call for blacks everywhere to assert themselves and claim power, Garvey's version of black Nationalism attracted a mass following that drew especially on urban workers and the middle class.

Historians have tackled many facets of Garvey's movement. David Cronon and others have used Garvey and the UNIA to analyze the conflicts and complexities among black leadership as they offered different approaches to realizing the potential of the rising militancy of the New Negro. Drawing fire from more moderate leaders who identified with the integration-oriented National Association for the Advancement of Colored People, Garvey was controversial in his own time for his denigration of the goal of social equality and his glorification of the ideal of racial purity. Socialist leaders like A. Philip Randolph also attacked Garvey for simplistic solutions that deflected African Americans from more radical critiques of the system.[33] Historians disagree over the extent of Garvey's radicalism and the nature of his movement. Tony Martin, in *Race First* (1976), as the title suggests, focuses on Garvey's black nationalism and sees the movement as a precursor to the nationalistic movements of the 1960s.[34] Judith Stein, in an impressively researched monograph, analyzes Garvey in the context of class relations. She finds his appeal linked to "the geography of black modernism." Whether in the urban United States, the Caribbean, or Jamaica, she argues, "Garvey's appeal received a hearing wherever economic development had destroyed old cultures and dangled the prospects of new prosperity." Stein emphasizes the attraction of Garvey's businesses, especially the Black Star Line navigation company, which symbolized this "entrepreneurial route to black progress." Describing it as "a modern economic enterprise blueprinted by older elites but supported by the masses in new organizations," she views the steamship company as Garvey's way to marshal the new black insurgency to provide the opportunity and recognition that were denied him and others like him."[35]

Like Stein, Robert Hill in his introduction to *The Marcus Garvey and Universal Negro Improvement Association Papers* (1983) stresses Garvey's emphasis on economic advancement, arguing that he inspired his followers with a black version of the gospel of success. But Hill also pays careful attention to the evolution of the movement, tracing it from one that emphasized confraternity and mutual benefit to one that was political and radical. In particular, Hill notes the influence of the upheavals of the World War I era, and especially the rise of Irish Nationalism, in shaping Garvey's ideas about black nationalism and the central role of a powerful, black-dominated Africa for uplifting blacks everywhere. Finally, Hill traces the shift in Garvey's thinking to an emphasis on racial purity that led him to criticize blacks like Du Bois who fought for political and social rights within mainstream society and to seek an alliance with the Klan and other white supremacists as sharing the same insistence on separation between the races.[36]

Yet another study offers a sense of the power of Garvey's ideology to attract a broad-based following. Lawrence W. Levine terms the UNIA a "revitalization movement," which anthropologist Anthony F. C. Wallace has defined as a "'deliberate, organized conscious effort by members of a society to construct a more satisfying culture.'" As they struggled to resolve the tension between the promises of American life and the realities of African American experience, a tension heightened by the expectations produced by the war years and black migration, African Americans were particularly accessible to a charismatic leader who could "provide a political channel and a global perspective for that [racial] consciousness." Garvey did not create black pride but rather articulated it, as he constantly reminded blacks of their proud African heritage and the legitimacy of their struggle for liberation. As Levine and others have noted, the historic context that made Garvey's message so vital to blacks in the United States was fueled in large part by the epic demographic changes of the "Great Migration," which created a large urban population with heightened expectations.[37]

Neither Marcus Garvey, the UNIA, the Harlem Renaissance, nor other examples of the New Negro would have been possible without the mass black migration to the cities in the second and third decades of the twentieth century. Historians' attention to this northward trek of over a million men and women has contributed substantially to urban history. It also represents a significant shift in African American historiography by supplementing the emphasis on the Civil War and slavery with studies of the twentieth-century urban experience. Despite differences in interpretation and emphasis, most historians who have examined cities as diverse as New York, Cleveland, Milwaukee, Philadelphia, and Chicago have emphasized the cruel contrast between the great hopes migrants had that wartime labor shortages could make northern cities a secular promised land and the reality of the conditions in the urban north that migrants encountered.[38] Social and economic discrimination in the 1920s solidified the ghettoization of African Americans in the North, as attitudes of white employers and most white unionists kept African Americans from making many inroads into the industrial jobs that could have been a gateway to mobility. Peter Gottlieb argues, for example, that for Pittsburgh migrants, "their overall status as unskilled, low-paid employees in the casual labor market left them more exposed to the threat of joblessness and destitution than in the years before the migration."[39] Violence was another common denominator for urban African Americans. The Chicago Race Riot of 1919, analyzed by William Tuttle, Jr., is just the most spectacular example of racial hostility that exploded in the cities as African Americans attempted to make their way in a new environment.[40] Institutionalized racism emerged in housing segregation and discrimination in schools, restaurants, and other public places. These urban studies also examined how tensions between the migrants and older settlers who resented newcomers out of fear intensified racism. As Joe Trotter notes of Milwaukee African Americans, "Established families keenly felt that the newcomers undermined their status and opportunities. They did not oppose migrants per se; rather, they opposed the unskilled, uneducated, and poor."[41]

Another productive approach to the Great Migration has been to examine the process itself. Thus in *Land of Hope* (1989), James R. Grossman has explored the push/pull dynamics behind the movement to Chicago. He uncovers the nature of southern life and economy that pushed men and women out of the South and details the lure of Chicago—its promise of education and "freedom" and, of course, its promise of jobs during World War I. Grossman's account is particularly noteworthy for its richly textured description of how well organized the migration was. The use of migration clubs, letter writing, and kinship networks kept the process of transplantation from being a completely alienating one. It was this organization that allowed many migrants to re-create community in new circumstances, forming their own churches, buying southern-style food, listening to blues performers sing songs about migration, and patronizing businesses run by their former neighbors. Thus they combined the comfort of the familiar with the excitement that urban life promised, a process that made it easier for them to cope with the disappointments they encountered in a city that did not measure up to their expectations.

Other scholars have reminded us that it was not just northern cities that were host to rural migrants. Carole Marks in *Farewell—We're Good and Gone* (1989), a work that emphasizes the proletarianization of the African American working class, argues that many of the northern migrants had first moved to southern cities, where they obtained job skills and learned to adapt to urban and modern ways, suggesting that many of the Chicago migrants were well equipped for urban industrial jobs that were generally denied them on the grounds that they were still rural peasants unused to the modern work place. In *In Their Own Interests* (1991), Earl Lewis presents the twenties as a period where the promise of the war years gave way to shrinking job opportunities and hardening lines of discrimination, prompting African Americans to turn inward and look to the "home-sphere" for sources of empowerment. Although Lewis notes the efforts of African Americans to pressure city officials into making civic improvements, he emphasizes the role of community and family in shaping their lives. Ironically, segregation led to a "measured autonomy" as it created an environment in which migrants "chose the people with whom they would interact, and in most cases they interacted with their own."[42] Lewis provides a particularly rich description of the process of "congregation"—of the combination of food, popular culture, religion, and visiting that helped to create a vibrant urban culture founded on a strong sense of the family. As other scholars have done, Lewis explores the key role of women in maintaining kinship and cultural continuity. Throughout, Lewis insists on the efforts of workers and middle class alike to act "in their own interests." As he puts it, "they remained actors in a fluid social drama."[43]

The struggle for empowerment of course has been a major theme in recent social history, and labor history of the 1920s is no exception as scholars have followed a more inclusive approach that focuses on groups outside the centers of power. They have recognized that any generalization about working-class experience is complicated by the extraordinary diversity of American laborers. Historians' focus has run the gamut from domestic servants to telephone operators, from textile workers to miners, from skilled manufacturing operatives to migrant farm workers. The labor force was a hierarchical one, where skill, race, nativity, and sex powerfully influenced opportunity. Few fully enjoyed the fruits of twenties prosperity, as Frank Stricker makes clear in "Affluence for Whom?" although wages and standard of living did improve for some, especially those at the top of the hierarchy. Moreover, underemployment and unemployment, as well as the general absence of any state protection, continued to place workers in an insecure position.[44]

The power of workers to better their circumstances was circumscribed by ongoing changes in the nature of work itself. Increased mechanization and rationalization of the shop floor—symbolized by Henry Ford's moving assembly line and the resultant "Ford miracle" of extraordinary productivity—meant that, more and more, industrial workers found themselves in jobs entailing less skill and less autonomy, and hence less bargaining power. Although many historians have addressed this development, the most comprehensive discussions are by Irving Bernstein, *The Lean Years* (1966), and David Montgomery, *The Fall of the House of Labor* (1987).[45] This process was far from new in the 1920s, but it did accelerate, especially as "scientific management" became widely adopted by the new class of managers that emerged as the corporate structure continued to evolve into a more bureaucratic and professionally run entity.[46] New procedures invariably aimed at extracting more work from employees, as *Like a Family* (1987), the oral history account by Jacquelyn Dowd Hall and others, makes clear:

> Southern mill hands remembered conditions that "just kept getting worse and worse." The "stretch-out" was their term for the cumulative changes that set them tending machines "by the acre," filled every pore in the working day, and robbed them of control over the pace and method of production. Work became a constant struggle to meet ever-increasing production quotas. "It looked like every time you got to where you could keep a job up," recalled Josephine Glenn, "they'd just add a little bit more to it. And you was always in a hole, trying to catch up."[47]

Shop-floor devices, such as the speed-up and time-motion studies, were accompanied by developments in personnel management designed to minimize labor turnover and union strength and to create a loyal work force. In the nation's largest corporations, managers extolled a new principle of management: welfare capitalism, which emerged well before World War I but flourished in the early years of the 1920s. In keeping with the optimistic tenor of employers and politicians who extolled the "new era," Stuart Brandes reports that proponents of welfare capitalism presented their programs as part of a new day of "humane, rationalized corporation as the chief instrument of social progress." The paternalistic programs of welfare capitalism, which included company unions, profit sharing, life insurance, and company softball teams, were offered as proof of corporate beneficence and enlightened labor policy.[48]

Many historians have contributed to our understanding of welfare capitalism, and in particular have sought to understand the responses of workers themselves to being managed. Brandes's *American Welfare Capitalism* is the basic general account; others (including Kim McQuaid, David Nye, and Gerald Zahavi) have examined its operation in specific companies. In answering the key question of whether welfare capitalism achieved management's aim of creating a docile and loyal work force, David Brody credits welfare capitalism with being a significant force in making labor and labor unions so passive in the 1920s. He comments that it "is comforting to think that welfare capitalism never was a success, never persuaded working men that they were best off wards of the employer," but that "the facts, however, suggest otherwise." Gerald Zahavi's study of the shoe manufacturing firm of Endicott Johnson concludes that welfare capitalism did work to an extent. Labor disturbances were low in comparison with elsewhere in the industry, and workers in oral history interviews recalled a degree of satisfaction and loyalty. But they also revealed that workers used manager's rhetoric to their own ends. Once having instituted various forms of welfare capitalism, managers found that workers considered benefits to be "what they were owed," not what they were given, and workers consistently put pressure on their employers to measure up to their promises of consideration for workers' opinions and needs: "Workers never quite viewed their loyalty in the terms that management defined it. They were never captive to paternalism." The Endicott Johnson experience suggests that workers were not so easily manipulated as managers expected and that their accommodation to welfare capitalism had its limits.[49]

As the debate over welfare capitalism suggests, another major theme for working-class history in this period is the weakness of organized labor and the concomitant power of their corporate employers.[50] World War I had followed years of industrial strife and union agitation, with significant success for the house of labor, and with war's end, labor unions continued to grow, so that by the 1920s they had doubled their prewar numbers. Although most of the pervasive strikes of 1919 were unsuccessful, organized labor entered 1920 militant, with membership at a high peak. From that point on a decline set in that was not significantly reversed until the early 1930s. While welfare capitalism may have contributed to the declining strength of unions, most historians also emphasize the more repressive side of the American political economy. The Red Scare, aided and abetted by corporate leaders who insisted that striking workers were evidence of the spread of Bolshevism, led to the severe repression of radical organizations and the undermining of unions. Its legacy throughout the decade helped to make labor unions suspect as "un-American." Moreover, an open-shop drive campaign began in earnest in 1919, and by the fall of 1920, there were open-shop associations in 240 cities. Historians, including Bernstein and Montgomery, have traced employers' use of blacklisting; the yellow-dog contract; industrial spying; and careful organization to keep unions at bay, and the policies underwritten by the Supreme Court that repeatedly undercut union tactics such as sympathy strikes and picketing. In this light, the weakness and the conservatism of unions can be better understood. As Montgomery puts it, "In the tight repression of the Coolidge era, all but a radicalized handful of workers reported quietly to whatever jobs they managed to hold, discarding their wartime aspirations as the folly of youth and directing their hopes and energies toward their homes, their children, and the esteem of their neighbors."[51] Unions thus were outflanked by the power of the corporation—not just on the shop floor but in the cultural, economic, and political arena as well.

Unions themselves, however, contributed to the dearth of labor organization in the 1920s. With radicals marginalized by the repression of the Red Scare, conservative leaders in the American Federation of Labor (AFL) increasingly headed the labor movement. These men tended toward "business unionism," a process in which unions began to replicate corporate hierarchy, with the leadership consolidating its position through bureaucracy at the expense of the rank and file. In addition, the AFL was dominated by craft unions that spoke primarily to skilled workers, a group increasingly less representative of American workers as technology and management undermined skill. The AFL leadership concentrated on maintaining benefits for its own skilled group and evinced little interest in organizing mass-production industries. Moreover, the racism and sexism that characterized most AFL unions was a major factor contributing to their failure to expand unions to under-represented groups, a point made by many historians who have examined workers among the Mexican, Asian, African American, and female population. As Dana Frank summed up the situation in Seattle, "Each moment at which the AFL movement redefined solidarity to include fewer and fewer members of the working class, it vitiated the movement's ability to counter employers' assaults."[52]

Despite organized labor's weakness in the 1920s, historians, especially those who have focused on the diversity of the work force, have uncovered pockets of resistance to employer power. Hall reports the opposition to scientific management in *Like a Family*: "Twice, when a time study man showed up at Erwin Mills in Durham," for example, "workers insisted that 'they did not want to be studied' and pushed him out a window."[53] There is also evidence of more overt, albeit unsuccessful, challenges. In California, a 1928 strike by unionized Chicano farm workers against melon growers was one of many that was suppressed by the increasingly powerful agribusiness sector, as Cletus Daniel demonstrates. Stephen Norwood documents the aggressive strike waged by New England female telephone operators in 1923. Routed by the superior power of the AT&T, the strike was remarkable for the aggressive, persistent effort of the strikers who combined their militancy with "boisterous, highly spirited behavior characteristic of young flappers."[54] In the South, textile workers were relatively quiet until the end of the decade, when workers in Elizabethton, North Carolina, the vast majority of them women, rebelled in a spontaneous strike. At that point, as Jacquelyn Dowd Hall explains, the United Textile Workers came in, and although the strike was lost, the incident contributed to a "Piedmont revolt" of union organizing and bitter, unsuccessful strikes that helped to lay the groundwork for depression-era militancy and unionization.[55] These strikers were harbingers of what was to come. In addition, as Hall's and Norwood's focus on women militants suggests, much of the richness of the new history of the 1920s stems from the growing body of literature that explores women's lives and experiences.

Ethnic and racial pluralism and the struggles of workers to negotiate the terrain of the twentieth-century workplace constitute key aspects of the modern side of the 1920s. "The New Woman"—so celebrated or vilified by her contemporaries—is another topic that historians have recently explored in great detail. Although they have found much that is modern, they have revealed continuities as well. Examining women's experience in the political, economic, and social arena, they have questioned the notion of liberation and radical change and have reminded us, as with any stereotype, to look beyond the image, to the diversity of American women.[56]

In politics, one of the central questions scholars have pursued is the aftermath of the suffrage movement. Why after such an impressive organizational triumph were women not able to translate their enfranchisement into the social reforms they had hoped for? Why did feminism falter? This lack of success was not for want of trying. Studies such as William H. Chafe, *The American Woman* (1972); Susan Felice D. Gordon, *After Winning* (1986); and Susan D. Becker, *The Origins of the Equal Rights Amendment* (1981) document the campaigns of organizations like the League of Women Voters and the Woman's Party to improve women's legal and economic status. Different campaign efforts met with piecemeal success on the state level, but the federal Equal Rights Amendment, introduced in 1924 by the Woman's Party, was a dismal failure. These studies also demonstrate the persistence of white women in promoting social reforms ranging from "protective" legislation for women workers to child labor laws, and city management reforms to the federal development of the Tennessee Valley. So significant were these efforts that both J. Stanley Lemons and Nancy Cott see them as key exemplars of the persistence of reform. As Lemons put it, they "sustained and promoted various causes in a conservative time until a more favorable climate for reform developed."[57]

Another group of women, until recently largely ignored, were the African American reformers who also helped to keep alive a reform spirit in inauspicious times. Both Paula Giddings, in *When and Where I Enter* (1984), and Rosalyn Terborg-Penn, in "Discontented Black Feminists," have traced the ongoing efforts of middle-class African American women to work on behalf of their race and their sex. Particularly important in the 1920s was the continued fight against lynching, which women participated in through the NAACP, and the effort, ignored by white women's organizations, to make suffrage—for both men and women—a reality in the South.[58]

A key term for the reform drive of the decade, however, was "effort." Not many permanent successes emerged and by the late 1920s, feminism and reform had stalled. As Estelle Freedman has pointed out in a valuable historiographical essay, most early historians of women in the 1920s tended to blame women themselves and their indifference to the vote for the stagnation of the women's movement; more recently, historians have explored the fate of feminism and reform with far more sophistication. They have emphasized that it was inextricably tied to the more general decline in reform spirit during the 1920s. While prosperity and consumerism may have deflected middle-class interest in social justice, equally important in this context was the Red Scare of 1919–20 with its red-baiting of reformers and their causes. Joan Jensen, in "All Pink Sisters," traces the origins of the famous "Spider Web Chart," a widely circulated document that purported to show the relationship between major women's organizations and the Bolshevik Revolution and demonstrates how damaging the fear of being labeled "red" was to women's organizations and to women's unity.[59]

Other problems were within the women's movement itself. Estelle Freedman has noted in "Separatism as Strategy: Female Institution Building and American Feminism, 1870–1930" that before the vote was won, women's exclusion from the public sphere had helped to define their unity. Among the upper- and middle-class white women, there was a separate political culture that gave an apparent cohesion to women activists. But by the 1920s, with the vote and increased participation in the work force, women were less segregated. With this, their areas of difference became more critical and made a unified feminism more difficult to achieve.[60]

Although many scholars have explored the impact of this diversity on feminism in the postwar era, the most significant is Nancy Cott's *The Grounding of Modern Feminism*. The narrow focus of the Woman's Party under Alice Paul led to associating "feminism" with support for the Equal Rights Amendment (ERA), a focus that excluded a wide range of women's issues. Thus African American women were rebuffed in their efforts to get white women's support for the implementation of the Nineteenth Amendment in the segregated South on the grounds that this was a race issue, not a women's issue. The interests of radical women like socialist Crystal Eastman—in sexual freedom, birth control, and the peace movement—also failed to find support within the mainstream. In addition, Cott brings fresh insights into the debilitating battle between the Woman's Party, with its support for the ERA, and "social" feminists who coupled support for women's rights with social reform and feared the impact of the ERA on "protective" legislation aimed at alleviating hardships for working-class women. ERA supporters, for their part, castigated "protective" legislation as damaging to their struggle to achieve absolute equality for women.

While divisions among women themselves were part of the story, Cott also makes it clear how difficult the prevailing attitudes toward women made it for a sustained interest in the feminist cause. Despite contemporaries' sense of a liberated woman, the popular media was overwhelmingly hostile to career women, calling them "the enemies of the home." The frequent celebration of women's new freedom was often an example of the co-optation of the rhetoric of women's rights, as Cott's quotation from an advertisement in the *Chicago Tribune* makes clear: "Today's woman gets what she wants. The vote. Slim sheaths of silk to replace voluminous petticoats. Glassware in sapphire blue or glowing amber. The right to a career. Soap to match her bathroom's color scheme."[61]

The media was also responsible for glamorizing the working girl of the 1920s, portraying her as independent and liberated, a theme picked up on by one of the most significant popular histories of the period, Frederick Lewis Allen's *Only Yesterday* (1931) in which he announced that women "poured out of the schools and colleges into all manner of new occupations." In Allen's account, this employment created the financial independence that led to the "slackening of husbandly and paternal authority," which in turn produced women's "headlong pursuit of freedom." Although contemporary social scientist Sophonisba Breckinridge challenged this interpretation, it was not until the 1970s that scholars paid much attention to women and work in this period and corrected the distortions Allen helped to promulgate.[62] Historians such as Alice Kessler-Harris and Leslie Tentler revealed that it was 1910, not 1920, that marked the significant upswing in women's participation in the work force and the increase in married women's paid labor. Moreover, the prewar years also saw the opening up of clerical work, which enticed more middle-class daughters into the labor market. This latter development has proved a rich field of study. Margery Davies, Lisa M. Fine, Susan Porter Benson, and Sharon Strom Hartman have traced developments in corporate and department store management that have contributed significantly to the history of business in this period in addition to the insights they have offered into the experiences of white-collar women workers.[63]

While many white middle-class women flocked to clerical work, some enjoyed the slight expansion into the professions, although for the most part opportunities were limited to the feminized professions of social work, nursing, teaching, and the like.[64] Opportunities for women of Japanese or Mexican ancestry and African American women, however, continued to be sharply restricted: they still were overwhelmingly relegated to domestic work. As Jacqueline Jones's *Labor of Love, Labor of Sorrow* (1985) and Paula Giddings's *When and Where I Enter* have demonstrated, northern migration and World War I did open up factory work, which had been the preserve primarily of European immigrant women, to African Americans. But for the most part, the factory jobs were the most unpleasant and lowest in status. Except in black-owned businesses, sales and clerical work was largely closed to African American women, and the handful of professional women, as Darlene Clark Hine suggests in *Black Women in White* (1989), met with extensive race and sex discrimination.[65]

Although there were significant differences between the opportunities offered women, all of these studies reiterate a point that held true for most women in the workplace. As Alice Kessler-Harris has argued, "Women were invited into the work force and again invited not to expect too much of it." Work for the most part was sex-segregated, and "women's work" was consistently underpaid and devalued. Despite the reality of the rising participation of women in the work force, popular attitudes tended to insist that women's proper role was in the home and that married women in particular did not belong in the labor market.[66]

Most historians have argued that despite the limitations of the work force, women were often able to use employment to shape a better life for themselves and their families and were generally not passive victims of employers or broad social forces. Susan Porter Benson argues that the female work culture produced by sex segregation led to at least a limited ability of white-collar workers to negotiate control of the workplace, especially in department stores. Elizabeth Clark-Lewis points out that even in domestic work, young African American migrants to Washington, D.C., shaped their experiences by moving out of live-in positions to day work which gave them more freedom. In another study of domestic workers, Evelyn Nakano Glenn suggests that women of Japanese descent found in their work a source of autonomy within the household.[67] Similarly, although some scholars have pictured young working women as so focused on their social life of consumption and courtships that they were indifferent to their jobs or any forms of resistance, others have uncovered significant pockets of militancy, as the work of Hall and Norwood discussed above indicates.

In the field of work, then, historians have fleshed out much of the early, superficial picture and offered fresh insights into business history, unionization, and the experience of work itself. Although the labor market was not a source of tremendous liberation, it was a significant indicator of changes in the lives of American women as they entered the twentieth century.

The reality of "liberation" has also been central to historians' approach to the sexual revolution so widely trumpeted in the 1920s. Here, too, a complex picture lies beneath the image. The roots of change in sexual mores clearly predates the era known as the jazz age. As early as 1913, one journal announced that the nation had "struck 'sex o-clock.'" But the 1920s certainly boasted the most dramatic symbol of the move away from the genteel restraints of Victorian middle-class culture: the flapper. Her bobbed hair and short skirts, her affection for cigarettes, drinking, and jazz dancing, all seemed to underscore young women's insistence on their right to sexuality and personal liberty. For unmarried middle-class youth, as Paula Fass has pointed out, "petting" was peer-sanctioned and pervasive.[68] Just as courtship changed, the ideal for middle-class marriage became the "companionate" marriage, which emphasized more equality between husband and wife and insisted on sexuality as central to a good relationship. Movies, advertisements, popular novels, and social scientists all reinforced this sense of changing sexual standards.

Historians, including Sheila Rothman, Beth Bailey, Estelle Freedman, John D'Emilio, and Elaine Tyler May, have confirmed contemporaries' sense of a changing sexual terrain.[69] In seeking its causes, they have offered a number of valuable insights. The emphasis on sexuality coincided with the trend of women seeking more freedom in their social life. At the forefront of this change were the working-class young women who by the turn of the century were seeking, in Kathy Peiss's words, "cheap amusements." Looking for an escape in part from parental authority and in part from the harsh conditions of work, many young women took advantage of the new urban amusements—dance halls, amusement parks, theaters. This unchaperoned, relatively anonymous environment inevitably led to more sexual experimentation. From another direction, by the 1920s, elite, radical women who clustered in bohemian centers like New York's Greenwich Village were also promoting a more sexualized personal life that included a rejection of bourgeois marriage. Many were "radical" feminists whose commitment to women's equality included the right to both economic independence and sexual satisfaction. Drawing upon the works of Sigmund Freud, Havelock Ellis, and Ellen Key, these bohemian radicals had great influence: they wrote novels, plays, and magazine articles that reached the middle-class parlor. Along with academic social scientists who were teaching the new sexual ideology in college courses, these women helped to spread new ideas about women's capacity for eroticism, a development accelerated as birth control became more widely disseminated. By the 1920s, these trends, emanating from the working class and intellectuals, had entered the mainstream, and the popular media had jumped on the bandwagon, exploring and celebrating the new sexuality.[70]

Although historians agree that sexual standards had undergone changes, they are cautious about the meaning of the new sexuality for women. Mary Ryan's article "The Projection of a New Womanhood," investigates cinematic images of the new, sexualized woman and argues persuasively that the new sexuality was accompanied by sexual objectification of women and by an association of sexuality with the commodities that women adorned their bodies with.[71] Other historians have emphasized the way in which popular media and social scientists portrayed the new sexuality, calling attention to it while at the same time reaffirming that a woman's goal in embracing it was marriage or the maintenance of marriage, a message that tamed female sexuality and kept it from threatening the social fabric. Thus Nancy Cott argues that the radical potential of earlier feminists' belief in sexual freedom had been co-opted by the media, with little of the egalitarian content. As she put it, "Advertising and mass media took up women's heterosexuality as their own agent, blunting the Feminist point that heterosexual liberation for women intended to subvert gender hierarchy rather than to confirm it."[72]

Scholars have also pointed out that the sexual revolution did not resonate the same for all women. Many women remained largely untouched by the new morality. As Estelle Freedman and John D'Emilio indicate, a very low rate of illegitimacy for Italian immigrant daughters persisted into the 1930s, suggesting that among that group, young women remained outside the peer culture that sanctioned sexual activity for unmarried women. Many women may have been profoundly affected by changing standards even if they did not embrace them. Elaine Tyler May has written about divorce cases in which traditionally reared wives could not accept the new sexual code, much to the dismay of their husbands, who had anticipated a highly sexualized marriage. The legacy of the Victorian moral code was not easily dismissed.

The emphasis on women's sexuality in the twenties also disconcerted many women's rights activists, for whom equality in sexual matters had never been an issue. These women, often shaped by Victorian notions of female sexuality, were critical of women's "abuse" of new freedoms. Having come of age in a time when homosocial bonding was especially common among educated, professional women, they were also disconcerted by the new psychology of sexuality that made close relationships between women suspect as homosexual. As Carol Smith Rosenberg has pointed out, it became increasingly common for popular observers to analyze militant feminists as repressed lesbians, a theme that Christina Simmons develops in "Companionate Marriage and the Lesbian Threat." For homosexual women, sophisticated urban environments gave them more opportunities to live the lives they wanted, but the relentless celebration of heterosexuality must have been disconcerting.[73] Although some studies have been done on lesbians in the 1920s, thus far the most significant book on homosexuality for this period is George Chauncey, *Gay New York* (1994). In exploring the origins and contours of New York's gay community, Chauncey not only writes about lesbians, but he also analyzes the more general question of the construction of masculinity and male sexuality, a field of study that is attracting increasing historical interest.[74]

For many African American women, the 1920s emphasis on sexuality was also problematic. Middle-class black women reformers traditionally had been eager to protect black women from sexual exploitation and to counter stereotypes of them as sexually permissive. This encouraged "dissemblance" according to Darlene Clark Hine in "Rape and the Inner Lives of Black Women in the Middle West." Hine argues that in their struggle to "counter negative stereotypes," many black women "felt compelled to downplay, even deny, sexual expression."[75] This tension about sexuality was also evident among the novelists of the Harlem Renaissance. Unlike many of their male counterparts, who tended to celebrate the "primitive" sensual side of black culture, women authors such as Nella Larsen and Jessie Fausset, as Paula Giddings and Barbara Christian have argued, were uncomfortable with this emphasis, especially when it touched on sexuality, because it seemed to reinforce unwanted stereotypes.[76] Turning away from novelists to blues singers, as Hazel Carby has done, can illuminate a strikingly different view of African American women's perception of their sexuality. While many blues songs entailed descriptions of a masochistic woman clinging to the man who "done her wrong," a significant body of songs, often written by the performers themselves, painted a different picture. Bessie Smith, Ma Rainey, Ida Cox, and Ethel Waters evoked an exuberant sense of women's enjoyment of their sexuality that spoke of resistance to sexual objectification and domination by men. Whether prescriptive or descriptive, these blues songs gave expression to black female desire that was distinct from that of their novelist sisters who focused on the burden of battling racial stereotypes.[77]

Scholarship on women in the 1920s has thus uncovered not liberation, but the hallmarks of themes that are at the center of twentieth-century women's history. The rigidly separated spheres for men and women were being eroded. In politics, the existence of a separate women's political culture was disappearing. Women activists, no longer part of a distinct separate sphere, became subsumed by the political parties, where they found little influence or power. In the workplace, the acceptability of employment for single women was a given by the 1920s. And despite the general disapproval of employed wives, the modern trend of their entering the work force was well in place, with its long-range implications for women and the family. Changing ideas about leisure and personal satisfaction that were an integral part of the consumer culture were evident in women's private lives, especially in the new emphasis on female sexuality. The fusion of sexuality with consumption also led to women's sexual objectification and encouraged women to measure their self-worth by the goods that adorned their bodies. The twenties, then, witnessed a coalescence of factors that did not make women free but did give their lives a modern contour.

The historians who have explored women's diverse experiences, the emerging consumer culture, ethnic and African American communities, and working-class life and labor in the 1920s have contributed significantly to our understanding of business, political, and labor history, of popular culture and reform, of family and sexuality. They have also been part of the broader enterprise of social history that has uncovered the experiences of ordinary people outside the main currents of history. Their scholarship has demonstrated that despite the constraints of their lives, these people—blues singers and domestic servants, African American migrants and intellectuals, immigrant workers and ethnic leaders, reformers, and consumers—have sought ways to empower themselves, however haltingly, in an increasingly complex, urban, and bureaucratic society in which the locus of power was becoming more and more remote. The 1920s is a particularly fertile period for examining these efforts, for the decade embodies so much of what was making America modern: the growth of cities and the tensions implicit in their racial and ethnic pluralism, the social and cultural meanings of changing roles for women, the significance of mass media in helping to construct a consumer culture, the implications of increasing corporate power, and the ramifications of transformations in the workplace. The historians discussed in this essay have contributed to their own specialized areas of scholarship but have also enlarged our view of the rich historical meanings embodied in Calvin Coolidge and his era.

NOTES

1. Henry F. May, "Shifting Perspectives on the 1920's," *Mississippi Valley Historical Review* 47 (1956): 405–27. Other valuable historiographical essays are Burl Noggle, "The Twenties: A New Historiographical Frontier," *Journal of American History* 53 (1966): 229–314; Charles W. Eagles, "Urban-Rural Conflict in the 1920s: A Historiographical Assessment," *Historian* 49 (1986): 26–48; Don S. Kirschner, "Conflicts and Politics in the 1920's: Historiography and Prospects," *Mid-America* 48 (1966): 219–33; Paul A. Carter, *The Twenties in America* 2d ed. (Arlington Heights, Ill., 1975); and the bibliographic essays in Ann Douglas, *Terrible Honesty: Mongrel Manhattan in the 1920s* (New York, 1995), and Lynn Dumenil, *The Modern Temper: American Culture and Society in the 1920s* (New York, 1995). I have not addressed the major overviews of the decade in this essay, but valuable works to consult are Michael E. Parrish, *Anxious Decades: America in Prosperity and Depression, 1920–1941* (New York, 1992); Stanley Coben, *Rebellion Against Victorianism: The Impetus for Cultural Change in 1920s America* (New York, 1991); Ellis Hawley, *The Great War and the Search for a Modern Order: A History of the American People and*

Their Institutions, 1917–1933 (New York, 1979); Paul A. Carter, *Another Part of the Twenties* (New York, 1977); William E. Leuchtenburg, *The Perils of Prosperity, 1914–1932* (Chicago, 1958; rev. ed., 1992); Roderick Nash, *The Nervous Generation: American Thought, 1917–1930* (Chicago, 1990; originally published 1970); Geoffrey Perrett, *America in the Twenties* (New York, 1982); and David A. Shannon, *Between the Wars: America, 1919–1941* (Boston, 2d ed., 1979). See also Lawrence W. Levine, "Progress and Nostalgia: The Self Image of the Nineteen Twenties," in *The Unpredictable Past: Explorations in American Cultural History* (New York, 1993), 195–96.

2. Of course, recent cultural and social historians have addressed other significant themes. A major body of work has focused on the Ku Klux Klan. See Nancy MacLean, *Behind the Mask of Chivalry: The Making of the Second Ku Klux Klan* (New York, 1994); Robert Alan Goldberg, *Hooded Empire: The Ku Klux Klan in Colorado* (Urbana, 1981); Leonard J. Moore, *Citizen Klansmen: The Ku Klux Klan in Indiana, 1921–1928* (Chapel Hill, 1991); Kathleen Blee, *Women of the Klan: Racism and Gender in the 1920s* (Berkeley, 1990); and Shawn Lay, *War, Revolution, and the Ku Klux Klan: A Study of Intolerance in a Border City* (El Paso, 1985). Moore's "Historical Interpretations of the 1920s Klan: The Traditional View and Recent Revisions" appears in Shawn Lay, ed., *The Invisible Empire in the West: Toward a New Historical Appraisal of the Ku Klux Klan of the 1920s* (Urbana, 1992), 17–38.

3. David Riesman, with Nathan Glazer and Reuel Denney, *The Lonely Crowd: A Study of the Changing American Character* (New Haven, 1950); Leo Lowenthal, "The Triumph of Mass Idols," in *Literature, Popular Culture, and Society* (Englewood Cliffs, N.J., 1961), 145–65; Warren I. Susman, "'Personality' and the Making of Twentieth-Century Culture," in *Culture as History: The Transformation of American Society in the Twentieth Century* (New York, 1973), 276; and T. Jackson Lears, "From Salvation to Self-Realization: Advertising and the Therapeutic Roots of the Consumer Culture, 1880–1930," in Richard Wightman Fox and T. Jackson Lears, eds., *The Culture of Consumption* (New York, 1983). In *The Twenties in America*, Paul Carter was the first to relate Riesman's and Lowenthal's ideas specifically to the 1920s.

4. The following discussion refers to only a few of the many valuable studies that enhance our understanding of the twenties and the consumer culture. See also Richard Butsch, *For Fun and Profit: The Transformation of Leisure into Consumption* (Philadelphia, 1990); Lewis A. Erenberg, *Steppin' Out: New York Nightlife and the Transformation of American Culture, 1890–1930* (Westport, Conn., 1981); *Mass Media Between the Wars: Perceptions of Cultural Tension, 1918–1941*, ed. Catherine L. Covert and John D. Stevens (Syracuse, 1984); Daniel Horowitz, *The Morality of Spending: Attitudes Toward the Consumer Society in America, 1875–1940* (Baltimore, 1985); Ronald Edsforth, *Class, Conflict, and Cultural Conflict: The Making of a Mass Consumer Society in Flint, Michigan* (New Brunswick, N.J., 1987); Douglas Gomery, *Shared Pleasures: A History of Movie Presentation in the United States* (Madison, 1992); Richard Schickel, *His Picture in the Papers: A Speculation on Celebrity in America Based on the Life of Douglas Fairbanks, Sr.* (New York, 1973).

5. Paula Fass, *The Damned and the Beautiful: American Youth in the 1920's* (New York: Oxford, 1977), 25, 292.

6. Robert Sklar, *Movie-Made America: A Cultural History of the Movies* (New York, 1975), 96.

7. Lary May, *Screening Out the Past: The Birth of Mass Culture and the Motion Picture Industry* (Chicago, 1980), 110, 112, 114.

8. Joan Shelley Rubin, *The Making of Middle/Brow Culture* (Chapel Hill, 1992), 104.

9. Vincent Vinikas, *Soft Soap, Hard Sell: American Hygiene in an Age of Advertisement* (Ames, Iowa, 1992), 107.

10. Roland Marchand, *Advertising the American Dream: Making Way for Modernity, 1920–1940* (Berkeley, 1985), 359. Another important work on advertising is Stuart and Elizabeth Ewen, *Channels of Desire: Mass Images and the Shaping of American Consciousness* (New York, 1982).

11. Jackson Lears, *Fables of Abundance: A Cultural History of Advertising in America* (New York, 1994), 169–71, 230, 233.

12. Lears, *Fables of Abundance*, 139.

13. Lawrence W. Levine, "The Folklore of Industrial Society: Popular Culture and Its Audience," *American Historical Review* 97 (December 1992): 1381.

14. Kathy Peiss, *Cheap Amusements: Working Women and Leisure in Turn-of-the-Century New York* (Philadelphia, 1986); Roy Rosenzweig, *Eight Hours for What We Will: Workers and Leisure in an Industrial City, 1870–1920* (Cambridge, Mass., 1983). See also Steven J. Ross, "Struggles for the Screen: Workers, Radicals, and the Political Use of Silent Film," *American Historical Review* 96 (1991): 333–67.

15. Lawrence W. Levine, *Black Culture, Black Consciousness: Afro-American Folk Thought from Slavery to Freedom* (New York, 1977). Ann Douglas, *Terrible Honesty: Mongrel Manhattan in the 1920s* (New York, 1995), 106–7.

16. Steven A. Riess, *City Games: The Evolution of American Urban Society and the Rise of Sports* (Urbana, 1989) is especially helpful on the ethnic and class context of sports, as is Rob Ruck, *Sandlot Seasons: Sport in Black Pittsburgh* (Urbana, 1987) and Don Rogosin, *Invisible Men: Life in Baseball's Negro Leagues* (New York, 1983). For other accounts of sports in the 1920s, see Benjamin G. Rader, *American Sports: From the Age of Folk Games to the Age of Spectators* (Englewood Cliffs, N.J., 1983); Ted Vincent, *Mudville's Revenge: The Rise and Fall of American Sport* (New York, 1981); Elliott Gorn and Warren Goldstein, *A Brief History of American Sports* (New York., 1993); and Douglas A. Noverr and Lawrence E. Ziewacz, "Sports in the Twenties," in *The Evolution of Mass Culture in America: 1877 to the Present*, ed. Gerald R. Baydo (St. Louis, 1982), 101–18; and Elliott J. Gorn, "The Manassa Mauler and the Fighting Marine: An Interpretation of the Dempsey-Tunney Fights," *Journal of American Studies* 19 (April 1985): 27–47.

17. See, for example, Earl Lewis, *In Their Own Interests: Race, Class, and Power in Twentieth-Century Norfolk, Virginia* (Berkeley, 1991); David Levering Lewis, *When Harlem Was in Vogue* (New York, 1981); Kathy J. Ogren, *The Jazz Revolution: Twenties America and the Meaning of Jazz* (New York, 1989); George M. Sánchez, *Becoming Mexican American: Ethnicity, Culture, and Identity in Chicano Los Angeles, 1990–1945* (New York, 1993); Richard K. Spottswood, "Commercial Ethnic Recordings in the United States," *Ethnic Recordings in America: A Neglected Heritage* (Washington, D.C., 1982).

18. Lizabeth Cohen, *Making a New Deal: Industrial Workers in Chicago, 1919–1939* (Cambridge, Mass., 1990), 135.

19. John M. Allswang, *A House for All Peoples: Ethnic Politics in Chicago, 1890–*

1936 (Lexington, Ky., 1971). See also Michael Walzer, Edward T. Kantowicz, John Higham, Mona Harrington, *The Politics of Ethnicity* (Cambridge, Mass., 1982); Howard Zinn, *La Guardia in Congress* (New York, 1959); J. Joseph Huthmacher, *Massachusetts People and Politics, 1913–1933* (Cambridge, Mass., 1959); Paula Eldo, *Governor Alfred E. Smith: The Politician as Reformer* (New York, 1983); Ronald H. Bayor, *Fiorello La Guardia: Ethnicity and Reform* (Arlington Heights, Ill.: Harlan Davidson, 1993); and David Burner, *The Politics of Provincialism: The Democratic Party in Transition, 1918–1932* (Cambridge, Mass., 1986).

20. John Higham, *Strangers in the Land: The Patterns of American Nativism, 1860–1925* (New York, 1955, 1989). The most comprehensive study of the Red Scare is Robert K. Murray, *Red Scare: A Study in National Hysteria, 1919–1920* (New York, 1955), while Stanley Coben offers a perceptive essay in "A Study in Nativism: The American Red Scare of 1919–1920." See also William Preston, Jr., *Aliens and Dissenters: Federal Suppression of Radicals, 1903–1933* (New York, 1963). On hostility to Asians and Mexicans, see Roger Daniels, *The Politics of Prejudice: The Anti-Japanese Movement in California and the Struggle for Japanese Exclusion* (New York, 1962); Yuji Ichioka, *The Issei: The World of the First Generation Japanese Immigrants, 1885–1924* (New York, 1988); Rodolfo Acuña, *America: A History of Chicanos*, 3d ed. (New York, 1988); David Montejano, *Anglos and Mexicans in the Making of Texas* (Austin, 1987); and Sánchez, *Becoming Mexican American.*

21. Leonard Dinnerstein, *Anti-Semitism in America* (New York, 1994); Leo P. Ribuffo, "Henry Ford and the International Jew," *American Jewish History* 69 (1980): 433–77; Lynn Dumenil, "The Tribal Twenties: 'Assimilated' Catholics' Response to Anti-Catholicism," *Journal of American Ethnic History* 11 (Fall 1991): 21–49. See also Marcia Graham Synott, *The Half-Opened Door: Discrimination and Admissions at Harvard, Yale, and Princeton, 1900–1970* (Westport, Conn., 1970).

22. Deborah Dash Moore, *At Home in America: Second Generation New York Jews* (New York, 1981). See also Henry L. Feingold, *A Time for Searching: Entering the Mainstream, 1920–1945* (Baltimore, 1945).

23. Sánchez, *Becoming Mexican American*, 125.

24. Elizabeth Ewen, *Immigrant Women in the Land of Dollars: Life and Culture on the Lower East Side, 1890–1925* (New York, 1985); John Bodnar, *The Transplanted: A History of Immigrants in Urban America* (Bloomington, Ind., 1987); John Higham, ed., *Ethnic Leadership in America* (Baltimore, 1978); Charles Shanabruch, *Chicago's Catholics: The Evolution of an American Identity* (Notre Dame, Ind., 1981); Robert A. Orsi, *The Madonna of 115th Street: Faith and Community in Italian Harlem* (New Haven, 1985); and Humbert S. Nelli, *Italians in Chicago, 1880–1930* (New York, 1970). See Dumenil, *The Modern Temper*, chapter 6.

25. Jean-Claude Baker and Chris Chase, *Josephine: The Hungry Heart* (New York, 1993); David Levering Lewis, *W. E. B. Du Bois: Biography of a Race, 1968–1919*, vol. 1 (New York, 1993); Martin B. Duberman, *Paul Robeson* (New York, 1988); E. David Cronon, *Black Moses: The Story of Marcus Garvey and the Universal Negro Improvement Association* (Madison, Wis., 1955). Arnold Rampersad, *The Life of Langston Hughes*, 2 vols. (New York, 1986); and Eugene Levy, *James Weldon Johnson: Black Leader, Black Voice* (Chicago, 1973).

26. Nathan Huggins, *Harlem Renaissance* (New York, 1971).

27. David Levering Lewis, *When Harlem Was in Vogue* (New York, 1981).

28. For women artists of the Renaissance, see Barbara Christian, *Black Women Novelists: The Development of a Tradition, 1892–1976* (Westport, Conn., 1980); Paula Giddings, *When and Where I Enter: The Impact of Black Women on Race and Sex in America* (New York, 1984); Maureen Honey, ed., *Shadowed Dreams: Women's Poetry of the Harlem Renaissance* (New Brunswick, N.J., 1989); Gloria T. Hull, *Color, Sex, and Poetry: Three Women Writers of the Harlem Renaissance* (Bloomington, Ind., 1987); and Cheryl A. Wall, "Poets and Versifiers, Singers and Signifiers: Women of the Harlem Renaissance," in *Women, the Arts, and the 1920s in Paris and New York*, ed. Kenneth W. Wheeler and Virginia Lee Lussier (New Brunswick, N.J., 1982).

29. Kathy J. Ogren, *The Jazz Revolution: Twenties America and the Meaning of Jazz* (New York, 1989), 117. See also Burton Nancy MacLean, *Behind the Mask of Chivalry: The Making of the Second Ku Klux Klan* (New York, 1994); Peretti, *The Creation of Jazz: Music, Race, and Culture in Urban America* (Urbana, 1992).

30. Arnold Rampersad, "Langston Hughes and Approaches to Modernism in the Harlem Renaissance," in *The Harlem Renaissance: Revaluations*, ed. Amritjit Singh, William S. Shiver, and Stanley Brodwin (New York, 1989), 65.

31. Douglas, *Terrible Honesty*, 90.

32. W. E. B. Du Bois, *The Souls of Black Folk* (Greenwich, Conn., 1961), v. An extensive annotated bibliography on the Harlem Renaissance is provided by Douglas in *Terrible Honesty*. Major works not enumerated above include Cary D. Wintz, *Black Culture and the Harlem Renaissance* (Houston, 1988); Houston A. Baker, *Modernism and the Harlem Renaissance* (Chicago, 1987); and Harold Cruse, *The Crisis of the Negro Intellectual: A Historical Analysis of the Failure of Black Leadership* (New York, 1967).

33. Emory J. Tolbert, *The UNIA and Black Los Angeles* (Los Angeles, 1980); E. David Cronon, *Black Moses: The Story of Marcus Garvey and the Universal Negro Improvement Association* (Madison, 1955).

34. Tony Martin, *Race First: The Ideological and Organizational Struggles of Marcus Garvey and the Universal Negro Improvement Association* (Westport, Conn., 1976).

35. Judith Stein, *The World of Marcus Garvey: Race and Class in Modern Society* (Baton Rouge, La., 1986), 273–74.

36. Robert A. Hill, "General Introduction," *The Marcus Garvey and Universal Negro Improvement Association Papers* (Berkeley, 1983), vol. 1, xxxv–xc.

37. Lawrence W. Levine, "Marcus Garvey and the Politics of Revitalization," in *The Unpredictable Past*, 115–16.

38. James R. Grossman, *Land of Hope: Chicago, Black Southerners, and the Great Migration* (Chicago, 1989); Carole Marks, *Farewell—We're Good and Gone: The Great Black Migration* (Bloomington, Ind., 1989); Joe William Trotter, Jr., *Black Milwaukee: The Making of an Industrial Proletariat, 1915–1945* (Urbana, 1985); Peter Gottlieb, *Making Their Own Way: Southern Blacks' Migration to Pittsburgh, 1916–1930* (Urbana, 1987); Kenneth Kusmer, *A Ghetto Takes Shape: Black Cleveland, 1870–1930* (Urbana, 1976); David Alan Levine, *Internal Combustion: The Races in Detroit, 1915–1926* (Westport, Conn., 1976); Gilbert Orofsky, *Harlem: The Making of a Ghetto: Negro New York, 1890–1930* (New York, 1963).

39. Gottlieb, *Making Their Own Way*, 112.

40. William M. Tuttle, Jr., *Race Riot: Chicago in the Red Summer of 1919* (New York, 1970). See also Arthur I. Waskow, *From Race Riot to Sit-in, 1919 and the 1960s*

(Garden City, N.Y., 1966). Herbert Shapiro, *White Violence and Black Response: From Reconstruction to Montgomery* (Amherst, Mass., 1988) goes beyond riots to discuss a variety of forms of violence and African American response.

41. Trotter, *Black Milwaukee*, 129.

42. Grossman, *Land of Hope*; Marks, *Farewell—We're Good and Gone*; Earl Lewis, *In Their Own Interests: Race, Class, and Power in Twentieth-Century Norfolk, Virginia* (Berkeley, 1991), 91.

43. Lewis, *In Their Own Interests*, 3. Two other studies that examine the South in this period are Lester C. Lamon, *Black Tennesseans, 1900–1930* (Knoxville, 1977); and I. A. Newby, *Black Carolinians: A History of Blacks in South Carolina from 1895 to 1968* (Columbia, S.C., 1973). For material on women and migration, see Jacqueline Jones, *Labor of Love, Labor of Sorrow: Black Women, Work and the Family, from Slavery to the Present* (New York, 1985) and Darlene Clark Hines, "Rape and the Inner Lives of Black Women in the Middle West: Preliminary Thoughts on the Culture of Dissemblance," in *Unequal Sisters: A Multicultural Reader in Women's History*, ed. Ellen Carol DuBois and Vicki L. Ruiz (New York, 1990), 292–97.

44. Irving Bernstein, *The Lean Years: A History of the American Worker, 1920–1933* (Baltimore, 1966). Frank Stricker, "Affluence for Whom?: Another Look at Prosperity and the Working Classes in the 1920s," *Labor History* 24 (Winter 1983): 5–33. Roy Lubove, *The Struggle for Social Security, 1900–1935* (Pittsburgh, 1968) discusses workmen's compensation and failures of other social security measures in the period before the Great Depression.

45. David Montgomery, *The Fall of the House of Labor: The Workplace, the State, and American Labor Activism, 1865–1925* (Cambridge, U.K., 1987); Bernstein, *The Lean Years*. See also James R. Green, *The World of the Worker: Labor in Twentieth-Century America* (New York, 1980) and Robert Zieger, *American Workers, American Unions* (Baltimore, 1994), 2d ed.

46. The material on scientific management and workers is voluminous. Dan Clawson, *Bureaucracy and the Labor Process: The Transformation of U.S. Industry, 1860–1920* (New York, 1980) analyzes the implications of scientific management for worker control. David F. Noble, *America by Design: Science, Technology, and the Rise of Corporate Capitalism* (New York, 1977) includes an examination of the role of engineers in reshaping ideas about management of the work force. Daniel Nelson, *Managers and Workers: Origins of the New Factory System in the United States, 1880–1920* (Madison, 1975) offers a useful overview.

47. Jacquelyn Dowd Hall et al., *Like a Family: The Making of a Southern Cotton Mill World* (Chapel Hill, 1987), 211.

48. Stuart D. Brandes, *American Welfare Capitalism, 1880–1940* (Chicago, 1976), 28.

49. Brandes, *American Welfare Capitalism*; David Brody, "The Rise and Decline of Welfare Capitalism," in *Workers in Industrial America: Essays on the Twentieth Century Struggle* (New York, 1980), 78; Gerald Zahavi, "Negotiated Loyalty: Welfare Capitalism and the Shoeworkers of Endicott Johnson, 1920–1940," *Journal of American History* 70 (1983): 611, 620. See also David E. Nye, *Image Worlds: Corporate Identities at General Electric, 1890–1930* (Cambridge, Mass., 1985); Kim McQuaid, "Owen D. Young, Gerald Swope, and the New Capitalism of the General Electric Company, 1920–1933," *American Journal of Economics and Sociology* 36

(1977): 323–34; Lizabeth Cohen, *Making a New Deal*; Brian Palmer, "Class, Conception, and Conflict: The Thrust for Efficiency, Managerial Views of Labor and the Working Class Rebellion, 1903–22," *The Review of Radical Political Economics* 7 (Summer 1975): 31–49; H. M. Gitelman, "Welfare Capitalism Reconsidered," *Labor History* 33 (Winter 1992): 5–31; Sanford M. Jacoby, *Employing Bureaucracy: Managers, Unions, and the Transformation of Work in American Industry, 1900–1945* (New York, 1985); and Norman J. Wood, "Industrial Relations Policies of American Management, 1900–1933," *Business History Review* 34 (1960): 403–20.

50. Irving Bernstein's account in *The Lean Years* is the most comprehensive discussion of workers and unions in the twenties. See also Foster Rhea Dulles and Melvyn Dubofsky, *Labor in America: A History*, 4th ed. (Arlington Heights, Ill., 1984); David Montgomery, *Workers' Control in America: Studies in the History of Work, Technology, and Labor Struggles* (New York, 1979). For a case study of management, see Robert Ozanne, *A Century of Labor-Management Relations at McCormick and International Harvester* (Madison, 1967).

51. Montgomery, *The Fall of the House of Labor*, 464.

52. Dana Frank, *Purchasing Power: Consumer Organizing, Gender, and the Seattle Labor Movement, 1919–1929* (Cambridge, U.K., 1994), 247. For African Americans, see material cited above and Sterling D. Spero and Abram L. Harris, *The Black Worker: The Negro and the Labor Movement* (Port Washington, N.Y., 1931). For Mexicans and Chicanos, see Acuña, *Occupied America*; Cletus E. Daniel, *Bitter Harvest: A History of California Farmworkers, 1870–1941* (Ithaca, N.Y., 1981); and Emilio Zamora, *The World of the Mexican Worker in Texas* (College Station, Tex., 1993). For Asian Americans, see Ronald Takaki, *Strangers from a Different Shore* (Boston, 1989).

53. Hall, *Like a Family*, 210.

54. Daniel, *Bitter Harvest*; Stephen H. Norwood, *Labor's Flaming Youth: Telephone Operators and Worker Militancy, 1878–1923* (Urbana, 1990), 282.

55. Jacquelyn Dowd Hall, "Disorderly Women: Gender and Labor Militancy in the Appalachian South," *Journal of American History* 73 (September 1986): 354–82.

56. A number of general studies deal with women in the 1920s. Besides Cott, *The Grounding of Modern Feminism*, see William H. Chafe, *The American Woman: Her Changing Social, Economic, and Political Roles, 1920–1970* (New York, 1972) and Dorothy M. Brown, *Setting a Course: American Women in the 1920s* (Boston, 1987).

57. J. Stanley Lemons, *The Woman Citizen: Social Feminism in the 1920s* (Urbana, 1975), 147; Cott, *The Grounding of American Feminism*. See also Chafe, *The American Woman*; Susan Felice D. Gordon, *After Winning: The Legacy of the New Jersey Suffragists, 1920–1947* (New Brunswick, N.J., 1986); Susan D. Becker, *The Origins of the Equal Rights Amendment: American Feminism Between the Wars* (Westport, Conn., 1981); Nancy Cott, "What's in a Name? The Limits of 'Social Feminism' or Expanding the Vocabulary of Women's History," *Journal of American History* 76 (December 1989): 809–29; William L. O'Neill, *Feminism in America: A History*, 2d rev. ed. (New Brunswick, N.J., 1989); William O'Neill, *The Woman Movement: Feminism in the United States and England* (Chicago, 1971); Ann Firor Scott, "After Suffrage: Southern Women in the Twenties," *Journal of Southern History* 30 (August 1964): 298–318.

58. Paula Giddings, *When and Where I Enter*; and Rosalyn Terborg-Penn, "Dis-

contented Black Feminists: Prelude and Postscript to the Passage of the Nineteenth Amendment," in *Decades of Discontent: The Women's Movement, 1920–1940*, ed. Lois Scharf and Joan M. Jensen (Westport, Conn., 1983), 261–78.

59. Estelle B. Freedman, "The New Woman: Changing Views of Women in the 1920s," in *Decades of Discontent*, 221–44; and Joan M. Jensen, "All Pink Sisters: The War Department and the Feminist Movement in the 1920s," in *Decades of Discontent*, 199–22.

60. *Feminist Studies* 5 (Fall 1979): 512.

61. Cott, *The Grounding of Modern Feminism*, 172.

62. Frederick Lewis Allen, *Only Yesterday: An Informal History of the Nineteen-Twenties* (New York, 1931), 80–81; Sophonisba Breckinridge, *Women in the Twentieth Century: A Study of Political, Social, and Economic Activities* (New York, 1970, reprint).

63. Alice Kessler-Harris, *Out to Work: A History of Wage-Earning Women in the United States* (New York, 1982); Leslie Woodcock Tentler, *Wage-Earning Women: Industrial and Family Life in the United States, 1900–1930* (New York, 1979); Susan Estabrook Kennedy, *If All We Did Was to Weep at Home: A History of White Working-Class Women in America* (Bloomington, Ind., 1979). On white-collar work, see Margery W. Davies, *Woman's Place Is at the Typewriter: Office Work and Office Workers, 1870–1930* (Philadelphia, 1982); Lisa M. Fine, *The Souls of the Skyscraper: Female Clerical Workers in Chicago, 1870–1930* (Philadelphia, 1990); Sharon Strom Hartman, *Beyond the Typewriter: Gender, Class, and the Origins of Modern Office Work* (Urbana, 1992); Susan Porter Benson, *Counter Cultures: Saleswomen, Managers, and Customers in American Department Stores, 1890–1940* (Urbana, 1988).

64. Barbara J. Harris, *Beyond Her Sphere: Women and the Professions in American History* (Greenwood, Conn., 1978).

65. Giddings, *When and Where I Enter*; Jacqueline Jones, *Labor of Love, Labor of Sorrow*; Darlene Clark Hine, *Black Women in White: Racial Conflict and Cooperation in the Nursing Profession, 1890–1950* (Bloomington, Ind., 1989). For Mexicanas and Chicanas, see Rosalinda M. Gonzalez, "Chicanas and Mexican Immigrant Families, 1920–1940," in *Decades of Discontent*, 59–84; and Albert Camarillo, *Chicanos in a Changing Society: From Mexican Pueblos to American Barrios in Santa Barbara and Southern California, 1848–1930* (Cambridge, Mass., 1979). For Japanese women, see Evelyn Nakano Glenn, *Issei, Nisei, War Bride: Three Generations of Japanese American Women in Domestic Service* (Philadelphia, 1986); Sucheng Chang, *Asian Americans: An Interpretive History* (Boston, 1991); and Ichioka, *The Issei*.

66. Kessler-Harris, *Out to Work*, 248.

67. Elizabeth Clark-Lewis, "'This Work Had an End': African-American Domestic Workers in Washington, D.C., 1910–1940," in *Women and Power in American History: A Reader*, vol. 2, ed. Kathryn Kish Sklar and Thomas Dublin (Englewood Cliffs, N.J., 1991), 195–208; and Glenn, *Issei, Nisei, War Bride*.

68. Fass, *The Damned and the Beautiful*.

69. Elaine Tyler May, *Great Expectations: Marriage and Divorce in Post-Victorian America* (Chicago, 1980); John D'Emilio and Estelle B. Freedman, *Intimate Matters: A History of Sexuality in America* (New York, 1988); Beth L. Bailey, *From Front Porch to Back Seat: Courtship in Twentieth-Century America* (Baltimore, 1988); Steven Mintz and Susan Kellogg, *Domestic Revolutions: A Social History of American Family*

Life (New York, 1988), 107–31; James R. McGovern, "The American Woman's Pre–World War I Freedom in Manners and Morals," *Journal of American History* 55 (September 1968): 315–33; and Joanne J. Meyerowitz, *Women Adrift: Independent Wage Earners in Chicago, 1880–1930* (Chicago, 1988).

70. Peiss, *Cheap Amusements*. On the theme of intellectuals and changing perceptions of women's sexuality, see Rosalind Rosenberg, *Beyond Separate Spheres: Intellectual Roots of Modern Feminism* (New Haven, 1982); June Sochen, *The New Woman: Feminism in Greenwich Village, 1910–1920* (New York, 1972); Ellen Kay Trimberger, "Feminism, Men, and Modern Love: Greenwich Village, 1900–1925," in *Powers of Desire: The Politics of Sexuality*, ed. Ann Snitown, Christine Stansell, and Sharon Tompson (New York, 1983), 131–52; and Paul Robinson, *The Modernization of Sex: Havelock Ellis, Alfred Kinsey, William Masters, and Virginia Johnson* (New York, 1976). For a discussion of birth control in the twenties, see David M. Kennedy, *Birth Control in America: The Career of Margaret Sanger* (New Haven, 1970); Linda Gordon, *Woman's Body, Woman's Right: A Social History of Birth Control in America* (New York, 1976); and Ellen Chesler, *Woman of Valor: Margaret Sanger and the Birth Control Movement in America* (New York, 1992).

71. Mary Ryan, "The Projection of a New Womanhood: The Movie Moderns in the 1920s," in *Our American Sisters: Women in American Life and Thought*, ed. Jean E. Friedman and William G. Shade, 3d ed. (Lexington, Mass., 1982), 500–18. On women and the movies, see also Lary May, *Screening Out the Past*, and Marjorie Rosen, *Popcorn Venus: Women, Movies, and the American Dream* (New York, 1973).

72. Cott, *The Grounding of Modern Feminism*, 152.

73. Carol Smith Rosenberg, "The Female World of Love and Ritual: Relations Between Women in Nineteenth-Century America," *Signs* 1 (Autumn 1975): 1–29; Christina Simmons, "Companionate Marriage and the Lesbian Threat," in *Women and Power in American History: A Reader*, vol. 2, ed. Kathryn Kish Sklar and Thomas Dublin (Englewood Cliffs, N.J., 1991), 183–94; Christina Simmons, "Modern Sexuality and the Myth of Victorian Repression," in *Passion and Power: Sexuality in History*, ed. Kathy Peiss and Christina Simmons (Philadelphia, 1989), 157–77; D'Emilio, *Intimate Matters*; Lillian Faderman, *Odd Girls and Twilight Lovers: A History of Lesbian Life in Twentieth-Century America* (New York, 1991); Freeman, "The New Woman"; May, *Great Expectations*.

74. George Chauncey, *Gay New York: Gender, Urban Culture, and the Making of the Gay Male World, 1890–1940* (New York, 1994).

75. Darlene Clark Hine, "Rape and the Inner Lives of Black Women in the Middle West: Preliminary Thoughts on the Culture of Dissemblance," in *Unequal Sisters*, 295.

76. Giddings, *When and Where I Enter*, and Christian, *Black Women Novelists*.

77. Hazel V. Carby, "'It Jus Be's Dat Way Sometime': The Sexual Politics of Women's Blues," in *Unequal Sisters*, 238–49.

4

Coolidge, Hays, and 1920s Movies

Some Aspects of Image and Reality

DANIEL J. LEAB

An uneasy duality marked and marred American life and culture during the 1920s, especially during the presidency of Calvin Coolidge. He served as president of the United States from the untimely, unexpected death of his predecessor, Warren Harding, at the beginning of August 1923, until March 4, 1929. He retired from office at the height of his great popularity. Coolidge had won reelection overwhelmingly in 1924 and was considered a shoo-in for reelection until he became the "unavailable man" when he did "not choose to run" again.[1]

During Coolidge's tenure as president, the United States experienced unprecedented material prosperity—with some notable exceptions in industries such as coal-mining, textile manufacture, and various branches of agriculture. That overall prosperity played out against a bitter, intense, internecine cultural warfare. Coolidge presided over a country in many ways in conflict with itself. The English critic Paul Johnson has summed up this conflict: "Americans during the Coolidge era viewed their native land as 'the last Arcadia' but one in which they felt increasingly threatened." A generation of Americans found themselves caught "between the continuity and discontinuity of history." The novelist F. Scott Fitzgerald, an icon of the age, exaggerated in 1923 when he described Americans as "a whole race going hedonistic." Yet traditional norms and values did come under heavy attack.[2]

Tradition had its vigorous defenders. And ultimately those holding opposing views found accommodation if not toleration or reconciliation. Arcadia came to grips with modernity. Myth and reality came to terms. As pundit Walter Lippmann presciently observed at the time: "we have attained a Puritanism de luxe in which it is possible to praise all the classic virtues while continuing to enjoy all the modern conveniences." The creation of image as never before in American history became the order of the day.[3]

Two important manifestations of that image making are Calvin Coolidge and movie morality. The depiction of Coolidge exemplifies sophisticated manipulation and utilization of both the traditional and newer media; the attempts to regulate movie morality and make its more salacious aspects palatable in a censorious society demonstrates the perceived need to deal with the movies, one of the most important of the new media (and one which by the end of the 1920s had become *the* American mass medium). A fascinating link between these two manifestations is Will Hays. Aptly described as "a surefooted front man," this Republican politico who supervised the GOP's winning Harding campaign in 1920 became the putative "czar" of the movie industry and helped fend off public censorship during that decade. Coolidge, Hays, and movie morality—each had a powerful impact on the public during the 1920s but an impact far removed in actuality because of a careful manipulation of reality in the context of Arcadia.[4]

Just months before Coolidge's death in January 1933, Frederick Lewis Allen, a shrewd chronicler of the 1920s, observed that the former president was "unobtrusive to the last degree." Allen dealt with Coolidge in a more kindly fashion than did many of his peers. A fellow observer of the times, the journalist and public figure George Creel, claimed that "sitting in the White House," the president was "distinguishable from the furniture only when he moved." *New Republic* editor Bruce Blivin declared that "Coolidge was saying little . . . solely and simply because he had little to say." The acerbic wit Dorothy Parker, when told of Coolidge's death, quipped in her usual brutal fashion "how can you tell?" H. L. Mencken in one of his newspaper columns dismissed Coolidge with the judgment that his "chief feat during five years and seven months" in the White House "was to sleep more than any President."[5]

Nor has Coolidge fared well with later generations of writers, intellectuals, and academics. Historians and other commentators on the 1920s American scene have continued to make negative judgments on the man and his style. The English Americanist Esmond Wright has characterized Coolidge as "overcomplacent," "inactive," "lacking in vision." The novelist Irving Stone in an essay entitled "A Study in Inertia" savaged Coolidge as a "do-nothing " indulging in "moronic puerility," who had "cut the umbilical cord between thought and speech." Historian William Leuchtenburg describes Coolidge as a man whose "taciturnity and inactivity in office" helped make the federal government "insignificant" during his presidency. The country, as one overview has put it, "wanted nothing done" and "he done it." Recently, Coolidge has been compared with Ronald Reagan, another popular president who has been the subject of much criticism, the argument being that both were men whose "approach to public problems rested on the application of a few broad, simple homilies," most notably that "the American social and economic order was basically sound." Bancroft Award winner Elizabeth Stevenson describes Coolidge as "small-scale, not of imagination, not hearty or spontaneous . . . saying a smart thing now or then."[6]

All these negative judgments—recently described as "the cult of Calvin Coolidge's personality"—undoubtedly owed a great deal to the contemporary media, which played up certain aspects of what has been termed "a dull original." One historian has summed up the response of many in declaring that the media process resulted in an "amazing metamorphosis" that created "a Coolidge image and a Coolidge myth." Tom Stokes, an erstwhile Pulitzer-Prize–winning Capitol Hill correspondent, recalled some years later that "it was really a miracle. He said nothing. Newspapers must have copy. So we grasped little incidents . . . and . . . created a character." The media created the image of the shrewd, pragmatic, laconic, efficient Coolidge known to history as "Silent Cal"—"sparing with words, economical in action."[7]

That image has not served Coolidge well since the 1920s. And at the time it allowed his detractors to pillory him as a symbol of everything they loathed about 1920s America. Coolidge never won them over, but throughout his lifetime and even after his death, he retained the affection overall of the American people. In 1928 a poll of schoolboys found that they most wanted to emulate Charles Lindbergh, the aviator hero of the day; Coolidge as a role model came in a distant second, but he significantly outscored such other contemporary icons as Henry Ford, Thomas Edison, and the new heavyweight champion, Gene Tunney. Nor did the collapse of "Coolidge Prosperity" after 1929 dramatically or even significantly reduce that positive response. Walter Lippmann noted this "political miracle" with some surprise: writing immediately after Coolidge's death in January 1933, as the nadir of the Great Depression rapidly approached with the U.S. economy grinding to a halt, Lippmann pointed out that the former president's "hold upon the American people . . . has endured, though the successes with which he was identified have proved to be illusions and have collapsed."[8]

That hold, like his career, depended on more than what many then and later called "Coolidge luck." His consistent good fortune in politics, which took him from town government in Northampton, Massachusetts, to the White House, resulted from what historian Allan Nevins has aptly summarized as "party loyalty, industry, and a grimly dependable caution." That often remarked-on caution as well as his much-heralded public reticence and widely discussed sardonic silence, even if artificially created and promoted, did serve him as "a protective armor," to use the words of one biographer, the influential newspaper editor William Allen White. The financier Bernard Baruch, according to one report, "was not alone in expressing astonishment at a host so unlike his public image." A Coolidge physician found the president to be "a man of silence" who could "talk voluminously when he had a mind to do so." A journalist in 1925 found to his surprise that after dinner the president and his male guests retired to a White House study for cigars and conversation, and "a man with a reputation for silence such as no man in public life ever possessed," displayed a "perfect willingness to talk freely, easily."[9]

Moreover, for all Coolidge's platitudinous official statements (e.g., "the chief business of America is business" or "the ultimate result to be desired is not the making of money, but the making of people"), he never completely lost the spark or interest that as a young man had led him to translate Dante's *Inferno* from the original. And his vaunted emotional restraint notwithstanding, Coolidge had, as one writer has recognized, "a surprising streak of sentiment." For over fifty years he carried a picture of his mother, who died when he was still a boy. He could not hide the continuing anguish caused by the unfortunate death in 1924 of his fourteen-year-old son from blood poisoning that resulted from an infected blister suffered while playing tennis on a White House court. He pressed the locket with his mother's hair into his dying son's hands.[10]

A passion, generally unknown to the public, marked his relations with his warm, gracious, and considerate wife. Coolidge bought many of his wife's clothes, and although well-known for his parsimony, was frequently extravagant in his purchases for her. A Washington society hostess of the day remarked with awe that the Coolidges "shared not only a room, but a bed." While vacationing with the president in the Dakotas in 1927, she returned inadvertently late for lunch from a hike with the veteran Secret Service agent who served as her bodyguard; a "vexed" and "impatient" Coolidge had the agent transferred immediately. Mrs. Coolidge told a friend that "the President disliked seeing and feeling that she was so much in another man's company."[11]

Coolidge's public persona not only belied the private man but also overshadowed his understanding and intelligent use of the mass media. The writer Michael Harwood believed that "he was probably one of the most frequently snapped men of his era" and the results were, as one historian puts it, "bizarre iconographies." Among the more well-known news photos are Coolidge glumly peering out from an Indian headdress of eagle feathers and the president stoically holding a ten-gallon hat while dressed in a full cowboy rig, including chaps with "Cal" on them. In another well-known photo, Coolidge wore New England farmer's overalls, but this effort proved embarrassing because, as historian John Lukacs notes, Coolidge wore them over "gleaming city shoes" and the photographer neglected to crop from the upper corner of the photo "the presidential . . . limousine, and the . . . chauffeur, cap in hand, respectfully waiting."[12]

The president and his advisers cared keenly about his public image, which they assiduously cultivated. Thus the president lent himself to promotions such as one dreamed up during the 1924 election campaign by Edward Bernays, one of the fathers of modern public relations. That "master huckster" (as the *New York Times* characterized him) acted on behalf of a client who hoped to obtain an influential job from the reelected president: Bernays argued that a presidential breakfast at the White House with a group of stellar actors and actresses would result in "nation-wide front page publicity." One of the president's chief advisers, his knowledgeable secretary C. Bascom Slemp, agreed and set up a breakfast date at the White House for a group headed by Al Jolson, a superstar of the era. A willing Coolidge, who, according to Bernays, "recognized the implications of this venture into image making," proved himself a genial, gracious host. After breakfast the actors and actresses adjourned to the White House lawn, where Jolson sang the campaign's theme song, "Keep Coolidge" ("He's never asleep, still waters run deep, so keep Coolidge! Keep Coolidge!"). The event, as Bernays later noted, "jutted out of" the routine circumstance, "made news," and "helped the public image of Calvin Coolidge."[13]

Coolidge knew how to use the press. As Lukacs remarks, Coolidge "delivered more speeches in four years than any other President before . . . him," or indeed than his immediate successor. He also held more press conferences than had any previous president. Coolidge met with reporters in small press conferences two or three times a week. As with his predecessors, questions had to be submitted in writing in advance. He was accessible but insisted on not being quoted directly, which meant in the words of one account that journalists had "to use such . . . references as 'sources close to the President' or 'a White House spokesman' to cover statements" by Coolidge, a technique used by him in 1926 when it was reported that he did not favor federal censorship of the movies. Coolidge did not escape criticism. The young American Communist leader Jay Lovestone in 1927 echoes the opinion and comments of many less radical journalists when he berated Coolidge for "hackneyed verbiage" and "vain-glorious boasting." Yet overall, the president handled himself skillfully, and the reporters responded accordingly. One of the surviving members of the Coolidge press corps spoke for many of his colleagues when in 1967 he asserted "we kinda liked the old coot."[14]

More important press figures such as editor White, wire-service head Frank Noyes, presslord William Randolph Hearst, influential columnist Mark Sullivan, and advertising executive Bruce Barton were entertained personally by the president—one result being, according to Nevins, that Coolidge "had more guests" than any previous White House occupant. On weekends he "frequently," as one report noted, made use of the presidential yacht *Mayflower* (a big ship: displacing 2000 tons, over 300 feet long, described in 1942 as equivalent to "a good sized modern destroyer"). Coolidge, who *Life* magazine maintained "loved" to utilize the vessel, would host his more important guests for a weekend cruise, "dropping down the Potomac Saturday afternoon, and coming back on Sunday." He would make use of the *Mayflower* not only in Washington, D.C. The ship's physician recalls the president entertaining Boston's leading newspapermen on a cruise starting in that city's harbor.[15]

The newer media also were cultivated and utilized intelligently by Coolidge. In his run for the presidency in 1924, for example, he made extensive use of the fledgling broadcasting industry with its rapidly growing audience. Slemp "arranged for the first radio broadcast of a State of the Union address" to Congress. The Republicans agreed (as did the Democrats, who met some weeks later) to allow their June 1924 convention in Cleveland to be broadcast live—"for the first time," as White points out, such "a great national gathering was heard upon the radio." TV producer Robert Saudek, then a thirteen-year-old boy, recalls listening to the convention: the speeches were "marred by static almost to the point of unintelligibility . . . yet . . . it was a glorious event." Some weeks after the convention, as was traditional then, came Coolidge's acceptance speech, which also was broadcast. (The GOP also got some mileage out of news photos showing Coolidge's aging father in tiny Plymouth, Vermont—the president's hometown—listening with some friends, all wearing earphones, on an early "wireless set" to his son speaking from Washington, D.C.). Coolidge concluded his 1924 re-election campaign with a broadcast address, the night before the election, to an audience estimated to exceed twenty million people.[16]

Film, like radio, burgeoned during the 1920s and had an increasingly powerful impact, a situation that Coolidge recognized and exploited. As with the unusual news photos, newsreel cameramen filmed him in a variety of unusual situations as well as in the course of more routine activities. He readily made himself available—so much so that at a mid-1920s Gridiron Club dinner he was satirized to the tune of "Boola Boola": "Mr. Coolidge went to Vermont upon a sunny day / The movies took his picture as he pitched the new-mown hay." About one cameraman Coolidge supposedly said "that man gets more conversation out of me than all Congress." On a week-long trip to Philadelphia in 1927, the president limited the size of his party but insisted on the inclusion of the "picture men."[17]

Coolidge embraced the new technology involved in making sound movies. He is the first president recorded speaking on film; there is a six-minute clip of his 1926 appearance in the collections of the National Archives. Indeed, the president for what has been described as "one of the momentous events in motion picture history" reenacted for a newsreel company "the presentation of the Congressional medal to . . . Lindbergh" for his solo flight to Europe. Coolidge also appeared in talking campaign films.[18]

His ease with the medium in part stems from his genuine liking for the movies. In 1910–11 as mayor of Northampton, he got passes to its movie houses and "enjoyed" using them. While governor of Massachusetts, he had vetoed a film censorship bill passed by the state legislature on constitutional grounds (an act "somewhat inconsistent" with previous Supreme Court rulings, according to one history). Coolidge believed, as he said at the 1923 Wheaton College commencement, that "the possibilities of the movie picture are just being realized." A few years later, a newspaper editorialized that the president felt "the Government should encourage" the movie industry.[19]

Both as vice president and president Coolidge held "movie previews" for family and friends. He arranged for movies to be shown on "the fantail" of the *Mayflower*, at the various "camps" he used for vacations, and at the White House. Movies included documentaries such as *Grass*, pictures of Zion National Park, and commercial hits such as *Beau Geste*, *Don Juan*, and *Mare Nostrum*. At the White House screening of *The Big Parade*, the twenty guests had the benefit of a forty-four-piece orchestra brought down from New York City. Predictably, Coolidge found comedies more "relaxing." A frequent guest at the Coolidge screenings recounted in 1925 after the showing of a Harold Lloyd comedy that he "never saw the President laugh more." A visit to the MGM studios in Hollywood occasioned one of the few recorded instances of Coolidge publicly laughing out loud. He visited the set of a Ramon Navarro film on which a trained bear "went on a rampage," ignoring his trainer; the Secret Service agents moved to get Coolidge off the set, but he stayed, becoming increasingly amused at the chaos caused by the bear, and "finally . . . nearly doubled up with laughter."[20]

During Coolidge's tenure as vice president and president, the American film industry was dramatically transformed. It did not completely shed the Victorian trappings that marked its beginnings a generation earlier. But it did become the social, cultural, and economic phenomenon that by the beginning of the 1930s marked the film industry as "big business" as well as *the* mass medium in the United States, one with worldwide influence. The so-called "Golden Age" of the movies in the 1930s had its roots in the transformation of the industry on many levels during the 1920s. As Lary May has cogently put it: "film innovators turned the once-crude peep show into a complex art form and multi-million-dollar business." By 1925 some have reckoned that the motion picture industry, with a capital investment in excess of $1.5 billion was "the nation's fourth largest business enterprise." Sound came in 1927 to about twenty thousand movie theaters with a seating capacity of some eighteen million.[21]

To offset the increasing criticism it faced in the early 1920s for the content of its product and the conduct of some of the leading performers, the industry turned to "self-regulation." Supposedly beneficial, this process, carefully publicized and marketed, served as a fig leaf to cover the creation of an oligopoly and the "policing" of those involved in the creative end of filmmaking. "Self-regulation" had its origins in the movie industry's response to the welter of proposed censorship and other regulations that came to the fore in the United States during the years immediately following the end of World War I in 1918. A variety of people and organizations had embraced coercive utopianism as a cure for perennial social ills. Prohibition probably remains the most notable example of the restrictive legislation that the putative reformers imposed on American society in their quest to control or eradicate influences, alien or domestic, judged to result in supposed deviant or immoral behavior. Attempts to restrict and regulate the film industry were part of a larger contest between conservative, traditional values and the urban-based move toward greater moral freedom.

What the social historian Robert Sklar has neatly summed up as "the genteel middle class cultural order" of pre–World War I America faced a vigorous, ultimately near-fatal challenge: Greenwich Village triumphed over Main Street; the "flapper" displaced the Gibson Girl; Prohibition was the law of a land where the newly established neighborhood speakeasy probably did more business than the outlawed corner saloon. For youth, as the perceptive historian Paula Fass has concluded, "a change in the norms" meant that "the tradition-oriented adult world of family and community" gave way as there was "a reorientation of behavior to new groups and institutions" such as the movies. John Lukacs has argued convincingly that "the movie culture of the 1920s" reflected the outcome of the contest between an older and contemporary America, and no way more so than in "the visible change in the physiognomy of the national ideal"—one important manifestation being "the craze for tango 'sheiks' . . . such as Rudolph Valentino.[22]

Given what today the networks and cable companies broadcast into our homes twenty-four hours a day, seven days a week, the films of that era appear relatively innocent. Yet to many they and the advertising for them seemed the height of licentiousness. In areas of Middle American morality such as Lexington, Kentucky, the city's dailies attacked the "gutter plays . . . that pander to what is the lowest and basest in human nature." Ellis Paxson Oberholtzer, chairman of the Pennsylvania Board of Censors—by "reputation the strictest board during this period," maintained that "we have been plunged into an abysmal morass of fornication, adultery, pandering, and prostitution."[23]

Unhappily, Oberholtzer's indictment in the context of that time had some substance. In 1920–21, for example, the industry did produce many Westerns and slapstick comedies—genres that enjoyed both critical and commercial success, domestically and overseas. But the various studios also continued to churn out the kind of films that so exercised Oberholtzer and his peers. Such films ultimately showed that those with moral shortcomings paid a price (often terrible). The ending might have, as one historian quipped, "loaded the scales in favor of Victorian virtue," but for the Oberholtzers of the day "the lesson went astray." Echoing the response of many, Oberholtzer sternly argued that "a few scenes" at the end do not offset "an hour and a half through the sewers of picturedom." On the whole, as a recent history tersely puts it, "sex and sex appeal provided the prime motif" of Hollywood films in these years. The 1920–21 schedule of releases included such films as *The Blushing Bride*, *The Good Bad Wife*, *Luring Lips*, *Short Skirts*, *Without Benefit of Clergy*.[24]

The content of these films often lived up to their titles. The 1920 film *Sex* (whose title the Pennsylvania censors forced the distributor to change to *Sex Crushed to Earth* "for screenings in that state") dealt with "a self-centered vamp who steals other people's husbands"; when asked by a wife "to free her husband," the vamp turns "a deaf ear"; her chief attraction is a reckless if sequential promiscuity. More than one studio knew how to use the Bible to produce a film that paired lust with religion. *The Queen of Sheba*, although set in the Biblical past, also dealt with "illicit love": this lavish 1921 feature loosely based on the Old Testament account of the queen's coupling with King Solomon, according to one report, had "the well-rounded actress" portraying the queen appearing in some scenes "wrapped in nothing much more than a few veils and a mass of imitation pearls."[25]

The director, Cecil B. De Mille, well characterized as "the industry's most influential trendsetter in the late 1910s and early 1920s," crammed flesh and passion into his films. De Mille's scenarist later claimed that these films were only trying "to include all the subtle manifestations of feminine charm which had come into vogue." But a challenge to traditional morality as well as a daring preoccupation with sex marked such commercially successful De Mille films as *Old Wives for New* (1918), *Don't Change Your Husband* (1919), *Why Change Your Wife* (1920), and *The Affairs of Anatol* (1921).[26]

The most notorious of De Mille's "vulgar comedies" (as a recent film history delineates them) was *Male and Female*—his filming of U.K. playwright James Barrie's ironic, slightly sardonic *The Admirable Crichton*, a comedy about the stranding on a deserted island of an upper-class British family along with their servants, including a butler whose natural talents ultimately lead to his taking charge. De Mille's film did end as in the play, with a rescue and the butler returning to his former station, but transformed the plot into what has been termed "an elaborately plushed up fantasy, . . . changing the butler into one of those I-was-a-king-in-Babylon types wallowingly admired by Gloria Swanson [playing an initially proper daughter] as a Virgin Slave wearing very little." Sklar argues that such films "angered moralists largely because they were popular with respectable middle-class audiences"—and *Male and Female* certainly was: the film cost $170,000 to produce and grossed over $1,250,000.[27]

The flights of lurid fancy that marked the industry's advertisements and publicity blurbs for many of its productions also proved extremely provocative. The producers of one film promised "brilliant men, beautiful jazz babies, champagne baths, midnight revels, petting parties in the purple dawn, all ending in one terrific smashing climax that makes you gasp." Another studio advertised boldly that its film contained "neckers, petters, white kisses, red kisses, pleasure mad daughters, sensation-craving mothers." As Frederick Lewis Allen correctly pointed out, "seldom did the films offer as much as their advertisements promised." But such ads and blurbs aroused the wrath of those concerning themselves with the morals of America, especially of its youth. The bluenoses "preferred to believe," in the words of political scientist Raymond Moley, even though their "eyes and ears told it otherwise," that America's "sons and daughters succumbed to the temptations of neither sex, alcohol, nor tobacco."[28]

Other temptations included substantial drug abuse. A 1921 report stated that "within a short time a whole new crop of picture favorites would be necessary because of the prevalence of drug addiction among the current stars." The actress Olive Thomas, once widely advertised as "the world's most beautiful girl," while on a long-delayed Paris honeymoon, died of an "accidental" drug overdose. She was found (by a floor waiter) sprawled naked on the floor of her suite at the Hotel Crillon "clutching a phial of mercury capsules—in those days somewhat venerated as a cure for syphilis." Such excesses marked and marred the life of the movie colony and were highlighted by an increasingly sensationalistic press.[29] That press, beset by ruinous competition, wanted more than the usual "fluff" that industry flacks had provided. Maintenance and increase of circulation demanded more "intimate details." The industry, ever anxious to ballyhoo its product and the men and women who created it, went to ever greater lengths. As Kevin Brownlow, among the most resourceful of the silent era's chroniclers, reports: "press agents staged fake suicides and other 'hoaxes' to push their stars and their pictures." Outrageous consumption, excessive life styles, unconventional romances—all were used as fodder to publicize the movies, and all led to further criticism of the industry. In effect, the hype boomeranged. The reformers used it for their own ends. Much of the public, as the social scientist Ruth Inglis makes clear, "began to resent . . . the . . . luxurious living, exotic parties, . . . the flaunting of traditional mores."[30]

Some of this resentment was not of the industry's making. Prostitutes in Los Angeles, on being arrested, often claimed to be "film extras" or called themselves "actresses"; the public read "again and again . . . of movie actresses being arrested as women of ill repute," but why, as Brownlow asserts, "was not explained." Newspaper stories would say "beautiful film star causes shooting affair at wild gin party" or "beautiful film stars . . . arrested in bawdy house." An industry apologist later argued with some justice that "scores of stories were fed to the public, but in not a single instance was an actress of even moderate prominence involved." But in the early 1920s, a series of what have been termed "not so private scandals" did involve some very important movie people and fed the already intense criticism of the industry.[31]

In March 1920, in what *Variety* characterized as an "ideal marriage," two of America's most popular and successful film stars wed—"America's Sweetheart" Mary Pickford and the dashing Douglas Fairbanks. They had been "linked romantically"—as it was put—for some years, although initially neither had been divorced. Almost immediately following the wedding, a scant four weeks after Pickford had gotten a Nevada divorce (the Fairbanks marriage had been dissolved in 1918), her former husband declared the divorce had been obtained by "fraud" and "collusion." The actor Owen Moore, who according to various reports had "tried to extort a large price for acquiescence" to a divorce from Pickford, also charged her with "insufficient residence" in Nevada. True enough, like many other women of the day who went to Nevada for a divorce, she was not a "bona fide" resident of the state. However, Pickford and Fairbanks, tagged as Hollywood's "royal couple," would easily have overcome the flurry of adverse criticisms if the situation had not become more serious. The press sat on the story until Nevada's attorney general, seeking political support from those anxious to reform Hollywood, sued to set aside the divorce decree. Eventually the Nevada courts sustained the divorce. But as Ruth Inglis points out, the affair for awhile "put the industry in an unfavorable light."[32]

The Arbuckle case proved much more sensational and had a devastating impact. Roscoe "Fatty" Arbuckle, although only in his early thirties in 1921, had been on-screen for nearly fifteen years. A one-time plumber's helper, he had gone from being a Keystone Kop to "a much-loved screen comic" despite his bulk: he weighed over three hundred pounds. It has been estimated that in his heyday, "next to Chaplin, Arbuckle was the world's most popular comedian." Talented, good-natured, uncomplicated, he liked to party. In July 1921 newspapers reported that in 1917 after a dinner for him at a Boston hotel, there had been a party at a suburban roadhouse that included what the press then euphemistically called "ladies of the evening," some of whom were under age. After the party, some of the "girls" had talked and what transpired threatened to become public knowledge in 1917: a fund of $100,000 had been raised and used then to deal with the situation and, as Terry Ramsaye in his history of the movies relates, "applied where it would do the most good in the least time." Press accounts of this four-year-old scandal—which did not center on Arbuckle (who apparently did not attend) and which resulted in the removal from office of the local district attorney—added fuel to the fires of criticism being directed at the industry.[33]

A few weeks after the Massachusetts story broke, Arbuckle became the center of "the worst Hollywood scandal of the decade." He had gone with some friends to San Francisco. On Labor Day 1921 in his suite of rooms at the St. Francis Hotel, a fairly wild party was going on (as one commentator later declared, "no one ever accused it of being good clean fun"). One of the guests, Virginia Rappe—a twenty-seven-year-old movie bit player, became a bloody mess, required medical treatment, and a few days later died in a hospital of a peritonitis infection resulting from a ruptured bladder. Virginia Rappe, who had a history of prostitution and had undergone five abortions in her early teens, was known as a "good-time girl." She had been alone in a bedroom with Arbuckle. Exactly what happened has been obscured by misleading if not false statements in the press as well as tainted testimony in court. Suffice it to say "a folk legend instantly arose that . . . Arbuckle had pushed a Coke bottle into Virginia Rappe's body during a sadistic sexual assault."[34]

After her death, Arbuckle resisted attempts to blackmail him. An ambitious San Francisco district attorney tried Arbuckle for manslaughter. Arbuckle was tried three times because two juries deadlocked. The first jury voted 10–2 for acquittal and was dismissed after forty-three hours; the second deliberated one hour longer but deadlocked 10–2 for conviction; the third jury took only minutes to acquit Arbuckle, and it then issued a statement declaring "acquittal is not enough for Roscoe Arbuckle. We find a great injustice has been done him."[35]

It was not only Arbuckle who stood trial, but the culture that the movie industry had fostered. The judge at Arbuckle's first trial summed up the situation when he declared that "we are not trying Roscoe Arbuckle alone . . . we are trying our present day morals; matters of . . . apprehension to every true love of an American institution." The old order—including those who supported the Harding-Coolidge ticket in 1920 and who in due course voted in 1924 for Coolidge, attracted by his succinctly stated putative social beliefs—fought hard in support of their values.[36]

Various middle-class organizations, such as the General Federation of Women's Clubs, undertook and published critical surveys of film content and advertising to support a push for federal censorship and regulation of the movies. The industry barely forestalled the proposed federal legislation. Against the backdrop of such events as the Pickford divorce, the Thomas death, and the Arbuckle case as well as other well-reported unsavory activities, the detractors of the industry called for Congressional investigations of film production, distribution, exhibition, and advertising. Appalled at what they considered Hollywood's licentiousness and corrup-

tion (likened to "floating down a sewer in a glass-bottom boat"), the reformers also attempted to act on the state and local levels. A recent history
of the drive for censorship reports that "in 1921 alone, solons in 37 states
introduced nearly 100 bills designed to censor motion pictures." That year,
despite the industry's best, desperate efforts, a "stringent censorship bill"
became law in New York, which became the sixth state to exact such legislation (others who acted earlier included Ohio and Pennsylvania). Because
of the importance of New York City as a marketplace—most films received
their premieres at "the city's prestige movie houses"—many in the industry
feared that the version of a film New York passed would become "the industry standard." The industry considered the enactment of the legislation
"a bitter defeat" and "a hard blow."[37]

Scandal had also wracked baseball: in September 1920 toward the end
of the season rumors about the "fixing" of the 1919 World Series proved
true and, in the vernacular of the day, "hit the press." Major league team
owners, anxious to reestablish what repeatedly was described as "the integrity of the game," appointed a "czar" with supposedly absolute power
over professional baseball's operations. Federal District Court Judge Ken-
esaw Mountain Landis—a chest-thumping, outspoken man who looked
"like a hillbilly Moses just down from Sinai"—had gained a reputation for
toughness and integrity by fining Standard Oil $29,240,000 in a freight
rebate case (a decision quickly reversed by a higher court). He furthered
his national reputation in 1918 when, after a mass trial, he passed stiff sentences on members of the Industrial Workers of the World who had out-
spokenly protested U.S. participation in World War I; one of those tried
remembers the judge resolutely "consigning almost a hundred men to
prison for a total of over 800 years." Landis, who as baseball commissioner
had less power than the press declared but much more than any successor,
quickly became an icon, what *Fortune* later defined as "the earnest of integrity that big league baseball offered up to a public that sharply reacted
. . . to the game's nastiest jam.[38]

The leaders of the film industry, like their baseball counterparts, recognized the urgent need to win over public opinion. One effort to this end
had been the establishment in 1916 of the National Association of the Motion Picture Industry, Inc., a loose collection of some production companies, which had, among other goals, planned to speak for the industry.
NAMI proved ineffective, never more so than in combating the drive for
censorship. Headed by William A. Brady, a veteran theatrical producer and
showman, NAMI "marshalled all its resources" against the New York censorship legislation, convincing the state's Conference of Mayors and AFL
head Samuel Gompers, among others, to publicly oppose the bill. And after
it passed, Brady and other NAMI members met with New York's governor
at length but failed to get it vetoed. After signing the bill, Governor Nathan

Miller told reporters that "it was the only way to remedy what everyone conceded had grown to be a great evil."[39]

The drive toward regulation concerned the industry, as did a spreading hostile attitude in Congress: one representative during a debate on a movie admissions tax declared to general approval that "any ignoramus who has the ability to make faces . . . makes motion pictures"; a senator lambasted movies made with "any ignorant girl who can make goo goo eyes." More important to the industry, however, was the fact that salacious films and others did not do well at the box office; public opinion seemed to have turned against movie-going. Movie audiences had increased steadily during the postwar recession, but now, while the economy revived, the movie industry slumped. According to a NAMI representative, testifying before the House Ways and Means Committee on elimination of the admission tax, just during June, July, and August 1921 "over 4,000 movie houses have actually closed their doors." *Harrison's Reports,* a trade newsletter, declared in July 1921 "we are in the midst of a financial depression unprecedented in the history of the motion picture industry" and a few months later lamented the plight of "exhibitors . . . facing the alternative of either closing the doors . . . and losing . . . entire investment, . . . or continuing to lose with the eternal hope of improvement." The Department of Commerce reported that in November 1921 total admissions had declined by $10 million from the same period a year earlier. An extensive poll in 1921–22 showed that of those theaters responding to queries "nearly one-third had been forced to lower prices recently."[40]

Various developments account for this unanticipated downturn, including greater competition for the leisure dollar. A burgeoning radio industry kept people at home. The increasing ownership of automobiles led families to diversions other than the neighborhood movie theater. Moreover, as Robert Sklar convincingly argues, "the total number of theaters had reached a saturation point." Because films and their creators had come into bad odor, children were discouraged from movie-going. In 1921, in what became a much cited article, the Columbia University psychologist Dr. A. T. Poffenberger found a direct connection between "motion pictures and crime"; he maintained that even those movies that show "the criminal brought to justice" color the imagination, especially of the young and the mentally deficient, so that "the moral goes unheeded"; he urged "preventive measures" not limited to censorship. A further complication resulting from declining box-office receipts and the publicity attendant on scandal was the reluctance "of many banks to supply needed capital to the industry," for the financial community responded "even more intensely" than did the average moviegoer, with scorn and hostility.[41] The film industry's most important executives, remembering, recounts an insider, "what baseball had done in a similar if not quite so desperate a plight," decided to employ a "special eminence . . . to redeem the repute" of their business. A half century later, a scholar summed up their efforts as a search for "a can of whitewash." The movie people explored various possibilities in their search for "a film czar," including Herbert Hoover, then an energetic, well-regarded secretary of commerce who had earned a splendid reputation for his handling of relief activities abroad during and after World War I. However, they settled on Will H. Hays, then serving as postmaster general in Harding's Cabinet. When queried about Hays's lack of knowledge about the movies, an industry spokesman said "Did Judge Landis know anything about baseball?"[42]

After some discussion among themselves, ten of the industry's most powerful executives (including Adolph Zukor, William Fox, Samuel Goldwyn, Carl Laemmle, and Lewis J. Selznick) had signed a "round-robin," dated December 2, 1921, inviting Hays "to become the active head of a national association of motion-picture producers and distributors" at a salary of $100,000 a year ($25,000 more than the president of the United States earned). They wanted, said the "round-robin," the movie industry "accorded the consideration and dignity to which it is justly entitled" and expressed confidence that Hays could assist in "careful upbuilding and a constructive policy of progress."[43]

After mulling over the offer, which did not come as a complete surprise (one of his subsequent aides, a long-standing friend, was involved in the process), Hays supposedly made up his mind to accept on Christmas day when he heard his son and two nephews arguing about who in "a game of cowboys" would play the western star William S. Hart. Later in his memoirs he said that "the text from the Scripture 'out of the mouths of babes and sucklings Thou has perfected praise' flashed through my mind." At the time he said "I accepted my post for three reasons—first because it offered a chance to engage in a public service; second, because it offered a chance to retire from politics; third, because I needed the money." He accepted formally on January 14, 1922, leaving the Cabinet a few weeks later: in March the newly organized Motion Picture Producers and Distributors Association, Inc. (MPPDA) opened its offices in New York City. It quickly came to be called "the Hays office." NAMI lingered briefly before going out of existence.[44]

The "Judge Landis of the movies" did not cut an imposing figure. Five-and-a-half-feet tall, spindly, with a reedy voice and what has been called a "ferret smile" on a face likened to that of "a startled mouse," his jug ears evoked ostensibly humorous comment (the satirist Ring Lardner, taking note of Hays's supposed early stint as a traffic cop, once unpleasantly asserted that when "the young man wished to stop northbound vehicles he faced north and nothing could pass"). Like many Americans of his age and background at that time, Hays had what has been called "a deep distrust of artists, foreigners, and intellectuals." His personal beliefs, he said, stemmed from "the Ten Commandments, self-discipline, faith in times of trouble, worship, the Bible, and the Golden Rule." Hays, however, also had a facile mind, great energy, and, according to a White House intimate, "the most orderly way of expressing himself." He also had an engaging disposition. It is typical of Hays's personality that although he was christened "William Harrison," he seems never to have used his given name, choosing to use the less formal "Will."[45]

Of the same generation as the seven-years-older Coolidge, Hays (who was forty-three years old in 1922) had made his way as an organization man. He had won office only once—being elected to a three-year term as city attorney of Sullivan, Indiana, his small home town. But he had gone from GOP precinct captain there in 1900 to Republican state chairman in 1914. Four years later, he became head of the party's national committee and in 1920 played an active role in the winning campaign of the Harding-Coolidge ticket. Among his other accomplishments as GOP chairman, he had broadened the party's financial base through a system of "decentralized giving" that encouraged "little contributions." During the 1920 campaign, he declared that nobody "should contribute more than a $1000.00 to the campaign." And few did, leaving the Republicans with a substantial deficit. During the later Congressional investigations of the Harding Administration, it turned out that Hays, following "the old political adage of not looking a campaign contribution in the mouth," had made use of "hot bonds" in order to reduce the campaign deficit.[46]

Although a participant in Harding's subsequently notorious poker evenings and appointed as "the natural reward for a man who had directed a successful campaign" (as a Brookings Institution study has put it), Hays certainly proved to be one of the better members of Harding's cabinet. He had a good record as postmaster general. The affable politico put his organizational skills into play and proved quite able, giving the Post Office Department what has been called "the most constructive leadership in more than two decades." To use his words, he was interested in "humanizing the service." Referred to by his colleagues as a "human perpetual motion machine," he lobbied for pay raises for the postal service, encouraged efficiency, attacked incompetence, implemented technological improvements, boosted morale, and built up the fledgling air mail system (which had been "in sore need of . . . redirection," to use one historian's words.)[47]

Hays remained as head of the MPPDA until 1945 when the industry decided (in John Gunther's words) "to . . . give it a thorough overhaul, and bring it up to date." Many industry leaders felt that the movies faced new problems. The industry still needed "a man with influence," but one from the business world and not a politician. But for over two decades, Hays had served the industry well as a marvelous front man and effective lobbyist. With his many deep-rooted social, political, and religious ties across the country, he had effectively if not always successfully worked hard on behalf of the industry. But for all his bicoastal activity on its behalf, he never cut his ties to Indiana. All during his many years as head of the MPPDA, he retained his law partnership with his brother Hinckle in the firm of Hays and Hays established by their father in Sullivan in 1869. In 1937 the *New York Times* reported that "he still calls Sullivan home, though he spends most of the year in New York City or Hollywood." After 1945 he carried on various business and legal activities in California and New York. He died in Sullivan in 1954.[48]

Just as Hays began his tenure as film "czar," another scandal rocked the film industry, further casting doubt on the morality of the movie industry and underscoring the arguments of those anxious to censor and regulate it. Sometime during the night of February 1, 1922, the director William Desmond Taylor was murdered in his Hollywood bachelor quarters. His African American, homosexual houseman found him in the morning lying dead beside the desk in his study with a bullet in his back. Prolific, competent, intelligent, the Anglo-Irish Taylor, in his mid-fifties, had begun his movie career in the United States before World War I as a stalwart actor. In 1915 he had taken up directing. He had a record of achievement as a filmmaker that has held up. Even so tough-minded and knowledgeable a critic as William Everson in discussing Taylor's 1920 version of *Huckleberry Finn* over a half century after its premiere called it a "superb" film, "possibly still the best screen adaptation of Mark Twain." Taylor's peers elected him head of the Motion Picture Directors Association. Suave, handsome, and elegant, he was considered a successful "man about town" and was played up by the press as having "gained wide social acceptance especially among lady stars." Journalists had a field day with stories about "a locked closet that supposedly contained dozens of items of women's lingerie, all tagged with initials and dates."[49]

Sixty years later, a study argued that all the press stories about his womanizing and possible drug connections were part of a studio smoke screen to cover up his homosexuality. Investigations of the murder at the time did reveal that he was a poseur whose real name was William Cunningham Dean Tanner. And in 1908 he had suddenly left New York City, a wife, a daughter, and a "flourishing" antiques business, to wander around America getting involved in various activities, including gold-mining, before settling down in Hollywood. On the night of his death, he had been visited by Mabel Normand, a feisty, vital star in her late twenties who supposedly was intimately involved with him. She had made her mark in Mack Sennett's Keystone Comedies (some directed by her when only twenty) alongside Arbuckle and Charlie Chaplin. She had severe drug problems, at which the press more than hinted. She was the last person outside the murderer to see Taylor alive and left his home about 9 P.M.; according to reports at the time, the director, "always thoughtful, lent her a book by Sigmund Freud when he observed some trashy literature in her limousine."[50]

The investigation also quickly implicated Mary Miles Minter, a beautiful star known as an "ethereal ingenue of high box office value"; in a few years, the twenty-year-old blonde had gone from being a popular child actress to becoming a serious rival to Mary Pickford, a challenge anchored by an unprecedented $1.3 million three-year contract she signed in 1919. Detectives did find intimate garments with an embroidered MMM at Taylor's as well as a note signed "Mary," declaring "Dearest: I love you – I love you – I love you," followed by a row of ten X's, presumably meant to be kisses (the last one two inches higher and "punctuated" by an exclamation point). Although claiming that she and Taylor were "just good friends," at the funeral home on the day of his internment, she kissed the corpse tenderly on the lips and later told the reporters that the dead Taylor had whispered, "I shall love you always, Mary."[51]

The sensationalist press was not alone in making much of the funeral (also attended by a grief-stricken Normand), Taylor's less than puritanical lifestyle, and the strong implications of drug involvement (supposedly Taylor in an attempt to end Normand's narcotics use had threatened to thrash her supplier). Arbuckle's second trial had ended in a hung jury a few days after Taylor's murder. The killing gave the press something new to exploit. The murder remained officially unsolved, although several plausible solutions have been set forth. Neither Normand nor Minter made a feature film after 1923. The latter retired into over sixty years of comfortable obscurity. Normand in January 1924 found herself involved in another shooting: Normand's chauffeur, an ex-con, was discovered standing over a badly wounded Hollywood oil heir, "holding a gun belonging to his boss." Normand died in 1930 ravaged by drink, drugs, and disease.[52]

Normand's second impressive stab at notoriety in 1924 did not make the same public stir as had the Taylor murder because of the impact of Hays. Notwithstanding the involvement of another high-priced female star, some obvious hanky-panky, the chauffeur's record as a "cocaine addict," and a victim with an impressive name (Cortlandt S. Dines, Jr.) and a bankroll to match it, the affair just faded away very quickly. Hays, a master of public relations and extremely well connected because of his political activities, had managed within a relatively short time to reach a modus vivendi with the press if not the reformers.[53]

Only months after the establishment of the Hays Office, Hays defused a possibly much more embarrassing situation. In January 1923, less than a year after the MPPDA's establishment, Wallace Reid—one of America's most popular stars—died of the effects of drug addiction amidst strong and probably correct rumors of studio involvement in the supplying of narcotics to the actor. A workhorse who for nearly a decade had appeared annually in a half dozen or more films (as opposed to the two or three made by his peers), Reid had an extraordinary and deserved box-office appeal. He was probably the last of what has been characterized as the "Arrow Collar stars," defined as "strong-jawed all-American figures" who exuded "stability, friendliness, optimism, reliability" and were "at home in overalls or evening clothes and . . . in a uniform." Reid also enjoyed great popularity with his peers. One actor recalled Reid as "one of the most charming, most lovable wonderful guys. . . . No ego there at all."[54]

Reid's studio did not wish to lose his services when he had an accident while filming; its doctor prescribed morphine to dull the pain. Reid became an addict. He could have been cured, but as a cameraman on Reid's pictures remembered, the actor "was altogether too good box office" so "the studio kept him supplied with more and more morphine." Reid's health broke and he died, not yet thirty-two.[55]

The press initially hinted strongly at the studio's complicity. Hays, seemingly open with the press, undertook a campaign of damage-control. He succeeded; newspapers dealt relatively kindly with Reid; typical was the response of the *New York Times*: "Wallace Reid Dies in Fight on Drugs . . . He Had Held Out Gamely." Mrs. Reid (the actress Dorothy Davenport), with a Hearst sob-sister in tow, attended a conference on narcotics in Washington, D.C., and then began work on an antidrug-use feature. Hays, as one historian has aptly noted, "gave special dispensation for this film, which violated most censorship codes, to be produced under the sponsorship of the Los Angeles Anti-Narcotic League." The reformers had been especially concerned about drug addiction in Hollywood: in discussing Reid's death, the popular weekly *Literary Digest* had referred to the town as "the graveyard of virtue."[56]

More than just a whiff of anti-Semitism was given off by a number of the Protestant clergymen among the reformers. To them the morality of the movies threatened Protestantism, for these clergymen America's traditional faith. They deplored the fact that, as Lary May points out, for a variety of reasons, Jews "held the reins . . . and virtually monopolized the market." This was an era when "anti-Semitism was a common practice" and unfortunately "a respectable belief," as Richard Maltby argues all too correctly. Thus even a contemporary "kinder" view of the impact of Jews on the film industry reads unhappily today: an early trade history praises Jews as "our best and most facile internationalists" and assumes that "the motion picture and the garment trade have a psychology in common to a marked degree." One leading Midwestern minister called upon Americans "to rescue the motion pictures from the hands of the devil and 500 un-Christian Jews."[57]

Few of the Protestant critics articulated their concern with the vehemence of the avowedly anti-Semitic *Dearborn Independent*, which asserted that "the whole secret of the movies' moral failure" was Jewish control of the industry; movies "are not American"; after all, their producers were "racially unqualified to reproduce the American atmosphere." Canon William Sheafe Chase, another alienated Protestant, in his *Catechism on Motion Pictures in Inter-State Commerce* (published by the "New York Civic League") drew not only on the *Dearborn Independent* but also on *The Protocols of the Elders of Zion*, which even in the 1920s had been discredited.[58]

The pious Hays, a Presbyterian Church elder and an announced teetotaler as well as being an Elk, a Moose, and a Rotarian, who described himself as "100 percent American" and as "raised in a Christian home," had the necessary "moral credentials" to defuse the preachments of such clergymen. He, as one history put it, "brought the respectability of mainstream middle America to a Jewish-dominated film industry." Hays managed to hold off the Fundamentalists and their allies in other Christian sects during the 1920s by striving to make the movies "respectable."[59]

Hays's first efforts toward this respectability included the creation, under the MPPDA, of a Committee on Public Relations. Hays invited over eighty of what he called "nationally organized associations for better things" to participate and send representatives to a committee that would "develop a program for the improvement of pictures." The MPPDA would meet the committee's expenses. It also, as a study by the Federal Council of Churches later discovered, paid "secret honoraria" to "civic, club, and church leaders for their cooperation"; in fact, between January 1928 and July 1929, a senior officer of the Federal Council itself "received an honorarium of $150 a month" for services defined as "the giving of advice concerning religious motion pictures." Initially the committee enlisted such religious, civic, fraternal, and professional organizations as the Boy Scouts, the Campfire Girls, the Daughters of the American Revolution, the National Education Association, the National Women's Trade Union League, the Russell Sage Foundation, the Salvation Army, and the Young Men's Christian Association. Significantly, many Protestant groups and outspoken reformers such as Canon Chase, all of whom still preferred censorship and regulation to cooperation with the industry, did not participate.[60]

Over a period of years, various groups joined and others left the committee, the defections stemming from concerns about the nature of the films produced by the industry. The Hays Office, according to its official history, did not set up this committee as "a trick, a scheme designed to call off the dogs"; Hays wanted these organizations "to work with him sympathetically in . . . cleaning up the movies." But over a period of years, various groups concerned about the film industry's product and activities defected, and a less sympathetic history notes that in 1925 the committee "dissolved itself and was absorbed into the formal structure of the Hays Office as the Department of Public Relations."[61]

The chairman of the committee's executive committee was a director of the prestigious Russell Sage Foundation. Hays drew on the foundation's resources to deal with a problem that long had vexed the industry and had resulted in a stream of continuing unfavorable publicity: every day men and women—seemingly of all ages, put preponderantly young—poured into Los Angeles looking for movie work and the "big break." For most, work as "extras" remained the limit of their success whatever their aspirations. A variety of fee-charging agencies (many of them unscrupulous) and phony but not inexpensive acting schools exploited these people. Hays "saw clearly," said a history of his activities at this time, "that the industry as a whole was indicted" for the wretched conditions in which these people "existed—with so many 'movie-struck' persons" competing for any kind of film job, poverty and crime awaited more than a few. Numerous young women turned to prostitution, and their arrests contributed further to Hollywood's sleazy reputation.[62]

At the behest of Hays, Mary Van Kleeck—head of the Russell Sage Foundation's industrial studies department and "one of the nation's leading experts on women's employment"—looked into the situation. Van Kleeck, apotheosized by Hays as "brilliant and experienced," went to Hollywood and worked with the State Industrial Welfare Commission. Her findings led in 1926 to the establishment of Central Casting, which charged no fee. Hays declared that this bureau would be "the only source of entry to film work" and would doom "the sleek-haired sheik vagrant . . . and the girls who dance without clothing on the beach, together with the whole coterie of hangers-on who have created the racy atmosphere around Hollywood." Central Casting did eliminate what Robert Sklar has described as "the long lines of aspirants outside studio gates" (an unhappy sight), and it refused to register what have been called "unsuitable applicants." But while publicly making another step in the "cleanup" of Hollywood, it did not end exploitation, inequities, or the casting couch.[63]

More circumspection by the stars became the order of the day. As long as an unattractive private life did not become public, private behavior generally escaped condemnation. "Soon after the Arbuckle case became front page news," reports Ruth Inglis, "the Universal company made it clear that all its studio contract players would be bound henceforth by clauses subjecting them to termination if accused, justly or not, of 'moral turpitude.'" Hays, a few months after signing on, announced with great fanfare the inclusion of such clauses in all studio contracts. Typically such a clause read: "The Artist agrees to conduct himself with due regard to public conventions and morals, and agrees he will not do or commit any act or thing that will being him into public hatred, contempt, or scorn, or ridicule public morals or decency or prejudice the Producer or the motion picture in general."[64]

What did it mean? One director facetiously said, "It would never do to have the Virgin Mary getting a divorce, or St. John cutting up in a night club." Not every drunk, addict, degenerate, or gay person lost his or her studio slot, but notoriety became a liability rather than an asset. As Hays declared, "Acquittal from a charge of larceny is no guarantee." When asked what would happen if a scandal erupted Elinor Glyn, then one of Hollywood's favorite British novelists, probably put it best: "whatever will bring in the most money will happen." The industry did clean house, but very circumspectly; as one writer reported, "players who had seriously compromised themselves disappeared quietly from the movie scene." An English investigative journalist later claimed that "an actual physical blacklist existed—I have seen a copy of it." Over two hundred names were listed. In any event, the studios took action only when it did not affect the box office.[65]

Indeed, "P.R." marked much of Hays's activities during the 1920s. Privately, many in Hollywood may have continued to lead wild lives, but Hays and his associates made strenuous efforts to set forth a very different view publicly, one more appealing to those who would reform and regulate the industry and its people. Hays, to use the words of one study, "advised studio publicity departments to play down the high salaries and luxurious living conditions of players and executives." In a 1924 fan magazine, writer Ruth Waterbury, describing Hollywood for *Photoplay*, declared that "a star who matters today cannot afford night life. There is little Bohemianism in the upper reaches of the movies. The work demands too much." The Hays Office strenuously encouraged a more wholesome view of Hollywood life.[66]

One result of this campaign was a book that blended a cross and a movie camera on its cover as it asked, "Can anything good come out of Hollywood?" The authors drew their answer from remarks by Dr. Wilsie Martin, pastor of Hollywood's First Methodist Church: Hollywood "is not a place east of Suez where there ain't no ten commandments. . . . It is a town of folks, some act, some write, some preach . . . some do nothing. . . . Hollywood is just a going American community." And the authors echoed in detail Dr. Martin's comments buttressing a view of Hollywood as "a place of beauty and peace" with well-chosen pictures of churches, schools, the Women's Club of Hollywood ("Sunday afternoon at the Studio Club . . . maintained for young girls just getting their start in the films"), actresses and their children (for "Mother Love runs as deeply in Hollywood as elsewhere"), and views of buildings containing "Hollywood's smokeless, odorless industry."[67]

Somewhat less saccharine and more realistic efforts also resulted. The trade journalist Tamar Lane penned a series of articles favorable to the industry that later was published as a book entitled *What's Wrong with Movies?* Lane, as did Hays, admitted that there might be "something wrong" with various individual players, directors, producers, exhibitors but in "l'envoi" to the book declaimed, "But the movies, themselves, bless them—*they* are all right." Lane also managed to attack a competing medium, arguing not wholly tongue-in-cheek that radio should be censored: "If . . . sinister tales dealing with crime are going to be broadcasted the proper eliminations must be made to prevent their being a pernicious influence" that "would undoubtedly start a new crime wave in the country."[68]

The studios' publicity machines echoed ten-thousandfold during the 1920s the guidelines laid down by Hays and his associates. They shamelessly catered to the lowest common denominator and occasionally won over even such acidulous intellectuals as Edmund Wilson. For all his skepticism about "stupid routine films," Wilson felt that a movie could have "possible educational value." Others embraced Hollywood much more enthusiastically. Fannie Hurst, the best-selling novelist and "sob sister of American fiction" went to Hollywood in the mid-1920s. She was feted by the studios and subsequently found an "art-industry" dedicated to bringing happiness, beauty, entertainment, and enlightenment to the universe. In words that must have brought joy to Hays, she enthused that "Athens in glorious Attic days was no more intent upon her classical mission than Hollywood." Hurst declared that "Hollywood is a promise. A gorgeous one."[69]

Hays pushed to implement that promise, which in different formats he preached throughout his tenure as head of the MPPDA. Over and over again he promised, as Frederick Lewis Allen recorded, that "all would be well." But all was not well—because in the final analysis Hays lacked power. The self-regulating censorship functions that his organization so effectively implemented after 1934 eluded him in the 1920s. Although sold to the American public as a "czar" (one wit subsequently dubbed him "czar of all the rushes"), Hays in reality was an employee of the film industry. He headed a trade association whose charter stated that its prime objective "is to foster the common interests of those engaged in the motion picture industry in the United States." As head of a trade association, Hays could cajole his employers, frighten them, or convince them, but during the 1920s, he certainly could not tell the studio heads what to do. Moreover, he was headquartered in New York City and spent relatively little time in Hollywood. His power, as Ruth Inglis points out, "came from his own prestige." As with Coolidge, the public view of Hays in the main belied reality.[70]

Hays never did manage to totally defuse the drive for federal regulation and government censorship on the state and local level. The reformers' campaign never ended, but Hays won some battles. In 1922 he carefully orchestrated in Massachusetts a campaign that resulted in an overwhelming defeat for the proponents of censorship. The previous year the state legislature had passed a bill providing for censorship and (as Hays ruefully described the situation) "a Massachusetts statute came before the voters for approval." In a state election in which more than 800,000 voters cast their ballots, censorship suffered defeat by over two-to-one; "the successful candidate for Governor," Hays pointed out, received "84,000 less than the 'no' vote on censorship." Hays had used successfully all the political tricks of the trade including telephone canvassing, specially established citizens' committees, and extensive lobbying of the press. The industry filled Massachusetts screens with filmed arguments against censorship, one of which featured the child star Jackie Coogan appealing to voters "to defeat the bill in the name of patriotism."[71]

What Raymond Moley in his official history of the Hays Office disingenuously described as "public education" did prove to be "the Waterloo of political censorship." In what has been the only state referendum ever held on film censorship in the United States, it was, as one history notes, "clear that the film industry had made the right decision in choosing Hays." The *New York Times* reported that Coolidge understood that "the character of the films has been improved and he now hears very little complaint about them. This improvement, the President believes, has been brought about to some degree by Will H. Hays." For the rest of the decade, no state except Connecticut, and then only briefly, enacted film censorship legislation.[72]

Yet the agitation continued, so much so that in 1926 Hays's good friend Calvin Coolidge spoke out publicly against federal censorship during Congressional hearings on a bill to create a Federal Motion Picture Commission in the Department of the Interior. The reason for this agitation lay in the movies' continuing assault on the country's supposed traditional moral values. The debauchery shown on screen, very mild by the standards of our day, infuriated the guardians of morality. Even the less censorious secretary of state, Charles Evans Hughes, argued that Hollywood movies present "a pernicious distortion . . . with respect to the way in which our people live and the prevalence here of vice and crime" and that these films affect our relations with other countries. But these films filled the theaters, even in Will Hays's Indiana. The Lynds in their classic study of "Middletown" (Muncie, Indiana) found that "sensational society films" packed Middletown's motion-picture houses week after week. *Down to the Sea in Ships*, a costly whaling adventure, however, failed to draw viewers because, as "the exhibitor explained, 'the whale is really the hero in the film.'"[73]

Given the stranglehold on film content that the Hays Office gained after 1934, when "self-regulation" proved an extremely effective form of censorship, his efforts during the 1920s highlight his incapacity as a moral censor and underscore the continued cry for censorship and regulation. The dichotomy arising from the differences between his perceived and actual powers became obvious shortly after his treatment of Arbuckle. In the Arbuckle case, Hays, as befit an extremely successful politician, operated very pragmatically. A few days after Arbuckle's acquittal in 1922, which did not still the shrill cries against the comedian, Hays banned his films. Hays may not have acted properly; he did not act without consulting the studio heads, but he did significantly enhance his credibility as a "czar." A studio executive summed up the public response: "The ban means that Will Hays is on the job, and that he does not intend to be a figurehead." Hays catered to the mindless campaign, redolent of the small-minded Puritanism that had shackled the United States with Prohibition, that wished to punish Arbuckle. The comedian's estranged wife, still anxious to help him, recalled pleading unsuccessfully with Hays to lift the ban; she later said "I've never seen a man in all my life that looked more like a rat dressed up in men's clothing than Will Hays."[74]

Subsequently, at Christmastime 1922, Hays did try to rescue Arbuckle, largely because the comedian's unreleased films "represented an investment of several hundred thousand dollars, all . . . sent to the scrap heap." But Hays and the studio bosses had seriously miscalculated public sentiment. His statement that "every man . . . is entitled to his chance to make good" resulted in a furor of criticism, not least from many of the organizations involved with the Committee on Public Relations. The head of the General Federations of Women's Clubs declared that, Arbuckle's acquittal notwithstanding, the testimony at his trial was of such a character as to bar him forever from appearing "before a decent self-respecting public."[75]

Indeed, the storm of protest has been called "one of the most vociferous and spontaneous outcries of public opinion ever aimed at the motion picture industry." Hays later described the outcry as a "sort of Dreyfus case in reverse." Mayors declared that they would suppress Arbuckle's films. Even William Jennings Bryan, for all his sympathy for Arbuckle, declared "his acquittal only relieved him of the penalty that attaches to a crime . . . The evidence showed a depravity entirely independent of the questions of actual murder. . . . He does not return like the Prodigal Son, but comes running back . . . inquiring for the fatted calf." The warden at New York State's Sing Sing prison continued to refuse to show Arbuckle's films to the inmates. Although some Arbuckle movies had been shown in outlying communities, Hays, practicing damage control, immediately made it clear that the ban remained, and the comedian's films remained unseen for years.[76]

This retreat typifies the MPPDA's stand during the Coolidge era. Hays kept announcing new guidelines, but the studio product, with its emphasis on sex, basically rendered them ineffective. The brouhaha over the possible distribution of the Arbuckle films had damaged the Committee on Public Relations. It died as a result of the defections that took place after a studio filmed the provocative novel *West of the Water Tower* despite strong protest from many of the committee's affiliates. Although watering down the novel somewhat, the 1924 film still involved illegitimacy, a dissolute clergyman, and small-town vindictive pettiness. Even a liberal trade newsletter declared, "There is not a redeeming feature in the picture; the hero is a weakling, the conduct of the small town folk toward the girl . . . is despicable . . . the narrow minded minister . . . is an unpleasant part."[77]

In order to fulfill his announced responsibility for keeping movies "clean," Hays now promulgated what came to be called the "Formula." Its genesis was an industry-wide "gentlemen's agreement" similar to that which NAMI earlier had effectuated. The Formula was intended to eliminate overt sex, excessive violence, ridicule of officials or religious beliefs, and salacious advertising or titles. Like most such agreements, it had little effect, especially given that the arrangement, as Richard Koszarski points out, "lacked any means of interpretation or enforcement." In early 1924 the directors of the MPPDA discussed what to do and passed a resolution, amplified in June, that called for the studios, among other things, "to exercise every possible care that only books or plays which are of the right type are used," and "to avoid using titles which are indicative of a kind of picture which should not be produced."[78]

Despite the vigorous efforts of Hays and his associates, the Formula also ultimately proved ineffective. No means of enforcement existed except, as has been pointed out, "Hays's powers of persuasion." A significant number of rejections did take place, over sixty in its first year of operation; each of which no doubt, had it been made, "would have brought intensified howls from the anti-movie lobby." But the Formula, as Moley makes clear, had "two fatal weaknesses: in addition to . . . voluntary observance," it did not apply to the bulk of scripts but only to those "based on material which already had appeared in book, play, or story form." For all that, the Formula remains significant as a major first step toward successful self-regulation—even if its critics did not realize that.[79]

In 1927 Hays tried again to deal with these critics. That year in June, the MPPDA adopted a report prepared by its staff in cooperation with studio officials. The report was primarily the work of Jason Joy—the former national secretary of the American Red Cross, who had been the only salaried member of the Committee on Public Relations. Circumspect, energetic, committed, Joy had been sent out to Hollywood in late 1926 to work with industry leaders there. Hays understood that "the distance between California (where the producers worked) and New York (where he worked) helped scuttle previous" efforts. Hays hoped that Joy would be more effective. One result was the report, with its eleven "don'ts" and twenty-six "be carefuls." With due fanfare these strictures were included in a "Code of the Motion Picture Industry" adopted at a conference held in October 1927 by the Federal Trade Commission. Except in being more detailed, the "don'ts" and the "be carefuls" did not differ much from NAMI's thirteen points and once again depended on voluntary compliance.[80]

The "don'ts" and "be carefuls" included a ban on nudity and profanity as well as the depiction of drug trafficking, white slavery, and sexual perversion. They urged "good taste" in presenting minorities, violence, criminal behavior, and the clergy. "What a marvelous scenario!" supposedly declared one foreign director when he read the list of "don'ts" and "be carefuls." Joy remained in Hollywood; during a period of nine months in 1927 producers consulted him on over 160 movies, and the next year he dealt with even more. But, as Moley points out, Joy's "painstaking efforts" had little effect: "despite the many modifications and rejections made under the 'Don'ts and Be Carefuls,' the residue left much to be desired . . . ; improvement . . . proceeded at a pace practically imperceptible to the naked eye."[81]

All through the 1920s, moviemakers flouted Hays, even if not always directly. A great deal has been made of the director Cecil B. De Mille's ability to present Bible-based Sodom and Gomorrah melodramas masquerading as cautionary tales, but he "anticipated the new moral climate." As one writer makes clear, the basic formula of his films and "of their countless imitators" depicted "sin graphically and entertainingly." De Mille's fondness for biblical stories was viewed "as a cover that allowed him to get away with scenes that would have been eliminated in a secular context." Thus his filmed life of Jesus (*King of Kings*, 1927) included a non-Biblical intimate relationship between a scantily clad Mary Magdalene and Judas Iscariot, and her haunting by the Seven Deadly Sins is shown with great zest in graphic sensual detail.[82]

The Hays Office proved no barrier to De Mille or his peers. Eric von Stroheim in his 1925 *Merry Widow* showed moviegoers, as one viewer reported, "a sexual fetishist who dies atop his bride on their honeymoon." *Variety* in discussing the 1926 major studio release, *Black Paradise*, commented on its "suggestive . . . hoochy-cooch scenes," described the finale's high point "when the heroine gets to show all her legs and 82 percent of everything else," and queried why "such stuff" is allowed to "ride through uncut." Another *Variety* reviewer, after describing what seemed to him "several direct attempts at obscenity" in the 1926 *Dance of Paris*, including a "girl dancer . . . having her clothes torn from her" by a mob of roues and "ladies . . . raped when posing as statues," concluded that "this piece of filth" from a major studio "in no way conforms to the recent Hays proclamation that the MPPDA is not making films which do not agree with the proprieties of the churches of America." A *New York Times* correspondent, reporting in 1927 on Hollywood films overseas, commented that "there are Americans who rarely go to the movies . . . at home, but on vacation abroad . . . may go to see an American film . . . and exclaim 'is this the sort of thing that is being shown night after night to our American youth?'"[83]

Hays himself contributed to the undercutting of the strictures he and his associates set forth. A gifted mediator and reconciler, he—as a journalist neatly said—"put harmony above everything." Notwithstanding the For-

mula and the Do's and Don'ts and Be Carefuls, the Hays Office allowed the
filming of *The Green Hat* by Michael Arlen, aptly described as the "Jacqueline Susann of his day," whose main character "became the very symbol of
the raunchy end-of-the-decade era." The Hays Office, recounts one history, "pursed its collective lips at plans in 1928 to film Arlen's novel, but financial temptation proved too great." The character was renamed, as was
the title, and the man who killed himself because of contracting venereal
disease still committed suicide in the film, but there was no mention of any
social disease. The year previous, as Paul Rotha, then a young radical film
critic, caustically pointed out, "It was Mr. Hays who so shrewdly decided
that Somerset Maugham's play *Rain*," with its emphasis on sexual desire,
"should not be made into a film . . . unless it were renamed *Sadie Thompson*,
thereby displaying a great moral sagacity."[84]

Much has been made of Hays's "hypocrisy"—critics called him "an in-
artistic prude who stifles the cinema's creative impulse." Any number of
film histories, in discussing the Hays Office, refer, as does David Robinson,
to its "kindergarten standards of propriety . . . which hamstrung any attempt to introduce adult themes . . . into pictures." Even so nuanced a historian as William Leuchtenburg has blasted the MPPDA head's insistence
"on false moralizations and the 'moral' ending." And such judgments appear to be absolutely correct in terms of the practices and impact of the
Hays Office after 1934 or even after the ineffective promulgation of the
1930 Production Code.[85]

In 1921, Will Hays—still immersed in GOP politics—astutely pointed
out to his peers that "at any time and under any Presidency . . . , the country
is colored by the personality" of the incumbent in the White House. For
Hays, that coloration was "one of the Presidency's most important functions." Coolidge seems instinctively to have understood that function and
to have understood that America in the 1920s did not want "a modern
man" as president. He presented himself to the United States as an embodiment of older virtues and thus could provide equaminity to a changing
America. As historian and one-time Dole and Reagan speechwriter Richard Norton Smith makes clear: "the cult of celebrity, the modern women's
movement, the decline of rural America's dominance—all had their genesis
in the Age of Coolidge"; his identification with the older virtues meant "his
countrymen moved forward even while gazing back with longing at a more
innocent society."[86]

During Coolidge's presidency, issues of class, race, and gender had a
pivotal impact on American society and culture. Publicly the seemingly
minimalist Coolidge concerned himself little with such issues, and perhaps
wisely, given the temper of the times. Nor did the president concern himself overly much with movie morality. But he did not overlook the movies,
or other media. He and his advisers used them to forge an image that did

not exactly belie reality but certainly manipulated it—and to good advantage for the president. The image that Coolidge projected took its coloration (to use Hays's concept) from aspects of his personality, but obviously there was more to the man than, for example, "Silent Cal" indicated. Coolidge, like others in the White House before and since, but with perhaps more success, controlled the image of himself. Thus, the spiffily dressed sailor (complete with yachting cap) frequently cruising on the presidential yacht got little play. Modern scholarship, although reinterpreting Coolidge's presidency, has not been kind to him. One historian recently dubbed him "the original Teflon President."[87]

But, at least, having been president of the United States, Coolidge cannot disappear from history. Will Hays, however, has now almost completely receded from view. For example, the fine book that accompanied the recent PBS series on American Cinema mentions Fatty Arbuckle but not Hays. Yet Hays certainly was a well-known and powerful figure in his day. As the 1920s child star Jackie Coogan later recalled, "Hays was like President Coolidge . . . he did have the power." Hays also knew how to use it. He was a very effective "fixer," to use the phrase of Senator S. W. Brookhart (R-Iowa), who declared in 1932 that Hays was "employed primarily to protect the industry against any sort of regulation through public action." Years later, one of the movie moguls who had signed the round robin offering Hays a job used kinder words, but in effect Adolph Zukor said the same thing: Hays "was a consummate diplomat . . . the seas upon which he embarked were exceedingly rough . . . he negotiated them with skill.[88]

Hays eventually through "self-regulation" did achieve an effective social and political censorship in the 1930s that lasted for a generation. But in the 1920s he was unable to implement the reforms he proposed, and they had almost no effect. The movies during the Coolidge era, like their Victorian antecedents, may have rushed to a moral judgment in the last reel. But overall, notwithstanding Hays's undoubted lobbying skills, 1920s American movies, as one historian recently put it, "exposed the Hays nostrums for what they were: the remedies of a quack."[89]

Calvin Coolidge and Will Hays are very much a part of the 1920s. They are significant figures in a bygone era. But in terms of image and reality they are up-to-date. The names of the players are different, but the issues remain the same.

NOTES

1. Michael E. Parrish, *Anxious Decades: America in Prosperity and Depression, 1920–1941* (New York: Norton, 1992), 204.

2. David R. Contosta and Robert Muccigrosso, *America in the Twentieth Century: Coming of Age* (New York: Harper and Row, 1988), 119; Fitzgerald quoted in Jonathan Daniels, *The Time Between the Wars: Armistice to Pearl Harbor* (Garden City, N.Y.: Doubleday & Co., 1966), 118.

3. Lippmann quoted in Parrish, *Anxious Decades*, 49.

4. J. C. Furnas, *Great Times: An Informal History of the United States, 1914–1929* (New York: G. P. Putnam Sons, 1974), 424.

5. Frederick Lewis Allen, *Only Yesterday* (New York: Harpers, 1931), 156; George Creel, *Rebel at Large* (New York: Putnam's, 1947), 264; Bliven quoted in Frederick J. Hoffman, *The Twenties: American Writing in the Postwar Decade* (New York: Collier Books, new rev. ed., 1962), 385. Parker quoted in Paul Boller, Jr., *Presidential Anecdotes* (New York: Oxford University Press, 1981), 235; Malcolm Moos, ed., *H. L. Mencken: A Carnival of Buncombe* (Baltimore: Johns Hopkins University Press, 1956), 135.

6. Esmond Wright, *The American Dream: From Reconstruction to Reagan* (Oxford: Blackwell Publishers, 1996), 234; Irving Stone, "A Study in Inertia," in Isabel Leighton, ed., *The Aspirin Age* (New York: Simon and Schuster, 1949), 151, 149; William E. Leuchtenburg, *The Perils of Prosperity* (Chicago: University of Chicago Press, 1958), 96; Thomas A. Bailey, *Presidential Greatness*, quoted in Boller, *Presidential Anecdotes*, 233; Parrish, *Anxious Decades*, 48; Elizabeth Stevenson, *The American 1920s: Babbitts and Bohemians* (New York: Collier Books, 1970), 115.

7. Stevenson, *The American 1920s*, 117; Stone, "A Study in Inertia," 145; Robert K. Murray, *The Harding Era* (Minneapolis: University of Minnesota Press, 1969), 499; Thomas L. Stokes, *Chips off My Shoulder* (Princeton: Princeton University Press, 1940), 139.

8. Roderick Nash, *The Nervous Generation: American Thought, 1917–1930* (Chicago: Rand McNally, 1970), 135; Allan Nevins, ed., *Interpretations by Walter Lippmann, 1933–1935* (New York: Macmillan, 1936), 365.

9. Allan Nevins, "Calvin Coolidge," *Dictionary of American Biography* (Supplement One, New York: Scribner's, 1944), 193; William Allen White, *A Puritan in Babylon: The Story of Calvin Coolidge* (New York: Macmillan, 1938), xiii; Myron M. Stearns, "Gentlemen, The President!" *McClure's Magazine* (June 1925), in Paul Carter, ed., *The Uncertain World of Normalcy: The 1920s* (New York: Pitman Publishing Co., 1971), 42; Richard Norton Smith, "The Price of the Presidency," *Yankee* (January 1996): 108; Dr. Joel Boone, *Papers*, vol. 21 (Library of Congress, Box 46): 6 (hereafter referred to as Boone).

10. Coolidge quoted in Parrish, *Anxious Decades*, 66; Richard Norton Smith, *An Uncommon Man: The Triumph of Herbert Hoover* (New York: Simon and Schuster, 1984), 41; Boone, vol. 21: 208.

11. Frances Parkinson Keyes, *Capitol Kaleidescope: The Story of a Washington Hostess* (New York: Harpers, 1937), 122; White, *A Puritan in Babylon*, 355–56, Boone, Box 46, vol. 21: 1927.

12. Michael Harwood, "Calvin Coolidge," *The American Heritage Pictorial History of the Presidents of the United States* (New York: American Heritage, 1968), 761 (on this page are to be found some prime examples of Coolidge snapped by news photographers); Page Smith, *Redeeming the Time: A People's History of the 1920s and the New Deal* (New York: McGraw-Hill, 1987), 104; John Lukacs, *Outgrowing De-*

mocracy: A History of the United States in the Twentieth Century (Garden City, N.Y.: Doubleday, 1984), 269.

13. Neal Gabler, "The Fathers of P.R.," *New York Times Magazine*, December 31, 1995, 28; February 20, 1962, draft of Edward Bernays, *Biography of an Idea* (Bernays papers, Library of Congress, Box 457), 3, 5, 9, 10. This pseudo-event did take place, but some of Bernays's account may be a bit fanciful since previous drafts have real problems with chronology.

14. Lukacs, *Outgrowing Democracy*, 269; Robert W. Desmond, *Crisis and Conflict: World News Reporting Between Two World Wars, 1920–1940* (Iowa City: University of Iowa Press, 1982), 130; Jay Lovestone, *The Coolidge Program: Capitalist Democracy and Prosperity Exposed* (New York: Workers Library, 1927), 4; quoted in Paul Carter, *The Twenties in America* (London: Routledge and Kegan Paul, 1968), 38.

15. Nevins, "Calvin Coolidge," 198; Stearns, "Gentlemen, the President!," 41; "Speaking of Pictures," *Life*, October 11, 1943, 11; Boone, Box 46, vol. 21: 379, 400.

16. Michael Medved, *The Shadow Presidents* (New York: Times Books, 1979), 180; White, *A Puritan in Babylon*, 298; Robert Saudek, "Program Coming in Fine. Please Play 'Japanese Sandman,'" *American Heritage* (August 1965): 24.

17. Boller, *Presidential Anecdotes*, 247.

18. Parrish, *Anxious Decades*, 74; Harold Brayman, *The President Speaks Off the Record: Historic Evenings with American Leaders, the Press, and Other Men of Power, at Washington's Exclusive Gridiron Club* (Princeton: Dow Jones Books, 1976), 160; Boone, Box 30, vol. 11: 5; Benjamin B. Hampton, *History of the American Film Industry from Its Beginnings to 1931* (New York: Dover, 1970; originally published 1931), 382–83.

19. Smith, *An Uncommon Man*, 41; Garth Jowett, *Film: The Democratic Art* (Boston: Little, Brown, 1976), 201; Calvin Coolidge, *The Price of Freedom* (New York: Scribner's, 1924); *United States Daily*, April 21, 1926, quoted in Howard T. Lewis, *The Motion Picture Industry* (New York: Van Nostrand, 1933), 379.

20. Keyes, *Capitol Kaleidoscope*, 129; "Speaking of Pictures," 11; Boone, Box 40, May 17, 1925, July 20, 1926, Box 46, vol. 21: 368, 581, 493, Box 30, May 16, 1925; Gary Carey, *All the Stars in Heaven: Louis B. Mayer's MGM* (New York: Dutton, 1981), 113–14.

21. Lary May, *Screening Out the Past: The Birth of Mass Culture and the Motion Picture Industry* (Chicago: University of Chicago Press, 1983), xii; Melvin Dubofsky et al., *The United States in the 20th Century* (Englewood Cliffs, N.J.: Prentice-Hall, 1978), 172.

22. Robert Sklar, ed., *The Plastic Age, 1917–1930* (New York: George Braziller, 1970), 2; Paula Fass, *The Damned and the Beautiful: American Youth in the 1920s* (New York: Oxford, 1977), 308–9; Lukacs, *Outgrowing Democracy*, 152.

23. Gregory Waller, *Main Street Amusements* (Washington, D.C.: Smithsonian Institution Press, 1995), 235; Ellis Paxson Oberholtzer, "Sex Pictures," in Gerald Mast, ed., *The Movies in Our Midst* (Chicago: University of Chicago Press, 1982), 195, 194.

24. Richard Koszarski, *An Evening's Entertainment: The Age of the Silent Feature Picture, 1915–1928* (New York: Scribners, 1990), 204–5; Oberholtzer, "Sex Pictures," 199; Barry Norman, *Talking Pictures* (London: BBC Books, 1987), 78; William Everson, *American Silent Film* (New York: Oxford, 1978), 152.

25. Patricia King Hanson et al., eds., *The American Film Institute Catalogue* . . . : *Feature Films, 1911–1920* (Berkeley: University of California Press, 1988), 822; Paul Sann, *The Lawless Decade* (New York: Crown, 1957), 66.

26. Sumiko Higashi, *Cecil B. De Mille and American Culture: The Silent Era* (Berkeley, Los Angeles: University of California Press, 1994), 160; Jeanie Mac Pherson quoted in Larry Ceplair, *A Great Lady: A Life of the Screenwriter Sonya Levin* (Lanham, Md.: Scarecrow Press, 1996), 34.

27. David Parkinson, *History of Film*, (London: Thames & Hudson, 1995), 42; Furnas, *Great Times*, 418; Robert Sklar, *Movie-Made America: A Cultural History of the Movies* (New York: Random House, 1975), 94.

28. Blurbs quoted in Allen, *Only Yesterday*, 101–2; ibid., 101; Raymond Moley, *The Hays Office* (Indianapolis: Bobbs-Merrill, 1945), 25.

29. Thomas obviously led an interesting life. Supposedly, an old lady in the lobby of the luxurious Ambassador Hotel in Los Angeles noticed a magnificent ring the movie actress wore and complimented her on it; Thomas said it was easy "to come by, honey, I got this for two humps with an old Jew in Palm Beach" (Selwyn Ford, *The Casting Couch* [London: Grafton Books, 1990], 47).

30. Kevin Brownlow, *Behind the Mask of Innocence* (New York: Knopf, 1990), 13; Ruth Inglis, *Freedom of the Movies* (Chicago: University of Chicago Press, 1977), 66–67.

31. Brownlow, *Behind the Mask of Innocence*, 13; Hampton, *History of the American Film Industry*, 287; Francis Russell, *The Shadow of Blooming Grove: Warren G. Harding in His Times* (New York: McGraw-Hill, 1968), 535.

32. Abel Green and Joe Laurie, Jr., *Show Biz: From Vaude to Video* (New York: Holt, 1951), 258; Tino Balio, *United Artists* (Madison: University of Wisconsin Press, 1976), 33; Terry Ramsaye, *A Million and One Nights* (New York: Simon and Schuster, 1964, originally published 1926), 806; Inglis, *Freedom of the Movies*, 67.

33. Kevin Brownlow, *The Parades Gone By* (New York: Knopf, 1969), 39; Ramsaye, *A Million and One Nights*, 806–7. What was later referred to as "an orgy of drink and lust" cost $100,000 because District Attorney Nathan A. Tufts of Middlesex County, referring to the movie moguls involved and their lawyers as "licentious Jews," informed them that "practices which might pass unnoticed in a large city could not be permitted in a small place like Woburn." The looming prosecution faded away on the payment of the $100,000. In 1921 Tufts was found guilty of corruption and ousted from office: David Yallop, *The Day the Laughter Stopped*, rev. ed. (London: Corgi Books, 1991), 81–85, 255.

34. Koszarski, *An Evening's Entertainment*, 206; David Thomson, *A Biographical Dictionary of Film*, 3d ed. (New York: Knopf, 1994), 21; Geoffrey Perrett, *America in the Twenties* (New York: Simon and Schuster, 1982), 225.

35. David Robinson, "Movies and Morals," *The Movie*, no. 8 (Leicester: Orbis Publishing, 1980), 141; Sann, *The Lawless Decade*, 68–69; jury statement quoted in Sann, 68–69.

36. Quoted in Furnas, *Great Times*, 422–23.

37. Ibid., 22; Leonard J. Leff and Jerold L. Simmons, *The Dame in the Kimono: Hollywood, Censorship, and the Production Code* . . . (New York: Grove Weidenfeld, 1990), 4; Jowett, *Film*, 157–58.

38. James Olson, *Historical Dictionary of the 1920s* (Westport, Conn.: Green-

wood, 1988), 31, 206; Furnas, *Great Times*, 393; Ralph Chaplin quoted in Stevenson, *The American 1920s*, 41; "Big League Baseball," *Fortune*, August 1937, 45.

39. Inglis, *Freedom of the Movies*, 86.

40. *Harrison's Reports*, December 3, 1921, p. 1 (quoting Senator Porter J. McCumber, R-N. Dak.); August 20, 1921, p. 136; July 16, 1921, p. 113; November 5, 1921, p. 180; January 23, 1922, p. 13.

41. Sklar, *Movie-Made America*, 82; A. T. Poffenberger, "Motion Pictures and Crime," in Mast, *The Movies in Our Midst*, 202; Janet Wasko, *Movies and Money* (Norwood, N.J.: Ablex Pub. Corp., 1982), 23.

42. Ramsaye, *A Million and One Nights*, 816; Sklar, *Movie-Made America*, 82; Miller quoted in Gregory D. Black, *Hollywood Censored* (New York: Cambridge University Press, 1944), 30; *New York Times*, December 9, 1921.

43. "Round-Robin" reproduced in Ramsaye, *A Million and One Nights*, 817.

44. Will H. Hays, *Memoirs* (Garden City, N.Y.: Doubleday, 1955), 325; Hays quoted in Gertrude Jobes, *Motion Picture Empire* (Hamden, Conn.: Archon Books, 1966), 234.

45. Russell, *The Shadow of Blooming Grove*, 365; Brownlow, *Behind the Mask*, 13; Lardner quoted in Leff and Simmons, *The Dame in the Kimono*, 5; Hays quoted in Phillip French, *The Movie Moguls* (London: Weidenfeld & Nicolson, 1969), 77; Boone, Box 46, vol. 21: 676; Stanley Coben, "Will H. Hays," *Dictionary of American Biography* (Supplement Five, New York: Scribner's, 1977), 280.

46. Murray, *The Harding Era*, 67; Russell, *The Shadow of Blooming Grove*, 636.

47. Laurin L. Henry, *Presidential Transitions* (Washington, D.C.: Brookings Institution), 190; Hays, *Memoirs*, 278; Murray, *The Harding Era*, 304; Donald Dale Jackson, *Flying the Mail*, Alexandria, Va.: Time-Life Books, 1982), 77.

48. John Gunther, *Inside U.S.A.* (New York: Harper, 1947), 51; Sklar, *Movie-Made America*, 296; *New York Times*, March 7, 1937, March 8, 1954. To use his words, Hays was interested in "humanizing the service" (Hays, *Memoirs*, 278).

49. Everson, *American Silent Film*, 150–51; Ephraim Katz, *The Film Encyclopedia* ("All-New Edition," New York: Harper Perrenial, 1994), 1335.

50. Sidney Kirkpatrick, *A Cast of Killers* (New York: E. P. Dutton, 1986), 3, 5, 19–20; Sann, *The Lawless Decade*, 70.

51. Furnas, *Great Times*, 422; the note is illustrated in Kirkpatrick, *A Cast of Killers*; Sann, *The Lawless Decade*, 71.

52. Graham Fuller, "Mabel Won and Lost," *The Movie*, no. 117, 2133.

53. Ramsaye, *A Million and One Nights*, 808.

54. Koszarski, *An Evening's Entertainment*, 276; Conrad Nagel in Bernard Rosenberg and Harry Silverstein, *The Real Tinsel* (New York: Macmillan, 1970), 278.

55. Brownlow, *Behind the Mask*, 139.

56. *New York Times*, January 2–4, 1924; *Literary Digest*, quoted in L. Hill and Silas Snyder, *Can Anything Good Come Out of Hollywood?* (Los Angeles: Times-Mirror Press, 1923), 1.

57. May, *Screening Out the Past*, 169; Rev. Wilbur Fiske Crafts quoted in Francis G. Couvares, "Hollywood, Main Street, and the Church: Trying to Censor the Movies Before the Production Code," *American Quarterly* 44 (1992): 589; Richard Maltby, *Harmless Entertainment* (Metuchen, N.J.: Scarecrow Press, 1983), 97.

58. "Jewish Activities in the United States," *The International Jew* (Dearborn,

Mich: Dearborn Publishing Co., 1927), 2:125; Ramsaye, *A Million and One Nights*, 483–87; "The Hays Office," *Fortune*, December, 1938, 72.

59. Hays quoted in Coben, 280; Hays, *Memoirs*, 324; Black, *Hollywood Censored*, 31; Jowett, *Film*, 165.

60. Will H. Hays, "The Motion Picture Industry," *Review of Reviews*, January 23, 1925, 79; Inglis, *Freedom of the Movies*, 108.

61. Moley, *The Hays Office*, 135; Inglis, *Freedom of the Movies*, 105.

62. Moley, *The Hays Office*, 213.

63. Eleanor Midman Lewis, "Mary Van Kleeck," in Barbara Sicherman et al., eds., *Notable American Women: The Modern Period* (Cambridge, Mass.: The Belknap Press of Harvard University Press, 1980), 708; *New York Times*, January 25, 1926; Robert Sklar, *Movie-Made America*, 84.

64. Inglis, *Freedom of the Movies*, 97; contract clause quoted in Brownlow, *Behind the Mask*, 17.

65. William De Mille quoted in Sann, *The Lawless Decade*, 74–75; Robinson, 141; Inglis, *Freedom of the Movies*, 97; Yallop, *The Day the Laughter Stopped*, 24, emphasizes this: he believes there is a direct link between the blacklisting of the 1920s and that of the Cold War era.

66. Inglis, *Freedom of the Movies*, 99; Ruth Waterbury, "Don't Go to Hollywood," in Mast, *The Movies in Our Midst*, 221.

67. Hill and Snyder, *Can Anything Good*, 1, 10, 22, 39, 60.

68. Tamar Lane, *What's Wrong with the Movies* (Los Angeles: The Waverly Co., 1923), 253–54.

69. Edmund Wilson, *The American Earthquake* (Garden City, N.Y.: Doubleday Anchor, 1958), 74; Fannie Hurst, "I Have Been to Hollywood," in *America: An Illustrated Display of Its Most Exciting Years—Writers and Writing* (Valencia, Calif.: American Family Enterprises, 1973), 21, 30–33. Hurst certainly had been won over. A few years earlier she had interrupted a critics' screening and had called the movie made of her novel, *Star Dust*, "cheap and tawdry." After viewing the film for an hour she had risen to apologize to those seeing "this so-called version of my novel" and had castigated Hollywood for producing "an affront to taste and intelligence" (*New York Times*, December 10, 1921).

70. Allen, *Only Yesterday*, 102; certificate of incorporation quoted in Moley, *The Hays Office*, 36; Inglis, *Freedom of the Movies*, 89.

71. Hays, *Review of Reviews*, 75–76; Frank Walsh, *Sin and Censorship: The Catholic Church and the Motion Picture Industry* (New Haven: Yale University Press, 1996), 27.

72. Moley, *The Hays Office*, 53–54; Walsh, *Sin and Censorship*, 28; *New York Times*, April 21, 1926. Although arguing that the taxes necessary to implement censorship in Connecticut "affected many theaters in the State which were facing bankruptcy," Hays and his staff agreed to give up their "fight for a repeal of the measure," having been assured that Republican state leaders and the governor "will bring pressure" on the General Assembly, which they did at the next session, and state censorship ended (*New York Times*, November 9, 1925).

73. *New York Times*, January 6, 1924; Robert and Helen Lynd, *Middletown* (New York: Harcourt Brace, 1929), 267.

74. *New York Times*, April 19, 1922; Walter Wanger, *You Must Remember This* (New York: Putnam, 1975), 40.

75. Hampton, *History of the American Film Industry*, 297; Moley, *The Hays Office*, 137; *New York Times*, December 21, 1922.

76. Jowett, *Film*, 173; Hays, *Memoirs*, 361; Bryan quoted in Andy Edmonds, *Fatty* (London: Futura, 1991), 253; Walsh, *Sin and Censorship*, 25.

77. *Harrison's Reports*, January 5, 1924, 2.

78. Koszarski, *An Evening's Entertainment*, 206–7; Moley, *The Hays Office*, 58.

79. Inglis, *Freedom of the Movies*, 113; Black, *Hollywood Censored*, 33; Moley, *The Hays Office*, 63.

80. Leff and Simmons, *The Dame in the Kimono*, 7; "The Don'ts and Be Carefuls . . . ," in Mast, *The Movies in Our Midst*, 213–14.

81. Paul Boller, Jr., and Ronald Davis, *Hollywood Anecdotes* (New York: Morrow, 1987), 212; Moley, *The Hays Office*, 65.

82. David Robinson, *Hollywood in the Twenties* (London: Zwemmer/Tantivy Press, 1968), 87; Walsh, *Sin and Censorship*, 52.

83. Leff and Simmons, *The Dame in the Kimono*, 6; *Variety*, June 23, March 31, 1926; *New York Times*, November 6, 1927.

84. *New York Times*, March 7, 1937; James Card, *Seductive Cinema* (New York: Knopf, 1994), 198; Paul Rotha, *The Film Till Now* (London: Cape, 1930), 32.

85. "The Hays Office," 72; Leuchtenburg, *The Perils of Prosperity*, 169; Robinson, *Hollywood*, 32.

86. Hays quoted in Paul Carter, *Another Part of the Twenties* (New York: Columbia University Press, 1977), 167; Smith, "The Price of the Presidency," 107.

87. Smith, "The Price of the Presidency," 107.

88. Yallop, *The Day the Laughter Stopped*, 526; Rotha, *The Film Till Now*, 33; Brookhart quoted in Maltby, *Harmless Entertainment*, 101; Adolph Zukor, *The Public Is Never Wrong* (New York: Putnam, 1953), 205. Coogan quoted in John Belton, *American Cinema/American Culture* (New York: McGraw-Hill, 1994), 94.

89. Leff and Simmons, *The Dame in the Kimono*, 6.

5

Calvin Coolidge, the Man and the President

ROBERT H. FERRELL

The man was president of the United States, and for many years people have asked how such a man, a Dickensian character, could be president, how he became so attractive to the American people that they would have given him another term in 1928 if he had asked for it. Perhaps the fault lay with the Boston department store owner, Frank W. Stearns, who sponsored Coolidge politically. Stearns it was who first talked his Amherst College friends into advancing Coolidge against the Harvard politicians who were dominating Massachusetts. In 1919 just after the Boston police strike and Governor Coolidge's pronouncement to Samuel Gompers about there being no right to strike against the public safety, Stearns raised his sights to the presidency; he sponsored a collection of Coolidge speeches entitled *Have Faith in Massachusetts*, bought sixty-five thousand copies from Houghton Mifflin, and gave them to anyone who could read. He said that Calvin Coolidge was as great as Abraham Lincoln. All this for what the Boston Brahmin and Harvard professor Barrett Wendell described as a "small, hatched-faced, colorless man, with a tight-shut, thin-lipped mouth, very chary of words."[1] This for a man who after marrying the most attractive girl in Northampton could be as offhand with her and their sons as he was with his constituents.

There also was a question of how this man could carry on the duties of president of the United States in an era like the golden twenties. Coolidge's entire personality stood against it. Alfred P. Dennis, who knew him from the turn of the century when Dennis was a history teacher at Smith College and the two ate at a boardinghouse, claimed he belonged to the eighteenth century and only found himself in the age of mobility—"light, heat and power distributed in an instant over copper wires, intelligence flashed across continents, under oceans and through the air in the twinkling of an eye, myriads of motor-cars darting to and fro on our public highways, a world on wheels, restless, avid, resistlessly pushing and struggling onward; fortunes made or lost in a day, big fees, high stakes."[2]

I

The Coolidge personality, let us face it, was not easy, and suffice to say that some of it was shyness, some of it was out of rural Vermont, and some derived from the pressures of high office. Some of it was attractive in a Plymouth Notch way, and this was what the American people saw and liked. Some of it was quite unattractive, and for the most part, they did not see it and hence could not know whether they liked it or not.

The shyness was undeniable. Judge Henry P. Field of Northampton, in whose office Coolidge studied law, said again and again that "Calvin is shy." It often was remarked what Coolidge himself said, that when he was a child and people were in the kitchen of the house at Plymouth Notch, he hated to go through the old kitchen door. "Every time I meet a stranger, I've got to go through the old kitchen door, back home, and that's not easy."[3] When he was president, he liked to have people around whom he had known. The assistant White House physician, Dr. Joel T. Boone, a lieutenant commander in the U.S. Navy, found that by navy custom, his tour of duty in the White House should be coming to an end. He spoke with the president about it, mentioning the possibility of serving with the marines in China. Coolidge listened, then took the cigar out of his mouth and said, speaking in his New England twang, "that it was very difficult for him to become acquainted with people, that he didn't warm up to people readily, and it took him quite a long time before he felt on a very familiar basis. He said I had been there ever since he became president . . ."[4]

Then there was rural Vermont, which surely accounted for his laconic nature. In Vermont the winters were cold, and the hot weather in summers was short-lived. Springs and autumns were diminished by cold nights. The climate did not lend itself to unmeasured conversation. Nor did the Vermont soil give much encouragement. Just to stay alive, people had to work hard. Before the actual work, they were preparing for it, girding themselves, and afterward they were tired. It was a straitened place. Luxury and leisure were not at hand. Coolidge's youth was only a century removed from the time of settlement, which was mostly after the Revolutionary War. Agriculture had just gotten started when the Erie Canal opened up the competition for western lands, and fields everywhere in New England passed back into wilderness, with only the stone walls of earlier times reminding visitors of what had been.

The laconic nature of the man was well known. He showed it even with his father. Boone one time was aboard the presidential yacht, *Mayflower*, and watched the president talking with his father, Colonel John Coolidge. As the sleek, beautiful ship built in the 1890s was cruising along—the ship that Coolidge's successor, Herbert Hoover, decommissioned as his first act of presidential economy—Boone saw Coolidge sitting on one end of the davenport with his father on the other end, with quite a space between them. They were looking out along the Potomac as the scenery was passing, not saying a word to each other. As Boone stood there, the president in his nasal twang and without looking toward his father, spoke out straight across the waters, "How is the sheep business?" Sheep were the only product of rural New England that made a profit.

Without turning his head toward his son and looking straight ahead, Colonel Coolidge said, "Good."

Another long pause, and the president inquired, "What are they bringing the pound?"

A sizable silence and his father replied with the price he was getting per pound for his sheep.[5]

The president's measured remarks baffled both his friends and his political associates, who needed to find out what was on the presidential mind. Stearns told the reporter Mark Sullivan that all the conversation he ever had with Coolidge would not make two days of the talk of ordinary men who were friends. Senator William M. Butler, who had been the Boston representative of the Republican leader in Massachusetts, the late Murray Crane, and had known Coolidge for many years, told Boone he often did not know how to take Coolidge because the president said so little that Butler was baffled. "He leaves one in suspense and in an indefinite state of mind, not knowing how to deduct from what the president tells one."[6] Butler was managing Coolidge's 1924 campaign, and at that moment Secretary of the Navy Curtis D. Wilbur had made a bad speech out West, and Butler was wishing the president would find a way to return Wilbur permanently to California, his home state, but did not know how to get the president to do the job. Secretary of Commerce Hoover, in 1927–28 and later as president, found himself exquisitely unable to get information out of Coolidge, at the outset about Hoover's own presidential ambitions, later about support for re-election in 1932. None of these individuals, confronting the president, wanted to talk about the sheep business, and that may have been part of the problem. But in the cases of Stearns and Butler, they were only seeking to advance Coolidge's purposes and needed to know what they were. Even Hoover was entitled to guidance.

Sometimes the president did not say anything at all. Everyone knows Stearns's tale of lament: When Coolidge spent his first day in the White House executive offices, after President Warren G. Harding passed on, the president called five times for Stearns. Each time, Stearns went in the presidential office, circled around, said nothing to Coolidge, who said nothing to Stearns. Even for Stearns, who had seen a great deal of Calvin Coolidge, this was unnerving. "A dog would have done equally well," he said disgustedly.[7] A state department official and Harvard man, who was perhaps sententious about the problem, wrote the American ambassador in London that the president "listens to what one has to say and makes no comment. But if the ideas expressed appeal to him he acts on them weeks or months later. They are always stored in his mind, to be used when the opportunity occurs."[8] It was an interesting observation if true, which only Coolidge knew.

From the tightness of Vermont, one can guess, came another quality other than brevity or silences, a quality not usually noticed by outsiders but altogether apparent within his family. This was a steely unwillingness to unbend, which took the form of refusing to do what would have made life much easier for everyone around him. Relations within the family circle, one would have thought, might not have possessed this quality. Yet such was the case.

When he courted Grace Goodhue in Northampton, he was strangely reticent. He should have been on his best behavior with Grace's friends but instead almost scared them. The stories of how he acted are well known and for the most part true, as Grace herself told most of them. She was such an opposite from him. In any sort of ordinary relationship, and perhaps simply from being around her, he should have unbent and become more like her—become, in a word, livable. She was such a good catch, as his boardinghouse friend, Dennis, observed. "I remember Grace Goodhue vividly," he wrote, "hardly out of her teens when she came to Northampton to . . . the Clarke School. A creature of spirit, fire, and dew, given to blithe spontaneous laughter, with eager birdlike movements, as natural and unaffected as sunlight or the sea, a soul that renders the common air sweet."[9] It may be that during the courtship when the couple were by themselves, Coolidge relaxed, but as soon as someone else came within their presence, he was stiff as a board. The Northampton description for him was that he was a "stick."

As he did not make any effort to get along with Grace's friends during what he must have realized was the important business of his courtship, neither did he try to make up to Mrs. Goodhue. She undoubtedly was difficult. Grace later told Dr. Boone that her mother had been a selfish person and did not want the marriage. He interjected that her mother had given her to the world. Mrs. Coolidge responded that she felt that fact, if it were a fact, had never impressed her mother. Mrs. Goodhue did not really care for her daughter's husband nor for that matter for the boys, John and Calvin, Jr. The president thought that Mrs. Goodhue's popularity in the newspapers was due to his own success and perhaps concluded that she might be grateful. But both during the courtship and afterward when his own political success might or might not have impressed Mrs. Goodhue, he refused to give an inch to his mother-in-law. He would not cater to her. He never wanted to stay long with her, and two days were long enough for any visit, indeed longer than he wanted.

He was not much more careful with his wife than he was with her mother. William R. Castle, Jr., of the State Department noticed how he walked ahead of his wife at White House musicals, observing to his diary, "I wonder whether he will continue to walk ahead of her when they leave the White House."[10] It was an elementary point of behavior. There were many other such lapses. He had a mischievous streak and when aboard the *Mayflower* may have refused to give his wife the guest list for this reason. It was very irritating to her, and if the purpose was mischief, he carried it much too far. She would step into a cabin and ask Boone who was on the list. Then she would go out and greet the guests.

The president did not want his wife to have anything to do with politics and pushed the point to ridiculous lengths. He was adamant on the subject, and it was not wise for her to speak about political issues in his presence. In this respect, she carefully watched the boundary he established. On one occasion two prominent women of one of the largest and most populous states in the country came by appointment to call and confer with her, and she saw them in the Red Room. When she joined the president for lunch, she told him of the call. He asked what they wanted, and she said it was a political interest. With quite a little irritation he snapped, "Did you tell them you didn't know anything about politics?" Mrs. Coolidge replied quickly, "They found that out in one minute, if not in two minutes."[11] It is of course well known that while in the Black Hills, Coolidge drove off one morning to his temporary office in a local high school some distance away, where he summoned reporters and gave them the typed-out slips announcing he would not run for the presidency the next year. Mrs. Coolidge knew nothing of the imminence of the event and only discovered what happened when her husband brought Senator Arthur Capper of Kansas home to lunch, and Capper told her after the lunch.

A real awkwardness within the family was the way in which the head of the family treated his sons. He told them what to wear. The boys brought home suits and other items they liked, and the decision was up to their father. The boys left the clothes laid out, suits on the bed, hats on the dresser, until their father came over from the executive offices for lunch. Coolidge had the boys try on the suits and unceremoniously did not ask which ones they liked. He pointed his finger at one suit and said, "You will take that one, John," and at another, "Calvin, you will take that one." He gave the same instruction for the hats, and then turned quickly and left the room.[12] He insisted that the boys wear galluses, or suspenders, rather than belts. He made them eat dinner in tuxedos. The latter requirement, the formality, was an expression of his respect for the presidency and the White House, but the rest of it, about the choice of clothes, had nothing to do with such matters.

There was a gulf between what Coolidge considered proper behavior and what the boys and his wife desired. Admittedly they lived in a goldfish bowl and had to be careful. When John was at Amherst, for example, he received a presidential letter advising him to go regularly to church—John had visited somewhere, perhaps seeing his "girl," Florence Trumbull, daughter of the governor of Connecticut, and had chosen (it is difficult to believe that Florence, whom he married, would have permitted this) to go to a nightclub on a Saturday night and sleep in the morning. The activity, and inactivity, had been in the newspapers, and the president did not like it. But it went beyond that sort of caution. When the *Mayflower* was in New England waters in 1925, Mrs. Coolidge would have liked to have young people aboard and entertain them with music and dancing and movies, parties of some sort. When she proposed this, the president would say, "What for? To spoil them?" She and John told Boone when they were at Swampscott that summer they would very much have liked to have a dance but raised the question, "What to do with father?"[13]

The tension could be almost unbearable. In the summer of 1926, Mrs. Coolidge did not want to go to the Adirondacks; however, the president not only decided to go but also refused to tell her when the departure would take place. Once there, he paid little attention to her. She wanted to have John there very much as Calvin, Jr., had died two years before, and the anniversary was coming up. Her husband made no promises. At last, in mid-August, John arrived, and Boone saw a gleam in Mrs. Coolidge's eyes as she gently watched her son.

Then there was the Coolidge temper, for the most part kept under wraps from anyone outside the family. This trait evidently came from his inability to express himself, which kept everything inward until an explosion took place, and from the mounting pressures on his time as he rose ever higher in his political offices. The truth was that whether in Northampton, Boston, or Washington, Coolidge was so busy pursuing his political responsibilities that he often had little time. In Northampton, the officeholding soon engrossed his days. In Boston, he stayed in a slovenly hotel known as the Adams House where he cooped himself up in a single room with an air shaft. He was home in Northampton on weekends for a single day, but so tired and irritable that he was hardly fit to live with. Calvin, Jr., was young at that time, and the boy's feelings did not turn into defiance, but in the case of John, relations were very awkward. His wife always was relieved when he returned to Boston.

In the presidency, Coolidge usually managed to shield his fits of anger from outsiders. When he was irritable, his assistants stayed away from him, and that helped. Once he tangled with an assistant who stood up to him, and he backed down. C. Bascom Slemp, a former Virginia congressman and a millionaire accustomed to careful treatment, who was his first presidential secretary, said that on one occasion Coolidge spoke brusquely to him, whereupon Slemp turned to the president and told him that no man heretofore had spoken to him that way, and it must not happen again. Coolidge, surprisingly, said he was sorry, that he had smoked too much the day before and that Slemp should not pay any attention to such manners. He said he knew he was "hard to get along with." [14]

The James Haley affair in the Black Hills in 1927 almost brought his tempered personality into public notice. During this summer vacation, the secret service agent assigned to Mrs. Coolidge went out with her on a hike and got lost, and the two of them returned an hour or two late. Haley had seen the president ignoring his wife. One time, he told Boone, Mrs. Coolidge got a fishhook in her finger, and the president looked at it and walked off. She had resorted to companionship and conversation and laughter with Haley, for lack of it with her husband. Doubtless Coolidge saw this and did not like it. Haley told Boone that when he returned late from the walk, the president had "blown up." [15] Coolidge sent Haley back to Washington. The affair got into the newspapers, although not in its full dimensions.

The family saw a good deal more temper than Slemp and Haley did. One time during the White House years, Mrs. Coolidge decided she would take up horseback riding and bought a riding habit and showed it to her husband. He was furious, hit the roof, shouted in anger, and told her to take it off and never let him see it again. Mrs. Coolidge later related a toned-down version of this affair to guests aboard the *Mayflower*, but it was a good deal worse than she described it.

Some of the presidential outbursts arose over the writing of speeches. Coolidge wrote his own speeches, unlike Harding who was the first but by no means the last of the presidents in the present century to employ a speechwriter, Judson C. (Jud) Welliver, for whom is named the Judson Welliver Society, a group of presidential speechwriters who hold annual meetings in the nation's capital. The group presently has a large membership. Coolidge did not write his speeches easily. "I always knew that there was some water in my well," he told Mark Sullivan, "but that I had to pump to get it. It is not a gushing fountain." [16] It may have been trouble over the State of the Union address of 1923 that disturbed relations between Coolidge and Slemp. It was a very important speech, as it set out Coolidge's campaign platform for election in 1924. The president already was troubled by Senate hearings over the Veterans' Bureau, the first of the so-called Harding scandals to emerge after his predecessor's death, and he may have heard rumbles of the Teapot Dome affair, which blew up a few days after the speech; he had a great deal on his mind.

Mrs. Coolidge said privately that, long before, she had found it was wise not to bother him or even be close to him when he was writing an important speech. "I let him alone as much as possible," she told Boone.[17] After the speech was ready, his nervous system seemed to level off.

Grace Coolidge once explained the presidential temper in detail to her physician. The president's grandmother, she said, had raised him, and he did not control his disposition as he should at all times. When he was merely tart, not furious, Grace Coolidge handled him by poking fun at him. One time the president thought he was being humorous with his naval aide, Captain Adolphus Andrews. He inquired if "public services" were being held aboard the *Mayflower* and wondered if it would not be better to hold "revival services" aboard her, to which Mrs. Coolidge observed to her husband, "Yes, if you will attend, they will do you good."[18] The president had been tart that morning. But when he was under strain, concentrating furiously, and likely to lose his temper, she had to act differently. On such occasions, she considered herself his "safety valve." She took the force that he might expend on others. Early in their married life she had learned that if he came home from his office amiable and affable, he might have exploded that day to some caller. If he came home irritable and nervous and blew off, she consoled herself because she knew he had not blown off to visitors or people in the office. Not long after they were married, she said, she knew she had to make a decision whether she could tolerate this kind of disposition, in other words, whether she loved him so greatly she could weather it.[19]

The president's personality was undoubtedly difficult to tolerate, and not merely for outsiders but for insiders. His were no easy ways. He was laconic or silent, and awkward, and tempered.

The result, both publicly and privately, beneath and behind the confusions, was nonetheless attractive. The White House under Grace and Calvin Coolidge was a pleasant place, where dinners and receptions were graciously handled and, contrary to impression, almost overflowing with food. While in the White House the Coolidges were most hospitable. They had more guests than were invited during any administration up to that time. Apart from relatives, close friends, and administration officials, Coolidge had 102 house guests in five years and seven months, compared to Taft who had 32 house guests in four years, Wilson who had 12 in eight years, and Harding who only had 5. People felt at home—and even the waspish Alice Roosevelt Longworth, when she learned that at long last she was pregnant, rushed to the White House, asked the head usher, Irwin H. (Ike) Hoover, where Grace Coolidge was, and then ran up the stairs calling, "Grace, Grace, I'm going to have a baby!"[20] The president's walking companion, Colonel Edmund W. Starling, came to see that the president's outward reticence and aloofness (Starling did not mention the temper) were only a protective shell, that he was very shy. In his way he was a sentimental man, embarrassed about showing it. He loved his wife deeply, if in his own way.

And she did him. When he died in January 1933, one wintry New England morning, and Starling learned of it, he dropped everything and took the first train for Northampton. When he came into the downstairs of the house, Grace Coolidge heard his voice and came hastily down the stairs. He took her in his arms, and she broke into tears.

2

When Coolidge became president, after the presidency of Harding who during his lifetime was very popular, not a few political leaders believed that Harding's successor could not handle the job. One of the western senators, Peter Norbeck of South Dakota, made light of his qualities, charging that he could "no more run this big machine at Washington than could a paralytic."[21] Norbeck had seen the way in which Coolidge as vice president had painted himself into a corner, become so inconspicuous he was invisible. Perhaps he remembered the story about a fire at the New Willard Hotel, where Vice President and Mrs. Coolidge maintained a modest apartment, and the guests considered them no more important, coming from Northampton, than their predecessors, Vice President and Mrs. Thomas R. Marshall who had resided at North Manchester, Indiana. According to the story, when the fire was announced the hotel's guests came down into the lobby in various states of undress, and at last, word was passed that the fire was out. Coolidge started upstairs, but the fire marshal halted him. "Who are you?" asked that functionary.

"I'm the vice president," Coolidge replied.

"All right—go ahead," said the marshal.

Coolidge went a step or two, only to be halted a second time. "What are you vice president of?" the marshal inquired suspiciously.

"I'm the vice president of the United States."

"Come right down," said the marshal. "I thought you were the vice president of the hotel."[22]

Norbeck thought him no man for the head of the government. "What we need," he opined, "is a regular Teddy Roosevelt house cleaning." He thought Senator Hiram Johnson could do the job; Johnson's record in California proved that. He described Coolidge as lacking "initiative and punch." The new president admittedly was judicial, "almost as judicial as Bill Taft." If Coolidge had any place in Washington, it was on the Supreme Court.[23]

Hoover and his reporter friend Sullivan agreed with this appraisal. Sullivan described Coolidge to Hoover as a man who became an office boy and then went up step-by-step. Hoover said, "Not a man to start a new corporation."[24]

But Hoover, like the country, was in a state of confusion. He had liked

Harding, who after all had brought him into the cabinet when his own situation as a member of the Wilson administration had left his Republican status unclear, and now in late 1923 he again was attempting to see where he fit into a new political picture.

Hoover and the country soon saw Coolidge as a worthy replacement. Not long after Harding's death, Hoover told Sullivan that Coolidge was a better administrator. "When you tell a thing to Coolidge he listens, takes it all in, and understands it promptly." Harding, he said, never cared for details. He trusted a cabinet member and took that individual's judgment. He would say, in jocular fashion, "What do you want today?" After barely listening, he would add, "All right; go ahead and do it." A little later another cabinet member would come in and have the same experience. Then the two things might conflict. Hoover said that would never happen with Coolidge.[25]

Coolidge's primeval point of administration, as he announced it in his *Autobiography*, consisted of "never doing anything that some one else can do for you."[26] It may have appeared as inaction, but it could well be, as Coolidge knew, far more effective than Hoover's administrative procedure, which was to have everything coming toward himself. Grace Coolidge, incidentally, was thoroughly aware of her husband's primeval point of administration, and one time unthinkingly took it out on their son, John. The time was the summer of 1926 when her husband had insisted on going to the Adirondacks. At last John had come. He was playing tennis, and a secret service man was picking up the balls. John's mother told her son that he was just like his father, never did anything when someone else could do it for him.

The rule had a large part in Coolidge foreign policy, which consisted mostly of chasing balls in imperial regions. "If there is a troublesome situation in Nicaragua, a General McCoy can manage it," wrote the president in his *Autobiography*. "If we have differences with Mexico, a Morrow can compose them. If there is unrest in the Philippines, a Stimson can quiet them."[27]

Domestically, in management of his cabinet, which included that corporation head, Hoover, Coolidge practiced his rule with a vengeance. According to Starling, who either was present at the scene or learned of it from his walking companion, one of Coolidge's secretaries, Edward T. (Ted) Clark, came in the office and asked if he could show the president a file of papers that Secretary of Labor James J. Davis wanted him to read. "He would like to know whether you agree with his decision," Clark said.

"I am not going to read them," the president said. "You tell ol' man Davis I hired him as Secretary of Labor and if he can't do the job I'll get a new Secretary of Labor."[28]

The president one day told his press conference that "the way I transact the cabinet business is to leave to the head of each department the conduct of his own business." In the cabinet, he did take up matters that required opinions of the members. But he did not consider that one member had any business advising another member. There were exceptions, and he may have been thinking of Hoover who always wanted to run two or three departments. Coolidge knew his rule had exceptions. He so advised the attendees at his press conference: "What I am telling you is a general principle."[29]

In regard to Hoover, Coolidge's friend Dennis wrote presciently, and it might have been after some conversation with his erstwhile boardinghouse friend:

> Mr. [Theodore] Roosevelt, whose restless genius kept him in a ferment of activity, would have taken the first train South when the Mississippi River broke its bounds. Mr. Wilson, a more intellectual man than Mr. Coolidge, embarked on an overseas expedition for the purpose of setting aright the affairs of the Old World. It is safe to say that Mr. Coolidge in like circumstances would not have budged from the White House. As to the Mississippi floods, he served the country better by remaining at home and deputizing Mr. Hoover, who specializes in floods and famines.[30]

With Congress, the president's *Autobiography* related a similar modus operandi: "About a dozen able, courageous, reliable and experienced men in the House and the Senate can reduce the problem of legislation almost to a vanishing point."[31] The remark was less believable than the Cabinet explanation, for Congress during the 1920s was almost unmanageable. Its emotional state was symbolized by the middle name of the junior senator from Iowa, of which the senator was proud: Smith Wildman Brookhart. President Woodrow Wilson had discovered that fact, and so had Harding; although having been a senator, Harding understood the congressional psyche and near the end of his life was beginning to get it in order. Coolidge, unfortunately, failed in this regard. He may have given up, in belief that nothing was to be done. He seems also to have had the quaint idea that all he needed to do was communicate his hopes and preferences and await Congress's pleasure.

In attempting to manage Congress, Coolidge instituted his well-known breakfasts, which bewildered most of the people who attended them. The food was excellent; it could not have been improved upon. There was a full-service menu, including griddle cakes served with Vermont maple syrup. The problem lay not in the food but the purpose of the drill, which—like the president to so many of his auditors—was inscrutable. There seemed no order of business, nothing beyond the free breakfast. The White House usher, Ike Hoover, who disliked Coolidge because the president refused to raise his salary (Hoover thought it was because Coolidge wanted to save the money and take it back to Northampton), claimed the invitees did everything possible to stay away. Senator Key Pittman of Nevada telephoned his excuse to Mrs. Pittman, who said a wheel had come off their car down the road. Senator Frederick Hale of Maine pleaded that his man had forgotten to call him. Senator Johnson averred that his barn had burned down (Hoover to the contrary, this was true; Johnson had rented a mansion with a barn, and the latter burned). One congressman, to Hoover's amusement, had been out all night and could not be found.[32]

Relying on the cabinet, less so on Congress, Coolidge also sought to use the newspaper press to support his administration against unbelievers, and in this regard, in his press conferences, he did well, setting a standard against which his predecessors appeared poorly and his successors until Harry S. Truman did only modestly well. In Coolidge's day the press conference attendance was small, perhaps a dozen reporters. Old-timers like Sullivan attended occasionally but seemed to have felt attendance harmed their dignity. A Harvard man, Sullivan complained to his diary about what he considered Coolidge's overconfidence, this at the beginning of the administration. In the metaphor of his conversation with Hoover, he wrote that Coolidge addressed the newspapermen as if he were president of a corporation reporting the current business. Desiring to be "a little malicious," which for Sullivan was not difficult, he amended his remarks, and said Coolidge was like the chief clerk of a corporation. The proceedings as he noticed them typically opened with the president sitting at his desk smiling and swinging his horn glasses in his fingers until the crowd was in. He then rose to face the reporters like a man in complete control. "I observe some newspaper man seems disposed to sit down," said the president. "Anybody who wants to can take my chair." One reporter, Gus Karger, a little malicious, said, "Does that go for anybody beside newspapermen?"[33] To Sullivan's displeasure, the president continued to conduct his press conferences like the president of the corporation that he was and referred to the little group of the faithful as "the class," sometimes treating them as pupils. They could not quote him, and so invented "the White House spokesman," whom newspaper readers gradually recognized as Coolidge. In 1927 the president held what he described as an "executive session" of the press conference and told the class to stop writing about the White House spokesman.[34] He held them firmly under classroom discipline. They had to submit questions in advance. If he did not like the questions, he forgot to answer them. One time he liked none of the questions, and the class watched in dismay as each slip of paper, held in the presidential hand, fluttered down on his desk, after which he said without a smile, "I have no questions today."[35]

A presidential activity that consumed far more time than the press conferences, requiring day after day of attention rather than attendance twice a week, was the writing of letters. To this task Coolidge again brought his prime administrative rule. Harding had dictated many letters, some of them quite long, but Coolidge hardly ever wrote one. He would sit at his desk, feet in a drawer, smoking a good Havana (he kept the good gift cigars and gave White Owls to visitors), and annotate letters. These sentiments the presidential staff translated into suitable answers. Sometimes comments were brief, such as "yes" or "no." President John Grier Hibben of Princeton University wrote to invite the president to receive an honorary degree. At the top of the letter, in the unmistakable rounded hand and Coolidgean black ink, was a single word: "Sorry." The headmaster of Mercersburg Academy, W. M. Irvine, Ph.D., L. L.D., at whose institution the Coolidge sons were in attendance, began to write chatty letters, and the president wrote on one of them, "Always glad to hear from you. C." When Irvine died in 1928, Coolidge wrote on a letter from the Mercersburg alumni association, "yes prepare letter C."[36]

Much of the president's routine was ceremonial. At 12:30, six days a week, he shook hands with an average of four hundred tourists. Sometimes he spoke to them: "Mawnin,'' he would say. Former President Taft, watching at an evening reception, described all this as "pump-handle work," in which, he said, Coolidge showed neither grace nor enthusiasm.[37] But he did it because he was too wise a politician not to. If he was too busy to shake hands, he would have the door opened to the presidential office, and people could file by and catch a glimpse of their tax dollars at work.

Luncheons usually were reserved for important visitors and gave no opportunity for relaxation. After luncheon, the president in good weather went out on the grounds and posed for photographs with groups, in bad weather arranged for photographs in the public rooms.

The science of public relations was rising to importance during the Coolidge era, having had encouragement from bond sales during the recent war, and the president did what he could to advance himself within its measurements. In 1924 he allowed the Republican national committee to employ the self-styled "public relations counsel" Edward L. Bernays to humanize him. It is not certain what Bernays did, but the president began to manage some extravagant things, such as having a White House breakfast for a group of New York theatrical people, after which they adjourned to the garden where Al Jolson led the guests in a song, "Keep Coolidge!" about voting for Coolidge.

> The race is now begun
> And Coolidge is the one,
> The one to fill the presidential chair.
> Without a lot of fuss
> He did a lot for us.
> So let's reciprocate and keep him there.

(Refrain)
Keep Coolidge! Keep Coolidge!
And have no fears
For four more years!
Keep Coolidge! Keep Coolidge!
For he will right our wrongs!
He's never asleep;
Still water runs deep.
So keep Coolidge! Keep Coolidge!
He's right where he belongs![38]

The guests and Mrs. Coolidge joined in the song. The humanizing must have worked, for Coolidge that year received a massive majority. After Bernays departed, the president continued to develop in this regard. During his western vacation in 1927, he not merely received a gift of a cowboy outfit from the Boy Scouts of South Dakota, bearing the initials C.A.L. down the chaps, but he wore it. Boone thought he regretted dressing in this regalia, also in an Indian headdress when he was designated by a tribe as "Chief Leading Eagle." The latter performance may have been necessary. The former, according to Mrs. Coolidge, was important to him. "He knew," she later wrote, "that he was making those boys happy at the cost of future criticism."[39]

Coolidge's speeches appear to have helped him. As mentioned, he took them seriously and did not consider them exercises in public relations—"bloviations," to use Harding's word—but opportunities to say where he and his administration stood. But beyond their point as statements, they were effective because of a piece of good fortune, the chance invention of "loud speakers," which came in at the end of the Wilson administration. Coolidge did not possess the lung power of such orators as William J. Bryan, who in the days before amplifiers could stand at a county courthouse and throw his voice three city blocks. Theodore Roosevelt possessed a high, shrill voice that carried across the heads of crowds. With the loud-speakers, Coolidge handled crowds as readily as Bryan and Roosevelt. It is an interesting point about Coolidge's speeches. When he was running for lieutenant governor of Massachusetts on the same ticket as Samuel W. McCall who was the party's candidate for governor, it was said that McCall could fill any hall, and Coolidge could empty it. The comment was no longer heard when Coolidge was president.

And what, lastly, was all this procedure, this careful management, this control of the executive branch of the government about? What was its purpose—was it nought but management?

Here the most recent biographer of Coolidge, Donald R. McCoy, whose book was published a generation ago, in 1967, has much to say. According to the biographer, the purpose of Coolidge's participation in government, from the very first political move he made, which was to run for the Northampton city council from his ward in 1898, was that "the citizen had an obligation to serve, to do good works." For him the most important area of service was politics, which held society together. Coolidge did not believe, as did the Republican Roosevelt, that his task was house cleaning. Put another way, it was not to sound alarms. His work, the reason for management, was to follow the Constitution and the laws of Congress and thereby carry out—serve— the will of the people.[40]

When Coolidge became prominent on the national scene while still governor of Massachusetts, his Amherst friend, Dwight Morrow, sought to give advice, perhaps with the thought that Coolidge as a national man might get Morrow out of J. P. Morgan and Company, where he was bored. In any event, he sought to advise Coolidge. He sent him four volumes by William Graham Sumner. Whether Coolidge read them must be a matter of doubt, though the governor told Morrow he read most of them. He regarded Sumner's commentaries as on-the-whole sound. But he took exception to the economist's claim that human existence was on the basis of dollars and cents "as he puts it." Sumner contended that economic principles came first, and thereafter democracy. He had little use, Coolidge wrote, for philosophy and religion. And then the telling comment: "He nowhere enunciates the principle of service."[41]

All this was visible in the speeches, which are in no sense as boisterous, as rolling in their phrases, summoning everyone to Armageddon, as were those of his great contemporary. Coolidge's were a series of statements, often short sentences. Sometimes the commentaries seemed commonplace, and yet there was just enough variation, enough novelty, that they were not. They were logical. They were not effervescences.

In defending service, Coolidge faced a host of unbelievers. Cynics thought it all a cover for ambition. To them the speeches meant nothing. Senator Johnson considered Coolidge an appalling hypocrite. He wrote his sons that he wished they could sit sometime for an hour with the president and size him up. "I really believe there never was a man in high position as politically minded. I do not think there is any principle or policy of government that for one instant will sway him when he believes his personal political fortune may be influenced." This was no nice estimate, the senator concluded, only the truth.[42] But against this comment, which of course the president never saw, Coolidge wrote Stearns of his determination to go ahead. Everything he did, he said, was going to be criticized and yet "I am going to try to do what seems best for the country, and get what satisfaction I can out of that."[43] Everything else, he said, could take care of itself.

NOTES

1. William Allen White, *Calvin Coolidge: The Man Who Is President* (New York: Macmillan, 1925), 114.

2. Alfred P. Dennis, *Gods and Little Fishes* (Indianapolis: Bobbs-Merrill, 1931), 169–170.

3. Claude M. Fuess, *Calvin Coolidge: The Man from Vermont* (Boston: Houghton Mifflin, 1940), 470.

4. Boone autobiography, Joel T. Boone Papers, vol. 21 (Library of Congress, Box 46): 505.

5. Ibid., 110.

6. Ibid., 503.

7. Fuess, *Calvin Coolidge*, 323.

8. William R. Castle, Jr., to Alanson B. Houghton, December 7, 1925, Box 3, Castle Papers, Herbert Hoover Presidential Library, West Branch, Iowa.

9. Dennis, *Gods and Little Fishes*, 25.

10. December 2, 1927, Houghton Library, Harvard University, Cambridge, Mass.

11. Boone autobiography, vol. 21: 183.

12. Ibid., 66.

13. Ibid., 459–63.

14. Ibid., 727–28.

15. Ibid., 849.

16. Sullivan diary, December 21, 1923, copy in Herbert Hoover Presidential Library.

17. Boone autobiography, vol. 21: 49.

18. Ibid., 468.

19. Ibid., 50–51.

20. Ibid., 318.

21. Gilbert C. Fite, *Peter Norbeck: Prairie Statesman* (Columbia, Mo.: University of Missouri, 1948), 114.

22. George Wharton Pepper, *Philadelphia Lawyer: An Autobiography* (Philadelphia: Lippincott, 1944), 202.

23. Fite, *Peter Norbeck*, 114.

24. Sullivan diary, Septemper 19, 1923.

25. Ibid., August 18.

26. *Autobiography of Calvin Coolidge* (New York: Cosmopolitan, 1929), 196.

27. Ibid., 197.

28. Edmund W. Starling and Thomas Sugrue, *Starling of the White House* (New York: Simon and Schuster, 1946), 209.

29. Press conference of April 16, 1937, in Howard H. Quint and Robert H. Ferrell, eds., *The Talkative President: The Off-the-Record Press Conferences of Calvin Coolidge* (Amherst: University of Massachusetts Press, 1964), 73.

30. Dennis, *Gods and Little Fishes*, 25.

31. Coolidge, *Autobiography*, 197.

32. *Forty-Two Years in the White House* (Boston: Houghton Mifflin, 1934), 127.

33. Diary, September 18, 1923; November 20, 1923.

34. Press conference of April 22, 1927, in Quint and Ferrell, eds., *The Talkative President*, 30.

35. Ibid., 21.

36. Hibben to Coolidge, January 15, 1924, reel 9, Coolidge private papers, Forbes Library, Northampton; Irvine to Coolidge, November 18, 1925, alumni association to Coolidge, August 31, 1928, reel 2.

37. Fuess, *Calvin Coolidge*, 327.

38. "Coolidge, Calvin," Box 457, Bernays Papers, Library of Congress. The occasion was October 17.

39. Introduction to "The Real Calvin Coolidge: A First-Hand Story of His Life," *Good Housekeeping*, February 1935, 20.

40. McCoy, *Calvin Coolidge*, 155, 294.

41. Ibid., 103.

42. To Archibald M. and Hiram W. Johnson, Jr., November 13, 1926, in Robert E. Burke, ed., *The Diary Letters of Hiram Johnson: 1917–1945*, 7 vols. (New York: Garland, 1983), vol. 4.

43. Letter of November 2, 1923, reel 4, Coolidge private papers.

6

The "Great Enigma" and
the "Great Engineer"

The Political Relationship of Calvin Coolidge and Herbert Hoover

GEORGE H. NASH

In the spring of 1923, Calvin Coolidge had been vice president of the United States for a little more than two years, but his hold on office was anything but sure. In the highest echelons of the Republican Party, speculation was rising that the enigmatic and laconic New Englander would not be renominated. Senators in his own party were said to be searching for someone else. Indeed, at the beginning of April a large contingent of Republican Progressives from the West—about forty members of Congress in all—publicly made it known that they wanted Assistant Secretary of the Navy Theodore Roosevelt, Jr., to replace Coolidge as the Republicans' vice presidential nominee in 1924.[1]

Coolidge's growing vulnerability was not surprising. Since taking his oath of office in 1921, he had made little impression on official Washington. To be sure, he had dutifully attended Cabinet meetings, presided over the Senate, and otherwise comported himself with propriety. But his impact upon public policy had been slight.

Then, just four months later, before the "Dump Coolidge" sentiment could crystalize, Warren Harding unexpectedly died, catapulting "Silent Cal" into the White House. Acutely aware that he was an accidental president, Coolidge felt morally bound to carry on Harding's policies until the next election. This in turn meant that the new president would keep his predecessor's Cabinet intact.

Among the Cabinet secretaries whom Coolidge thus retained was a man just two years younger than he, a man who was already making a powerful impression on the Republican administration: Secretary of Commerce Herbert Hoover. Since entering the Cabinet in 1921 over the bitter objections of the Republican old guard, Hoover had rapidly established himself as one of the ablest and most influential of Harding's advisers. Within months, Hoover had transformed his hitherto quiescent Cabinet agency into a bureaucratic dynamo. A tireless exponent of efficiency, he had launched a national campaign to eliminate waste in industry, an effort that included literally hundreds of Commerce Department–sponsored conferences on product standardization and related subjects. With Harding's approval, he had taken the initiative in the development of regulatory frameworks for the pioneering industries of civil aviation and radio. In the field of labor relations, he had played a key role in the settlement of the traumatic national coal and railroad strikes of 1922 and in the elimination of the twelve-hour day in the steel industry in 1923. Waterway development, farm relief, and foreign trade: into these fields, and more, Hoover had energetically ventured, usually with the admiring support of the president. Hoover is "the smartest 'gink' I know," Harding had remarked one time to a friend. In the president's Cabinet only Secretary of State Charles Evans Hughes had wielded comparable influence. Not surprisingly, on Harding's final western trip in 1923, Herbert Hoover had gone with him and had helped to ghostwrite some of the president's last official utterances.[2]

If the serious, hard-driving Hoover and the genial, flaccid Harding had been an unlikely political twosome, the pairing of Hoover and Calvin Coolidge was to be, if anything, stranger still. In 1895 each man had graduated from college: Coolidge from Amherst on the east coast, Hoover from Stanford University in California. From that point on, their careers could hardly have been more divergent. Hoover had become a globe-trotting mining engineer and financier who later calculated that he had spent a total of two years of his life on ships at sea. Coolidge had become a lawyer and politician in a small city only ten miles from his alma mater. By 1914 Hoover had traveled around the world several times, including such exotic locales as the Australian outback, the jungles of Burma, and China during the Boxer Rebellion. Coolidge, by contrast, had traveled outside the United States only once—to Montreal, Canada, for his honeymoon—and had otherwise journeyed rarely, if ever, more than a hundred miles from his adopted hometown of Northampton, Massachusetts. In World War I and its aftermath, Hoover had become an associate of Woodrow Wilson, a participant in the Versailles peace conference, and a humanitarian responsible for saving millions of Europeans from hunger and death. Coolidge, in the same period, had ascended the "escalator" of elective office in Massachusetts.

Each man was a hereditary Republican. In 1920 each had been a dark horse candidate—and thus a rival of the other—for the Republican presidential nomination that ultimately went to Harding. But here, too, their differences overshadowed their commonality. In 1912 Hoover had supported Theodore Roosevelt's Bull Moose campaign for the presidency. In 1918, as a leading member of President Wilson's wartime administration, he had publicly endorsed Wilson's call for the return of a Democratic Congress in the off-year election. In 1920 he had first declared himself an "independent progressive" before affirming a Republican affiliation. During this same period, Coolidge had been a paragon of party regularity and, by 1920, a symbol of safety and conservatism.[3]

These distinctions in background and career experience were reinforced by profound differences in the two men's temperaments. Hoover was a veritable workaholic, filling his calendar with appointments from morning till night and using lunches and dinner parties for intense discussions of public business. It was not uncommon for him to converse with thirty different visitors in a single afternoon. Coolidge, who in his boyhood had seemed destined to die young of tuberculosis, had a much less robust constitution and was obliged to conserve his energy constantly. Thus, as president, Coolidge received no visitors in the afternoon (except upon request) and required as much as ten hours of sleep per day. Concern for his fragile health was one of the motifs of Coolidge's presidency.[4]

In part, no doubt, because of these basic physiological dissimilarities, the two men's approaches to governance differed markedly. Coolidge's speeches were often patriotic homilies, long on idealism and devoid of controversy. Secretary of Commerce Hoover's speeches tended to be policy statements, replete with data and proposals for action. Coolidge was legendarily cautious and vigilant. "I have never been hurt by what I have not said," he once declared.[5] Secretary Hoover, though he could be equally cautious, nevertheless generated an unending blizzard of speeches, congressional testimony, and press releases, all carefully compiled by his office staff into reference volumes that they called the "Bible." Coolidge was a competent and well-informed chief executive who generally preferred, when a problem arose, to delegate it to the appropriate governmental agency. Hoover, as secretary of commerce (and, later, as president) would delegate, too—and then immerse himself in the troublesome matter anyway. Coolidge's "ideal day," H. L. Mencken once remarked, "is one on which nothing whatever happens." Hoover's ideal day—nay, his typical day—was marked by incessant activity at a pace few men could equal.[6]

The two men also responded very differently to criticism. When Coolidge entered public life, he decided (he once told a visitor) that he would not let abuse annoy him any more than he could help.[7] Hoover was just the opposite. Widely known for possessing one of the thinnest political skins in Washington, he sedulously kept track of all press criticism of himself and sought (usually through surrogates) to rebut what he labeled "smears" and "mud." On one occasion early in Coolidge's presidency, Hoover angrily complained to the president about editorial criticism of the secretary of commerce in *Wallaces' Farmer*. "Do you mean to say," Coolidge replied, "that a man who has been in public life as long as you have bothers about attacks in the newspapers?" "Don't you?" Hoover retorted, citing a savage critique of Coolidge in a recent issue of the *American Mercury*. "You mean that one in the magazine with the green cover?" Coolidge answered; "I started to read it, but it was against me, so I didn't finish it."[8] Imbued with an "emotional need to take things easy,"[9] Coolidge, wherever possible, tried to avert stress and risk. Hoover, in his own words, had a "naturally combative disposition"[10] and an eagerness to take command.

Even the two men's political philosophies seemed to reflect their unlike temperaments. To Coolidge, the purpose of government was not to do good but "to prevent harm." When governments attempted to "do good," he told a friend, "they generally got themselves and other people into trouble."[11] "A great many times if you let a situation alone it takes care of itself," the president told a news conference in 1924.[12]

Hoover, by contrast, was an avid "policy wonk" with a passion to implement his ideas. "I know how to make money and that no longer interests me," he remarked one time to a friend. "I don't fully know how Government may best serve human beings. That does interest me."[13] If Coolidge (in Hoover's slightly disdainful words) was "a real conservative, probably the equal of Benjamin Harrison,"[14] Hoover was a trained engineer. And engineers are taught to alter their environment, not leave it alone.

Between the instinctively noninterventionist Yankee president and his instinctively interventionist secretary of commerce, then, there lay a considerable experiential, psychological, and even philosophical gulf. "If you see ten troubles coming down the road," Coolidge told Hoover, "you can be sure that nine will run into the ditch before they reach you and you have to battle with only one of them." "The trouble with this philosophy," Hoover later wrote, "was that when the tenth trouble reached him he was wholly unprepared, and it had by that time acquired such momentum that it spelled disaster."[15]

With all of these disparities in outlook, some measure of friction between the two men was well-nigh inevitable. When Hoover entered the Harding Cabinet, some had predicted that the aggressive secretary of commerce would soon be out of office. Hoover had indeed clashed with a number of his fellow Cabinet officers, some of whom regarded him as a bureaucratic meddler.[16] One Treasury Department official labeled him "Secretary of Commerce and Under-Secretary of all other departments."[17] Still, he had managed to get along with his tolerant boss in the White House, and that had sufficed. But now Hoover's benevolent patron was gone, and a new chief executive was in charge. Would the ubiquitous secretary of commerce have the same success with Coolidge as he had enjoyed with Warren G. Harding?

For the next five-and-a-half years the "Great Enigma" in the White House and the "Great Engineer" at the Commerce Department dominated the American political landscape.[18] Although some of the vagaries of their interaction are no doubt lost to history, the record is sufficient to disclose the basic pattern. Behind the façade of official etiquette and party regularity, one finds an evolving and increasingly tense relationship. By exploring its contours and intricacies, we may illuminate some of the political dynamics of a far from placid decade.

Hoover's early contacts with Coolidge showed every sign of cordiality and cooperation. Barely two months after President Coolidge took office, his secretary, C. Bascom Slemp, wrote to Hoover: "I can not tell you how many things I feel we are dependent on you about." When Coolidge unveiled his legislative program in his first State of the Union address on December 6, 1923, many of his recommendations reflected Hoover's interests. Even more significantly, when Coolidge submitted his first budget to Congress a few days later, Hoover's Department of Commerce was one of only two Cabinet agencies to escape the president's budget-cutting axe.[19]

In the months ahead, other manifestations of presidential support for Hoover occurred. One of Hoover's most ambitious goals as secretary of commerce was the development of America's inland waterways: a project that he believed would yield enormous economic benefits. Already, in 1921, President Harding had appointed him chairman of a commission to negotiate an interstate compact for taming the Colorado River. Another component of Hoover's vision was construction of a seaway that would link the Great Lakes with the Atlantic Ocean. On March 14, 1924, President Coolidge appointed him chairman of the St. Lawrence Commission of the United States, with authority to negotiate with its Canadian counterpart. One more arrow had been added to Hoover's expanding quiver of governmental responsibilities.[20]

Still another area where Hoover and Coolidge found common ground was agricultural policy, the most contentious (and, for the Republican Party, the most divisive) issue of the 1920s. In the aftermath of World War I, the nation's corn and wheat belt had plunged from prosperity into recession, exacerbated by surplus production. As the crisis lengthened, farmers and their Congressional allies clamored for federal assistance. Much of their agitation crystalized into support for a massive interventionist proposal known as the McNary-Haugen bill, under which a U.S. government export corporation would buy surplus crops at a remunerative domestic price and sell them abroad at whatever price the foreign market offered. Hoover vehemently opposed the price-fixing McNary-Haugen plan, which he considered thoroughly unsound. Instead, he argued for credit reform and a nationwide system of voluntary marketing cooperatives by the farmers themselves, with the assistance of a federal marketing board. Hoover clearly was no disciple of laissez-faire, but he vigorously objected to overt governmental price-fixing and direct governmental operation of business. "No one can sit in the middle of the Federal Government and watch the operation of bureaucracy, even in its best sense," he said in 1927, "and have any confidence whatever as to its ability to buy, sell, and distribute commodities and services."[21]

By the spring of 1924, an early version of the McNary-Haugen bill was before Congress, and Coolidge's Cabinet was split. Secretary of Agriculture Henry C. Wallace openly favored the legislation; Hoover emphatically did not. On this and other issues (including bitter jurisdictional disputes between the two agencies), the two men's differences had degenerated into bureaucratic warfare. Coolidge did not intervene in their feuding. With an eye, probably, on the coming presidential election and the farm vote, the president refrained from definitive comment on the McNary-Haugen bill. But from the legislation that he *did* support in 1924—including encouragement of marketing cooperatives—there is little doubt that his position on farm relief was much closer to Hoover's than to the McNary-Haugenites'. Although the McNary-Haugen bill was defeated in Congress in June 1924 (thanks in part to Hoover's influence with Congress), it would come up again and again in the next four years. In the initial battle to defeat it, a bond had been forged between Hoover and Coolidge. It was to be the most important and consequential bond of their relationship.[22]

In the early months of Coolidge's presidency, Hoover had another opportunity to cement his ties to his new chief. In November 1923, California's prickly Progressive Republican senator, Hiram Johnson, announced that he would seek the Republican presidential nomination in 1924. Since Coolidge also was presumed to be a candidate (a surmise that he soon confirmed), an intraparty brawl seemed in the offing. Johnson was already an arch-enemy of his fellow Californian, Hoover, who had challenged him in California's presidential primary in 1920 and whose supporters had been trying ever since to remove Johnson as an obstacle to Hoover's presidential ambitions. With Hoover's assistance, his California faction swung into action in behalf of Coolidge's candidacy. Hoover himself publicly endorsed the president shortly before the California primary. When the votes were counted in California, Coolidge had administered a humiliating defeat to Johnson, thereby clearing the last hurdle to an easy nomination. More gratifying, perhaps, to Hoover, his well-organized supporters had secured his ascendancy over Johnson in the California Republican Party: a decisive step in Hoover's own quest for the White House.[23]

As it happened, Hoover nearly found himself on the ticket as Coolidge's running mate in 1924. As the Republican national convention convened in

Cleveland that June, the only uncertainty was the party's choice for vice president. Hoover's name was prominently mentioned as a possibility. But Coolidge was reportedly averse to Hoover's leaving the Cabinet and at any rate wanted Senator William Borah of Idaho to balance the ticket. In the wee hours of the morning of June 12, Coolidge's campaign manager, William M. Butler, notified party leaders that this was Coolidge's wish and that the hitherto resistant Borah would accept.[24]

Now followed nearly twenty-four hours of confusion that may have changed the course of American history. Awakened at his home in the middle of the night, Borah announced emphatically that he would not accept a vice presidential nomination. With the Idaho maverick out of the picture, Butler floated the name of another progressive, Judge William Kenyon of Iowa. Unable to stomach a man they deemed too radical and irregular, party hierarchs demanded that President Coolidge personally request Kenyon's selection. Contacted at the White House by telephone, Coolidge (who had previously adopted a "hands off" attitude toward the matter) declined to comply. The lid was now very much off the kettle.

The first ballot for vice president ended inconclusively. Then, on the second ballot, the delegates stampeded to former Governor Frank Lowden of Illinois, only to have him telegraph the convention a few hours later that *he* would not accept the nomination. Desperate to contain the deepening disarray, Butler now ordered that Hoover be chosen as Coolidge's running mate. It was too late. Throughout the convention many party leaders had resented the tactless ways of Butler, and now they took their revenge. On the third ballot they nominated Charles G. Dawes, who received 682½ votes to 234½ for Hoover. The bulk of Hoover's support came from California, Massachusetts (controlled by Butler), and southern delegations controlled by the Coolidge administration. On the final ballot, Hoover had been the candidate of the Coolidge forces, and he had lost.[25]

There is no evidence that Butler had designated Hoover on any direct instructions from the White House. But it is unlikely that Butler would have tried if he had thought that President Coolidge would disapprove. For his part, Hoover pronounced himself "more than happy" at Dawes's selection and privately asserted that his own "greatest opportunity for public service lay elsewhere."[26] It is, in fact, hard to envision such a hyperactive man spending the next four years presiding over the U.S. Senate.

In the ensuing presidential contest, Hoover actively campaigned for the Coolidge-Dawes team. In late October, the secretary of commerce even ghostwrote a presidential telegram (which Coolidge then issued under his own name) endorsing federal development of the Colorado River, including "a great dam at Boulder Canyon or some suitable locality."[27] And when Coolidge was elected in a landslide, Hoover was quick to telegraph his congratulations. Coolidge replied that he was "deeply grateful to you for all

that you have done in behalf of the cause for which we both stand." This exchange was more than a formality. A few days after the election, Coolidge
asked Hoover to remain in the Cabinet. The secretary of commerce eagerly
accepted.[28]

Two months later, however, a curious new development occurred. Just
before the November election, Hoover's antagonist, Secretary of Agriculture Henry C. Wallace, had died in office. Seizing the opportunity to install
a more compatible man in his place, Hoover immediately recommended
that the president appoint William Jardine of Kansas, an economist "opposed to all paternalistic legislation" (meaning McNary-Haugenism).[29] Instead, Coolidge appointed another individual who would serve ad interim
for a few months.

Then, on January 15, 1925, Coolidge informed the press that he was con-
sidering transferring Hoover himself to the Department of Agriculture. Using his official disguise of "White House Spokesman," Coolidge announced
that the Secretaryship of Agriculture was a very important post at the present time and that he (Coolidge) was seeking a man of large business experience who could fill it and institute a plan of cooperative marketing (Hoover's
favorite solution to the farm crisis). Coolidge's public courtship of Hoover
was surprising behavior for a man who was generally secretive about his appointments. Even more extraordinary was Hoover's public announcement
the next day that, yes, Coolidge *had* offered him the Secretaryship of Agriculture but that he had declined it.[30]

Historians have generally considered Coolidge's unusual job offer as
evidence of his confidence in Hoover and of their ideological compatibility
on farm policy. Indeed, this was the case. But there may have been more to
this denouement than met the eye. A few days earlier, Coolidge had announced that Ambassador to Great Britain Frank B. Kellogg would shortly
replace Charles Evans Hughes as secretary of state—a move that completely stunned official Washington. For months, rumors had circulated
that Hughes might soon retire, and many political figures had believed that
Hoover would succeed him. According to the *New York Times*, there was no
evidence that Hoover was disappointed at being passed over for the more
elevated Cabinet position. But if a political insider at the Republican National Committee was correct, Hoover was more than disappointed; he was
furious. According to this source (who was evidently very close to Coolidge), Hoover was so upset at the selection of Kellogg—who he felt had
slighted him on some matter in the past—that he immediately wrote a letter
resigning from the Cabinet. Hoover was persuaded not to send the letter,
and an intermediary notified the White House of the crisis. To assuage
Hoover's angry ego, President Coolidge promptly offered him the Secretaryship of Agriculture and permission to disclose this fact publicly.[31]

If this version of the event is correct, it revealed how highly Coolidge regarded his secretary of commerce and how much the president wished to retain him in the Cabinet. It also may be evidence for a rumor that was to recur repeatedly in Washington in the next two years: that Hoover, with his heart set ultimately on the presidency, wanted badly to be secretary of state.

The net result of the January 1925 offer was that Hoover emerged with enhanced bureaucratic prestige. In the end, Coolidge made Jardine (Hoover's candidate) secretary of agriculture. Unlike the deceased Wallace, Jardine worked well with the secretary of commerce, whose sphere of influence once again expanded.

On March 4, 1925, Calvin Coolidge took the presidential oath of office for a new term. No longer Warren Harding's legatee, the man from Vermont was now chief executive in his own right, and his priorities were not necessarily those of his secretary of commerce. Coolidge's prized goals were tax-cutting, debt reduction, and economy in government—conservative goals. The Cabinet officer on whom he most relied to implement them was Secretary of the Treasury Andrew Mellon. As the economic boom known as "Coolidge prosperity" took hold in the mid-1920s, Mellon's influence at the White House flourished.

This did not mean that Hoover's influence necessarily waned. In size, reputation, and effectiveness, the Department of Commerce continued to grow. Between 1921 and 1928, the department increased its staff by more than 50 percent and almost doubled its congressional appropriation. In 1925, in response to Hoover initiatives, President Coolidge transferred the Patent Office and Bureau of Mines from the Department of the Interior to the Department of Commerce. In aviation, radio, labor disputes, settlement of the Allies' World War I debts, and much else, Hoover was in the very thick of the federal government's policy making.[32]

By late 1925, the nation's press had begun to take notice. The Washington correspondent of the *New Republic* doubted "whether in the whole history of the American government a Cabinet officer has engaged in such wide diversity of activities or covered quite so much ground [as Hoover]. . . . There is more Hoover in the administration than anyone else. Except in the newspapers and the political field there is more Hoover in the administration than there is Coolidge." A few weeks later a lengthy profile in the *New York Times Magazine* reached the same conclusion: "No man in the Administration plays so many parts" as Hoover.[33]

If Coolidge resented his secretary of commerce's ubiquity, there was as yet no sign of it. In April 1925, for instance, Coolidge invited Hoover (among others) to spend a weekend cruising down the Potomac River on the presidential yacht, the *Mayflower*. Throughout the Coolidge years, in fact, the two men conferred frequently on public affairs—often for an hour or more at a time, at the White House, after dinner. To all appearances the relationship between them was businesslike and amicable.[34]

Temperamentally, of course, the gap between them persisted. While Hoover appreciated Coolidge's "high intellectual honesty," "moral courage," and other personal qualities, he surely found the Yankee president a little too conservative for his taste. Coolidge, wrote Hoover years later, was "a fundamentalist in religion, in the economic and social order, and in fishing." To the horrified disdain of Hoover (an expert fly fisherman), Coolidge, when he took up fishing as president, initially baited his hook with worms.[35]

Yet for all the evidence that the secretary of commerce was a valued member of the Coolidge administration, in late 1925 and 1926 signs multiplied that Hoover was becoming disenchanted. One source of his anxiety was growing speculation in the stock market and real estate—trends fueled, in his opinion, by the "easy money" policies of the Federal Reserve Board. Unwilling, because of his Cabinet status, to intervene directly with the Fed, he persuaded Senator Irvine Lenroot to address a set of sharp inquiries to Federal Reserve officials. (Hoover helped to draft Lenroot's questions.) Hoover himself, without mentioning the Fed by name, publicly criticized Wall Street's "fever of speculation" in his December 1925 review of economic prospects for 1926. Lenroot's letters (with their not-too-subtle hint of a possible Congressional investigation) may have caused the Federal Reserve Board to tighten its monetary policy for a time. It certainly revealed Hoover in a characteristic role: the bureaucratic wirepuller, working discreetly through willing intermediaries. The developing bull market, however, drew no remonstrance from the White House.[36]

On other fronts, too, Hoover was growing restive. In mid-1926, he complained privately that Coolidge was not being a sufficiently energetic leader, particularly in the ongoing struggle over farm relief. In 1925 and early 1926, Hoover conducted a loud campaign against foreign monopolies, notably the British rubber control policy known as the Stevenson Plan. His agitation infuriated the State Department. To at least one official in the department, Hoover's very public denunciation of the British was a blatant attempt to further his presidential ambitions.[37]

Resentment of Hoover's "self-advertising" began to build in Washington in early 1926, especially at the State and Treasury departments. To William R. Castle, Jr., a senior State Department official, Hoover's "whole campaign at the present time" was "a personal publicity campaign" designed to establish him as "the great figure in American life, the one man in the Administration who has completely at heart the good of the American people. He seems to be insanely ambitious for personal power." In Washington, in December 1925, a report circulated that Hoover had been promised the Secretaryship of State the following June, in return for promising not to interfere in the presidential campaign of 1928.[38]

This sensational rumor was probably false. But there is little doubt that

Hoover's recent burst of newspaper publicity had rankled some Republican leaders. According to a profile of Hoover in the New York *World* some months later, the Republican Party's "delegate slatemakers" were saying that no man since Theodore Roosevelt had such a large entourage of "personal press agents" as Hoover.[39]

Did Calvin Coolidge share this developing sentiment? The record, predictably, is silent. But Coolidge was an assiduous reader of the press, and in his own papers at the Library of Congress is the very New York *World* article just cited. "HOOVER BOOSTED AGAIN AS LEADER," ran the headline. "Called Best Fitted Man for Presidency but Professional Politicians, Generally, Fight Shy of Him." Most interestingly of all, perhaps, the *World* article contained a direct quotation from Coolidge's good friend and booster, Dwight W. Morrow: "If the President is not a candidate [in 1928] the logical Republican nominee is Herbert Hoover." At the top of this clipping, deposited today in the Coolidge Papers, someone wrote: "File here under Hoover," and so it was. Someone in the White House was watching the secretary of commerce.[40]

A month later, the *New York Times* published a glowing profile of the secretary of commerce as a veritable "one man Cabinet." More than any other person in American history, it said, either inside or outside the government, Hoover was "the recognized leader of all business America." Although the *Times* quoted Hoover's closest associates as insisting that he was "utterly without political ambition" and that his aspirations were "satisfied in his present position," the *Times* reported that Hoover "probably would not grumble" if he were "kicked upstairs."[41]

For his part, despite his private reservations about his chief, Hoover continued to play the role of loyal lieutenant. When, in mid-1926, a friend suggested that Hoover resign and escape Washington for awhile, the secretary of commerce replied that he had this in mind but that he first had much to do for the Administration before the November 1926 elections. In the ensuing campaign, he spoke vigorously for Republican candidates from coast to coast and hailed President Coolidge's "great work" for "national rehabilitation." By being such a good political soldier, Hoover could, perhaps, allay conservative Republican doubts about his party regularity. He could also win points with his boss in the White House.[42]

By the end of the campaign, there were signs that he needed to do just that. In mid-October, Secretary of the Treasury Mellon somehow got the notion that Hoover was refusing to campaign in Massachusetts, where President Coolidge's closest political friend and adviser, William M. Butler, was embroiled in a desperate race for the Senate. Anxious to dispel this dangerous impression, Hoover made a written denial to the president. At the request of Coolidge's secretary, Hoover sent a letter to Massachusetts publicly endorsing Butler.[43]

A few days later, while on a campaign tour in the West, Hoover received a startling telegram from the president—the first known sign of discord between them: "Press reports indicate you are going to make addresses and hold conference on matters that come under the Interior Department. I suggest that you take no action of that kind until you have conferred with Secretary Work and me. Acknowledge." Hoover was stunned. "Not a word of truth in the report given you," he wired back; "have never heard of any such question." "Greatly mystified," he asked Secretary of Interior Hubert Work to find the source of the "pollution."[44]

What had happened? Earlier in the year, in speeches on the west coast and elsewhere, Hoover had unveiled a comprehensive scheme for the development of the nation's water resources. Years later, Hoover disclosed in his *Memoirs* that President Coolidge was "not very enthusiastic" about certain of these proposals because of their high cost, and in fact refused to sanction some of them. Then, in the waning days of the 1926 election campaign, press reports circulated that advocates of a Columbia River basin development project were organizing to promote their cause in Congress and that a "waterways bloc" would be active in the next Congressional session. The press reports also evidently suggested that Hoover was going to confer with some of these activists. To Coolidge, already at war with a feisty "farm bloc" over McNary-Haugenism, the thought of battling yet another special interest group eager to spend taxpayers' money must have been anathema. It evidently displeased him that Hoover was apparently in league with these interests—and on an issue seemingly outside his jurisdiction.[45]

In a lengthy telegram to Work and a lengthier letter to Coolidge, Hoover insisted that he had done nothing to exceed his statutory authority, to encroach on the Interior Department's turf, or to misstate the official water policy of the Administration. He pointed out that Coolidge himself, in messages to Congress, had already formally endorsed all but one of Hoover's specific water development projects. He even suggested that creation of a "bloc" to support Coolidge's water proposals would be a good thing. He also denied having any improper contacts with the Columbia River enthusiasts. Perhaps Hoover did not yet realize that Coolidge was not as enamored of expensive public works projects as his engineer at the Department of Commerce. In a terse reply, Coolidge acknowledged Hoover's letter and enclosures. The president did not say, however, that he believed Hoover's elaborate explanations.[46]

Hoover never forgot the admonitory telegram that the man in the White House dispatched to him in October 1926. It was an unmistakable lesson to the "one man Cabinet" that if he was not careful, he could alienate his boss. In the months ahead, Hoover did not cease to be a useful servant to his president. But the trajectory of their friendship had definitely reached its zenith.[47]

. . .

Early in 1927, Hoover had an opportunity to help the president when Congress passed a new version of the McNary-Haugen farm bill. Relying in part upon ammunition supplied by the commerce secretary, Coolidge vetoed the legislation. This did not mean that Coolidge was thrilled with Hoover's alternatives (he was not). But at least in their opposition to what they perceived as a noxious panacea, the two men shared common ground.[48]

Behind the scenes, however, new evidence of friction between the president and his secretary of commerce soon appeared. Once again the issue was waterway development. In his annual message to Congress, Coolidge had pronounced himself in favor of the "necessary legislation" to expedite development of the lower Colorado River.[49] On Capitol Hill, this legislation had taken the form of the Swing-Johnson bill, which would authorize $125,000,000 for a gigantic dam at Boulder Canyon. The Swing-Johnson bill was vehemently opposed by private power interests, who argued that it would permit the federal government to generate and sell electricity at the dam site on an unprecedented scale in direct competition with private enterprise. Partly for this reason, the bill was bottled up in the House of Representatives Rules Committee.

Enter now Richard B. Scandrett, Jr.—friend of Calvin Coolidge, nephew of Dwight Morrow, vice president of the American Gas and Electric Company, and opponent of the Swing-Johnson bill. On a trip to Washington in early January, Scandrett called upon his old friend Bertrand H. Snell, chairman of the House Rules Committee. Snell had his own reasons for delaying the bill, but he told Scandrett that he was under great pressure from Hoover to release it so that the full House could take action. And Hoover, Snell presumed, was representing the White House.

The eager young Scandrett told Snell that the bill was in conflict with the 1924 Republican Party platform, which had stoutly opposed government enterprise in competition with the private sector. Hoover, who was also militantly opposed to socialism, evidently did not share the private power companies' interpretation of the bill's potential. In any event, Scandrett and Snell promptly prepared a memorandum—which Scandrett swiftly delivered to the White House—stressing the bill's socialistic character, its alleged incompatibility with past Republican pronouncements, and Hoover's *approval* of the bill in his conversations with members of Congress. According to Scandrett, when Coolidge learned what Hoover was doing, the president was "mad as the devil."[50]

Coolidge's irritation may have been matched by Hoover's own. On January 21 the secretary of commerce told a friend that big business, basking in prosperity and favored by the Coolidge administration, had become arrogant. In fact, he added, big business needed to be curbed more now than in Theodore Roosevelt's day. Among Hoover's grievances was the opposition of big business to the creation of a Boulder Dam.[51]

It was not domestic policy, however, but foreign policy—coupled with Hoover's apparent political ambition—that provided the occasion for the most public and most dangerous display of presidential displeasure in their entire relationship. Early in 1927, Secretary of State Frank B. Kellogg was seventy years old. Known as "Nervous Nellie" to his detractors, Kellogg had never been popular in official Washington, and speculation had often sprouted that he would not remain long in his post. When the tense and irritable secretary of state took a vacation in February, rumors flew that he would soon quit because of ill health. The White House denied the report.[52]

By the beginning of April, rumors of Kellogg's impending resignation were again swirling in the nation's press, along with suggestions that Herbert Hoover would succeed him. The Baltimore *Sun* reported that it was "well known" that Hoover would like to hold the preeminent Cabinet position and that it was "no secret" that his friends were ready to "exert influence" for him at the "proper time." A few days later, the *Washington Post* declared that Hoover would become secretary of state within a few weeks and that Dwight Morrow would succeed him at the Commerce Department. Meanwhile, up in Boston, the *Independent*—edited by Hoover's former secretary, Christian Herter—opined that Kellogg's days "seem numbered" and that Hoover "stands head and shoulders above all others" as the best person to inherit Kellogg's job.[53]

To at least one Washington observer, the rising flood of Kellogg-will-go rumors suggested a deliberate campaign to drive him into retirement. Indeed, there is some evidence that one of Hoover's closest associates had been endeavoring to do just that in order to create a vacancy for Hoover. For its part, the White House stoutly denied the sensational reports of a Cabinet shakeup. Coolidge himself disclaimed any knowledge that Secretary Kellogg intended to resign. Some days later, the president was reported to be "weary" and "exasperated" by the incessant suggestions that Hoover replace Kellogg in order to "redeem" the State Department's lost "prestige."[54] Hoover, of course, kept mum, at least publicly. Whatever his hopes, he told a close friend on April 3 that there was no chance that Kellogg would leave. In the next twelve days, however, something evidently happened to change Hoover's assessment. On April 15, on a trip to New York City, he confided to the same friend that he might become secretary of state.[55]

As it turned out, April 15, 1927, was to be a very eventful day in Washington. For some time the Coolidge administration had been grappling with a dangerous crisis in China, where civil war, revolution, and anarchy had created pressures for American and European intervention. In response to the murderous Nanking Incident in March, the United States had joined other powers in dispatching an identic note to the Chinese government demanding compensation for the loss of foreign lives and property in the Nanking riots.

Then, on April 15, the *Washington Herald* carried a banner headline on page one: "CABINET IS SPLIT OVER CHINA POLICY. . . . HOOVER FEARS KELLOGG ERRS BY FAILURE TO TRY LONE HAND." According to the *Herald*'s article, Hoover had spoken out in a Cabinet meeting against a policy of joint diplomatic action with Great Britain and other foreign powers against China. Nevertheless, the State Department had gone ahead and issued a diplomatic protest identical to that of the British. The *Herald* quoted Hoover as denying any "official" differences between Kellogg and himself. But it noted that the tales of a policy rift between them had revived rumors that Hoover wanted to succeed the ailing secretary of state.[56]

The *Washington Herald*'s sensational story was quickly denied on all sides. The *New York Times* found "no foundation whatever" for the claim that Hoover was the "chief objector" to Kellogg's China policy. Hoover himself soon blamed the leak on Secretary of the Navy Curtis Wilbur, who had evidently told some correspondents that *he* did not approve the identic note. Worried about his indiscretion, Wilbur (according to Hoover) then told the newsmen not to publish it. One of the journalists wrote a story about Cabinet dissension anyway, without mentioning Wilbur by name. After that story appeared, *other* journalists, whom Wilbur had not briefed, leaped to the inference that the dissident Cabinet officer must be Hoover. The tale quickly acquired new momentum.[57]

Hoover's version of the episode may or may not have been correct.[58] But even if true, in a sense it no longer mattered. Now the president of the United States had *two* embarrassing stories on his hands—China and the Hoover/Kellogg rumors—and he did not like it one bit.

On April 15, only hours after the *Herald*'s article hit the streets, Coolidge held his semiweekly news conference. He was not in an affable mood. With unusual bluntness, the president denied that his Cabinet was in any way divided over China policy. "All members of the Cabinet," he declared, had agreed with Secretary Kellogg's actions in that area. In fact, the president noted pointedly, Hoover had been "the warmest advocate in the Cabinet of identic notes." Coolidge then proceeded to scold the press about "speculation" concerning the United States government's attitude toward delicate foreign problems like the crisis in China. And then, without warning, the angry president added a stinging announcement: "While I am on that, I might state again that Mr. Kellogg isn't going to resign. If he does resign, Mr. Hoover will not be appointed Secretary of State."[59]

What had happened? The usually self-controlled Coolidge was certainly not immune to fits of temper, as members of his official family knew. But why now? According to one source, during the press conference a reporter accidently stepped on Coolidge's dog, provoking a severe presidential tongue-lashing. From then on, it was said, the president had been in a foul mood. This happenstance may have added to the asperity of the president's remarks, but it certainly did not dictate their substance. Something more had prompted the chief executive's explosion, and not a few of the correspondents who emerged from the press conference thought they knew what it was. The president of the United States, they believed, was jealous of his secretary of commerce.[60]

Coolidge's remarkable press conference—and above all, his apparent slap at Hoover—unleashed a typhoon of controversy in the nation's press. The Baltimore *Sun* called it "the most unusual, even the most sensational, incident" in the nearly four-year-old Coolidge presidency. According to the *Washington Post*, no other political utterance of Calvin Coolidge had evoked as much curiosity as this. Politicians, pundits, editorialists, and White House spin doctors promptly endeavored to explain what he meant. On the one side, it was claimed that Coolidge (1) had intended no rebuff at all; (2) in fact, esteemed Hoover highly; (3) considered Hoover too valuable as secretary of commerce to transfer to the Department of State; (4) wanted his secretary of state to be a lawyer; and (5) meant to rebuke press rumor mongering about Hoover, not Hoover himself. According to this thrust of interpretation, the president's choice of words was merely a case of Vermont plain speaking, not meant to convey any reproach.[61]

Other commentators were not so convinced. It was one thing for the president of the United States to be irritated at misleading reports of disagreements in his Cabinet and at the incessant gossip that his secretary of state would soon resign. But why did Coolidge then curtly say, without a word of further explanation, that Hoover would not succeed Kellogg *even if* Kellogg resigned? To the columnist Frank R. Kent, the truth was that Coolidge *did* intend to rebuke Hoover. To Kent (who detested Coolidge), "The truth is that with Mr. Coolidge and the small group of intimates who surround Mr. Coolidge there is and has been for a long time considerable jealousy of Mr. Hoover—and that fact has been well known and widely talked of in Washington." According to Kent, the "White House" had been intensely annoyed a year or so earlier when newspaper correspondents had begun habitually to refer to Hoover as the "Economic President of the United States."[62]

Chagrined at the uproar he had instigated (or so the press now reported), President Coolidge moved quickly to quell it. On April 16, he invited Hoover (who was then in New York City) to have breakfast with him in Washington, D.C., the next morning. Thoroughly upset by the president's published remarks, Hoover returned to the capital immediately. The next morning, Easter Sunday, he joined Secretary of the Treasury Mellon, among others, for breakfast with the president. Nothing happened. Hoover sat at Coolidge's left, and Mellon at his right, but no clarification, no apology, not one word about politics emanated from the president's lips. Hoover and the other invitees left more perplexed than ever.[63]

If Coolidge thought that his little gesture would placate the secretary of commerce and satisfy the press, he miscalculated. By now Hoover's friends and political supporters were reported to be incensed at the still unexplained presidential barb. The White House breakfast, which one correspondent dubbed "one of the strangest Easter feasts on record," only strengthened the speculative fever.[64]

With Washington abuzz in gossip over the "Hoover mystery" and with the *New York Times* (among others) practically demanding a clarification, President Coolidge held his next regularly scheduled press conference on April 19. Now, once and for all, he tried to put the incident to rest:

> I didn't speak of Mr. Hoover's abilities the other day. I had rather assumed that that would be assumed by the conference. His reputation is so well established in this country, and indeed abroad, for ability and executive achievement that I doubt very much if I should be able to shake it even if I wished to. Certainly, I have no desire to do that and shouldn't want to be thought so lacking in appreciation of a man of his abilities as to think that he wasn't well qualified for any position in the Cabinet that he would be willing to accept. Of course, the place that he is in now is one of great importance and of constantly increasing importance, not only on account of our domestic commerce, but on account of our foreign commerce, which under his direction and encouragement has very greatly increased and shows promise of further increase in the future.[65]

The next day the President's explanation was front page news across the country. Never before, apparently, had the "White House Spokesman" spoken so admiringly about anyone in his administration. Pro-Coolidge papers hailed his tribute to his secretary of commerce, and the whiff of political scandal soon subsided—although not before 221 separate newspaper editorials across the country had commented on the incident. Still, nothing Coolidge had said in explanation could quite conceal one fact: whatever the tone of his original remark, its substance remained unmodified. He had no intention of making Hoover his secretary of state.[66]

The Hoover-Coolidge relationship now returned to outward normalcy. Only three days after the president's quasi-apology before the press, he appointed Hoover chairman of a Cabinet committee to coordinate relief efforts for victims of flooding in the lower Mississippi Valley. This was no perfunctory assignment; the Mississippi River flood of 1927 was the worst natural disaster in American history. More than three hundred thousand people were forced to flee their homes and live in tent cities. That spring and summer, Hoover threw himself with characteristic zeal into organizing the public/private response to the unprecedented emergency. His leadership won him the applause of the nation and new status as a humanitarian hero. In a letter to the engineer-turned-public servant in June, Coolidge himself praised Hoover's "great service" and told him: "I do not think of any one else that was equipped to handle it as you have done." In this same letter, Coolidge even invited Hoover to visit him during the summer at the presidential vacation site in South Dakota, if Hoover should happen to be "going west at any time."[67]

For his part, Hoover seemed anxious to furbish his credentials as a loyal lieutenant. The secretary of commerce was undoubtedly aware of the pervasive belief in political circles that Coolidge was annoyed by the maneuverings of Hoover's friends to advance his presidential prospects and by press reports that Hoover would be Coolidge's choice to succeed him in 1928. Hoover also undoubtedly realized that any presidential ambitions he harbored could be crushed forever if he antagonized the sometimes irascible man in the White House.[68]

In the spring and summer of 1927, then, as speculation intensified about whether Coolidge would run again, Hoover did his best to proclaim his fealty. He was *not* a candidate for the presidential nomination, he told a visitor in May (who promptly informed the *New York Times*). The secretary of commerce said he was convinced that Coolidge would run again, be renominated, and win reelection. In mid-July, in Chicago, he declared: "No, I will not be a candidate. I am for Mr. Coolidge, who, I am sure, will be our President for four more years."[69]

Under the circumstances, Hoover could not have been entirely pleased when the *Des Moines Register*, on April 27, published a cartoon by J. N. Darling. The cartoon depicted a horde of pedestrians, all in the likeness of Hoover, crossing the street and creating a traffic jam. The pedestrians were identified as Hoover the secretary of commerce, Hoover the radio commissioner, Hoover the farm economist, Hoover the labor arbitrator, and more. The stopped vehicles were labeled "Sec. Kellogg," "Sec. Mellon's car," and "Congress." Standing in the middle of the parade, and acting as a traffic cop, was Calvin Coolidge, dressed as a policeman. The title of the cartoon was "The Traffic Problem in Washington, D.C."[70]

There is no evidence that Coolidge saw or commented upon this artistic suggestion that Hoover was *the* dynamic figure in Washington. Nor, apparently, did Coolidge comment in May when Hoover publicly clashed with Kellogg over the question of whether the U.S. government should restrict private American loans to foreign countries for purposes that the U.S. government deemed nonproductive. (Hoover was in favor of such a policy). A few weeks later, however, Hoover's intimate friend Hugh Gibson (fresh from a visit to Washington) provided a hint that all was not well beneath the surface. According to Gibson, President Coolidge was thoroughly irritated by the accolades Hoover was receiving for his Mississippi flood relief work. Certainly some in the Coolidge wing of the GOP were worried by the adulation that Hoover was gaining in the deep South, whose delegates might be a decisive factor at the next Republican national convention.[71]

On July 20, Hoover arrived at the Black Hills of South Dakota, where he briefed the vacationing president about the Mississippi Valley's flood recovery needs. The atmosphere seems to have been anything but cordial. At first the president had planned to remain at his quarters in the State Game Lodge and let his visitor come to him. Then Coolidge changed his mind and motored to the train station at Custer. But when Hoover stepped off the train, it was a Secret Service agent who met him; the president did not get out of his car. When Hoover came over to the waiting automobile, Coolidge greeted him without a smile. Later, the two men were chauffeured to the president's office in Rapid City. On the entire drive (thirty miles), neither man spoke to the other.[72]

It is impossible to know the source of the president's displeasure—if, indeed, displeasure it was. The president may have been bothered by the possibility that his omnipresent commerce secretary would demand a special session of Congress to appropriate extra money for flood relief—a course Coolidge strongly opposed. In the president's view, sessions of Congress always produced "agitations" that disturbed business. In any case, Hoover could not have been comforted by his host's frosty reticence or by the spate of political rumor mongering that the visit generated. Questioned by the press, Hoover angrily denied a report that he was about to resign and run for president regardless of Coolidge's intentions. "I am desirous and willing to serve under and with President Coolidge," he insisted.[73]

More and more, conjecture about Hoover's and Coolidge's ambitions was coloring the news coverage about the two men. No doubt with relief, Hoover departed from the Black Hills on July 21 and headed to his beloved California. Less than two weeks later, on August 2, he was vacationing at the Bohemian Grove north of San Francisco when a telegram arrived from the Associated Press. It said: "President Coolidge issued statement as follows Quote I do not choose to run for President in 1928 Unquote Please telephone or telegraph your views of Presidents statement."[74]

Suddenly the path to the White House was open. Or was it?

In reconstructing the next phase in the Coolidge-Hoover relationship, it may help to recall that Coolidge was both a stubborn Vermont Yankee and a lover of practical jokes. Certainly this least flamboyant of presidents must have relished the perplexity that his cryptic announcement produced in the nation's political elite. What did the president mean, and how much did he mean it? Had he really forsaken another term? Would he accept a draft, if offered, at the next convention? Would he publicly endorse someone else?[75]

Coolidge's stunning thunderbolt posed immediate problems for Hoover. Already under suspicion at the White House for his pushiness, the secretary of commerce could ill afford to look overly ambitious, at least not until the president's own intentions were certain. Hoover therefore immediately instructed his supporters to lie low and informed the press of his "regret" at Coolidge's statement. "I still believe," said Hoover on August 3, that Coolidge "should be renominated and re-elected."[76]

A few weeks later, when both men were back in Washington, Hoover called at the White House and tried to obtain some clarification. The secretary of commerce explained that since August 2 he had been inundated with "urgings" that he now seek the presidency. Despite this, Hoover declared that he thought Coolidge should run again. If the president would give the signal, Hoover said, he would steer his supporters into a "Draft Coolidge" effort. Hoover further offered to "stop the movement toward myself" if there were "any possibility" that Coolidge could be persuaded to accept renomination. The president answered that Hoover "ought not to stop it." When Hoover asked whether Coolidge's Black Hills declaration was "absolutely conclusive," however, the president "made no direct reply."[77]

Denied the positive assurance that he sought, Hoover felt obliged to confine his presidential maneuverings that autumn to "unofficial" activities by his friends. But if for Hoover the future still seemed murky, for Coolidge, apparently, it was altogether clear. Sometime in the autumn of 1927, the president was out on one of his frequent strolls in downtown Washington with his Secret Service escort and friend, Edmund W. Starling. Suddenly the "little fellow" (as Starling called Coolidge) spoke:

> Well, they're going to elect that superman Hoover, and he's going to have some trouble. He's going to have to spend money. But he won't spend enough.
>   Then the Democrats will come in and they'll spend money like water. But they don't know anything about money. Then they will want me to come back and save some money for them. But I won't do it.[78]

If this anecdote is accurate (and there is no reason to doubt its essence), it was one of the most prescient remarks Calvin Coolidge ever made.

Then, on December 6, in an address before the Republican National Committee, the president broke his public silence. Prior to this speech, Hoover had gone to him again, informing him that there was "great demand" that he continue in office and that, if Coolidge would give his assent at the RNC meeting, the party would surely "go along unanimously." Ever anxious to demonstrate his loyalty, Hoover stressed that he did not want Coolidge to feel constrained by the activities of Hoover's friends. According to Hoover, Coolidge "made no very definite statement" except to give him some campaign advice. Instead, the president reserved his next bomb-shell for the speech he gave to the RNC:

> This is naturally the time to be planning for the future. The party will soon place in nomination its candidate to succeed me. To give time for mature deliberation I stated to the country on Aug. 2 that I did not choose to run for President in 1928.
> My statement stands. No one should be led to suppose that I have modified it. My decision will be respected.
> After I had been eliminated the party began, and should vigorously continue, the serious task of selecting another candidate from among the numbers of distinguished men available.

Once more the inscrutable figure in the White House had delivered an oracular pronouncement. This time, for most observers, its meaning seemed plain. Still, the president did not state what he would do if, in defiance of his apparent wishes, the Republican national convention should draft him anyway. On that slim reed of uncertainty, much of the politics of the next six months would pivot.[79]

The campaign of 1928 now got underway in earnest. By early February, Hoover was ready to announce his candidacy publicly. But before he did so, he went to the White House yet again. He told the president that he (Hoover) was under pressure to enter the presidential primary in Ohio, where Senator Willis had already come out as a favorite son. Hoover then asked Coolidge directly whether he intended to place his name on the Ohio primary ballot. The president replied in one word: "No." Hoover then asked whether *his* name should go on the Ohio ballot. The president replied in two words: "Why not?"[80]

With Coolidge's acquiescence, then (though hardly his blessing), Hoover publicly affirmed his candidacy for president on February 12, 1928. Somewhat disingenuously (for a man already working at full throttle behind the scenes for his objective), Hoover asserted his "conviction" that he should not "strive for the nomination." For this reason, he said, and because of his "obligations as Secretary of Commerce," he would make no "personal campaign." Hoover thereupon pledged that if he received the nomination he would "consider it my duty to carry forward the principles of the Republican party and the great objectives of President Coolidge's policies—all of which have brought to our country such a high degree of happiness, progress and security." Interestingly, Hoover did not precisely promise to carry forward Coolidge's policies—only the *objectives* of those policies. It was a subtle distinction that may have been deliberate.[81]

Certainly one Coolidge policy that Hoover did *not* approve was the president's indifference toward—if not outright encouragement of—the

surging stock market. By early 1928, prices on the New York Stock Exchange had advanced to record levels, abetted by a staggering growth in
brokers' loans. In January, the amount of such loans held by member banks
of the New York Federal Reserve system approached an unprecedented $4
billion, an increase of about a billion dollars in just twelve months. On January 6, President Coolidge was asked at a news conference whether the
amount of these loans was now dangerously high. Relying upon information from his Treasury Department, the president replied that he saw no
signs that the amount was "large enough to cause particularly unfavorable
comment." Upon hearing this presidential benediction, the stock market
soared again.[82] When Hoover heard it, he was incredulous. Turning to an
aide, he asked: Did Coolidge say *that?*[83]

Actually, Coolidge himself had qualms about the enormous credit expansion that was driving the stock market upward. But for a variety of reasons he declined to intervene. As he put it to a relative a few days later, "I
regard myself as the representative of the government and not as an individual." When "technical matters" arose, he said, he turned them over to
the appropriate government agency and used the resulting feedback as the
basis for his official stance. That, however, "does not prevent me from
thinking what I please as an individual." And, as an individual, he considered any loan obtained for "gambling in stocks" to be an "excessive loan."
Herbert Hoover's conception of the presidential office was to be far more
interventionist.[84]

Meanwhile, Coolidge's attitude toward Hoover was becoming more
critical. In the autumn of 1927, the President startled William R. Castle,
Jr., of the State Department by remarking that he did not consider Hoover
a very good adviser on State Department affairs. It was probably during this
period that someone asked Coolidge what he thought of his secretary of
commerce. The president replied, "How can you like a man who's always
trying to get your job?" In the wake of the Mississippi River flood disaster,
Coolidge began privately to disparage Hoover as the "miracle worker" and
"wonder boy."[85]

Publicly Coolidge remained scrupulously neutral in the developing presidential campaign. He even issued further renunciatory statements. In
March, he declined a request from the Republican State Central Committee of Wyoming that he run again. A month later he insisted that a write-in
movement for him in the Massachusetts primary be discontinued. His letter strongly intimated his displeasure at "Draft Coolidge" drives occurring
in other states. Officially, at least, Coolidge was out of the contest and doing nothing to confer advantage on any would-be successor.[86]

Privately, however, an agitated Hoover was not so sure. Hoover was
fully cognizant that much of the opposition to his candidacy was coming
from men who were plotting for a deadlocked convention and a last-minute

draft of Coolidge. As early as December 1927, Hoover believed that agents of the Republican national chairman were constantly telling Coolidge false stories about Hoover and that Coolidge was reacting angrily. A few months later, Hoover appeared to agree with the report of a friend that Coolidge was hostile to his secretary of commerce. It is impossible to know the substantive basis for these perceptions. But Hoover believed (as he later wrote a friend) that Coolidge considered him a "somewhat dangerous 'liberal.'" Hoover also believed that Coolidge preferred Senator Charles Curtis of Kansas for the nomination, and he expected Coolidge to say so publicly. From day to day, then, Hoover was condemned to live in fear that the "little fellow" would in some way deprive him of the great prize.[87]

By early May, Hoover was far in the lead in the quest for delegates but by no means certain of a majority. For a final time, he made a plea to the president. I now have about 400 delegates, he told Coolidge. But if you will allow your name to be placed in nomination, I will release my delegates and tell them to vote for you. Hoover was certain that Coolidge would then be nominated. According to Hoover, the president replied that this (in Hoover's words) was "a fine offer, but it should not be done." As for the claim of 400 delegates, the president remarked, "If you have 400 delegates, you better keep them." He said no more.[88]

Once again, the "Great Enigma" had given his caller little relief from nervous tension, but Hoover might have derived hope from a conversation that Coolidge had at nearly the same time with Senator James Watson, a "favorite son" candidate who had recently been conspiring to renominate the president. You and Charles Hilles [a leading pro-Coolidge Republican in New York] "are bad boys, and I want you to behave yourselves," Coolidge lectured. "I have studied it all over and have finally concluded that I do not want that nomination."

"But suppose the Convention nominates you, then what?" Watson asked. Ducking this "hypothetical" question, Coolidge explained why he did not want to be president again. "I fitted into the situation that existed right after the war, but I might not fit into the next one," he said. After the war, the American people had wanted "rest"; he had given it to them, and they had prospered. But now, new circumstances were arising. "From this time on, there must be something constructive applied to the affairs of government, and it will not be sufficient to say, 'Let business take care of itself.'" "I do not feel that I am the man" to "meet the demand" for "affirmative" action that will soon arise, said Coolidge. "Somebody can do it, but I do not want to undertake it." Watson warned Coolidge that if he did not accept the nomination, Hoover would surely be selected. "Well," Coolidge replied, "that is a matter for the Convention to decide."[89]

Meanwhile, in Washington, D.C., the McNary-Haugen monster had once again reared its head. Only weeks before the Republican convention

was to assemble, the Congress enacted yet another version of this farm relief panacea so loathed by both Coolidge and Hoover. On May 23, President Coolidge vetoed the measure. In a scathing message whose ferocity
astonished the press, Coolidge excoriated the "vicious," "dangerous," "re-
pugnant," "fantastic," "delusive," "preposterous," and "intolerable" fea-
tures of the McNary-Haugen bill. His veto was promptly sustained.[90]

For Hoover, the president's rebuff of McNary-Haugenism contained
both good and bad news. On the one hand, it highlighted a critical issue on
which he was in accord with Coolidge and the more conservative elements
in the Republican Party. It also threw a roadblock in front of Hoover's rivals for the nomination, some of whom had endorsed the controversial legislation. On the other hand, the divisive controversy now threatened to be-
devil the national convention and even to ignite the defection of the farm
belt states to the Democrats. In the aftermath of the president's stinging
veto, enraged McNary-Haugenites vowed to carry the fight to the convention floor in Kansas City. The governor of Nebraska called for one hundred thousand farmers to march on the convention and "demand their
rights."[91]

In a bid to quell the threatened agrarian rebellion, Secretary of Agriculture Jardine asked the president in May to send a special message to Congress urging enactment of an alternative farm bill sponsored by Jardine and
Hoover. In this way, the farm states could be appeased. Coolidge apparently did not care for the alternative bill. Or perhaps he did not care to confer so obvious a favor on the leading contender for the nomination just
weeks in advance of the party's decision. For whatever reason, Coolidge
was not to be moved. When Jardine asked him outright to send the special
message in support of the farm bill as a favor to Hoover (the presumptive
nominee), the president exploded: "That man has offered me unsolicited
advice for six years, all of it bad!"[92]

The final weeks before the convention were a time of high but covert
drama, as pro- and anti-Hoover forces attempted to smoke out the sphinx
in the White House. Hoover's agony was excruciating. He was so close to
success, yet possibly so far. Pacing the floor in anxiety at one point, he ex-
claimed to an adviser, "Everything is all right. The Kansas City situation
seems to hold no element of doubt. But the thing that gets me is the man
there in the White House. What is his game? What cards will he play and
how?" Deeply disturbed by Coolidge's continuing silence, Hoover arranged on June 8 to debrief a certain friend after the friend had lunched
with the president. The friend could only report afterward that Coolidge
had given no hint of his political plans. That very same day, Andrew Mellon, chairman of the powerful Pennsylvania delegation, asked the president
whether there was any possibility that he would change his mind about the
nomination. According to Mellon, the chief executive "looked down his

nose and almost snarled his reply." "He speaks of his position and cannot change," Mellon wrote in his diary. "Is in accord with me on Hoover." What this probably meant was that Coolidge had reached the same conclusion that Mellon had: Without a draft of the president, Hoover's nomination was inevitable.[93]

Despite tremendous pressures, then, Coolidge refused to give the signal that even then could have stopped Hoover. Nor, despite repeated pleadings, did he succumb to demands that he anoint an anti-Hoover candidate or help the anti-Hoover coalition "get together." "I refused to interfere," Coolidge told a friend two years later. "There was no way for me to do so without creating a situation that would lead to my own nomination. I was determined that that should not happen."[94]

Still, in ten long, agonizingly suspenseful months, he had never issued a "Sherman statement." He had not once said unequivocally that he would refuse to accept the nomination if it were tendered to him. Why not? Because, he asserted in his autobiography, such a statement would not have been "in accordance with my conception of the requirements of the Presidential office." (Just what these were, he did not say.) "I never stated or formulated in my own mind what I should do in such circumstances," he added, "but I was determined not to have that contingency arise."[95]

In the end, Coolidge did not have to face this supreme crisis of renunciation. On the eve of the balloting in Kansas City, William Vare, the boss of Philadelphia, bolted to Hoover, splitting the hitherto uncommitted Pennsylvania delegation and making any further "Stop Hoover" movement hopeless. The anti-Hoover front quickly collapsed. Coolidge himself, through his secretary Everett Sanders, requested the pro-Coolidge leaders of several state delegations not to vote for him, and they obeyed.[96]

Yet if Coolidge did not want the nomination, he was not necessarily gratified by the convention's outcome. As it happened, the president was on his way by train to Wisconsin for a summer vacation when the Republican Party chose his successor. Coolidge was in bed when, late on the evening of June 14, Hoover swept to a first ballot victory in Kansas City. The next morning, Coolidge received the news in Wisconsin, and the Secret Service agent who was with him never forgot his reaction. His face betraying anger, the president bluntly ordered the agent to get him a bottle of whiskey.[97]

At this point, one might ask: if Coolidge was so unenthusiastic about Hoover, why did he not try in some way to thwart Hoover's pursuit of the great prize? First, Coolidge appears to have sincerely believed that a sitting president should not, in most cases, attempt to influence the selection of his successor. The candidate, he later wrote, "should be the choice of the people themselves." To all external appearances, Coolidge scrupulously adhered to these convictions. A second, less abstract reason may also have intruded: the absence of acceptable, first-class alternatives. Andrew Mellon was too old. Charles Evans Hughes was not interested. Vice President Charles Dawes openly favored McNary-Haugenism and had even helped the fight for it in the Senate; besides, Coolidge had other reasons for detesting him. Frank Lowden of Illinois—an open and formidable contender —also embraced the McNary-Haugen plan, even endorsing it just six days before Coolidge's veto. By this act, Lowden made it impossible for eastern, conservative Coolidgeites to support him. Coolidge later opined that had Lowden not made that ill-timed endorsement, he might well have wrested the nomination away from Hoover.[98]

There were other candidates, of course—favorite sons and such—but these were small fry, and Coolidge did not care for some of them, either. Hoover was not the only presidential aspirant whom the president disliked. And even if he secretly preferred Senator Curtis (as both Hoover and Curtis thought), for Coolidge there was still the hurdle of principle mentioned above.[99]

This dearth of acceptable rivals of Hoover in 1928 (acceptable, that is, to party conservatives) underscores the centrality of the McNary-Haugen controversy in Republican politics in the 1920s. On this, one of the key litmus test issues of the day, Hoover and Coolidge stood on the same side of the ideological divide. Without this essential common ground between them, it is doubtful that Hoover could have become Coolidge's successor.

Coolidge's first official response to Hoover's convention victory was a telegram that in form, at least, was more than adequate: "You have been nominated for the most important position in the world. Your great ability and your wide experience will enable you to serve our party and our country with marked distinction. I wish you all the success that your heart could desire. May God continue to bestow upon you the power to do your duty." Only one phrase—the wish for "all the success that your heart could desire"—carried a possible hint of reproach. Was this an oblique reference to what in Coolidge's eyes was Hoover's overweening ambition? If so, no one seems to have noticed. Hoover's reply to Coolidge's wire was equally dignified: "I am greatly touched by your telegram. During the last seven years you have given me unremitting friendship and my greatest hope is that it will continue to sustain me in this new task. Your high sense of duty and your devotion to public service will always be for me an inspiration." To the Republican national convention, Hoover pledged "to uphold the traditions of the Republican Party so effectively exemplified by Calvin Coolidge." On the surface, all seemed well.[100]

In the next several months, however, the now familiar Coolidge/Hoover pattern repeatedly manifested itself: public correctness, private strain. One source of tension was uncertainty over whether Hoover would visit the president in Wisconsin on a trip west to California. Early in July, reports circulated in Washington that the secretary of commerce would do so. Coolidge, who had issued no such invitation, was displeased and let the press know it: "I have no definite engagement to meet Mr. Hoover. I have no information of any kind or description as to whether he is coming here. I should assume, though, that if he was coming he would say something to me about it." The next day Coolidge's lack of knowledge of Hoover's plans was duly reported in the press. Taking the hint, the secretary of commerce speedily asked the president for an opportunity to visit him and discuss "some matters of importance in connection with the campaign." Coolidge promptly invited Hoover and his wife to stay at the president's vacation lodge on his visit.[101]

On July 16, the Republican nominee and Mrs. Hoover arrived at the presidential retreat in the Wisconsin woods. At the outset, at least, it was an awkward encounter. When the two men met, the president was unsmiling and his handshake "the usual matter of course greeting for which he is famous." It was left to the two wives to do the smiling. A few minutes later, Coolidge and Hoover sat solemnly for the photographers. When asked by one of them to carry on a conversation, the president turned to Hoover and made some remark. Hoover smiled but made no reply. The president spoke to him again. Once more his guest smiled but said nothing. Turning to the photographers, Coolidge said, "I am sorry. I am willing, but I cannot make Mr. Hoover keep up his end of the conversation." This was a switch: Silent Cal unable to get Hoover to speak! Mrs. Coolidge and Mrs. Hoover were greatly amused. Eventually, at the president's prodding, Hoover held an informal news conference but said nothing about politics.[102]

The remainder of the Hoovers' two-day sojourn went well; so, at least, Coolidge told his next news conference. Much of the time the president and his guest spent fishing, a recreational activity that required neither of them to say much to the other. "He is a more expert fisherman that I am," Coolidge afterward confided to the press. But when asked whether he could be quoted on this, the president declined.[103]

One issue that the two apparently did not resolve during Hoover's visit was the timing of his resignation as secretary of commerce. Hoover had informed Coolidge of his desire to leave in a note on June 30 and had formally tendered his resignation on July 5. But Coolidge seemed in no hurry to accept it. He informed the press twelve days later that there was some Commerce Department business that he wanted Hoover to "look into a little" before the resignation became official. Was Coolidge, in this subtle way, letting Hoover know that he was still president? One cannot be sure.[104]

Hoover now went on to California, where, on August 11, he formally accepted his party's nomination in a ceremony in the Stanford University football stadium. The event was carried on nationwide radio, but Coolidge did not listen. At the time of Hoover's address, the president was out fishing—a datum that was quickly reported in the press. In fact, Coolidge did not send Hoover a congratulatory telegram for three days—and then only after his failure to do so had been noted in the newspapers. When it came, the presidential felicitation was but two sentences long: "Your speech ranks very high in political discussion. I congratulate you upon it and upon the reception which has been given to it by the country."[105]

Seven days later, Coolidge finally accepted the resignation of his secretary of commerce. In a parting telegram of thanks, the president asserted that Hoover's service had been "of great benefit to the commercial life of the Nation" and that Hoover's knowledge of "the mechanics of business and government" was "unsurpassed." "It will always be a satisfaction to me," wrote Coolidge, "to have had the benefit of your wise counsel in meeting the problems which have arisen during my administration. My best wishes will always attend you in the broader field to which you have been called." On its face it was a decent encomium, but many Republican politicians were disappointed. To them the president's message seemed "lacking in fervor."[106]

If Hoover now hoped that Coolidge would participate actively in the fall campaign against the Democrats, he soon learned differently. On August 29, the nominee asked Coolidge by letter to deliver at least two nationally broadcast speeches for the Republicans. But when Coolidge returned to Washington from Wisconsin in September, he indicated that he had reached no decision about his campaign role. He told visitors that he did not consider it dignified for a president to deliver political speeches during a campaign. Theodore Roosevelt, he pointed out, had made no partisan speeches for Taft in 1908, nor had Woodrow Wilson for his party's standard bearer in 1920. If this was indeed Coolidge's sole reason for not hitting the hustings, it showed how exalted was his conception of the office he held.[107]

Olympian dignity, of course, was not what Republican activists were seeking in the frantic autumn of 1928. By mid-October, Coolidge's reticence about the GOP ticket had become a source of comment in the press and of considerable discomfiture among Republican leaders. Would "the White House sphinx," or would he not, deliver a speech for the party? No one seemed able to find out. To be sure, in late September the president had sent a message to a Massachusetts party leader endorsing Hoover, but the endorsement had been embarrassingly formal. As one observer noted, Coolidge's "recommendation was like that one gives an employe whose departure is welcome to the endorser." Day by day the mystery mounted. Could it be, as some Democrats were openly suggesting, that the man in the White House did not really care who succeeded him? Once again, as the *New York Times* editorialized, Coolidge was "most secretive when the politicians are almost neurotic at being kept so long on needles and pins."[108]

All this speculation probably delighted the attentive reader of newspapers who inhabited the presidential mansion. Once more Coolidge the Silent was proving himself a master of suspense.

On November 1, Hoover called upon his president one more time before heading to California to vote. As the Movietone cameras recorded the scene on the White House lawn, Coolidge said: "Good-bye, Mr. Hoover. I wish you a pleasant trip to California and a safe return. Good-bye and good luck." Replied Hoover: "Good-bye and thank you, Mr. President." Nothing more.[109] But the press did not know that Hoover and Coolidge were secretly planning one last Coolidgean surprise. Since the president was unwilling to make campaign speeches, Hoover conceived the idea of a dramatic presidential telegram to the candidate late in the campaign.[110] Coolidge agreed, and on November 2—only four days before the election—he telegraphed a message in some of the most effusive words he ever wrote:

> I have just heard your St. Louis speech with great satisfaction. It is the concluding address of a series which have disclosed a breadth of information, a maturity of thought, and a soundness of conclusion on public questions never surpassed in a previous presidential campaign. You have had the knowledge and judgment which enabled you to tell the people the truth. You have been clear, candid and courteous, demonstrating your faith in the people and your consciousness that the truth has a power and conclusiveness of its own which is always supreme. All the discussion has only made more plain the wisdom of the plans you have proposed for solving our political, economic, and social problems. You have shown your fitness to be President. I wish to congratulate you on the high quality of your leadership. You are able, experienced, trustworthy, and safe. Your success in the campaign seems assured and I shall turn over the great office of President of the United States of America to your keeping, sure that it will be in competent hands in which the welfare of the people will be secure.[111]

The telegram at once evoked large headlines, as both men surely knew that it would. Hoover was grateful. Republican leaders were jubilant and relieved. Not everyone, of course, was ecstatic. The *New York Times* wondered, "If the President wanted to promote the success of his sometime subordinate, why was he so unconscionably long in bringing himself to do it?"[112] Nevertheless, no one could charge that Coolidge, a faithful party man, had failed to do his political duty. And when, on November 6, Hoover was overwhelmingly elected, Coolidge telegraphed his "cordial congratulations": "The success of our party with your election to the Presidency and the endorsement of the Administration are of great satisfaction to me. With this endorsement I can now retire from office in contentment."[113]

The president's term, however, still had four months to run, and he was

known to be very touchy about his prerogatives. No doubt with these sensi-
tivities in mind, Hoover proposed on November 1 that he take a semi-
official goodwill tour of Latin America after the election. Coolidge was
willing to accommodate the president-elect, although the correspondence
between them betrayed a hint of disharmony. The thrifty president evidently wanted Hoover to sail on a U.S. Navy cruiser; Hoover insisted upon
and ultimately received a battleship. And so, from November 19, 1928,
until early January 1929, Hoover not only stayed out of Washington; better
still, he stayed out of the country.[114]

On January 9, back in Washington at last, the president-elect conferred
at the White House at Hoover's request and began planning his new regime. A few days later, Hoover headed to Florida for a vacation; he returned
to the capital in mid-February, a full two weeks in advance of his inauguration. Both of these visits were contrary to recent precedent; Wilson and
Harding had not set foot in the capital until the eve of *their* inaugurations.
If Coolidge perceived Hoover's visits as undue encroachment, he evidently
did not say so. To all appearances, contacts between the chief executive and
his successor-in-waiting were (in one newspaper's words) "entirely correct
and friendly." Coolidge even gave Hoover some "fatherly" advice about
managing the White House: "You have to stand every day three or four
hours of visitors. Nine-tenths of them want something they ought not to
have. If you keep dead-still they will run down in three or four minutes. If
you even cough or smile they will start up all over again."[115]

Still, signs were appearing that a new political era was at hand, and Coolidge could not have been entirely happy at the prospect. Throughout his
term, the frugal executive had gotten along with one White House secretary (a senior position, not a clerical one). On January 21, Hoover asked
Coolidge to recommend to the Congress the appropriation of money to
hire two more. Coolidge went along with this request. But if Washington
scuttlebutt was correct, during these final weeks, as problems came to his
desk, Coolidge began to remark, "We'll leave that to the wonder boy."[116]

One such problem—in Hoover's eyes, at least—was the continuing,
dizzy advance of the stock market: that "mad orgy of speculation" (as he
later called it) that had begun in 1927. Upon returning from Latin America
in January 1929, Hoover had been "appalled" (as he subsequently put it) by
the extent to which share prices had risen during his trip. The nervous
president-elect promptly called upon Coolidge and urged him to ask the
Federal Reserve Board "to put the brakes upon the mis-use of credit for
speculative purposes." Although Coolidge (said Hoover) "could not believe
that anything was really wrong," he did authorize Hoover to raise the issue
with the Federal Reserve Board. Hoover did so. According to him, the
Board instituted some restrictions on the speculative use of credit and "got
out warnings" that briefly cooled the "market fever." But to Hoover's cha-

grin, at a press conference some days later president Coolidge made "a bullish statement" that set off the market stampede all over again. By the time Hoover took office, it was too late (he later claimed) to do much to curb the market's "madness."[117]

Hoover's account may have been self-serving, but it did limn the contrast between his approach to the economy and Coolidge's. According to Hoover, his predecessor as president was "a strict legalist" who held that the Federal Reserve Board "had been created by the Congress entirely independent of the Executive and that he could not interfere." Hoover had no such aversion to "jawboning" the Fed, either personally or through surrogates.[118]

On March 4, 1929, fulfilling an ambition that had touched his soul for a decade or longer, Herbert Hoover became president of the United States. For an hour and a half during the ceremonies, he and Calvin Coolidge stood, sat, and walked side by side without saying a word to each other. In his inaugural address, Hoover politely paid tribute to his predecessor: "For wise guidance in this great period of recovery the nation is deeply indebted to Calvin Coolidge." When the ceremonies at the Capitol were over, the two men said goodbye, and the new president left for the White House. The ex-president took a train home to New England, where, for the rest of his days, he lived.[119]

Coolidge's exit from Washington did not mean that he had permanently left the national stage, however much he (and Hoover) may have desired it. For the next four years, as New Era prosperity curdled into depression, the puzzling Yankee in Northampton, Massachusetts, cast a troubling shadow over his successor.

As the Great Depression set in and intensified, talk of replacing Hoover in 1932 with another candidate circulated widely among Republican leaders. Hoover could never be sure when a challenge to his renomination might erupt from his party's conservatives (or, for that matter, from Republican Progressives). Hoover knew painfully well that Coolidge could have taken the prize from him in 1928 at any time and that the Coolidge faction of the party had only grudgingly acquiesced in Hoover's selection. The man in the White House therefore kept an anxious watch on the sage of Northampton.

The new president's uneasiness about his predecessor may have been reciprocated, if Washington gossip was at all on the mark. According to one hostile source, Coolidge was decidedly unhappy when Hoover, in his very first economy move, put the presidential yacht, the *Mayflower*, in mothballs. When Hoover, in another act of symbolic frugality, removed two unused riding horses from the White House to nearby Fort Myer, Coolidge supposedly gibed, "Yes, I s'pose they'll eat less hay at the fort than they will at the White House."[120]

Publicly, of course—and by now we should not expect otherwise—Hoover and Coolidge maintained a carefully respectful relationship. If the former president had reservations about his successor's policies, he did not discuss them in public. Nor did Coolidge undercut the incumbent with plans of his own to combat the depression, despite incessant pleadings that he do so. "I won't do it," he said. "I refuse to be a Deputy President."[121]

As it happened, Hoover need not have fretted about Coolidge's plans for 1932. Ever the party loyalist, and burdened by failing health, the former president had no intention whatever to run again. In late 1931 he wrote: "A retired President ought to be an example of loyal support to his successor." "In an emergency like the present," he added, "the responsible elements of our party should offer a solid front in their support of the President. That is the course I propose to pursue." The following spring he gave no encouragement when die-hard Coolidgeites attempted to draft him for the national ticket, either as president or vice president. Hoover and his supporters easily quashed the abortive insurrection.[122]

And now, in the last election campaign he would ever see, it was Coolidge's turn to be the loyal lieutenant. There was no question at all about his sentiments. "I think it would be a great calamity if Mr. Hoover was not reelected and I cannot believe that he will be defeated," he wrote to a close friend. As a contribution to the cause, he published "The Republican Case" in the *Saturday Evening Post* in September. Hoover, he said, should be reelected "for what he has done and for what he has prevented." Hoover was "safe and sound." In a note of thanks, Hoover said he found it difficult to express his "full feeling of appreciation" for Coolidge's article.[123]

But Hoover and his increasingly desperate associates wanted more. Throughout the summer and autumn, emissaries from the White House and other quarters beseeched Coolidge to make speeches to save the party from disaster. At first he resisted; his ailing throat would not stand it, he said. But the former president relented when told that his party was going to be defeated and that he must be seen to have been one of the fighters for the losing cause. "I am always ready to share the fate of my party," he replied. A few weeks later he appealed for Hoover's reelection at a rally in Madison Square Garden. Hoover was overjoyed. With almost pathetic gratitude, he thanked Coolidge for this "warming remembrance from a true friend."[124]

Coolidge, in fact, had not been well when he spoke in New York and had been afraid that he would be unable to finish. Upon learning of the ex-president's physical difficulties, President Hoover quickly dropped plans for Coolidge to deliver a campaign address in Chicago.[125] In the end, Coolidge did manage to speak again publicly—on the night before the election, on nationwide radio, from his home in Northampton. For the last time, he faithfully performed his duty according to the code by which he had lived:

> When the American people make a major decision like the election of a President they do not offer themselves to the highest bidder. . . . In all our history we have never deserted our President because we were not making money. . . . Promises and good intentions are not enough. We cannot afford rash experiments. . . . For nearly twenty years our President, Herbert Hoover, has been serving our country and the world. Measured by accomplishments he holds commanding rank. . . . All the teachings of common sense require us to reelect President Hoover. . . . From my knowledge of President Hoover, after sitting at the Cabinet Table with him for eight years, after considering the difficulties he has encountered and the policies he has proposed, I believe that he is the best man for us to entrust with the Presidency in this great emergency.[126]

It was a classically conservative case for a man he had once disparaged as a meddlesome liberal.

Two months later, Calvin Coolidge died suddenly. Herbert Hoover was shocked by the news. The president immediately issued a proclamation and attended the funeral in Northampton. "I feel I no longer fit in with these times," Coolidge had said just weeks before his death. About to be consigned to exile himself, Hoover soon felt the same way. Perhaps partly in gratitude for Coolidge's valiant contribution to the Republican campaign of 1932 when his uncertain health was failing, Hoover in the years to come tended to suppress the depth and detail of their past differences. To one correspondent in 1934, he even denied that there had ever been any "friction" between Coolidge and himself. *De mortuis nil nisi bonum?* Not quite. In Hoover's *Memoirs* and elsewhere, explicit and implicit criticism of Coolidge can be found. But the acute, underlying sense of vexation—which Hoover and Coolidge had often felt about each other—was lacking in Hoover's later reminiscences. Long after his predecessor passed away, Hoover perpetuated the patina of diplomatic correctness that had marked their relationship in life.[127]

And what more need now be said? Leaving aside differences of personality and ideology, the Coolidge/Hoover relationship illustrated this point: Political parties are alliances of factions. Only three times in the twentieth century—1908, 1928, and 1988—has an elected candidate of one party succeeded in office an elected incumbent of the same party.[128] Such intraparty successions can be fraught with peril, for they entail the ascendancy of a new faction *within the coalition*. In a subtle sense, the recent victory at the polls becomes perceived as a factional triumph more than an all-party success. Trouble can soon result, over redistribution of patronage and much else. If Coolidge had been a younger man and less of an organization man, the Republican Party might have engaged in factional warfare in 1932 as it did in 1912 and 1992 and for some of the same reasons. The convoluted Coolidge-Hoover story illustrates something else. The Republican Party of the 1920s was no monolith. In the nuances of these two men's relationship, we can see in microcosm some of the political fault lines of a decade far more intriguing than is usually perceived.

NOTES

1. *New York Times*, April 4, 1923, 1; [Ray Thomas Tucker], *The Mirrors of 1932* (New York, 1931), 65; James E. Watson, *As I Knew Them* (Indianapolis and New York, 1936), 233.
2. *New York Times*, August 5, 1923, 5; Robert K. Murray, *The Harding Era: Warren G. Harding and His Administration* (Minneapolis, 1969), and Robert K. Murray, "Herbert Hoover and the Harding Cabinet," in Ellis W. Hawley, ed., *Herbert Hoover as Secretary of Commerce: Studies in New Era Thought and Practice* (Iowa City, 1981), 19–40.
3. For Coolidge's background, see Claude M. Fuess, *Calvin Coolidge: The Man from Vermont* (Boston, 1940); Donald R. McCoy, *Calvin Coolidge: The Quiet President* (Lawrence, Kansas, 1988); Donald R. McCoy, unpublished paper, "Herbert Hoover's Relations with Warren G. Harding and Calvin Coolidge," delivered at George Fox College, October 1993 (copy in possession of the author).
4. R. V. Oulahan, "Hoover, the Handy, Plays Many Parts," *New York Times Magazine*, November 22, 1925, 3; Henrik Booraem V, *The Provincial: Calvin Coolidge and His World, 1885–1895* (Lewisburg, Penn., 1994), 36–37.
5. John Hiram McKee, *Coolidge Wit and Wisdom* (New York, 1933), 121.
6. "Memoirs of Robert G. Simmons" (typescript, n.d.), 15, in Robert G. Simmons Papers, Herbert Hoover Library, West Branch, Iowa; H. L. Mencken, *A Carnival of Buncombe* (Baltimore, 1956), 124.
7. James H. MacLafferty, "A Visit to Calvin and Grace Coolidge at 'the Beeches,' Northampton, Massachusetts, September 24, 1930" (typescript, n.d.), 7, in James H. MacLafferty Papers, Herbert Hoover Library.
8. Russell Lord, *The Wallaces of Iowa* (Boston, 1947), 253.
9. McCoy, *Calvin Coolidge*, 290.
10. George H. Nash, *The Life of Herbert Hoover: The Humanitarian, 1914–1917* (New York, 1988), 370.
11. Dwight Morrow to J. P. Morgan, Jr., ca. August 19, 1927, quoted in Harold Nicolson, *Dwight Morrow* (New York, 1935), 291.
12. Howard H. Quint and Robert H. Ferrell, eds., *The Talkative President: The Off-the-Record Press Conferences of Calvin Coolidge* (Amherst, Mass., 1964), 9.
13. A. H. Ulm, "Hoover Emerges as a Cabinet," *New York Times*, September 19, 1926, sec. 4, 1.

14. Herbert Hoover, *The Memoirs of Herbert Hoover*, vol. 2, *The Cabinet and the Presidency* (New York, 1952), 56.

15. Ibid., 55–56.

16. Brand Whitlock diary, February 26, 1921, in Allan Nevins, ed., *The Journal of Brand Whitlock* (New York, 1936), 652; Murray, "Herbert Hoover and the Harding Cabinet," 30–33; Edward L. Schapsmeier and Frederick H. Schapsmeier, "Disharmony in the Harding Cabinet: Hoover-Wallace Conflict," *Ohio History* 75 (Spring-Summer 1966): 126–36, 188–90.

17. Oswald Garrison Villard, "Presidential Possibilities: IV. Herbert C. Hoover," *The Nation* 126 (February 29, 1928): 235.

18. The use of the epithets "Great Enigma" for Coolidge and "Great Engineer" for Hoover may be seen in *Mirrors of 1932*, 56.

19. C. Bascom Slemp to Herbert Hoover, October 19, 1923, "President Coolidge: 1923, October," Commerce Papers, Herbert Hoover Papers, Herbert Hoover Library; McCoy, *Calvin Coolidge*, 200–2.

20. Hoover, *Memoirs*, 2: 115–16, 122; Calvin Coolidge to Hoover, March 14, 1924, "President Coolidge," Commerce Papers, Hoover Papers.

21. Hoover's remarks before Business Men's Commission on Agriculture, National Industrial Conference Board, April 15, 1927, Public Statements File, Hoover Papers.

22. McCoy, *Calvin Coolidge*, 234–35; Edgar Rickard diary, January 23, 1925, Hoover Library.

23. *New York Times*, November 20, 1923, 21; Hoover, *Memoirs*, 2: 56; Ralph Arnold, "Laying Foundation Stones: Part II," *Historical Society of Southern California Quarterly* 37 (September 1955): 243–60; Richard Dale Batman, "The Road to the Presidency: Hoover, Johnson, and the California Republican Party, 1920–1924" (Ph.D. dissertation, University of Southern California, 1965), 239–305; Hoover telegram to *California Republican*, April 26, 1924, "President Coolidge," Commerce Papers, Hoover Papers.

24. Mark Sullivan diary, March 25, 1924, Mark Sullivan Papers, Hoover Institution Archives, Stanford University; *New York Times*, May 29, 1924, 1; June 8, 1924, sec. 1, 3; June 10, 1924, 1–2; June 11, 1924, 1.

25. Coverage of the Republican national convention can be found in the *New York Times* and other newspapers for June 10–13, 1924. See also "The Old Guard Plunges Through," *Independent* 112 (June 21, 1924): 329–30, for an account probably written by Hoover's friend and former secretary, Christian Herter, as well as McCoy, *Calvin Coolidge*, 245–47.

26. *New York Times*, June 13, 1924, 1; Hoover to Grosvenor Clarkson, June 21, 1924, "Clarkson, Grosvenor," Commerce Papers, Hoover Papers.

27. Hoover to C. Bascom Slemp, October 7, 1924; Slemp to Hoover, October 8, 1924. Both in Calvin Coolidge Papers, case file 482, Library of Congress, and in "President Coolidge," Commerce Papers, Hoover Papers.

28. Hoover to Coolidge, November 5, 1924, and Coolidge to Hoover, November 5, 1924, "President Coolidge," Commerce Papers, Hoover Papers; Mark Sullivan diary, November 18, 1924, Sullivan Papers; *New York Times*, November 21, 1924, 3.

29. Hoover to C. Bascom Slemp, November 3, 1924, "President Coolidge," Commerce Papers, Hoover Papers.

30. *New York Times*, January 16, 1925, 1, January 17, 1925, 1, 2. Privately Hoover worried that if he became secretary of agriculture he would be unable to win the loyalty of that department's bureau chiefs for at least two years. Edgar Rickard diary, January 23, 1925, Hoover Library. Some of the late Secretary Wallace's associates had been bitter opponents of Hoover—and vice versa.

31. *New York Times*, January 17, 1925, 1; William R. Castle, Jr., diary, April 15, 1925, microfilm copy at the Hoover Library.

32. Ellis W. Hawley, "Herbert Hoover, the Commerce Secretariat, and the Vision of an 'Associative State,' 1921–1928," *Journal of American History* 61 (June 1974): 116–40; Coolidge, executive order 4239, June 4, 1925, "President Coolidge," Commerce Papers, Hoover Papers. See also Joseph Brandes, *Herbert Hoover and Economic Diplomacy: Department of Commerce Policy, 1921–1928* (Pittsburgh, 1962); Hawley, *Herbert Hoover as Secretary of Commerce*; Carl E. Krog and William R. Tanner, eds., *Herbert Hoover and the Republican Era: A Reconsideration* (Lanham, Md., 1984); R.V. Oulahan, "Hoover, the Handy, Plays Many Parts"; Philip T. Rosen, *The Modern Stentors: Radio Broadcasters and the Federal Government, 1920– 1934* (Westport, Conn., 1980); Robert Zieger, *Republicans and Labor, 1919–1929* (Lexington, 1969); and Benjamin D. Rhodes, "Herbert Hoover and the War Debts, 1919–33," *Prologue* 6 (Summer 1974): 130–44.

33. "Washington Notes," *New Republic* 44 (September 2, 1925): 43; Oulahan, "Hoover, the Handy, Plays Many Parts," 3.

34. *New York Times*, April 26, 1925, sec. 1, 25; Hoover, *Memoirs*, 2: 55; Richard Scandrett, "Remembering Calvin Coolidge: An Oral History Memoir," *Vermont History* 40 (Summer 1972): 209.

35. Hoover to Arthur McKeogh, January 23, 1935, Herbert Hoover Collection, Box 314, Calvin Coolidge folder, Hoover Institution Archives; Hoover to William Allen White, January 25, 1938, Post-Presidential Individual File, Hoover Papers; Hoover, *Memoirs*, 2: 55–56.

36. Hoover, *The Memoirs of Herbert Hoover*, vol. 3, *The Great Depression* (New York, 1952), 7–10; Herbert F. Margulies, "The Collaboration of Herbert Hoover and Irvine Lenroot, 1921–1928," *North Dakota History* 45 (Summer 1977): 40–41; Herbert F. Margulies, *Senator Lenroot of Wisconsin: A Political Biography, 1920–1929* (Columbia and London, 1977), 391; *New York Times*, December 31, 1925, 4.

37. Rickard diary, June 29–30, 1926, September 25–26, 1926; Brandes, *Herbert Hoover and Economic Diplomacy*, 84–128; Brandes, "Product Diplomacy: Herbert Hoover's Anti-Monopoly Campaign at Home and Abroad," in Hawley, ed., *Herbert Hoover as Secretary of Commerce*, 186–214; William R. Castle, Jr., to Alanson B. Houghton, January 7, 1926, "England: January–March 1926," William R. Castle, Jr., Papers, Hoover Library; Castle diary, January 21, 1926.

38. Castle to Houghton, January 7, 1926; Castle diary, December 4, 1925, January 7 and 11, 1926.

39. Castle diary, December 4 and 5, 1925; New York *Evening World* article by Robert Barry, August 18, 1926, Coolidge Papers, case file 3.

40. Robert Barry article.

41. Ulm, "Hoover Emerges as a Cabinet."

42. Rickard diary, June 29–30, 1926; *New York Times*, October 17, 1926, 1, 3, and October 23, 1926, 9.

43. Hoover to Coolidge, October 19, 1926, "President Coolidge," Commerce Papers, Hoover Papers; *New York Times*, October 23, 1926, 9.

44. Coolidge to Hoover, October 25, 1926, and Hoover to Coolidge, October 25, 1926, Coolidge Papers, case file 3; [?] Burlew, telegrams (in behalf of Hoover) to Hubert Work, October 26 and 28, 1926, Coolidge Papers, case file 3.

45. Hoover, *Memoirs*, 2: 56, 112–16; Work to Hoover, October 28, 1926, "President Coolidge," Commerce Papers, Hoover Papers; Hoover to Work, October 29, 1926, Coolidge Papers, case file 3.

46. Hoover to Work, October 29, 1926, Hoover to Coolidge, November 2, 1926, Coolidge Papers, case file 3; Coolidge to Hoover, November 9, 1926, Coolidge Papers, case file 3.

47. In his *Memoirs*, Hoover stated that it was after a speech of his in Seattle on August 21, 1926, on "water conservation" that President Coolidge sent him a "sharp telegram . . . objecting on the ground that my proposals would improperly increase expenditures" (*Memoirs*, 2: 56). I have found no Coolidge-to-Hoover telegram fitting this description. Hoover's recollection here was probably inaccurate. In all likelihood, he was referring to the presidential telegram (quoted in my text) that he received in Tulsa, Oklahoma, on October 25, 1926.

48. A draft presidential veto message, heavily edited by—and apparently written by—Hoover, is in "President Coolidge," Commerce Papers, Hoover Papers. It is dated February 14, 1927. At the top of the page, in Hoover's handwriting, are the words: "Next to Final Draft Sent President Feb. 16_1927." A comparison of this draft with Coolidge's final veto message (February 25, 1927) shows that Coolidge used some of Hoover's sentences and paragraphs. Coolidge thus incorporated parts of Hoover's draft verbatim. See also McCoy, *Calvin Coolidge*, 308–10, 324.

49. Coolidge message to Congress, December 7, 1926, printed in *New York Times*, December 8, 1926, 14–15.

50. Richard B. Scandrett, Jr., to Dwight W. Morrow, February 26, 1927 (plus enclosures), Dwight W. Morrow Papers, Series 1, Box 41, folder 25, Amherst College Archives; Scandrett, "Remembering Calvin Coolidge," 209; Richard B. Scandrett, Jr., oral history (typescript, ca. 1966), 205–7 and supplemental memorandum, 11–12 (regarding Hoover and the Boulder Dam), Cornell University Libraries.

51. Rickard diary, January 21, 1927.

52. *New York Times*, March 5, 1927, 2.

53. Baltimore *Sun* clipping, March 31, 1927, copy in Clippings File, Hoover Papers; press summary for March 1927, Clippings File, Hoover Papers; *Washington Post*, April 3, 1927, sec. 1, 1, 4; *Independent* 118 (March 26, 1927): 325–26.

54. Daily Press Summary, April 6, 1927, 6, Clippings File, Hoover Papers; [Charles W. Hilles], memorandum regarding George Barr Baker, May 14, 1927, in Dwight W. Morrow Papers, Series 1, Box 26, folder 14; *New York Herald Tribune*, April 4, 1927, 5; transcript of President Coolidge's news conference, April 5, 1927, in Press Conferences of Calvin Coolidge, the Forbes Library, Northampton, Massachusetts; Baltimore *Sun* clipping, April 17, 1927, Clippings File, Hoover Papers.

55. Rickard diary, April 3 and 15, 1927.

56. *Washington Herald*, April 15, 1927, 1, clipping attached to Daily Press Summary for April 15, 1927, Clippings File, Hoover Papers.

57. Ibid.; *New York Times*, April 15, 1927, 4, April 16, 1927, 6; Castle diary, April 21, 1927.

58. For a report that it was Wilbur (not Hoover) who initially objected to Kellogg's China policy, see *New York Herald Tribune*, April 20, 1927, 1.

59. Transcript of President Coolidge's news conference, April 15, 1927, Press Conferences of Calvin Coolidge, Forbes Library.

60. Rickard diary, April 16, 1927. According to "T.R.B." in the *New Republic*, the word "jealousy" was "on the lips of every correspondent who came out of the White House conference" on April 15. *New Republic* 50 (May 4, 1927): 300. The possibility that Coolidge was jealous of Hoover also appeared in articles in the Baltimore *Sun* (including Frank R. Kent's column "The Great Game of Politics") on April 17, 1927. Copies in Clippings File, Hoover Papers. On May 6, 1927, Clinton W. Gilbert published an article headlined "Why People Are Jealous of the Secretary of Commerce" in the *New York Post*. A copy of this item is in "President Coolidge—Statement to the Press . . . ," Commerce Papers, Hoover Papers.

61. Baltimore *Sun* clipping, April 17, 1927, in Clippings File, Hoover Papers; press summary entitled "President Coolidge's Statement on the Secretaryship of State" (April 18, 1927), Clippings File, Hoover Papers. For other examples of this cluster of interpretations, see *New York Times*, April 16, 1927, 1, 6; *New York Herald Tribune*, April 17, 1927, sec. 1, 1, 3; *Boston Post* clipping, April 17, 1927, in "President Coolidge—Statement to the Press . . . ," Commerce Papers, Hoover Papers; *New York Times*, April 19, 1927, 8; press summary entitled "The President's Statement on the Secretaryship of State" (April 20, 1927), Clippings File, Hoover Papers; "Back Stage in Washington," *Independent* 118 (May 21, 1927): 541.

62. Frank R. Kent, "The Great Game of Politics," Baltimore *Sun*, April 17, 1927, copy in Clippings file, Hoover Papers.

63. *Boston Post* clipping, April 17, 1927; press summary for April 18, 1927, Clippings File, Hoover Papers; *New York Times*, April 17, 1927, sec. 1, 4, and April 18, 1927, 21; Rickard diary, April 16, 1927; New York *World*, April 18, 1927, 1, 2.

64. *New York Times*, April 19, 1927, 8; Baltimore *Sun* clipping, April 19, 1927, in "President Coolidge—Statement to the Press . . . ," Commerce Papers, Hoover Papers; press summary entitled "The President's Statement on the Secretaryship of State" (April 20, 1927), 1, in "President Coolidge—Statement to the Press . . . ," Commerce Papers.

65. New York *World*, April 18, 1927, 1, 2; *New York Times*, April 19, 1927, 8; Mark Sullivan's column in Portland *Morning Oregonian*, April 19, 1927, copy in "President Coolidge—Statement to the Press . . . ," Commerce Papers, Hoover Papers; transcript of President Coolidge's news conference, April 19, 1927, in Press Conferences of Calvin Coolidge, Forbes Library.

66. Press summary entitled "The President's Statement on the Secretaryship of State" (April 20, 1927); Hoover's staff's press summary and tabulation for the month of April 1927 (especially 13–15), in Clippings File, Hoover Papers. According to "T.R.B." in the *New Republic*, Coolidge neither retracted the "slur" nor removed "the ban on Hoover for promotion." *New Republic* 50 (May 4, 1927): 300. For a similar observation, see New York *World*, April 20, 1927, 2.

67. *Washington Post* clipping, April 23, 1927 (with annotations), in "Mississippi Valley Flood—Relief Work—Miscellaneous—1927—April," Commerce Papers, Hoover Papers; Bruce A. Lohof, "Herbert Hoover, Spokesman of Humane Efficiency: The Mississippi Flood of 1927," *American Quarterly* 22 (Fall 1970): 690–700; Coolidge to Hoover, June 20, 1927, "President Coolidge," Commerce Papers, Hoover Papers.

68. Press summary entitled "The President's Statement on the Secretaryship of State" (April 20, 1927), 2; *New York Herald Tribune*, April 17, 1927, sec. 1, 1, 3; *New York Times*, May 9, 1927, 23.

69. *New York Times*, May 8, 1927, sec. 1, 9, May 9, 1927, 23, and July 21, 1927, 13.

70. *Des Moines Register*, April 27, 1927, 1.

71. Charleston, South Carolina, *Post* editorial, May 5, 1927, copy in "President Coolidge—Statement to the Press . . . ," Commerce Papers, Hoover Papers; New York *Sun* editorial, May 5, 1927, copy in Morrow Papers, Series 1, Box 34, folder 18; Hoover, *Memoirs*, 2: 89–90; Rickard diary, June 3, 1927; New York *World*, July 21, 1927, 5.

72. New York *World*, July 21, 1927, 5; George C. Drescher oral history (1967), 6, Hoover Library. Drescher was a Secret Service agent who accompanied the president and Hoover on the drive to Rapid City.

73. *New York Times*, July 22, 1927, 3; also see July 21, 1927, 13.

74. Associated Press telegram to Hoover, August 2, 1927, "President Coolidge," Commerce Papers, Hoover Papers.

75. For Coolidge's love of practical jokes (and its significance for understanding him), see Booraem, *The Provincial*, 44, 162–63, 204–5, and McCoy, *Calvin Coolidge*, 157–58. Hoover, in his *Memoirs*, 2: 190, recalled that Coolidge "certainly enjoyed the amazing volume of curiosity and the discussion that his statement had evoked and apparently did not want to end it. Nor did he ever do so."

76. Rickard diary, August 3, 1927; *New York Times*, August 4, 1927, 1.

77. Hoover to William Allen White, January 25, 1938; Hoover, *Memoirs*, 2: 190.

78. Edmund W. Starling, *Starling of the White House* (New York, 1946), 263.

79. Hoover to William Allen White, January 25, 1938; *New York Times*, December 7, 1927, 1.

80. Donald R. McCoy, "To the White House: Herbert Hoover, August 1927–March 1929," in Martin L. Fausold and George T. Mazuzan, eds., *The Hoover Presidency: A Reappraisal* (Albany, 1974), 29–49, 197–99; Rickard diary, February 11, 1928; Hoover, *Memoirs*, 2: 191.

81. Rickard diary, February 11, 1928; *New York Times*, February 13, 1928, 1, 2.

82. Coolidge statement to the press, January 6, 1928, in Quint and Ferrell, eds., *The Talkative President*, 137–38; *New York Times*, January 7, 1928, 2, January 8, 1928, sec. 1, 1.

83. Bradley Nash oral history (1968), 79–80, Hoover Library. Nash dated this incident as probably occurring in the autumn of 1927, but the episode seems to have occurred on January 6, 1928. See also Hoover, *Memoirs*, 3: 13, note 8.

84. McCoy, *Calvin Coolidge*, 319–20; William Allen White, *A Puritan in Babylon: The Story of Calvin Coolidge* (New York, 1938), 390–91. According to Hoover, Coolidge was a "strict legalist" who "insisted that the [Federal] Reserve Board had

been created by Congress entirely independent of the Executive and that he could not interfere." Hoover disagreed. Hoover, *Memoirs*, 3: 11.

85. Castle diary, October 4, 1927; George Creel, *Rebel at Large* (New York, 1947), 265–66; White, *A Puritan in Babylon*, 353.

86. *New York Times*, March 22, 1928, 1, 8 and April 21, 1928, 1, 5. Coolidge later wrote: "In the primary campaign I was careful to make it known that I was not presenting any candidate." Coolidge, *The Autobiography of Calvin Coolidge* (New York, 1929), 245.

87. Rickard diary, December 31, 1927, May 6, 1928; Hoover, draft letter to William Allen White, January 25, 1938, Post-Presidential Individual File, Hoover Papers; Henry L. Stoddard, *It Costs to Be President* (New York and London, 1938), 89.

88. Hoover to William Allen White, January 25, 1938; Hoover, *Memoirs*, 2: 193.

89. Watson, *As I Knew Them*, 255–56.

90. *New York Times*, May 24, 1928, 1, 20, 21, and May 26, 1928, 1; McCoy, *Calvin Coolidge*, 327.

91. *New York Times*, May 24, 1928, 1.

92. White, *A Puritan in Babylon*, 400.

93. Ibid., 401; Rickard diary, June 8, 1928; Robert J. Rusnak, "Andrew W. Mellon: Reluctant Kingmaker," *Presidential Studies Quarterly* 13 (Spring 1983): 275.

94. Stoddard, *It Costs to Be President*, 91.

95. Coolidge, *Autobiography*, 243–44.

96. Ibid., 244, 246; *New York Times*, June 15, 1928, 2, and April 10, 1929, 60; New York *Evening Post* article, April 9, 1929, copy in Clippings File, Hoover Papers; Charles D. Hilles to Cyril Clemens, August 23, 1944, Calvin Coolidge Papers, Miscellaneous Collection, Box 2, folder 10, Forbes Library.

97. Drescher oral history, 4–5; *New York Times*, June 16, 1928, 2.

98. Coolidge, *Autobiography*, 245; Stoddard, *It Costs to Be President*, 91–93; *New York Herald Tribune*, May 18, 1928, 7.

99. "If Coolidge disliked Herbert Hoover, it must be remembered that he disliked many men." McCoy, *Calvin Coolidge*, 391; Hoover, draft letter to William Allen White, January 25, 1938; Hoover, *Memoirs*, 2: 194.

100. Coolidge to Hoover, June 15, 1928, Calvin Coolidge Personal Files, PPF 1360, Forbes Library; Hoover to Coolidge, June 15, 1928, "Coolidge, Calvin," General Correspondence, Campaign and Transition Papers, Hoover Papers; Hoover, *Memoirs*, 2: 196.

101. *New York Times*, July 4, 1928, 2; Coolidge statement to the press, July 3, 1928, Press Conferences of Calvin Coolidge, Forbes Library; Hoover to Coolidge, July 5, 1928, Everett Sanders to Hoover, July 7, 1928, Hoover to Sanders, July 7, 1928, Calvin Coolidge Personal Files, PPF 1360; Sanders to Hoover, July 9, 1928, Coolidge Papers, case file 3.

102. *New York Times*, July 17, 1928, 1, 2; New York *World*, July 17, 1928, 1, 2.

103. Transcript of Coolidge press conference, July 17, 1928, in Press Conferences of Calvin Coolidge, Forbes Library.

104. Hoover to Coolidge, June 30 and July 5, 1928, "Coolidge, Calvin," General Correspondence, Campaign and Transition Papers, Hoover Papers; transcript of Coolidge press conference, July 17, 1928.

105. *New York Times*, August 14, 1928, 24; Coolidge to Hoover, August 14,

1928, "Coolidge, Calvin," General Correspondence, Campaign and Transition Papers, Hoover Papers.

106. Coolidge to Hoover, August 21, 1928, "Coolidge, Calvin," General Correspondence, Campaign and Transition Papers, Hoover Papers; *New York Times*, August 22, 1928, 1, 2.

107. Hoover to Coolidge, August 29, 1928, Calvin Coolidge Personal Files, PPF 1360; *New York Times*, September 14, 1928, 6, September 15, 1928, 4, and November 4, 1928, sec. 1, 1.

108. *New York Times*, September 30, 1928, sec. 1, 1, October 5, 1928, 3, October 6, 1928, 18, October 7, 1928, sec. 3, 1, 2, October 20, 1928, 16, and October 26, 1928, 24.

109. Ibid., November 2, 1928, 2.

110. E. D. Adams, "Notes on Hoover" (November 6 and 7, 1928), E. D. Adams Papers, Box 8, Stanford University Archives.

111. Coolidge to Hoover, November 2, 1928, "Coolidge, Calvin," General Correspondence, Campaign and Transition Papers, Hoover Papers. Printed in *New York Times*, November 3, 1928, 1.

112. Hoover to Coolidge, November 3, 1928, Coolidge Papers, case file 4450; *New York Times*, November 4, 1928, sec. 1, 1, and November 5, 1928, 22.

113. Coolidge to Hoover, November 7, 1928, "Coolidge, Calvin," General Correspondence, Campaign and Transition Papers, Hoover Papers.

114. Castle diary, July 6, 1928; transcript of Coolidge press conference, November 9, 1928, Press Conferences of Calvin Coolidge, Forbes Library; *New York Times*, November 10, 1928, 2; Coolidge to Hoover, November 8 and 9, 1928; Hoover to Coolidge, November 8 and 9, 1928. The Coolidge-Hoover exchanges are in Coolidge Papers, case file 4450. See also Hoover, *Memoirs*, 2: 211.

115. *New York Times*, January 10, 1929, 1, January 22, 1929, 28, February 17, 1929, sec. 3, 1, 2; Everett Sanders memorandum for Mrs. Coolidge, January 15, 1929, Coolidge Papers, case file 4450; Hoover, *Memoirs*, 2: 55.

116. Hoover to Coolidge, January 21, 1929 (plus enclosure), Everett Sanders to Hoover, January 21, 1929, Sanders memorandum, January 21, 1929, Coolidge Papers, case file 4450; *Mirrors of 1932*, 61.

117. Hoover, *Memoirs*, 2: 56; Hoover to William Allen White, January 25, 1938. See also Hoover, *Memoirs*, 3: 16–17.

118. Hoover, *Memoirs*, 3: 11.

119. *New York Times*, March 5, 1929, 5, 6.

120. *Mirrors of 1932*, 59; *New York Times*, March 23, 1929, 1.

121. Richard Norton Smith, "Calvin Coolidge: The Twilight Years," in *The Real Calvin Coolidge*, no. 4 (Plymouth, Vermont, 1986), 26.

122. Calvin Coolidge, "Party Loyalty and the Presidency," *Saturday Evening Post* 204 (October 3, 1931): 3–5, 102. For anti-Hoover maneuverings of certain Coolidge supporters in 1932, see James H. MacLafferty diary, June 9, 1932, MacLafferty Papers, and Edward T. Clark to Coolidge, June 11, 1932, in John L. Blair, ed., "The Clark-Coolidge Correspondence and the Election of 1932," *Vermont History* 34 (April 1966): 86–88.

123. Coolidge to Edward T. Clark, September 21, 1932, in "Clark-Coolidge Correspondence," 99; Calvin Coolidge, "The Republican Case," *Saturday Evening*

Post 205 (September 10, 1932): 3–5, 68–70, 72; Hoover to Coolidge, September 7, 1932, "Coolidge, Calvin," President's Personal File, Hoover Papers.

124. Stoddard, *It Costs to Be President*, 136–39; *New York Times*, October 12, 1932, 1, 16; Hoover to Coolidge, October 12, 1932, "Coolidge, Calvin," President's Personal File, Hoover Papers; Edward T. Clark to Coolidge, October 13, 1932, in "Clark-Coolidge Correspondence," 104. For Coolidge's concern about his inability to make speeches because of his throat, see "Clark-Coolidge Correspondence," 99, 105, 106.

125. Coolidge to Clark, October 26, 1932, in "Clark-Coolidge Correspondence," 106; Fuess, *Calvin Coolidge*, 460: Hoover to Fuess, August 22, 1938, in Fuess, *Calvin Coolidge*, 460–61.

126. Coolidge's speech to the nation on November 7, 1932, in *Campaign Speeches of 1932 by President Hoover [and] Ex-President Coolidge* (Garden City, N.Y., 1933), 262–68.

127. Theodore G. Joslin diary, January 5 and 7, 1933, Hoover Library; Hoover to Mrs. Calvin Coolidge, January 5, 1933, "Coolidge, Calvin," President's Personal File, Hoover Papers; Coolidge interview, December 14, 1932, in Stoddard, *It Costs to Be President*, 145; Hoover to William Allen White, January 25, 1938; Hoover to Arthur McKeogh, November 7, 1934, Herbert Hoover Collection, Box 314, Coolidge folder, Hoover Institution Archives.

128. I am not referring to presidential succession following the death or resignation of the incumbent but to succession by election. In the case of succession as a result of a presidential death, of course, factional troubles can also become acute. The woes of Harry Truman and Lyndon Johnson are notable examples.

7

The American Economy of the Interwar Era

Growth and Transformation from the Great War to the Great Depression

MICHAEL A. BERNSTEIN

> After all, the chief business of the American People is business.
> They are profoundly concerned with producing, buying, selling,
> investing, and prospering in the world.
>
> CALVIN COOLIDGE

> The three great causes most favourable to production are, accu-
> mulation of capital, fertility of soil, and inventions to save labour.
> They all act in the same direction; and as they all tend to facili-
> tate supply, without reference to demand, it is not probable that
> they should either separately or conjointly afford an adequate
> stimulus to the continued increase of wealth, which can only be
> kept up by a continued increase of the demand for commodities.
>
> THE REVEREND T. R. MALTHUS

The economy of interwar America certainly manifested the energies and
instincts of a people "profoundly concerned with producing, buying, selling, investing, and prospering." Yet it also exhibited, in time, a system of
production and distribution that increasingly had difficulty maintaining a
balance between supply and demand—the ultimate consequences of which
were an inability to "afford an adequate stimulus to the continued increase
of wealth" and a decade of unprecedented instability and unemployment.
Even so, during most of the 1920s, Americans would have been hard-
pressed to anticipate the exceptional economic difficulties of the thirties.
The boom years of the twenties, perhaps uniquely epitomized in the opti-

mism and hard-headed realism of the "Coolidge era," encouraged many in
the belief that the future was indeed bright and uncomplicated.

There is perhaps no better place to start than the year 1921—when Babe
Ruth hit fifty home runs while playing major-league baseball in the Bronx.[1]
Like Ruth, and his team the New York Yankees, the national economy was
destined for bigger and better things later in the decade. From 1920 to 1929,
total manufacturing output rose a bit over 50 percent, an aggregate figure
that masked even more rapid rates of growth in major sectors of the economy. Primary manufacturing grew at a rate of 2.5 percent per year; end-
product manufacturing increased 4 percent per year throughout the decade. By 1929, the economy of the United States produced four-tenths of
the world's coal, seven-tenths of the world's petroleum, a third of the
world's hydro-electric power, half the world's steel, and virtually all of the
world's natural gas. In the same year, the nation consumed as much electricity as the rest of the world combined. In 1919, 6.6 million cars and almost 900,000 trucks were registered in the United States; ten years later,
the figures had increased remarkably, to 23 million automobiles and 3.5
million trucks. The impact that this growth of the automotive sector had
on associated industries can be well imagined. That broad-based development was further stimulated by outlays on state and national highway networks that increased surfaced road mileage some nine times, from 350,000
miles in 1919 to 3,272,000 miles in 1929. We might also consider that from
1922 to the time of the stock market crash seven years later, radio sales increased on the order of 1400 percent, again with associated linkages with
other sectors—not the least important of which was advertising, an activity
that in 1927 contributed $3.3 billion to the gross domestic product. This
was also the era in which motion pictures became a multimillion dollar enterprise; in 1929, national income originating in the motion picture industry accounted for $440 million.[2]

Labor productivity in manufacturing rose close to 63 percent during the
1920s, an event that contributed to the spectacular performance of profits
in that sector—that is, roughly a 60 percent improvement over the course
of the decade. Other examples of the unique prosperity of the era were a
doubling of expenditures on public education, an increase of approximately
100,000 hospital beds nationwide, a notable decrease in the rate of morbidity, and impressive improvements in the quantity and quality of the foodstuffs comprising the national diet. The national index of gross output of
livestock and food crops rose almost 20 percent from 1921 to 1929. The
number of persons supplied with food per farm worker rose from an average of 8.3 to 9.8 in the same time period.[3]

These are but a few data that demonstrate, in some respects, that the
twenties were a period in which the American economy showed great health
and maturity. Yet even though the decade witnessed important advances in

industrial output, structure, and technology, as well as significant changes in the composition of national output, it also came to represent a period of widespread hardship in agriculture and of new and precarious developments in America's international trade position.

Of the twenties, one noted historian said that they were years in which "the business man was the dictator of our destinies ousting the statesman, the priest, the philospher, as the creator of standards of ethics and behavior and bec[ame] the final authority on the conduct of American society." And they were the years during which a president (namely, Coolidge) could say: "The man who builds a factory builds a temple, the man who works there worships there." A sign outside a church during this decade said "Come to church. Christian worship increases your efficiency." But it was also an era that ended with a well-known and well-worn joke: "What's that [one would say seeing a line of people on the street] . . . a breadline or a bank?"[4]

Thus, this era was generally a period of confidence and assurance. Yet, there were also some worms in the woodwork. The twenties were hard years for workers and investors in the textiles, shipbuilding, and shoe and leather sectors. The rise of synthetic textiles, such as rayon and nylon, virtually decimated the wool and silk industries, for example. In the 1930 *Census of Manufactures*, certain enterprises, such as blacksmithing, wheelwrighting, coopering, and cabinet-making, had been all but obliterated, replaced by factory-methods or new products. New sectors were included that had never before been listed in previous censuses, such as automobiles, telephones and telegraph, and chemicals.[5]

With electrification progressing every year, industry increasingly dispersed from what previously had been stationary power sources. A new phase of regional development thereby arose with characteristic unevenness and frictional difficulties. Cotton mills, for example, moved south and west as the northern division of the industry went into secular decline. This regional development pattern is documented in table 1. Most striking in that pattern was the Pacific region's good fortune relative to others, along with the West South Central region's impressive growth performance, especially in value-added, changes clearly indicative of the growing importance and impact of petroleum refining in those parts of the country.[6]

Technological unemployment was a major problem in this era, creating pockets of severe hardship in affected sectors. As some major manufacturing sectors became less and less capable of sustaining employment for significant proportions of the national labor force, service industries began to play an increasingly larger role in the provisioning of jobs. The growth of service enterprise, in entertainment, recreation and tourism, education, insurance, health care, and communication was indeed a singularly notable sign of the "mature capitalism" characteristic of the Coolidge era.[7]

Interwar American prosperity was also exemplified by large increases in

TABLE I.
Indexes of Regional Development in 1925 (1914 = 100)

Region	Number of Factories	Number of wage earners	Value-added by industry
New England	101.1	99.2	233.5
Middle Atlantic	99.3	107.2	262.0
East North Central	107.2	141.3	304.1
West North Central	102.8	122.6	244.6
South Atlantic	98.1	121.6	299.7
East South Central	106.1	143.0	252.2
West South Central	111.7	129.8	307.1
Mountain	110.6	127.7	222.4
Pacific	139.1	179.9	344.1

Source: Committee on Recent Economic Changes, *Recent Economic Changes*, 1: 209.

discretionary expenditures on consumption goods. As shown by large increases in consumer debt, it is clear that in the twenties the era of installment buying had arrived.[8] Total consumer debt in 1920 was $3 billion of constant purchasing power; by 1929, that figure had risen to almost $7.2 billion.[9] Home appliance sales, especially of the refrigerator, were a central part of this expansion in consumer obligations—all of which were, in turn, crucially dependent upon the continuing proliferation of a nationwide electrical grid to power these new domestic amenities. Cosmetics and tobacco companies similarly enjoyed year after year of impressive sales growth. The automobile brought with it the demise of the "Mom-and-Pop" grocery store, and its replacement by shopping malls and that distinctively American institution, the supermarket. While the delivery of foodstuffs to the nation may have thus become more and more homogeneous with the growth of large-scale marketing organizations and stores, the compositon of the products made available became increasingly varied. Consider this description of consumptions habits in the twenties: "The diet of today contains an unprecedented proposition of elements appealing to the appetite, the senses of sight, taste, and smell, and other aesthetic desires. It is strikingly diversified in the individual mean, from meal to meal, from day to day, from season to season."[10]

National consumer expenditure patterns had also begun to change before World War I, although the war itself had tended to mask this new trend. With the prosperity of the 1920s, however, this movement became more evident. Consumption data for the 1920s reveal demand patterns of singular importance for our understanding of the interwar American economy. Between 1923 and 1929, for example, the share of consumer spending devoted to clothing fell from 17 percent to 15.1 percent. For housing and utilities, the proportion declined from 20.4 percent to 17.9 percent. The share of payments going to transportation equipment and related services was roughly stable. Increasing percentages of demand expenditures were allocated to food products, tobacco, household appliances and operations, medical care and insurance, recreation, and education.[11]

The share of American income expended on appliances, other household equipment, and household operations rose throughout the interwar years. In 1914, 9.3 percent of real consumption spending was devoted to such categories; by the end of the twenties, the proportion reached 11.9 percent. The trend actually continued into the thirties. Other evidence confirms the impression afforded by the consumption share figures. Eight percent of American families owned washing machines in 1920; by 1930, 24 percent did. Thirty-five percent of American farms had washing machines by 1941, as did 44 percent of the rural nonfarm population. The percentage of families with mechanical refrigeration capacity rose steadily from 1910 to 1940. Nine percent of American homes had vacuum cleaners by 1920; the figure rose to 30 percent by 1930. A quarter of American homes owned radios in 1925. The share rose to 40 percent in 1930. Americans enjoyed new household comforts as increasing numbers of them purchased vacuum cleaners, washing machines, refrigerators, ranges, dishwashers, irons, toasters, coffee makers, radios, and other new products. These changes went hand in hand with the introduction of electricity to American homes. The percentage of households with electricity rose from 35 percent to 68 percent during the twenties.[12]

Finally, during the "New Era" of the twenties, expenditures on personal care, recreation, and amusement rose from 14.3 percent in 1914 to just over 17 percent by the mid-twenties. The evidence indicates that the real expenditure shares rose for several major groups of nondurable and service goods such as personal appearance services, laundries, theatres, and hotels; social and cultural activities such as education, charity payments, and organizational dues; and utility services such as electricity, residential natural gas, and telephones.[13]

It should also be noted that variations in consumer demand during the interwar years were facilitated by changes in the role of women in the national economy and in family life. The entry of women into the American labor force during the interwar years arose, in part, out of a redefinition of an adequate standard of living—to include, for the first time, domestic appliances, automobiles, commercial entertainment, and other services. New expectations regarding appropriate family income levels thus encouraged more women to enter the labor market, a phenomenon that was both a cause and effect of the rising availability and utilization of home appliances.[14]

Mass production and standardized processes were the order of the day during the New Era. The twenties were, in many respects, the decade of

"High Taylorism," and people in the twenties witnessed the beginning of large and routine commitments, by major firms, to industrial research and development. Production, in most major sectors of the economy, came to be divided into four stages: management, design, tool-making, and productive operation. Forward and backward linkages were not lacking to contribute toward the establishment of a virtuous circle of industrial progress. (For example, with the automobile came roads, and with the roads came service stations, diners, hotels, campsites, and other tourist and recreational facilities.)[15] The "machine-age" of the twenties brought a wider distribution of standardized products across the nation, thereby closing the gap between rural and urban (not to mention regional) manners, dialects, styles of dress, and of life. This helped to forge what some have understood to be a cohesive national culture, but others have viewed that process more cynically. "When work was laid aside for amusement," wrote Charles and Mary Beard, "the masses listened to manufactured music, watched moving pictures portray with endless reiteration identical plots and farcical acts. . . . When they gratified their thirst for the open country, they did so in standardized automobiles wheeling along standardized highways, past standardized signboards and standardized soft-drink huts, to conventional places of entertainment packed with masses of their kind." To be sure, the overwhelming majority of Americans experienced dramatic improvements in the quality and quantity of the goods and services that framed the material side of their lives. As for the impact these positive changes in material welfare may have had on cultural diversity and variety, the tools of economic analysis are ill-suited to the task of rendering an unambiguous assessment.[16]

    The era of standardized production also brought with it a New Era that focused on corporations and significant changes in industrial structure. Corporations steadily expanded their role in the manufacturing sector, as table 2 shows, most notably increasing their share of the actual number of operating establishments from a bit less than one-third to close to one-half within ten years. There was a discernible wave of mergers, as table 3 documents, the bulk of which were of the horizontal variety. Many mergers in the 1920s appear to have been oriented toward achieving national scale in advertising and product distribution; no particular sector or group of sectors seems to have been predominantly affected.[17]

    Although there are no reliable concentration-ratio data for the period, some investigators have inferred a decrease in the economy's competitiveness over the course of the twenties. Generally speaking, there were (in the manufacturing sector) large increases in the number of workers per establishment, especially in aircraft, automobiles, and asbestos products; in the amount of horsepower employed in each plant; and in the value of output per establishment—all signs of potential capital concentration and rising barriers to entry in the affected industries.[18] Wages, as a percentage of

TABLE 2.
Corporate Share in Manufacturing

	1919	*1929*
Number of Establishments		
Total (1000s)	290.1	211.0
Owned by corporations (1000s)	91.5	101.8
Corporate percentage share	31.5	48.3
Number of Wage-Earners		
Total (1000s)	9096.4	8838.7
In corporations (1000s)	7875.1	7945.5
Corporate percentage share	86.6	89.9
Value of Output		
Total ($ millions)	62,418.0	70,435.0
Owned by corporations ($ millions)	54,745.0	64,901.0
Corporate percentage share	87.7	92.2

Source: U.S. Department of Commerce, *Fifteenth Census of the United States* [*Census of Manufactures: 1929*] (Washington, D.C.: U.S. Government Printing Office, 1933), 1 ("General Report"): 95.

TABLE 3.
Percentage-Distribution of Mergers by Type, 1926–1930

Horizontal	75.9
Vertical	4.8
Conglomerate	19.3

Source: Committee on Recent Economic Changes, *Recent Economic Changes*, 1: 84 and Staff Report of the F.T.C., *Economic Report on Corporate Mergers*.

value-added in manufacturing, followed a falling trend in this period, as table 4 shows. The concomitant rise in the profit share also implies a diminution of competitive structure. Finally, table 5 documents the boom in issues of new equity—the well-known symptom of the age. The stock market boom faltered, as one can see, in the recessions of 1921 and 1926. But these fluctuations did not fully obstruct the secular advance, nor did they prevent the unprecedented acceleration of 1927 to 1929.

The stock market boom was massive, exhilarating, and (in far too many cases) foolish. Margin-buying was the rule not the exception; in these days prior to the establishment of a Securities and Exchange Commission, brokers often allowed as much as 80 percent of the value of a stock purchase to be borrowed. That such margins were frequently extended in the absence of any formal check on the credit-worthiness of the customer involved,

TABLE 4.
Share of Wages as Percentage
of Value-Added in Manufacturing

1919	42.1
1921	45.0
1923	43.0
1925	40.4
1927	39.9
1929	36.9
1931	36.9

Source: U.S. Department of Commerce, *Sixteenth Census of the United States [Census of Manufactures: 1939]* (Washington, D.C.: U.S. Government Printing Office, 1940), 2, part 1 ("Reports by Industries"): 20.

TABLE 5.
Corporate Equity Issues

1919	1436
1920	1002
1921	265
1922	570
1923	659
1924	829
1925	1153
1926	1087
1927	1474
1928	2961
1929	5924
1930	1503

Source: U.S. Department of Commerce, *Census of Manufactures*, selected years.

only increased the enormous danger of the practice as a whole. So confident were brokers and the public of the market's rise that transactions took on the character of a drunken flush. Banks and corporations were not immune from the passions (and stupidity) of the day; they too placed reserve funds on call in the market. Following the stock market collapse in October of 1929, brokers called in their margin accounts, and many banks found themselves pushed into bankruptcy, forced to close their doors to depositors as liquid assets dwindled. Individual bank failures then generated runs on other banks, as depositors more generally became nervous about the security of their accounts. When the day of reckoning came, both large firms and old pensioners would feel the pain.

Interestingly enough, in 1925 a boom began in real estate in south Florida that seemed to foretell in miniature the fortunes of Wall Street a few years later. A speculative fever broke out in the buying of properties on Florida's southeastern "Gold Coast," only to be blown apart shortly thereafter as investors became hesitant about their commitments. The results were for many catastrophic. To be sure, the stock market definitely played a role in the debacle of the 1930s but, as one noted economic historian of the interwar era put it, "The stock market crash in the autumn of 1929 precipitated the depression about in the sense that one more [person] climbing onto a crowded raft sinks it, but the weight of previous comers must not be forgotten."[19]

American agriculture had seen better years than the twenties. The recovery of European competitors after the Great War had removed the basis for the affluent prices of American crops (especially corn, cotton, and wheat) that had prevailed during the hostilities. What's more, an understandable apprehension of future struggles in Europe prompted some continental governments to pursue autarky with respect to agricultural products. This simply furthered the erosion of the American farmer's market. Nine years of protectionist trade policy in Washington did not help matters. Three successive rises in duties were legislated during the 1920s, culminating in the ill-conceived Hawley-Smoot Tariff Act of 1930.[20] The foreign retaliation that these measures inevitably encouraged further depressed agriculture's prospects. These challenges to the fortunes of American cultivation were uniquely related, in large measure, to the postwar political and economic landscape. Other factors were, however, linked with supply considerations.

The stimulation of the World War I years had hastened not only the absolute expansion of cultivation in the United States, but also the more rapid introduction of mechanized techniques that served to improve per-acre yields. Moreover, the substitution of internal combustion engines for draft animals released close to 25 percent of the total national acreage in crops to the production of human foodstuffs rather than animal-fodder—this, in addition to the deterioration in the demand for animal feeds that the increasing use of farm tractors exacerbated.[21]

Wartime had also brought, through its impact on the markets for agricultural output throughout Europe, hasty decision-making, resulting in soil exhaustion and erosion. In large measure, the blame for poor land management can indeed be laid entirely at the farmers' feet, for the fertilizer industry had performed fairly well (despite the war's impact on the ocean transport of necessary nitrates and guano). Capital invested in fertilizer manufacturing rose almost 8 percent between 1919 and 1929, and total expenditures for fertilizer and lime increased from $165 million in 1915 to $300 million fourteen years later.[22] Even so, the full emergence of scientific agriculture and agronomy lay yet in the future.

Finally, as if these woes were not enough, rising trends in the prices of transportation services and in the increasing wages of farm hands worked to the farmer's detriment.[23] On the basis of all this, we might expect table 6 to tell an even *more* distressing story than it does; even so, the numbers are not reassuring. As the time-series on the ratio of prices received by farmers for their products to the prices they paid for production inputs and consumption needs shows, the twenties did not bring the prosperity and growth-mania to the heartland that they bestowed upon the cities and industrial towns. A 1925 survey of the nation's agricultural households shows that only 10 percent of these homes had running water (although, remarkably, some 75 percent of them had natural gas or electricity, while 38 percent had telephone service).[24]

Interwar discontent on American farms, although not as passionate or sustained as at the end of the nineteenth century, expressed itself often

TABLE 6.
Indexes of Farm Prices (1910–1914 = 100)

	Prices received	Prices paid	Received/paid
1919	209	205	102
1920	205	206	99
1921	116	156	75
1922	124	152	81
1923	135	153	88
1924	134	154	87
1925	147	159	92
1926	136	156	87
1927	131	154	85

Source: Committee on Recent Economic Changes, *Recent Economic Changes*, 2: 600–1.

pragmatically in movements to establish more cooperatives (which had been exempted from the antitrust laws) that could control the timing of crop movement to market, grade and standardize output, bargain over received prices and assessed costs, and (in some cases) jointly advertise. The success of these amalgamations was, however, spotty. Yet, they may have influenced Congress in 1927 when, in a bold display of economic nationalism, it passed the McNary-Haugen Act (after two Coolidge vetoes) to provide for the overt dumping of America's agricultural surpluses abroad.[25]

Labor's fortunes got off to a shaky start after World War I. Aside from the falling-off in military production, shifting strength in worldwide markets and technical advances, most notably in tool and machine production, contributed to layoffs.[26] The end of the war in 1918 initiated a massive strike wave, peaking in the 1919 steel strike in which 365,000 workers struck for union recognition followed by the walkout of nearly 400,000 coal miners. The strikes, however, did not go well for workers. Corporate managers broke the steel strike, and the industry remained unorganized until the late 1930s. The United Mine Workers survived but were forced to accept contract terms that severely weakened the union. In general, organized labor was in retreat during the decade. The decade saw the nation's first consciously restrictive immigration policies (save for the Chinese Exclusion Act of the preceding century) put into effect in 1921 and 1924.[27] Although the driving force behind immigration restriction lay elsewhere, most labor unions lobbied for these acts both ethnophobically and with the more mundane motive of restricting the labor supply and thus bolstering pay rates.

As the decade passed, the opportunities for workers, although not for unions, improved after the instability and difficulty of the early years. In 1914, the average annual wage for a laborer (in 1929 dollars) was $613. By

1928, wages had more than doubled. Table 7 shows a little weakness in average weekly earnings for some selected industries after the downturn of
1921, but no serious deterioration thereafter. From 1921 to 1929, the price
level fell by a total of 4 percent; the real wage rose at an impressive annual
rate of 2.1 percent.[28] No doubt all this had something to do with the relative calm in industrial relations that prevailed during the last half of the
decade. Table 8 offers some evidence in this regard.

We have only a few reliable data on unemployment rates for the 1920s.
Although annual earnings showed improvement through the decade, recall
table 4 concerning labor's share in manufacturing value-added. Those
statistics have an ominous quality about them. Although the doctrine of
high wages had gained widespread acceptance after its most publicized introduction by Henry Ford in the automobile industry, changes in income

TABLE 7.
Average Full-Time Weekly Earnings
(Selected Industries) (in 1929 $s)

1919	28.78
1920	32.57
1921	27.62
1922	26.04
1923	27.58
1924	27.51
1925	27.45
1926	27.03
1927	27.09

Source: Committee on Recent Economic
Changes, Recent Economic Changes, 2: 433.

TABLE 8.
Indexes of Industrial Disputes (1916 = 100)

	Industrial disputes	Employees involved
1919	96	260
1920	90	91
1921	63	69
1922	29	101
1923	41	47
1924	33	41
1925	34	27
1926	27	21
1927	19	22

Source: Committee on Recent Economic Changes,
Recent Economic Changes, 2: 491.

distribution, and in the competitive structure of American industry, do give reasons for pessimism regarding the longer run vitality of the interwar economy. In 1920, the top 5 percent of recipients in the United States received a bit over 25 percent of income; by the end of the decade, their share had risen to 32 percent. From 1923 to 1929, per capita disposable income for the lower 93 percent of the non-farm population fell by 4 percent; the top 1 percent of the income distribution enhanced their share by 63 percent. Ironically, and prophetically, the special presidential Committee on Recent Economic Changes, chaired by then Commerce Secretary Herbert Hoover, would write but months before the 1929 stock market crash that "[u]ntil comparatively recent times, the problem of industry was to produce a sufficient quantity to supply the demand. Today the problem of industry is largely that of disposing of its products."[29]

The decade of the twenties witnessed progressive advances in social legislation on behalf of working people. The 1920 Industrial Rehabilitation Act provided aid for the victims of industrial accidents, and the 1921 Sheppard-Towner Act appropriated $1.5 million for public hygiene and health instruction in the states. Congressional acts of 1924 brought new controls to bear upon the practice of child labor. The goal of the eight-hour day was fast becoming a reality as well.

On the international scene, the United States became a creditor nation for the first time—thanks to the Great War. As Broadus Mitchell noted, the "United States entered the war a net debtor to foreign countries to the extent of $3 billion, and emerged a net creditor, *exclusive of Allied debts*, to the extent of $6 billion."[30] This fact, along with "the economic consequences of the peace,"[31] prevented the United States from pursuing economic, if not political, isolation. World finances were significantly destabilized by the provisions of the Versailles Treaty. The principal irritant consisted of a dangerous circle of obligations and risks in which (as epitomized in the Dawes Plan of 1924) the United States lent funds to Great Britain, France, and Germany, while German reparations were needed to allow the Allies to liquidate their American debts. By 1928, American banks were already quite wary of the situation. Yet their predictable and understandable response, cutting back on loans to European governments, merely made the situation worse. In addition, the protectionist policies of the period not only weakened many foreign economies, insofar as their borrowing could not be made good by their exports, but they also hurt U.S. domestic markets by lowering the demand for the nation's exports.[32] Even so, as table 9 shows, U.S. involvement in direct foreign commitments rose sharply during the twenties. Needless to say, a rather straightforward analysis would link these data with Washington's increasing obstreperousness abroad—in the interwar diplomatic and legal battles with Mexico over her land reform policies that culminated in the one-sided Treaty of Bucareli in

TABLE 9.
United States Direct Investment Abroad (in billions of constant $s)

1914	5.0
1919	9.7
1924	15.1
1927	17.9
1929	21.5

Source: *Historical Statistics of the United States*, part 2, series U26, 869.

1923, in the State Department's insistence that the Five-Power Treaty of 1922 (signed by Britain, France, Italy, Japan, and the United States) include a reaffirmation of the "Open Door" policy in China, and in the renewed intervention of U.S. Marines in Nicaragua in 1926.

The paradoxes of American trade policy during the twenties were profound. For the U.S. economy to continue to supply increasing amounts of farm and manufacturing output to world markets, further credits had to be extended to foreign economies in order to sustain the growth of demand. At the same time, foreign governments, in receipt of American loans, faced increasing debt-maintenance and principal-installment payments for those obligations. Their incentive was thus to foster higher rates of exports to the United States, in the absence of which they would have had seriously to consider the outright repudiation of their notes.

In the face of these strained circumstances, the American government found itself in a quandary regarding trade policy. On the one side, bankers were eager to see Washington sustain a free trade agenda so that their international loans would be made good by the improved export performance of their foreign debtors. On the other, manufacturers believed themselves to be the major losers in any policy setting that weakened their protection with respect to imports from overseas. Meanwhile, American farmers felt altogether left out of the bargain insofar as trade protection invited foreign retaliation against their exports while a free trade policy invited potentially ruinous competition from resurgent primary-product competitors elsewhere in the global economy. This turmoil in the political economy of national trade policy during the twenties was never resolved.[33]

The robust achievements of the American economy of the 1920s have traditionally and understandably been overshadowed by the dramatic collapse of 1929 and the severe depression that followed. It is not, therefore, surprising that a significant portion of the extant scholarship on the causes of the Great Depression have focused on developments in the twenties for explanations. The economy of the interwar era was indeed Janus-faced. On the one side, high rates of growth and remarkable technological and institutional advancements were the very core of what is known, in collective memory, as the "roaring twenties." On the other, certain deep-seated weaknesses and tendencies set the stage for the worst economic crisis in the nation's history.

In some respects, many scholars have viewed the collapse of the thirties as an outcome implicit in the boom of the twenties. The unbridled expansion of values in financial markets, it was claimed, necessitated an ultimate reckoning by means of a general sell-off. A more comprehensive formulation of this argument directly confronted the question of why financial markets collapsed when they did. Looking to the political and institutional distortions created by the Treaty of Versailles, some writers argued that the depression was an inevitable consequence. The demise of the gold standard in international trade, and the ensuing demands by France and the United States that Germany make her war reparations payments in gold rather than goods and services, created a net gold flow into the United States that led to an explosion of credit. Extremely unstable financial arrangements emerged thereby in the twenties, especially in mortgage markets. Because many banks in the relatively unregulated environment in which they operated at the time were committed to questionable loan contracts, when the adjustment of the stock market occurred with a general collapse in values, an implosion of the banking system was quick to follow.[34]

Some scholars have rejected the excessive credit and speculation argument on the grounds that it abstracted too boldly from real events in the interwar economy. Indeed, business cycle indicators turned down before the stock market crashed; a softness in construction activity was apparent in 1928, and indices of industrial production started to fall by the summer of 1929. Such critics as John Kenneth Galbraith held that "cause and effect run from the economy to the stock market, never the reverse. Had the economy been fundamentally sound in 1929 the effect of the great stock market crash might have been small [and] the shock to confidence and the loss of spending by those who were caught in the market might soon have worn off."[35]

The literature that focused on long-run factors in the American depression was distinctive in holding that the New York Stock Market crash of 1929 was less important than certain developments in the economy that had deleterious impacts throughout the interwar period. Some authors have argued that, during the twenties, the distribution of national income became increasingly skewed, lowering the economy's aggregate average propensity to consume. Others have focused on a secular shift in the terms of trade between primary products and manufactured goods, due to the uneven development of the agricultural and industrial nations. This change in the terms of trade, they argued, created a credit crisis in world markets when bad crop yields occurred in 1929 and 1930. At the same time that agricultural economies were losing revenue because of poor crops and declining world demand, the developed economies were contracting credit for the developing nations and imposing massive trade restrictions such as the Hawley-Smoot excise. As the agricultural nations went into a slump, the industrialized countries (most notably the United States) lost a major market for their output. Hence, the downturn of 1929 became more and more severe.[36] Industrial organization economists have sought an explanation of the depression in the increasing extent of imperfect competition in the American economy of the early twentieth century.[37] Downward inflexibility of prices after the crash of 1929, caused by the concentrated structure of American industry and the impact of labor unions, intensified the effective demand problem and prevented the price system from reaching a new equilibrium at full employment. "Sticky prices" further limited the already constrained purchasing power of consumers, and to the extent that noncompetitive pricing predominated in the capital goods sector, producers were less willing to buy new plants and equipment. Excessive real wages, held up by union pressure and New Deal policy, further contributed to persistent disequilibrium in labor markets. Price and wage inflexibility thus inhibited the recovery of both final product demand and investment demand.[38]

There were several weaknesses in all these theories. Those authors who focused on an increasingly unequal distribution of income or on administered pricing did not marshal unambiguous evidence to make their case, nor did they specify precisely how such factors came to life in the interwar economy. While some investigators claimed to have demonstrated a relative price inflexibility in concentrated economic sectors during the 1930s, their critics were unconvinced. Insofar as the aggregate price level fell by one-third in the early thirties, they argued, how inflexible could the general price system have been? The sticky prices thesis also relied on an assumption of perfect competition in all markets other than those where the imperfections existed. If this assumption were relaxed, the thesis did not hold. As Michal Kalecki pointed out, if "sticky wages" were responsible for the length of the depression, it followed that a reduction in wages would have eliminated the persistent disequilibrium. If, however, there were imperfections in product markets as well, a reduction in nominal wages would have lowered real wages, thereby exacerbating the effective demand crisis. Only if price adjustments were general and followed very quickly by increased investment would the sticky prices thesis concerning the thirties hold.[39]

The terms of trade argument similarly had a major flaw. The major weaknesses in the American economy of the interwar period were domestic, and the collapse of demand on the part of primary product exporting nations was not highly relevant. America's dependence on foreign markets was not significant in the interwar years. During the 1920s, exports as a share of the nation's gross national product had annually averaged only a bit over 5 percent. A fall in export demand then could not have played a major role in worsening or prolonging the Great Depression.[40]

Continued research on secular mechanisms in the interwar American economy necessarily relied upon work on cyclical processes in modern economies. A leading investigator held that three major cycles of economic activity in the United States (and Europe) coincidentally reached their nadir in the time between the world wars.[41] These cycles were (1) the Kondratieff, a wave of fifty or more years associated with the introduction and dispersion of major inventions, (2) the Juglar, a wave of approximately ten years' duration that appeared to be linked with population movements, and (3) the Kitchin, a wave of about forty months' length that had the appearance of a typical inventory cycle.

These efforts were paralleled by those of other eminent researchers. One in particular, a future Nobel Laureate, was successful in documenting the existence of waves of some fifteen to twenty years in length. These periodic swings demonstrated that in the United States and other industrialized countries "development during the nineteenth and early twentieth centuries took the form of a series of surges in the growth of output and in capital and labor resources followed by periods of retarded growth." Significantly, "each period of retardation in the rate of growth of output . . . culminated in a protracted depression or in a period of stagnation in which business cycle recoveries were disappointing, failing to lift the economy to a condition of full employment or doing so only transiently."[42]

Most, if not all, of this particular literature was concerned with the explicit dating of the long swings that appeared in the data. It seemed clear that these swings involved changes in resource endowments (including the size of population) and alterations in the intensity of resource utilization.[43] The specific behavioral mechanisms that could account for such phenomena (and their precise manifestation in the United States in the 1930s) were necessarily the focus of continued debate. It is in this context that one can understand the large literature on "secular stagnation" that ultimately emerged in many scholarly assessments of the Great Depression itself.

Broadly speaking, the so-called stagnation theorists of this century grouped into those who evinced a "Schumpeterian pessimism" about the declining incidence of innovations and new technologies and those who shared a "Keynes-Hansen pessimism" concerning the shrinkage of investment outlets owing to a decline in the rate of population growth.[44] Both groups agreed that stagnation or, as it was sometimes called, economic maturity involved a "decrease of the rate of growth of heavy industries and of building activity . . . [and] the slowing down of the rate of growth of the total quantity of production, of employment, and usually of population. It [also involved] the rising relative importance of consumer goods." They also believed that "the appearance of industrial maturity raise[d] profound questions concerning the ability of an enterprise system to produce a progressive evolution of the economy."[45]

The "Keynes-Hansen" pessimism held that as population growth fell off, and as major markets in housing, clothing, food, and services consequently contracted, outlets for new investment were quickly limited to those created by the introduction of new technology or new products. To the extent that recovery from a depression required investment outlays above and beyond the level of depreciation allowances, an upturn would be dependent on the availability, in an adequate volume, of opportunities in new industries and processes. If these were not forthcoming, as some stagnation theorists believed was true of the 1930s, the only avenue out of the slump would be deficit spending to augment consumer purchasing power.[46]

There was a serious inadequacy in the arguments concerning economic maturity and population. The theory conflated population with effective demand. As one critic put it: "It is sometimes maintained that the increase in population encourages investment because the entrepreneurs anticipate a broadening market. What is important, however, . . . is not the increase in population but in purchasing power. The increase in the number of paupers does not broaden the market. For instance, increased population does not mean necessarily a higher demand for houses: without an increase in the purchasing power the result may well be crowding of more people into the existing dwelling space."[47] A more systematic theory had to argue that, for secular reasons, the purchasing power of the population, rather than the size of the population itself, fell in advanced capitalist systems. It was also true that most of the secular stagnation literature did not address the impact of demographic changes on the population's age structure and thereby on the composition of final demand. For instance, one could argue that as the rate of population growth (and immigration) fell in the 1920s, the resulting increase in the age structure raised the economy's marginal propensity to save, thus slowing the growth rate of consumption. Moreover, an older population would most likely have slowed the expansion of such important industries as automobiles and residential construction.[48]

Much like the population theory, the variant of the stagnation theory that focused on the decline of innovation and technical change as factors in the distress of the thirties embodied many inconsistencies and questionable assertions. The lower rate of technical change and the decline in the number of major innovations, which were posited as primary causes of the inability of the economy to recover in the course of the Great Depression, were deemed to be exogenous factors resulting from the state of technical knowledge at the time.[49] Little justification of this position was offered. Furthermore, meager attention was given to a seeming contradiction in the argument. If during the thirties little technical change took place, why did not the eventual reduction in the amount of capital equipment available (owing to firm exits and the periodic obsolescence of plants) result in a revival of capital goods output?[50]

There was one further objection to the technology argument that was apparent to some of the stagnation theorists themselves. There was an implicit assumption made that new innovations were always of the capital-using type; thus, had innovation occurred in the thirties, net investment demand would have absorbed large capital outlays thereby generating a robust upturn. But if innovations were capital saving, this argument foundered. Heavy investment in earlier stages of economic growth (in, for example, railroads, motor cars, and housing) may have given way (in later periods) to newer forms of investment in managerial technique and information processing. These latter innovations may not have absorbed very large amounts of investment expenditure at all. While they may have therefore improved the organization and efficiency of production, their impact on aggregate spending would not have been adequate to the task of systematic stabilization.[51]

Josef Steindl, a relatively unknown European economist, provided the most sophisticated version of the economy maturity idea—and, in doing so, he provided insight into the workings of the American economy throughout the interwar period as a whole. Not surprisingly, he did so in part by explicitly situating the Great Depression in the United States within a long-term development framework. His work linked economic stagnation directly with the behavior of capitalist enterprise, thereby avoiding the mechanistic qualities of many of the stagnation arguments as well as their frequent appeals to exogenous factors. His version of the maturity thesis was that long-run tendencies toward capital concentration, inherent in capitalist development over time, led to a lethargic attitude towards competition and investment. Specifically, the emergence of concentrated markets made difficult, and in some cases impossible, that expulsion of excess capacity required for revival.[52]

What is central to the stagnation thesis (in all its forms), and what endows it with much of its appeal, is the conception of long-term alterations in industrial structure that make the economy as a whole more incapable both of recovering from cyclical instability and of generating continued growth. The emergence of oligopolistic market structure is taken to be inherent in the process of capitalist development insofar as that process is coterminous with the development of large-scale manufacturing techniques. Economic maturity and the threat of stagnation result because the growing incidence of "[o]ligopoly brings about a maldistribution of funds by shifting profits to those industries which are reluctant to use them."[53] In order to escape stagnation, capital must be redistributed either to more competitive sectors or new industries, although such shifts can only proceed (given the difficulties of obtaining technical knowledge and goodwill in new product lines) with time lags.

The weaknesses in the stagnation theory literature do not, of course, ob-

scure the importance of its contribution to an understanding of the interwar American economy. That importance derives from the fact that it attempts to situate the interwar decades within a larger historical framework.
In this context, the Great Depression may be viewed as the outcome of
an interaction between cyclical forces dating from 1929, and tendencies of
long-run development spanning a half century or more.

Precisely because it stands on the threshold of the Great Depression,
and thereby of the war years and the dramatic prosperity of the 1950s, the
American economy of the 1920s remains of great interest to historians and
economists. While scholarly agreement on the causes and consequences of
the economic volatility of the era will no doubt remain elusive, there is
clearly unanimity of opinion regarding the significance and curiosity of the
epoch.

In 1927, as the economy embarked on the final phase of one of the most
fantastic booms in its history, the New York Yankees fielded a team that
similarly achieved enormous success. Known to their opponents as "Mur-
derers' Row," they won 110 games in a 154-game season. Lou Gehrig batted .373 and drove in 175 runs. Babe Ruth accomplished his destiny hitting
60 home runs while batting .356. Two other teammates hit over .300 and
compiled over 100 runs-batted-in apiece. The team had one 22-game winner on its pitching staff, two 19-game winners, and one 18-game winner.
No one fielded less than .936, and Gehrig himself converted a record 1,662
chances while averaging an astounding 11 chances per game. At the World
Series that concluded the season, the Yankees swept the Pittsburgh Pirates
in four games.[54] These numbers seem fantastic, as well they might. A similar wonderment greets the economic historian who examines the 1920s.

After 1927, the fortunes of both the New York Yankees and of the
American economy took many turns. The nostalgia for the twenties, however, continually increased. As for Yankee fans, so for all who struggled
through the years that followed, the "good-old days" would be fondly remembered and sorely missed. One could, to be sure, look forward to future
pennants and World Series. Yet never again would the horizon seem so
endless, the order of things so secure, nor the confidence of the adoring
multitudes so justified.

NOTES

I am most grateful for comments on earlier versions of this essay from Richard
Challener, Michael Edelstein, Steven Hahn, Carol Heim, William Parker, Michael
Parrish, Peter Temin, and David Weiman; for the exemplary research assistance of
Abraham Shragge II; and for funding support provided by the Committee on Re-
search of the Academic Senate of the University of California, San Diego.

1. J. L. Reichler, ed., *The Baseball Encyclopedia*, 5th ed., (New York: Macmillan, 1982), 1302.

2. U.S. Department of Commerce, *Historical Statistics of the United States: Colonial Times to 1970* (Washington, D.C.: United States Government Printing Office, 1975), part 2, series P13–14, p. 667, part 2, series Q56 and Q148–150–162, pp. 716 and 110, part 2, series T444 and T8, pp. 856 and 839; Committee on Recent Economic Changes of the President's Conference on Unemployment, *Recent Economic Changes* (New York: McGraw-Hill, 1929), 1: xi, 79; Robert S. McElvaine, *The Great Depression: America, 1919–1941* (New York: Times Books, 1984), 17.

3. *Historical Statistics of the United States*, part 2, series W30, p. 950, part 1, series H486, p. 373 and series B332, p. 78, part 1, series B149, p. 58, part 1, series K414–429, p. 499, and series K407, p. 498; George Soule, *The Prosperity Decade: From War to Depression, 1917–1929* (New York: Holt, Rinehart and Winston, 1962), 321. Statistics on mortality rates were not compiled systematically until 1933. The death rate for tuberculosis is taken here as a proxy for morbidity rates.

4. Charles A. Beard and Mary R. Beard, *The Rise of American Civilization* (New York: Macmillan, 1961 [1921]), 2: 700; and McElvaine, *The Great Depression*, 16.

5. Some 75,000 jobs in cotton textiles alone were lost between 1920 and 1930. There was also an 80 percent drop in employment in shipbuilding and ship repair—accounting for a total of 94,000 positions liquidated. In the shoe and leather sectors, declines in employment ranged from a loss of 5.3 percent in the footwear trades to almost 63 percent in leather products as a whole. *Historical Statistics of the United States*, part 1, series D233–682, pp. 143–45, series D175, p. 139, series D651–657, p. 145, and series D508 and 624, pp. 143 and 145; Committee on Recent Economic Changes, *Recent Economic Changes*, 163–65.

6. See *Historical Statistics of the United States*, part 1, series D233–682, pp. 144–45, and series M54–67, p. 586.

7. On technological unemployment calculations, see *Historical Statistics of the United States*, part 1, series 85–86, p. 135, and Committee on Recent Economic Changes, *Recent Economic Changes*, 2: 469, 1: 92, and 2: 328. Also see Soule, *The Prosperity Decade*, 215–17; David Weintraub, "Unemployment and Increasing Productivity," in National Resources Committee, *Technological Trends and National Policy* (Washington, D.C.: National Resources Committee, 1937), 83; National Industrial Conference Board, *Management Almanac* (1945), 18–27; and U.S. Bureau of Labor Statistics, *Technical Memorandum No. 16* (July 13, 1944), and *Technical Memorandum No. 20* (July 4, 1945).

8. See Martha L. Olney, *Buy Now, Pay Later: Advertising, Credit, and Consumer Durables in the 1920s* (Chapel Hill: University of North Carolina Press, 1991).

9. See *Historical Statistics of the United States*, part 2, series X409, p. 989.

10. Committee on Recent Economic Changes, *Recent Economic Changes*, 1: 77.

11. See J. Frederic Dewhurst and Associates, *America's Needs and Resources* (New York: The Twentieth Century Fund, 1947), 80–82; and William H. Lough, *High-Level Consumption* (New York: McGraw-Hill, 1935), appendix A. Also see *Historical Statistics of the United States*, part 1, series G470–494, p. 320, as well as my *The Great Depression: Delayed Recovery and Economic Change in America, 1929–1939* (New York: Cambridge University Press, 1987), 173–74.

12. See Stanley Lebergott, *The American Economy* (Princeton: Princeton University Press, 1976), 272–88, 355.

13. See Lough, *High-Level Consumption*, 43.

14. Winifred D. Wandersee, *Women's Work and Family Values, 1920–1940* (Cambridge: Harvard University Press, 1981), chap. 2.

15. On Taylorism see Daniel Nelson, *Frederick W. Taylor and the Rise of Scientific Management* (Madison: University of Wisconsin Press, 1980); David Noble, *America by Design: Technology and the Rise of Corporate Capitalism* (New York: Knopf, 1977); and, of course, Frederick W. Taylor, *The Principles of Scientific Management* (New York: Harper and Brothers, 1911), as well as his *Scientific Management* (New York: Harper and Brothers, 1947).

16. *The Rise of American Civilization*, 760; also see 745–63.

17. See Committee on Recent Economic Changes, *Recent Economic Changes*, 1: 217; and Soule, *The Prosperity Decade*, 148–49.

18. *Historical Statistics of the United States*, part 2, series Q565 and 573, p. 768, series P68–69 and 73, p. 681, and series P1 and 10, p. 666, as well as part 1, series D505 and 623, 143–45.

19. The quote is Broadus Mitchell's, *Depression Decade: From New Era Through New Deal* (New York: Holt, Rinehart and Winston, 1961), 59. Also, on the stock market crash, see for example Soule, *The Prosperity Decade*, 290–314; Charles A. Beard and Mary R. Beard, *The Rise of American Civilization*, 729–31; Milton Friedman and Anna J. Schwartz, *A Monetary History of the United States, 1867–1960* (Princeton: Princeton University Press, 1963); Robert Sobel, *Panic on Wall Street: A History of America's Financial Disasters* (New York: Macmillan, 1968); and his *The Great Bull Market: Wall Street in the 1920s* (New York: Norton, 1968).

20. On tariff policies see Albert U. Romasco, *The Poverty of Abundance: Hoover, the Nation, the Depression* (New York: Oxford University Press, 1965), and Elliot A. Rosen, *Hoover, Roosevelt and the Brains Trust: From Depression to New Deal* (New York: Columbia University Press, 1977).

21. *Historical Statistics of the United States*, part 1, series J52–55, p. 433, series K392 and 396, p. 497, series K407–410–412, p. 498, series K502–550, pp. 511–17, and series K415–416 and K420–421, p. 499. Also see William Parker's chapter on "Agriculture," in Lance E. Davis et al., *American Economic Growth: An Economist's History of the United States* (New York: Harper and Row, 1972), 369–417.

22. *Historical Statistics of the United States*, part 1, series K192–194, p. 469, and part 2, series P155, p. 685.

23. Committee on Recent Economic Changes, *Recent Economic Changes*, 1: 278, and *Historical Statistics of the United States*, part 1, series K176–177 and K182, p. 468. Also Soule, *The Prosperity Decade*, 229; Mitchell, *Depression Decade*, 183; and Secretary of Agriculture, U.S. Department of Agriculture, *Yearbook of Agriculture, 1928* (Annual Report for the Year 1928) (Washington, D.C.: United States Government Printing Office, 1928), 250. On credit problems that faced American farmers in the 1920s, see Lee J. Alston, "Farm Foreclosures in the United States During the Interwar Period," *Journal of Economic History* 43 (December 1983): 885–903. On the relative weakness of the banking sector in rural areas, see David C. Wheelock, "Regulation and Bank Failures: New Evidence from the Agricultural Collapse of the 1920s," *Journal of Economic History* 52 (December 1992): 806–25.

24. See Soule, *The Prosperity Decade*, 250; as well as U.S. Department of Agriculture, *Yearbook of Agriculture, 1928*, 45.

25. On "McNary-Haugenism," see Soule, *The Prosperity Decade*, 246–47; Mitchell, *Depression Decade*, 184–85; McElvaine, *The Great Depression*, 148; and William A. Williams, *The Tragedy of American Diplomacy* (New York: Norton, 1988), 110–12.

26. Soule, *The Prosperity Decade*, 81–85; *Historical Statistics of the United States*, part 2, series Y457–463, p. 1114; and E. J. Hovenstine, Jr., "Lessons of World War I," *American Academy of Political and Social Science Annals* 238 (March 1945), 180–87.

27. These new laws were the Quota Act of 1921 and the Immigration Act of 1924. See Committee on Recent Economic Changes, *Recent Economic Changes*, 2: 426–28.

28. See *Historical Statistics of the United States*, part 1, series D723–727, p. 164.

29. The quotation is taken from Committee on Recent Economic Changes, *Recent Economic Changes*, 1: 81. The income distribution data are taken from Simon Kuznets, *Shares of Upper Income Groups in Income and Savings* (New York: National Bureau of Economic Research, 1953), 637; Jeffrey G. Williamson and Peter H. Lindert, *American Inequality: A Macroeconomic History* (New York: Academic Press, 1980), 315–16; and Robert J. Lampman, *Changes in the Share of the Wealth Held by Top Wealth-Holders, 1922–56*, N.B.E.R. occasional paper 71 (New York: National Bureau of Economic Research, 1960). More recent investigation of income shares during the 1920s has been undertaken by Gene Smiley. See his "Did Incomes for Most of the Population Fall from 1923 through 1929?," *Journal of Economic History* 43 (March 1983): 209–16, as well as his collaborative research with Richard Keehn on "Federal Personal Income Tax Policy in the 1920s," *Journal of Economic History* 55 (June 1995): 285–303. In "New Estimates of Income Shares During the 1920s," presented at the "Calvin Coolidge and the Coolidge Era" conference and published separately in this volume, Smiley offers new figures on income shares suggesting less change than Kuznets's earlier estimates.

30. Emphasis added. Mitchell, *Depression Decade*, 6. Also see Soule, *The Prosperity Decade*, 252–55.

31. With acknowledgments, of course, to John Maynard Keynes, *The Economic Consequences of the Peace* (London: Macmillan, 1920).

32. Keynes, *The Economic Consequences of the Peace*, 113–225. Also see, on the Dawes Plan, McElvaine, *The Great Depression*, 34.

33. For overviews of interwar international trade and finance, see Barry Eichengreen: *Golden Fetters: The Gold Standard and the Great Depression, 1919–1939* (New York: Cambridge University Press, 1992); *The Collapse of the World Financial System, 1919–1939* (New York: Oxford University Press, 1992); and *Elusive Stability: Essays in the History of International Finance, 1919–1939* (New York: Cambridge University Press, 1993).

34. See Irving Fisher, *The Stock Market Crash—and After* (New York: Macmillan, 1930); and his *Booms and Depressions: Some First Principles* (New York: Adelphi, 1932), 85–110. Also see J. A. Schumpeter, "The Decade of the Twenties," *American Economic Review* 36 (May 1946): 1–10; C. R. Noyes, "The Gold Inflation in the United States, 1921–1929," *American Economic Review* 20 (June 1930): 181–98; C. E. Persons, "Credit Expansion, 1920 to 1929, and Its Lessons," *Quarterly Journal of Economics* 45 (November 1930): 94–130; and J. Viner, "Recent Legislation and the

Banking Situation," *American Economic Review* 26 (March 1936): 106–7. Lionel Robbins, *The Great Depression* (London: Macmillan, 1934), 51–54.

35. From John K. Galbraith, *The Great Crash, 1929* (Boston: Houghton Mifflin, 1972), 93, 192. Also see W. Arthur Lewis, *Economic Survey, 1919–1939* (Philadelphia: Blakiston, 1950), 52; G. H. Moore, *Statistical Indications of Cyclical Revivals and Recessions*, N.B.E.R. Occasional Paper 31 (New York: National Bureau of Economic Research, 1950), 10–11; E. A. Erickson, "The Great Crash of October, 1929," in H. van der Wee, ed., *The Great Depression Revisited: Essays on the Economics of the Thirties* (The Hague: Martinus Nijhoff, 1972), 10.

36. Seymour Harris, *Saving American Capitalism: A Liberal Economic Program* (New York: Knopf, 1948); Paul M. Sweezy, *The Theory of Capitalist Development* (New York: Monthly Review Press, 1968); W. Arthur Lewis, *Economic Survey, 1919–1939* (Philadelphia: Blakiston, 1950), 55–56; Charles P. Kindleberger, *The World in Depression: 1929–1939* (Berkeley: University of California Press, 1973), 292–93; and Vladimir P. Timoshenko, *World Agriculture and the Depression*, Michigan Business Studies 5 (Ann Arbor: University of Michigan Press, 1933): 541–43.

37. See Gardiner C. Means, "Price Inflexibility and the Requirements of a Stabilizing Monetary Policy," *Journal of the American Statistical Association* 30 (1935), and Gardiner C. Means and Adolf A. Berle, *The Modern Corporation and Private Property* (New York: Harcourt, Brace and World, 1968).

38. Lloyd G. Reynolds, "Producers' Goods Prices in Expansion and Decline," *Journal of the American Statistical Association* 34 (1939): 32–40; and W. L. Thorp and W. F. Crowder, "Concentration and Product Characteristics as Factors in Price-Quantity Behavior," *American Economic Review* 30 (1941): 390–408.

39. See Michal Kalecki, *Studies in the Theory of Business Cycles* (New York: August M. Kelley, 1969), 40–59.

40. See *Historical Statistics of the United States*, part 2, series U201–206, p. 887.

41. See Joseph A. Schumpeter, *Business Cycles: A Theoretical, Historical, and Statistical Analysis of the Capitalist Process* (New York: McGraw-Hill, 1939), 2: 905–1050.

42. See Simon Kuznets, "Long Swings in the Growth of Population and in Related Economic Variables," *Proceedings of the American Philosophical Society* 102 (1958): 25–52; Moses Abramovitz, "The Nature and Significance of Kuznets Cycles," *Economic Development and Cultural Change* 9 (1961): 225–48; and Richard A. Easterlin, *Population, Labor Force, and Long Swings in Economic Growth: The American Experience* (New York: National Bureau of Economic Research, 1968).

43. See Abramovitz, "The Nature and Significance of Kuznets Cycles," 241.

44. See William Fellner, "Full Use or Underutilization: Appraisal of Long-Run Factors other Than Defense," *American Economic Review* 44 (1954): 423–33. However, also note his earlier "The Technological Argument of the Stagnation Thesis," *Quarterly Journal of Economics* 55 (1941): 638–51.

45. The quotations are taken from G. E. McLaughlin and R. J. Watkins, "The Problem of Industrial Growth in a Mature Economy," *American Economic Review* 29 (1939): 1–14.

46. See Alvin H. Hansen, "Economic Progress and Declining Population Growth," *American Economic Review* 29 (1939): 1–15; and John Maynard Keynes, "Some Economic Consequences of a Declining Population," *Eugenics Review* 29 (1937): 13–17. A complete, if rather polemical exposition of the stagnation thesis

may be found in George Terborgh, *The Bogey of Economic Maturity* (Chicago: Machinery and Allied Products Institute, 1945).

47. From Michal Kalecki, *Studies in Economic Dynamics* (London: George Allen and Unwin, 1943). Also see A. R. Sweezy, "Population Growth and Investment Opportunity," *Quarterly Journal of Economics* 55 (1940): 64–79.

48. Some evidence on these matters is presented in Robert M. Coen and Bert G. Hickman, *An Annual Growth Model of the U.S. Economy* (New York: North-Holland, 1976). Also see R. B. Zevin, "The Economics of Normalcy," *Journal of Economic History* 42 (1982): 43–52.

49. See Alvin H. Hansen, *Full Recovery or Stagnation?* (New York: Norton, 1941), 279ff.; and Michal Kalecki, "Observations on the Theory of Growth," *Economic Journal* 72 (1962): 134–53.

50. As admitted by Michal Kalecki, *Selected Essays on the Dynamics of the Capitalist Economy, 1933–1970* (Cambridge: Cambridge University Press, 1971), 30.

51. See Michal Kalecki, *Theory of Economic Dynamics: An Essay on Cyclical and Long-Run Changes in Capitalist Economy* (New York: Monthly Review Press, 1968), 159; and Hansen, *Full Recovery or Stagnation?* 310, 315.

52. See Josef Steindl, *Maturity and Stagnation in American Capitalism* (New York: Monthly Review Press, 1979), chaps. 2–5, 9, 13; and Josef Steindl, *Small and Big Business: Economic Problems of the Size of Firms* (Oxford: Basil Blackwell, 1945), 48–54, 63–66. Similarly, see Kalecki, *Studies in Economic Dynamics*, 92; and *Theory of Economic Dynamics*, 159.

53. From Steindl, *Maturity and Stagnation in American Capitalism*, xv.

54. See *The Baseball Encyclopedia*, 229, 889, and 1302. For the record, Tony Lazzeri batted .309 and drove in 102 runs; Bob Meusel hit .337 with 103 runs batted in. Waite Hoyt pitched victoriously in 22 games; Urban Shocker had 18 wins. The two 19-game winners were Wilcy Moore and Herb Pennock.

8

New Estimates of Income Shares During the 1920s

GENE SMILEY

Introduction

The 1920s were a prosperous period with what appeared to be sustained growth. From the cyclical peak of 1923 to the cyclical peak in 1929, real per capita incomes rose by 2.13 percent per year. After the recovery from the 1920–21 depression, the rate of unemployment averaged 3.3 percent per year, and the highest rate was in 1924 at 5.0 percent. Of course, we now know that this growth was not sustained. Economic activity began to contract in the early summer of 1929, and following the collapse of the booming stock market in September and October 1929, the American economy disappeared into the black hole of the Great Depression.

Among the theories offered to help explain the Great Depression was one based on the growing inequality in the distribution of income.[1] To the critics, this trend indicated that the prosperous twenties were not as prosperous as they may have seemed on the surface and that the growing income inequality may have contributed to the onset of the contraction by depressing consumption spending and increasing savings, leading to weakened growth in aggregate demand.[2] However, this alone seems inadequate to explain the timing of the contraction. In addition, if the "high" savings rates were reducing the rates of return on investment, then interest rates should have fallen, leading to a reduction in the savings of higher income recipients and an increase in their consumption spending while investment spending fell.[3]

Estimates of Income Shares in the Twenties

Whatever its causal relationship to the Great Depression, changes in the distribution of income during the 1920s (as during other periods) have always been of interest because of the obvious significance they had for the welfare of the individuals in the society. Examination of this topic was enhanced with the publication of Simon Kuznets's seminal 1953 work, *Shares of Upper Income Groups in Income and Savings*.[4] Kuznets's masterful study was begun in the late 1930s, but the bulk of the work was completed between 1946 and 1950. It achieved standards in the analysis of the distribution of income that many current studies fail to achieve. Kuznets used the estimates of the shares of upper-income groups to examine the social and economic characteristics of upper income groups and their effect on savings in the American economy. It quickly became the definitive work on income distribution in the interwar American economy.[5]

Kuznets developed two variants of income shares. The *Economic Income Variant* was designed to approximate "the payments to individuals that are associated with the participation of individuals or their property in production whose net result is measured in national income."[6] Not all of this income was available to individuals to spend because of income taxes. In addition, individuals could also spend the excess of gains over losses from the sales of assets even though this did not arise from the current production of national income. Subtracting federal income taxes paid and including the excess of gains over losses realized from the sales of assets yielded Kuznets's *Disposable Income Variant*.

These income share estimates were developed from two data sources: estimates of aggregate national income and data reported by individuals filing federal income tax returns. Only the highest income recipients filed income tax returns during the twenties, so shares of total economic or disposable income for the top 1 percent, 2 and 3 percent, 4 and 5 percent, and 6 and 7 percent of the nonfarm population could be estimated.[7] The shares of the lower 93 percent of the nonfarm population during the twenties were then estimated as the residuals, though Kuznets chose to do little with these share estimates in his study.

Kuznets's Conclusions

Kuznets found large changes in disposable income shares for the nonfarm population during the twenties. The per capita disposable income share of the top 1 percent of the nonfarm population fell from 13.13 percent in 1919 to 12.78 percent in 1923 and then jumped to 19.07 percent by 1929. For the top 7 percent the share rose from 29 to 30.26 percent between 1919 and 1923 and then increased sharply to 38.71 percent by 1929. Accordingly, the share of disposable income of the lower 93 percent of the nonfarm population fell from 71 percent in 1919 to 69.74 percent in 1923 and then rapidly declined to 61.29 percent in 1929.[8]

Kuznets's more accurate and detailed data portrayed an economy with rapidly increasing income inequality during the 1920s. And the story grew worse. Kuznets had estimated the current dollar per capita incomes of the upper-income percentiles during this period but did not do so for the lower 93 percent of the nonfarm population.[9] In 1977, Charles Holt employed Kuznets's data to fill in this gap.[10] He estimated nominal and real per capita incomes for the upper-income nonfarm percentiles and for the lower 93 percent of the nonfarm population. The estimates provided rather startling results. It was not simply that there was increasing income inequality during this prosperous period. Rather all of the gains were conferred on the few in the upper tail of the income distribution and on those who were farmers. Between the cyclical peak in 1923 and the cyclical peak in 1929, the real per capita incomes of the lower 93 percent of the nonfarm population fell 4 percent, and, in fact, the current dollar per capita incomes of this group fell 2 percent over these years. In contrast, the real per capita incomes of the top 1 percent rose 63 percent between 1923 and 1929 while the real per capita incomes of the second through seventh percentiles rose 23 percent.[11] The implication was clear. The mass of the urban population in the United States grew absolutely worse off during the twenties while the "prosperity belonged to the urban upper-income classes and the farmers."[12]

Biases in Kuznets's Share Estimates

These results were at odds with the prevailing view of the twenties. It is one thing to find that there was growing income inequality but quite another to argue that for the mass of the nonfarm population real and nominal incomes declined during the twenties. By the early 1980s, research suggested that Kuznets's share estimates overstated the rise in inequality.[13] As indicated above, Kuznets constructed his estimates of income shares from federal income tax return data and separate estimates of national income. He assumed that income reported on the federal tax returns was an accurate reflection of the income received by the upper-income groups. Any legal avoidance or illegal evasion of income taxes would obviously lead to an understatement of income, but Kuznets suggested that these were most likely to occur with lower-income households on the boundary of filing and not filing, or on the boundary of a somewhat higher-rate tax bracket. If this were the case, then it would have little (if any) noticeable effect on the income shares of the upper-income nonfarm population. Kuznets made no mention of any problems with tax avoidance by individuals in higher-income tax brackets.[14]

Any systematic trend of changes in tax avoidance, for example, would bias the changes in income shares. Suppose that tax avoidance among higher-income individuals tended to diminish during the twenties. Such a trend would lead to a greater growth in incomes reported on income tax returns than actually occurred because a portion of the growth in incomes would simply represent the movement of assets and the income they produce from nontaxable activities into taxable activities. Because the incomes and income shares of the lower 93 percent of the nonfarm population were estimated as a residual, if the growth of incomes and income shares of the upper-income nonfarm population are overstated, then the decline in the income and income shares of the mass of the nonfarm population must similarly be overstated. The evidence, in fact, suggests that this is what happened.

The United States enacted its first permanent federal income tax in 1913. The initial rate was a low 1 percent of net income but was transformed into a slightly progressive rate structure by the imposition of a surtax on incomes in excess of $20,000. This surtax rate rose to 7 percent on all net income in excess of $500,000. In 1916, the United States Congress raised income tax rates as it prepared for war, and with the advent of war, federal personal income tax rates skyrocketed. The normal tax rate rose from 1 percent in 1915 to 6 percent in 1918 while the surtax rate on $50,000 net income rose from 2 percent in 1915 to 35 percent in 1918, and the surtax rate on $500,000 net income rose from 6 percent in 1915 to 75 percent in 1918. Following the war, federal personal income tax rates were reduced. Rates were reduced slightly in 1919, and much larger cuts were made in 1921, 1924, and 1926. For 1925, federal personal income tax rates were reduced to 1.5 percent for the lowest taxable net income class with the highest marginal rate being 25 percent on net incomes in excess of $100,000.[15]

It has been argued that the dramatic tax rate increases from 1916 to 1918 led higher-income individuals to take steps to avoid the higher personal income taxes.[16] By 1919, President Woodrow Wilson and his treasury secretary, Carter Glass, called for tax rate cuts. They argued that, for the upper-income groups, rates above 70 percent could not be collected and had "passed the point of productivity," actually bringing about a reduction of taxes collected on the upper-income groups.[17] In fact, the possibility of income tax avoidance by higher-income individuals was known when the income tax law was enacted. Because individuals had used corporations to avoid income taxes during the Civil War, the 1913 legislation contained a provision that all profits, whether distributed or not, should be included in estimating taxable income. Because of increasing tax avoidance, Congress, in 1916, voted to tax stock dividends on their cash value and in 1918 voted to treat personal service corporations as partnerships so that all earnings, whether distributed or not, were subject to the income tax. Federal personal income taxes could also be avoided by placing wealth in tax exempt state and local securities.

Both Democrats and Republicans recognized the extent of the income tax avoidance that had taken place as rates had been increased, and there was general agreement that this had reduced the taxes collected from the upper-income population. However, there was a difference of opinion as to what the source of the income tax avoidance was and on how to reduce the practice. Democrats generally argued that corporations were a more important source of tax avoidance and that they could be controlled so that rates would not need to be cut as much and a more progressive rate structure maintained. Led by Andrew Mellon, secretary of the treasury under Presidents Warren G. Harding and Calvin Coolidge, Republicans argued that the tax exempt securities were a more important source, and the only effective way to reduce this income tax avoidance was to sharply reduce the rates. The Democrats were not able to enact effective ways to control tax avoidance through corporations, and tax rates were cut in 1921 and 1924. Finally, after the Republicans gained greater control of Congress in the 1924 elections, Coolidge and Mellon introduced tax cuts that reduced the rates to the levels they had initially proposed. Federal income tax revenues actually increased after the tax rate cuts in 1924 and again in 1926, and there was a shift in the share of income taxes paid away from the lower-income taxpayers to higher-income taxpayers over the decade.[18]

The evidence is persuasive that income tax avoidance grew when rates were increased between 1916 and 1918 and was reduced when income tax rates were cut in 1921, 1924, and 1926. Therefore, some of the growth during the twenties in incomes reported on the federal income tax returns filed by income taxpayers was due to the reduction in income tax avoidance. Because Kuznets made no adjustments for this, it means that the growth in income shares of upper-income individuals during the twenties is overstated as is the decline in income shares of the lower 93 percent of the nonfarm population during that decade.

New Estimates of Income Shares in the Twenties

To obtain a truer picture of the income share of the upper-income nonfarm population during the twenties, the changes in reported income due to changes in sheltering incomes from federal income taxes have to be eliminated. It is possible to create estimates of income shares that do this, and this chapter reports the conclusions derived from these new estimates.[19]

The first step is to estimate what the number of income tax returns in each net-income class would have been if there were no changes in tax avoidance behavior. Only the upper tail of the income distribution was subject to federal income taxes during the twenties. If taxpayers increasingly sheltered wealth to avoid federal income taxes as rates rose and moved wealth out of tax shelters as rates declined, then there would be a negative

TABLE I.
Shares of Disposable Income for Selected Percentiles of the Nonfarm Population, 1919–1929

Year	Top 1 percent		Top 2–3 percent		Top 4–5 percent		Top 6–7 percent		Lower 93 percent	
	Revised Estimates	Kuznets's Estimates	Revised Estimates	Kuznets's Estimates	Revised Estimates	Kuznets's Estimates	Revised Estimates	Kuznets's Estimates	Revised Estimates	Kuznets's Estimates
1919	19.093	13.13	7.727	7.08	4.781	4.58	4.572	4.20	63.827	71.00
1920	18.279	12.09	8.530	6.72	5.732	4.64	4.735	4.10	62.724	72.45
1921	20.810	14.02	9.345	8.16	6.008	5.85	5.037	4.40	58.801	67.57
1922	20.009	14.38	8.733	7.61	5.480	5.58	4.039	4.68	60.729	67.75
1923	20.927	12.78	9.408	8.19	5.623	5.20	4.830	4.08	59.212	69.74
1924	19.822	14.10	9.181	8.43	5.693	5.29	5.148	4.53	60.156	67.64
1925	21.542	16.71	9.289	8.57	5.671	5.90	4.928	5.23	58.569	63.59
1926	23.601	16.39	9.454	8.47	6.128	5.84	4.556	5.12	56.261	64.19
1927	22.929	17.50	8.828	8.6	5.750	5.79	4.833	5.13	57.660	62.98
1928	22.015	19.40	8.768	8.71	5.577	5.92	4.923	5.23	58.716	60.74
1929	24.598	19.07	9.649	9.01	5.706	5.73	4.814	4.90	55.233	61.29
Trend coefficient: 1919 to 1929	0.515[a]	0.703[a]	0.094[c]	0.191[a]	0.042	0.108[b]	0.023	0.111[a]	-0.655[a]	-1.113
Trend coefficient: 1923 to 1929	0.600[b]	1.081[a]	-0.020	0.109[a]	0.003	0.098[c]	-0.021	0.134[c]	-0.562[c]	-1.420[a]
Change in share: 1923 to 1929	3.671	6.29	0.241	0.82	0.083	0.53	-0.016	0.82	-3.979	-8.45

Source: Gene Smiley, "Technical Appendix: New Estimates of Income Shares During the 1920s" (October 1995), table 6, and Simon Kuznets, *Shares of Upper Income Groups in Income and Savings* (New York: National Bureau of Economic Research, 1953), table 122.

The trend coefficient is β in the regression, % SHARE = α + β(YEAR), where % SHARE is the percent share of disposable income and YEAR is the year for that percentage income share.

[a] Significantly different from zero at the 1 percent significance level.
[b] Significantly different from zero at the 5 percent significance level.
[c] Significantly different from zero at the 10 percent significance level. Significance tests based on a two-tail *t* test.

relationship between income tax rates in a net-income tax class and the number of returns in that class after controlling for other variables. Multiple regression analysis permitted this relationship to be estimated. Then, holding tax rates constant while allowing the other variables to take their actual values each year from 1919 through 1929 provided estimates of the number of income tax returns that would have been filed if there had been no changes in tax avoidance behavior. For each year for each net-income class, the ratio of the estimated to the actual number of returns was multiplied by each type of income (employee compensation, entrepreneurial income, dividends, and so forth) to provide adjusted estimates of the economic income for each net-income tax class. The number of persons represented by the returns in each net-income tax class could be similarly estimated. With these new estimates of the economic income and population in each net-income tax class in each year, it was possible to follow Kuznets's procedures and re-estimate all income shares and per capita incomes for the nonfarm upper-income percentiles and the lower 93 percent of the nonfarm population.[20]

New Evidence on Changes in Income Shares in the Twenties

Table 1 presents the revised estimates of shares of disposable income for the upper-income nonfarm percentiles and for the lower 93 percent of the nonfarm population. For comparison, Kuznets's share estimates are also presented.

All of the revised estimates of income shares for the upper percentiles are higher than Kuznets's original estimates. The revised estimates were based on constant marginal tax rates that were in effect in 1916. These rates were considerably lower than rates in 1928 and 1929. For example, the 1916 marginal rate on $2,000 net income was zero percent, but 1.5 percent in 1928. The marginal rate on $10,000 net income in 1916 was 2 percent, but 5 percent in 1928. At $50,000, the 1916 marginal rate was 4 percent, but 18 percent in 1928, and at $100,000, net-income taxpayers faced a marginal rate of 6 percent in 1916 and 24 percent in 1928. Reducing the tax avoidance behavior by the use of constant, lower marginal rates increases the income shares of the upper nonfarm percentiles and reduces the income shares of the lower 93 percent of the nonfarm population.

Although the revised income shares are higher than Kuznets's shares, they do not increase as rapidly during this period. From 1919 through 1929, the trend coefficient for Kuznets's estimates indicates that their share rose 0.703 percent per year, while the trend coefficient for the revised estimates shows that their share rose 0.515 percent per year. The first business cycle peak after the severe depression of 1920–21 was in 1923. Perhaps a

TABLE 2.
Real Per Capita Disposable Incomes for Selected Percentiles of the Nonfarm Population, 1919–1929

Year	Top 1 percent		Top 2–3 percent		Top 4–5 percent		Top 6–7 percent		Lower 93 percent	
	Revised Estimates	Kuznets's Estimates	Revised Estimates	Kuznets's Estimates	Revised Estimates	Kuznets's Estimates	Revised Estimates	Kuznets's Estimates	Revised Estimates	Kuznets's Estimates
1919	$13,832	$9,211	$2,799	$2,484	$1,732	$1,606	$1,656	$1,473	$497	$536
1920	12,411	7,959	2,896	2,212	1,946	1,527	1,607	1,349	458	513
1921	12,796	8,372	2,873	2,436	1,847	1,747	1,549	1,314	389	434
1922	14,035	9,803	3,063	2,594	1,922	1,902	1,771	1,595	458	497
1923	16,223	9,629	3,647	3,085	2,179	1,959	1,872	1,537	494	565
1924	15,053	10,511	3,486	3,142	2,162	1,972	1,955	1,688	491	542
1925	16,782	12,724	3,618	3,263	2,209	2,246	1,919	1,991	491	521
1926	18,516	12,595	3,708	3,254	2,404	2,244	1,787	1,967	475	530
1927	18,098	13,541	3,484	3,327	2,269	2,240	1,907	1,985	489	524
1928	18,094	15,681	3,603	3,520	2,292	2,393	2,023	2,114	519	528
1929	20,972	15,725	4,114	3,715	2,432	2,362	2,053	2,020	506	543
Trend Coefficient:										
1919 to 1929	762.35[a]	796.76[a]	113.61[a]	141.44[a]	64.95[a]	88.13[a]	43.65[a]	81.87[a]	5.64[c]	3.52
Trend Coefficient:										
1923 to 1929	773.04[a]	1051.61[a]	53.61	96.79[a]	38.54[b]	73.04[a]	23.82	81.96[b]	3.21	−3.25
Percentage Change:										
1923 to 1929	29.28%	63.31%	12.80%	20.40%	11.61%	20.60%	9.62%	31.44%	2.59%	−3.82%

Source: Smiley, "Technical Appendix," tables 8 and 10.

The trend coefficient is β in the regression, $Y_{PC} = \alpha + \beta(\text{YEAR})$, where Y_{PC} is the real per capita disposable income and YEAR is the year for that real per capita income.

[a] Significantly different from zero at the 1 percent significance level.
[b] Significantly different from zero at the 5 percent significance level.
[c] Significantly different from zero at the 10 percent significance level. Significance tests based on a two-tail *t* test.

more appropriate comparison is to compare the business cycle peak in 1923 with the business cycle peak in 1929. The peak in 1923 is comparable to that in 1929 and is less affected by the real and financial distortions resulting from the First World War. Between 1923 and 1929, the revised estimates show the income share of the top 1 percent growing an average of 0.60 percent per year while Kuznets's estimates show this share growing an average of 1.081 percent per year.

Similar changes are found for the second and third, fourth and fifth, and sixth and seventh upper-income percentiles as shown in table 1. For each percentile, the trend coefficient for the revised estimates is much smaller than the trend coefficient for the Kuznets's estimates. This is especially true for 1923–29, where the trend coefficients for the revised estimates are not significantly different from zero.

These characteristics are mirrored in the shares of the lower 93 percent of the nonfarm population. Whereas the revised estimates show considerably smaller increases in income shares for the upper-income nonfarm percentiles, the decline in the income shares of the lower 93 percent is much smaller for the revised estimates than for Kuznets's estimates. The rate of decline in the revised share estimates between 1919 and 1929 is only 59 percent of the rate of decline in Kuznets's share estimates. Over the 1923–29 period, the revised share estimates declined at less than half the rate at which Kuznets's share estimates declined.

These revised share estimates present a different picture of changes in the distribution of income during the twenties. They continue to show an increase in income inequality; however, it is considerably less than Kuznets's original income shares estimates showed. The primary group gaining income shares was the top 1 percent of the nonfarm population, especially between 1923 and 1929. The primary group losing income shares was the lower 93 percent of the nonfarm population, though their share loss was considerably smaller.

Real per capita incomes for these percentiles are shown in table 2. The real per capita incomes of the upper 1 percent grew much faster than for any other percentile, though the rate of growth was slower for the revised estimates than for Kuznets's estimates. Over the 1919–29 period, Kuznets's estimates show an average annual growth of nearly $797 in real per capita income for the upper 1 percent, while the revised estimates show an average annual growth of just over $762 a year.[21] Between 1923 and 1929, Kuznets's estimates show real per capita incomes growing nearly $1,052 a year while the revised estimates show a growth of $773 a year. According to Kuznets, by 1929 real per capita incomes of the upper 1 percent were 63.31 percent higher than in 1923, while the revised estimates show these real per capita incomes were only 29.28 percent higher in 1929 than in 1923. For the other upper-income nonfarm percentiles (the second and third, fourth and fifth, and sixth and seventh percentiles), similar declines in the growth of real per capita incomes are found using the revised estimates rather than Kuznets's estimates. Once again, as with the income shares, the 1 percent of the nonfarm population in the extreme end of the upper tail of the income distribution enjoyed most of the gains in income during the twenties.

But it now appears that the population in the upper-income percentiles did not enjoy all of the gains in real income during the twenties.[22] The real per capita incomes of the lower 93 percent of the nonfarm population grew at an average rate of $5.64 a year between 1919 and 1929 according to the revised estimates, but only $3.52 a year according to Kuznets's estimates. Between 1923 and 1929, the revised estimates show that the real per capita incomes of the large low-income group increased by 2.59 percent while Kuznets's estimates show that their real per capita incomes fell by 3.82 percent over this period. According to the revised estimates, a family of four in this percentile would have seen their family income increase by $48 between 1923 and 1929.[23] Though the gain is small, nonetheless it is an increase and, with the revised estimates, it is no longer possible to say that the mass of the nonfarm population lost income during the booming twenties.

Speculations on the Sources of Income Share Changes

These revised estimates suggest that the rise in inequality was less than Kuznets's estimates found. The lower 93 percent of the nonfarm population do appear to have experienced increases in their real per capita incomes during the twenties, though their incomes grew much more slowly than for individuals in the upper nonfarm income percentiles. It is possible to speculate on some of the sources of this rise in inequality that the revised estimates show. The two most likely sources are adjustments from the First World War and the growth in realized capital gains during the twenties.

The First World War appears to have interrupted a long-term trend of rising inequality according to Jeffrey Williamson and Peter Lindert.[24] This is suggested by their examination of unskilled and skilled wages as well as other data. Lee Soltow used the income tax return data from 1866 to 1871, from 1894, and from 1913 on to examine income inequality among the upper-income groups.[25] He found, *among the upper-income groups*, that there appeared to be a slight decline in inequality in the 1913–16 period compared to the 1866–71 period. Like Williamson and Lindert, Soltow found that inequality within this group declined dramatically in 1918 and 1919. It fell even lower, on average, in the 1920–24 period before rising sharply, on average, in 1925–29.[26] There seems to be general agreement that income inequality fell during the First World War as "workers . . . gained income shares at the expense of the 'rentier classes,' those who depended on earnings from investments."[27]

The reasons for this are not hard to find. Government controls tended to reduce property incomes and raise wages. In 1916, in a highly controversial move, President Wilson convinced Congress to reduce the workday in the railroad industry from ten to eight hours with no reduction in pay.[28] The Adamson Act was supposed to avert a threatened railroad strike. With the door opened, federal government intervention into markets increased sharply during the First World War.

The federal government took over and operated the railroads and telegraph. Boards were created to control and direct activity in markets considered crucial. Prices were fixed to aid the government in its purchases. Huge and complex excess profits taxes were imposed to be certain that firms did not profit from the war. Conscription reduced the labor supply just as the demand for labor was rising, and this helped to push up real wages. To reduce labor strife, the federal government encouraged the recognition of unions and collective bargaining between unions and employers.[29] Because of a 1912 law mandating an eight-hour day for firms engaged in government contracts and the War Department's discouraging firms from employing workers for ten hours a day, the eight-hour day became more widespread.[30] The Department of Labor began compiling a price index (the Consumer Price Index) that was used to adjust wages so as to maintain real wages. The authorities controlling wages allowed even larger increases "for the more poorly paid workers, on the basis of the principle that everyone should be able to afford a family budget representing a 'minimum of health and decency.'"[31] Salaried workers, however, whose incomes were normally higher, saw their real incomes fall because "they did not engage in collective bargaining, and there were no boards to alter their compensation as the cost of living rose."[32]

It is not difficult to understand why there was a sharp decrease in measured income inequality during the First World War. One would expect that after the war, some of these changes would be reversed. With the end of the war and demobilization, the demand for labor fell and the supply of labor rose, tending to reduce real wages. With the end of the war, many controls were removed or reduced tending to allow property incomes to rise. The federal government's support of labor unions diminished as it was no longer necessary to minimize labor strife to increase war output. The failure of a strike to organize the steel industry and growing employer resistance to unions (the "open shop" movement) led to the onset of declining labor union membership and influence. Therefore, in the early 1920s, as market relationships were restored, there would have been some rise in income inequality back toward the prewar conditions. The question is how much was this increase and how long did it take to eliminate the unusual conditions brought on by the war? Soltow's data suggest that this must have been completed by the mid-1920s because the inequality measure in the 1925–29 period was essentially the same as for the 1913–16 period.[33]

The other major influence in the twenties was the great stock market boom of the last half of the decade. Clearly this conferred large increases in disposable income on those who realized capital gains during the boom. It is possible to make some crude calculations to measure the maximum contribution of the excess of gains over losses on asset sales toward inequality changes in the twenties. To do this, the shares of disposable income are re-estimated completely excluding the adjustment for the excess of gains over losses on the sales of assets. With these share estimates and total disposable income excluding the excess of gains over losses on asset sales, per capita incomes for the various percentiles can be re-estimated. These estimates are presented in table 3.

Consider first the income shares of the top 1 percent. Excluding the excess of gains over losses on asset sales, their income share essentially had no trend over either 1919–29 or 1923–29. By 1929, the share for the top 1 percent would have been 19.371 percent rather than 24.598 percent. The share for the top 2 to 3 percent, top 4 to 5 percent, and top 6 to 7 percent all show significantly rising shares over the 1919–29 period. However, the gains are all concentrated in the 1919–22 period since there are no significant trends in their shares over the 1923–29 period. For the lower 93 percent of the nonfarm population, their income share tends to fall over the period, but the trend is not significant. Though neither trend coefficient is significantly different from zero, the trend coefficient is smaller in the 1923–29 period than in the 1919–29 period, suggesting a more pronounced fall in their income share from 1919 through 1922. In 1929, the share of the lower 93 percent of the nonfarm population would have been 59.741 percent rather than 55.233 percent if the excess of gains over losses on asset sales had not been included.

There are similar changes in real per capita incomes. For all of the percentiles, there are significantly positive trends over the 1919–29 period, but not the 1923–29 period. For the top 1 percent, their real per capita incomes would have increased about $211 per year rather than $762 per year. By 1929, the real per capita incomes of the top 1 percent would have been about $15,395 rather than $20,972. The changes are less pronounced for the top 2 to 3 percent, top 4 to 5 percent, and top 6 to 7 percent. For each percentile, the per capita incomes are reduced somewhat, but the trends are very similar to those when the excess of gains over losses on asset sales are included. For the lower 93 percent of the nonfarm population, the per capita incomes are essentially the same with and without the excess of gains over losses on asset sales.

These speculations suggest that between 1919 and about 1922, the in-

TABLE 3.
Income Shares and Per Capita Incomes for the Nonfarm Population Excluding
the Adjustment for the Excess of Gains Over Losses on Individuals' Asset Sales

Year	Top 1%	Top 2–3%	Top 4–5%	Top 6–7%	Lower 93%
A: Income Shares					
1919	18.398%	7.463%	4.694%	4.541%	64.905%
1920	18.065	8.101	5.523	4.660	63.651
1921	20.671	9.178	5.945	5.014	59.192
1922	18.760	8.525	5.474	5.077	62.164
1923	19.295	9.366	5.682	4.843	60.814
1924	18.053	9.006	5.685	5.177	62.079
1925	17.722	9.019	5.743	5.093	62.423
1926	20.259	9.396	6.173	4.706	59.466
1927	19.250	8.784	5.907	4.901	61.158
1928	16.913	8.703	5.768	5.152	63.465
1929	19.371	9.571	5.980	5.157	59.741
Trend:					
1919–29	−0.023	0.120[b]	0.080[b]	0.038[c]	−0.222
Trend:					
1923–29	−0.019	−0.008	0.044	0.025	−0.061
Change:					
1923–29	0.076	0.385	0.298	0.314	−1.074
B: Per Capita Incomes					
1919	$13,075	$2,652	$1,668	$1,613	$496
1920	12,050	2,702	1,842	1,554	457
1921	12,634	2,805	1,817	1,532	389
1922	12,869	2,924	1,877	1,741	459
1923	14,544	3,530	2,142	1,825	493
1924	13,292	3,316	2,092	1,906	491
1925	13,007	3,310	2,108	1,869	493
1926	15,091	3,500	2,299	1,753	476
1927	14,375	3,280	2,205	1,830	491
1928	12,920	3,324	2,203	1,968	521
1929	15,395	3,875	2,376	2,049	511
Trend:					
1919–29	211.00[b]	99.64[a]	63.25[a]	43.62[a]	6.10[b]
Trend:					
1923–29	113.46	36.46	36.46[b]	27.04	4.00
Percentage Change:					
1923–29	5.85%	9.77%	11.69%	13.02%	3.57%

Sources and Derivations: See text.
  For the explanation of the trend coefficients see the notes to tables 1 and 2.
  [a] Significantly different from zero at the 1 percent significance level.
  [b] Significantly different from zero at the 5 percent significance level.
  [c] Significantly different from zero at the 10 percent significance level. Significance tests
based on a two-tail *t* test.

creased inequality resulting from the changes in income shares were primarily due to the elimination of changes initiated by the First World War, especially the federal government's imposition of market controls. These changes tended to restore the income distribution that existed prior to the war. From 1923 on, the changes in income shares were driven primarily by the stock market boom and the increasing excess of gains over losses on asset sales of the high-income groups, especially the top 1 percent of the nonfarm population.

Conclusions

Simon Kuznets's study of the income shares of upper-income groups in the interwar period is and will remain a masterful study. However, it now seems clear that his estimates of income shares during the twenties are biased because he failed to adjust for the changes in tax avoidance behavior of taxpayers, particularly the higher-income taxpayers, during this decade. The rise in income inequality was less pronounced than Kuznets found. In particular, the lower 93 percent of the nonfarm population did not experience decreases in their real and nominal per capita incomes after the recovery from the 1920–21 depression. Though their real income growth was much slower, it did grow along with the real per capita incomes of the nonfarm upper-income percentiles.

The increases in inequality that appear in the revised estimates for the 1920s seem to have been driven by two factors. First, there was an initial rise in inequality after the temporary rise in equality during the war. This ended about 1922. For the rest of the decade, the rising inequality was primarily driven by the booming stock market as the excess of gains over losses on asset sales explain much of the differences in real per capita income growth.

Finally, it must be admitted that these estimates are quite crude and, hopefully, will be improved in the future. The estimates would be improved if there was better information on how the holdings of tax exempt state and municipal securities by the upper-income groups changed as tax rates changed in the twenties. If tax rates had been constant at lower rates, this surely would have had real effects on the economy. Interest rates, savings, and the allocation of investment spending might well have been different. This would likely have had effects on national income, and a more sophisticated analysis would take this into account. However, even with the crudity of these income share estimates, it now appears that the gains of the twenties were more broadly based than Kuznets's share estimates suggest. The mass of the nonfarm population *did* see increases in their real incomes, and the rise in inequality was less pronounced than previously thought.

NOTES

This paper has benefited from comments by members of the Economic Faculty Seminar at Marquette University and, especially, Richard H. Keehn and Peter Temin. The author is solely responsible for all remaining errors and omissions.

1. For an early quantitative evaluation of the growing income inequality in the twenties, see George Soule, *Prosperity Decade: From War to Depression, 1917–1929* (New York: Holt, Rinehart, and Winston, 1947), 317. Soule relied upon data developed by Arthur Burns, *Twenty-Sixth Annual Report of the National Bureau of Economic Research* (New York: NBER, 1946), 30–38.

2. The point is frequently noted. For example, the recent textbook of Hughes and Cain mentions this but does not suggest that it started the contraction. (Jonathan Hughes and Louis Cain, *American Economic History*, 4th ed. [New York: Harper Collins, 1994], 425–26.) It has also been emphasized by Peter Fearon, though Fearon notes that this does not explain why it was in 1929 when the economy turned down. [Peter Fearon, *War, Prosperity, and Depression: The U.S. Economy, 1917–45* (Lawrence: University of Kansas Press, 1987), 151–52.]

3. The magnitude of such an effect would, of course, depend upon the interest elasticity of consumption and savings and the length of time that adjustments took. However, as long as there was some interest elasticity of consumption and savings demands, then the compensating adjustments would occur. Given the rise in interest rates in the late 1920s, this scenario hardly seems plausible.

4. Simon Kuznets, *Shares of Upper Income Groups in Income and Savings* (New York: NBER, 1953).

5. This study owes a great debt to Kuznets's work. It builds upon and is based upon Kuznets's masterful study. The calculations for this study consumed more than six months of work with three months in the summer of working exclusively on these calculations using computer spreadsheets for the complex linked calculations. It is hard to imagine making these calculations by hand as Kuznets and his assistants did in the late 1930s and late 1940s.

6. Kuznets, *Shares*, xxxii.

7. Kuznets developed income share estimates for the total population and the nonfarm population. Separate estimates of per capita incomes for the farm population were available and indicated that nominal and real per capita incomes for this group rose from 1921 through 1929, though never reaching the unusually high level reached in 1919. With separate estimates of farm incomes available, it was possible to separate these out and estimate the incomes of the nonfarm population to provide greater detail on income shares. See Kuznets, *Shares*, 292.

8. All percent income shares are from Kuznets, *Shares*, table 122.

9. Ibid., table 122.

10. Charles F. Holt, "Who Benefited from the Prosperity of the Twenties?" *Explorations in Economic History* 14, no. 3 (July 1977): 277–89.

11. Ibid., table 4, 285.

12. Ibid., 285.

13. See the following: John Mueller, "Lessons of the Tax-Cuts of Yesteryear,"

Wall Street Journal, March 5, 1981; James Gwartney and Richard Stroup, *Tax Rates, Incentive Effects and Economic Growth* (Manuscript in possession of the author, 1981), chap. 3; Gene Smiley, "Did Incomes for Most of the Population Fall from 1923 Through 1929?" *The Journal of Economic History* 43, no. 1 (March 1983): 209–16. Also see: Richard H. Keehn and Gene Smiley, "Tax Avoidance in the 1915–1929 Era," *Essays in Economic and Business History: The Journal of the Economic and Business Historical Society* 13 (1995): 157–67; and Gene Smiley and Richard H. Keehn, "Federal Income Tax Policy in the 1920s," *The Journal of Economic History* 55, no. 2 (June 1995): 285–303.

14. Kuznets, *Shares*, chap. 11, section 2, 437–41.

15. Roy D. and Gladys C. Blakey, *The Federal Income Tax* (New York: Longmans, Green, and Co., 1940), table 20, p. 512, and table 21, pp. 514–15.

16. This is discussed in detail in Smiley and Keehn, "Income Tax Policy in the 1920s." The following discussion will draw upon that paper.

17. Andrew Mellon, *Taxation: The People's Business* (New York: Macmillan, 1924), 128–30.

18. See Smiley and Keehn, "Income Tax Policy in the 1920s," for a more complete discussion of this.

19. Gene Smiley, "Technical Appendix: New Estimates of Income Shares During the 1920s," Manuscript, Department of Economics, Marquette University, Milwaukee, Wisconsin 53201–1881 (October 1995). This paper is available from the author.

20. Two sets of revised income shares were estimated in the "Technical Appendix." One set includes interest income from tax exempt securities while the other set excludes interest income from tax exempt securities. In the early 1920s, Republicans argued that tax exempt securities were a method of avoiding taxes and that tax rate reductions would reduce tax avoidance, implying that the holdings of tax exempt securities by upper-income groups would decline. Democrats argued that corporations were the primary source of tax avoidance. Kuznets assumed that all tax exempt securities were *always* held by the upper-income individuals. If this is correct, then tax avoidance was primarily through corporations, and the income shares should be calculated including this income. If Republicans were correct, then individual holdings of tax exempt securities should have declined as tax rates fell, and when returns are estimated to eliminate changes in tax avoidance behavior (with relatively low and constant tax rates), the income from tax exempt securities should be reduced, though not necessarily eliminated. However, it seems plausible to assume that upper-income individuals always held the bulk of tax exempt securities. Though the differences in rates of return on high-grade tax exempt municipal securities and AAA corporate bonds diminished during the 1920s, corporate bonds still carried about a 0.5 percent higher rate of return by the end of the twenties. (For evidence on this, see Smiley and Keehn, "Income Tax Policy in the 1920s," 292–93.) Thus, it seems plausible that even as income tax rates fell, most of the tax exempt securities were still held by upper-income taxpayers. Therefore, the data used in this analysis includes interest income from tax exempt securities.

21. If these annual dollar incomes were stated as percentages of the base year real per capita incomes, then the revised estimates would show a considerably smaller

growth compared to Kuznets's estimates as a result of the large differences in initial levels of real per capita incomes for this percentile.

22. Though farmers saw a rise in real per capita incomes from 1923 through 1929, between 1919 and 1929 their real per capita incomes fell. Real per capita incomes of farmers were $373 in 1919 but $295 in 1929. (Kuznets, *Shares*, 292; and *Historical Statistics of the United States: Colonial Times to 1970* (Washington: GPO, 1976), series E-135.

23. Between 1923 and 1928 this increase would have been $100 for a family of four.

24. Jeffrey Williamson and Peter Lindert, *American Inequality. A Macroeconomic History* (New York: Academic Press, 1981), chap. 12.

25. Lee Soltow, "Evidence on Income Inequality in the United States, 1866–1965," *The Journal of Economic History* 29, no. 2 (June 1969): 279–86.

26. The inverse-Pareto slope coefficient declined from an average of 0.70 in 1866–71 to 0.685 in 1913–16. The coefficient fell to 0.61 in 1919 and to 0.60 in 1920. On average, it was 0.55 in 1920–24 and 0.67 in 1925–29. Note that the 1925–29 average is almost back to the 1913–16 average. (Soltow, "Evidence," 282.)

27. Hughes and Cain, *American Economic History*, 416.

28. Robert Higgs, *Crisis and Leviathan: Critical Episodes in the Growth of American Government* (New York: Oxford University Press, 1987), 116–21.

29. Soule, *Prosperity Decade*, 67–68.

30. Ibid., 72.

31. Ibid., 74.

32. Ibid., 76.

33. Soltow, "Evidence on Income Inequality," 282.

SELECTED REFERENCES

Blakey, Roy D., and Gladys C. Blakey. *The Federal Income Tax* (New York, 1940).

Burns, Arthur. *Twenty-Sixth Annual Report of the National Bureau of Economic Research* (New York, 1946).

Fearon, Peter. *War, Prosperity, and Depression: The U.S. Economy, 1917–45* (Lawrence, Kans., 1987).

Garrett, W. *Government Control over Prices* (Washington, D.C., 1920).

Gwartney, James, and Richard Stroup. *Tax Rates, Incentive Effects and Economic Growth* (Manuscript, 1981).

Higgs, Robert. *Crisis and Leviathan: Critical Episodes in the Growth of American Government* (New York, 1987).

Historical Statistics of the United States: Colonial Times to 1970 (Washington, D.C., 1975).

Holt, Charles F. "Who Benefited from the Prosperity of the Twenties?" *Explorations in Economic History* 14 (July 1977): 277–89.

Hughes, Jonathan, and Louis Cain. *American Economic History*, 4th ed. (New York, 1994).

Keehn, Richard H., and Gene Smiley. "Tax Avoidance in the 1915–1929 Era," *Essays in Economic and Business History: The Journal of the Economic and Business Historical Society* 13 (1995): 157–67.

Kuznets, Simon. *Shares of Upper Income Groups in Income and Savings* (New York, 1953).

Mellon, Andrew. *Taxation: The People's Business* (New York, 1924).

Mueller, John. "Lessons of the Tax-Cuts of Yesteryear," *Wall Street Journal*, March 5, 1981.

Paglin, Morton. "The Measurement and Trend of Inequality: A Basic Revision," *The American Economic Review* 65 (September 1975): 598–609.

Smiley, Gene. "Did Incomes for Most of the Population Fall from 1923 Through 1929?" *The Journal of Economic History* 43 (March 1983): 487–93.

Smiley, Gene. "Technical Appendix: New Estimates of Income Shares During the 1920s," Manuscript, Department of Economics, Marquette University, Milwaukee, Wisconsin 53201–1881 (October 1995).

Smiley, Gene, and Richard H. Keehn. "Federal Personal Income Tax Policy in the 1920s," *The Journal of Economic History* 55 (June 1995): 285–303.

Soltow, Lee. "Evidence on Income Inequality in the United States, 1866–1965," *The Journal of Economic History* 29 (June 1969): 279–86.

Soule, George. *Prosperity Decade: From War to Depression, 1917–1929* (New York, 1947).

Williamson, Jeffrey. "American Prices and Urban Inequality Since 1820," *The Journal of Economic History* 36 (June 1976): 303–33.

Williamson, Jeffrey, and Peter Lindert. *American Inequality: A Macroeconomic History* (New York, 1981).

9

America and the World in the 1920s

WARREN I. COHEN

The most important point to remember about the 1920s is that the United States was not isolated and that its foreign policy was not "isolationist." Indeed, the era marked the greatest peacetime involvement in world affairs in American history. The United States emerged from the war as the world's leading power and its number one creditor nation. At the Department of State and in the Department of Commerce, striking new levels of professionalism had been reached, providing the nation with the apparatus to use its wealth and power abroad. Decisions made in Washington, on Wall Street, and in the offices of various nongovernmental organizations across the country had an enormous impact on the rest of the globe—an expansion of American influence and interests on a scale unprecedented in American history.

A generation of Americans was misled about the 1920s by advocates who wanted U.S. participation in a world organization and then labeled the decade an isolationist interlude because of the failure of the United States to join the League of Nations. That failure was indeed regrettable, but as indicated in the work of Stephen Schuker, Michael Hogan, Melvyn Leffler, and Joan Hoff Wilson, international relations were not confined to the Geneva offices of the League.[1] The United States of the 1920s was an imperial power with colonies and protectorates in the Caribbean and across the Pacific. It had trade and investment interests on each of the globe's continents, not excluding Africa. And as Emily Rosenberg has demonstrated, American culture also spread rapidly in this era.[2]

We have all learned in recent years that the study of foreign affairs involves much more than the examination of the political and military activities of governments. One simple illustration derives from the fact that the automobile culture of the 1920s depended in large part on access to oil and rubber. Fearful of dependency on foreign cartels, American businessmen, supported by their government, sought new oil concessions all over the globe, succeeding in Canada, Venezuela, Iraq, Bahrain, Kuwait, and the Dutch East Indies.[3] Threatened by British dominance of rubber supplies, the U.S. government and the Firestone Corporation developed new rubber plantations in Liberia.[4] No troops were necessary; nor was membership in an international organization essential for coping with the overseas concerns of the United States as it expanded its interests in four continents.

The Caribbean and Central America provide the most obvious evidence of U.S. activity beyond the borders of the forty-eight states. American military forces could be found in Cuba, Puerto Rico, Panama, Haiti, Nicaragua, and the Dominican Republic. The stars and stripes flew over the Virgin Islands as well. In all of these possessions or protectorates, indigenous regimes functioned subject to the pleasure of Washington's representatives. Cuba, Haiti, and the Dominican Republic were required by law to obtain U.S. approval before they could borrow from foreign bankers.

In some of these and in other countries of Latin America, multinational corporations headquartered in the United States played exceptionally important roles, United Fruit being only the most obvious of these. Mining companies committed the most capital abroad in the 1920s with Latin America as the recipient of the greatest increase in U.S. investment. The Guggenheims replaced British capital with their own as they sought nitrates, copper, lead, zinc, and tin in Chile, Peru, and Bolivia.[5] United Fruit, which had the worst reputation for meddling in the internal affairs of host countries and disrupting local societies, had a larger budget in Costa Rica than the national government. In Honduras, the corporation financed a revolution.[6]

Guggenheim and United Fruit needed little help from the U.S. government. Pan American, on the other hand, received critical support from the Department of State, which viewed Latin America as a preserve to be controlled by the United States.[7] It did not want air links falling into European hands. The strategic value of controlling the airways received at least nominal consideration. The Pan American case is probably the only one in which the government's role was crucial. Remember, however, that those who were its *objects* rarely distinguished between the exercise of official and private American power. To them, it was all Yankee imperialism: the United States was the source of their discontent.

Bear in mind that in addition to their depredations, some of these corporations contributed significantly to public health programs, transportation, and housing in order to provide a healthy and reliable work force. The Guggenheims in particular had a good reputation for building schools in remote areas. Mira Wilkins argues that "Central American bananas, Chilean copper, and Venezuelan oil became valuable resources *only* because foreign companies were ready and able to take large risks, to supply sizable amounts of money, and to offer technical knowledge and skills."[8] Obviously, the corporations involved were not eleemosynary institutions. The point simply is that in the pursuit of profit, they affected every society they touched, and some of these in very important and beneficial ways.

The United States' involvement in Mexico and Nicaragua in the 1920s also demonstrates the importance of the American role in Latin American affairs. Subsequent to the revolution of 1911, the Mexican Constitution of 1917 had claimed subsoil rights for the Mexican people at a time when 40 percent of the land and 60 percent of the oil industry was owned and controlled by citizens of the United States. It also contained provisions protecting labor that were perceived by American businessmen as a threat to their profits. Washington supported the claims of its citizens against the conflicting rights of the Mexican people. To advance the cause of American investors, the United States withheld recognition from the Mexican government. The Mexican government of Alvaro Obregon wanted recognition for the legitimacy it would confer at home and abroad. More to the point, it needed recognition in order to borrow capital from foreign investors, most of whom in the 1920s were likely to be U.S. citizens. The Mexicans wanted to deal, but the Department of State did not. In 1922, Thomas W. Lamont of J. P. Morgan and Co. rode to the rescue. His ultimate concern was the collection of Mexico's debt to American bondholders, requiring a prior political settlement. Bondholders, unlike the oilmen and mining interests, didn't give a damn what the Mexicans did about subsoil rights or the protection of labor or new taxes on oil—that could be used to pay the debt. In 1923, Lamont brokered the Bucareli Agreements, a deal between the two governments that excluded previously developed land from the Constitutional provisions and provided compensation for expropriated land. Calvin Coolidge then recognized the Mexican government.[9]

A few years later, after a new Mexican president, Plutarco Elias Calles, renewed the threat to U.S. oil interests, enraged some Americans with his attacks on the Catholic Church, and had the audacity to meddle in Nicaraguan affairs, the Coolidge administration considered sending in the troops. Assistant Secretary of State Robert E. Olds accused the Mexicans of spreading Bolshevism in Central America, and Secretary of State Frank Kellogg sounded the same tocsin before the Senate Committee on Foreign Relations. Once again, it was J. P. Morgan and Company that came to the rescue, averting war and resolving the crisis. This time Lamont had substantial help from the American peace movement and his partner, Dwight Morrow, who went to Mexico as ambassador. The peace movement, led by Frederick Libby of the National Council for the Prevention of War (NCPW) and the Federal Council of Churches of Christ in America, mobilized the media and public opinion in opposition to the use of force against Mexico.

Morrow helped Calles out of the mess he had gotten himself into with the Catholic Church and persuaded him to dilute plans to nationalize all subsoil rights without compensation. By March 1928, the U.S. Department of State announced that there were no longer any outstanding differences with Mexico.[10] The postwar climate, although hardly isolationist, was strongly antiimperialist, largely the result of the efforts of the peace movement.[11] Muckraking techniques, successful in stimulating prewar domestic reform, were applied to foreign policy issues. American diplomacy to resolve problems with Mexico had been welcomed by the peace movement. The threat to use force against Mexico provoked public and congressional opposition, fanned by peace activists such as Libby of the NCPW.

The Caribbean was still perceived as an American lake, and it was hard to find a threat to the hegemony of the United States in the region. Britain and Germany had been greatly weakened by the war, and efforts to evoke the specter of Bolshevism in Mexico had produced mostly laughter. If the principle of self-determination that Wilson had proclaimed meant anything, it was time to apply it in the American sphere. The retreat from imperialism began in the Dominican Republic in 1924 as U.S. Marines withdrew, and political power was transferred from the U.S. Navy to Dominican leaders—although the United States retained significant control of Dominican finances.

Withdrawal from Nicaragua proved more difficult. The marines came home in 1925, but a bloody civil war broke out shortly afterward, and U.S. forces returned to Nicaragua in 1926. In the absence of public support for the use of force, Coolidge sent Henry Stimson to devise a peaceful political settlement that would result in a viable government acceptable to Washington.[12] Stimson decided the answer was free elections, supervised by the United States. U.S. Marines would maintain order until a Nicaraguan constabulary was trained to take over. Elections managed by the United States in 1928, 1930, and 1932 were deemed fair by the major parties in Nicaragua, but a split between Generals Anastasio Somoza and Augusto Sandino, both associated with the Liberal Party, precluded peace. Somoza became the hated dictator whose family maintained order for forty years. Sandino took to the hills in rebellion, plagued the U.S. Marines, and became a folk hero. It was not until January 1933 that the last of the marines came home.

Struggling to find a means of maintaining an order friendly to U.S. interests in Latin America at a time when the American public had little tolerance for presidential warmaking, the United States was prepared to surrender the hemispheric police powers Theodore Roosevelt had claimed in his notorious "corollary" to the Monroe Doctrine. No U.S. president or secretary of state, however, was willing to renounce the right to intervene. Much as the United States wanted to be a Good Neighbor, it retained the desire for hegemony in the region. Washington in the 1920s was unquestionably more sensitive to Latin American fears and aspirations than it had been earlier in the century, but the Coolidge administration abandoned little of the U.S. empire in the western hemisphere.[13]

One country often overlooked in the story of American expansion in the 1920s is Canada. No crisis, domestic or international, called attention to United State's northern neighbor. But Canada in the 1920s was the world's second largest importer of goods from the United States. In 1922, U.S. investors overtook their British counterparts to dominate Canadian capital markets. The Big Three automakers overwhelmed and destroyed the native auto industry. General Electric controlled Canada's largest electric company, and American subsidiaries produced more than two-thirds of Canada's electrical equipment. U.S. drugstores, five-and-dime, and grocery chains spread across the country. International Nickel, the largest mining company in Canada and producer of 90 percent of the world's nickel, was American-owned. Once a British colony, Canada was perilously close to becoming part of the American empire.[14]

East Asia provides an even better test of the argument that the United States was intensely involved in world affairs in the 1920s. The Philippines, the promise of eventual independence notwithstanding, remained a colony. American economic power contributed mightily to Japan's empire on the continent while American diplomacy, political influence, and military might —specifically the U.S. Navy—contained Japanese ambitions. The unresponsiveness of American bankers to pleas to finance China's modernization efforts left millions of Chinese to starve. The refusal of the United States to support other imperial powers in China eased Jiang Jieshi's path to dominance over most of his country. Whether Americans acted or chose not to act, their decisions often determined who prospered and who failed, who lived and who died.

Led by Japan, Asia increased in importance as a market for American goods. By the period 1926–30, approximately 12 percent of U.S. exports were going to Asia, more than twice the percentage for the prewar years of 1910–14.[15]

The administration of Woodrow Wilson, in its last hours, had recreated the four-power banking consortium designed to lend money to the Chinese government. But Lamont, who had negotiated the agreement on behalf of the Department of State, disappointed his government in the years that followed by denying the desired loans. He and his Morgan partners were more interested in the highly profitable, low-risk loans they could extend to Japan than they were in stimulating Chinese-American trade or the investments of American industrialists.[16] Efforts by Secretary of Commerce Herbert Hoover to facilitate trade and investment in China failed to produce the results of which publicists and officials dreamed.[17] But it was not for lack of trying.

The government of the United States was not successful in creating a coherent, sensible foreign economic policy. Ideological obstacles, such as the unwillingness to have the U.S. Treasury lend money to foreign governments, limited the role the government could play. Special interest groups blocked Harding and Coolidge administration efforts in the national interest, as when bankers subverted efforts at loan controls. But certainly the leaders of those two administrations understood the need for Washington to play a larger role in world economic affairs, to provide direction at home and leadership abroad.

Japanese officials had grand schemes for developing East Asia using American money and Japanese brains. The determination of American bankers to finance Japanese imperialism in Manchuria met with occasional opposition from the Department of State. In particular, the U.S. government tried to prevent American capital from being used to the detriment of American entrepreneurs competing with the Japanese. Wall Street, however, preferred the sure profits of dealing with Japanese government entities like the South Manchuria Railroad. Led by Lamont, the bankers were able to redesign the loans to make them acceptable. There were limits to the bankers' patriotism, and they consistently laundered funds intended to develop Japan's overseas empire. The U.S. government was rarely a match for Lamont's ingenuity.[18]

On the diplomatic level, the Harding administration quickly demonstrated that absence from the League of Nations did not preclude the United States from playing a major role in working for peace, especially in East Asia. In 1921, the United States invited all nations with interests in the region (except for Soviet Russia) to a conference in Washington aimed at easing tensions between the United States and Japan, mitigating Japanese imperialism in China, and forestalling an arms race. At the conference, Secretary of State Charles Evans Hughes and his staff performed brilliantly. They won concessions from Japan for U.S. interests in the Pacific island of Yap, obtained the abrogation of the troubling Anglo-Japanese alliance, succeeded in reaching agreement on a major naval arms limitation agreement, and gained international acceptance of American views of the best way to protect China from further imperialist encroachment. The conference was a great triumph for the United States and created a Pacific system that endured for most of the remainder of the decade—until undermined by the Chinese Nationalist revolution and the Japanese response to it.[19]

As Sun Zhongshan and Jiang Jieshi, with Soviet assistance, led their forces northward from Guangzhou to subordinate warlords and imperialists to their national purpose, the American government was generally indifferent, sometimes hostile. On one occasion, it sent warships to prevent Sun from seizing the customs surplus at Guangzhou. Americans in China enjoyed imperial privileges, including immunity from Chinese law. At home there was little public awareness of the situation, certainly not of what it might cost to maintain those privileges.[20]

In May 1925, an incident in Shanghai led to a spontaneous outburst of antiforeign sentiment that raged throughout China, fanned by Nationalist and Communist agitators. The Chinese revolutionaries demanded an end to imperialist privilege, not least an end to the stationing of foreign troops on Chinese soil, foreign gunboats in Chinese waters. J. V. A. MacMurray, the U.S. minister in China, urged rejection of Chinese demands. The American Chamber of Commerce in Shanghai called for a show of force. But the American public was in no mood to use force against a poor country so that a few businessmen and missionaries might enjoy profit and privilege abroad. The use of American power was not an option available to the Coolidge administration.[21]

By January 1927, the Coolidge administration had indicated its willingness to revise its treaty relationship with China and surrender at least some of the privileges Americans enjoyed there. In March, the House of Representatives overwhelmingly passed a resolution calling for negotiations to give the Chinese what they wanted. What could be retained through negotiation might be kept; what had to be fought for would be abandoned.

An attack by Nationalist forces on foreigners in Nanjing that included the murder of the American vice president of Nanjing University provoked bombardment by American and British gunboats and forced postponement of a diplomatic solution. It took a year before settlement of that incident could be negotiated and the diplomatic approach resumed. President Coolidge then declared that the Chinese Revolution was a worthy imitation of the American Revolution, an entirely praiseworthy effort by the Chinese to unite their country and free it from foreign domination. In July 1928, the United States and China signed a new treaty granting tariff autonomy to China and constituting recognition of Jiang's government.[22]

Washington had been slow to recognize the imperatives of the situation, slow to respond to Chinese nationalism. When the revolution finally impinged on the consciousness of American leaders, they understood they would have to yield, the advice of the American minister to China and the American business community there not withstanding. The ability of the Nationalists and the Communists to mobilize the masses meant that retention of the privileges of empire would require the sustained use of force, would mean American casualties in numbers that few in the United States would have found tolerable. Instead, the Coolidge administration retreated, sought rapprochement with the Chinese revolutionaries, allowing Americans once more to view themselves as "champions of the sovereign rights of China."

More remote from American interests was the revolution in Russia. Wilson's initial delight with the overthrow of the tsar's regime in March

1917 had evaporated when the Bolsheviks seized power in November. Wilson never conceded the legitimacy of Lenin's Soviet government and refused to recognize it. But despite the hostility of the Great Powers, the Bolsheviks prevailed in the ensuing Russian civil war.

Soviet leaders had little hope of softening Wilson's heart; they were optimistic, however, about doing business with his successors. Within the limits of their understanding of American political culture, they expected Republicans to be more responsive to economic inducements. A number of prominent Republicans favored recognition, but Secretary of State Hughes rejected the idea, repelled by Soviet leaders' repudiation of the debts of their predecessors and Moscow's support for an American Communist Party dedicated to the overthrow of the government of the United States. If American protests were to no avail, then Washington would use the only weapons available to it: nonrecognition and discriminatory trade practices.[23] For the United States in the 1920s, Russia was of little relevance. The Soviets posed no threat to American security, and they were of minimal economic importance. Despite the Red Scare in the closing months of the Wilson administration, despite widespread antiradicalism across the country, the American Communists frightened few. Their existence and that of the Soviet regime served as useful instruments for reactionary forces in American society, but there was little genuine concern—and little interest in Russia.

Still, Soviet leaders reached out to American businessmen, hoping to exploit the profit motive for political and development purposes. In the course of the 1920s, they had considerable success, especially in obtaining American financing and technology for Russian modernization. The persistent inability of the American government to harness foreign economic policy to political policy worked to Soviet advantage.

During Coolidge's presidency, hundreds of concession contracts were signed between Soviet authorities and American capitalists. The Soviet Amtorg Trading Corporation maintained an office in New York and purchased large quantities of American products. By 1928, a fourth of all foreign investment in Russia was American. By 1930, Americans also led all exporters to the Soviet state with a 25 percent market share. Averell Harriman, a central figure in Cold War relations between the United States and the Soviet Union, received a billion-dollar manganese concession. The Hammer family, Armand and his father Julius, opened a pencil factory in Soviet Russia and diversified their efforts with an asbestos mining contract and art dealing.[24] The Ford Motor Company also developed strong links with Russia. In 1925, more than a third of the tractors exported by Ford went to the Soviets. By 1927, 85 percent of the tractors used by Russian farmers had been manufactured by Ford. In 1929, Henry Ford signed a contract to facilitate the creation of a Soviet auto and truck industry, enabling the Russians to create an imitation Model A. Other major corporations such as DuPont, General Electric, and International Harvester signed agreements with the Soviet government for trade and the transfer of technology. And hundreds of American engineers, agricultural and steel industry specialists, went to Soviet Russia in the 1920s to help modernize the Soviet economy.[25]

Clearly, American capital and technology contributed enormously to the development of the Soviet economy in the 1920s. It was probably essential to the success of Moscow's first Five Year Plan. Equally obvious is the fact that the government of the United States, despite general hostility to Bolshevism, made no effort to prevent the transfer of important technology to the Soviet state. It was not the practice of the American government to coordinate trade with political policy in peacetime. Washington was just beginning an awkward effort to persuade bankers to subordinate their loans to what political leaders perceived to be the national interest. Moreover, the experience of dealing with a state-controlled economy was new and few American officials understood the way in which such an economy could be manipulated for political ends.

In sum, during the 1920s, the American government remained unfriendly toward the Soviet state but allowed private interests free rein to assist in the modernization of the Soviet economy. The Bolsheviks were viewed with contempt rather than fear. Coolidge and his advisers would have liked to see the Bolshevik regime disappear. They did not fear it enough to advocate any action to eliminate it. As the economic power of the United States grew, it penetrated even the Soviet state and influenced the development of that country. The larger role of the United States in world affairs in the 1920s is as evident in the Soviet Union as anywhere else in the world—and in few places was it more benign.

At home, as well as elsewhere in Europe, there was ample evidence of increased American interest and involvement in world affairs. In addition to the peace movement that played a role in bringing about the Washington Conference and the Kellogg-Briand pact and restrained gunboat diplomacy in Latin America and China, the Council on Foreign Relations was created in the 1920s. The first separate school for the study of world affairs was established at Georgetown University in 1919. In 1925, Johns Hopkins University and the Department of State opened their own schools to train Americans for careers in international relations. And the Fletcher School of Law and Diplomacy came into being in 1932.[26]

In the 1920s, the power and influence of the United States grew throughout the world. This expansion was most evident when measured in terms of economic interests. It was also visible in the efforts of the government to bring stability to Europe and East Asia, as well as to traditional areas of concern in Latin America. Directly or indirectly, Washington participated in nearly every important international meeting of the era and acted responsibly, with considerable success in achieving American goals. Despite its regrettable failure to join the League, the United States was the world's leading power and the dominant actor on the global stage.

NOTES

1. Stephen Schuker, *The End of French Predominance in Europe: The Financial Crisis of 1924 and the Adoption of the Dawes Plan* (1976); Michael J. Hogan, *Informal Entente: The Private Structure of Cooperation in Anglo-American Economic Diplomacy, 1918–1929* (1977); Melvyn P. Leffler, *The Elusive Quest: America's Pursuit of European Stability and French Security, 1919–1933* (1979); Joan Hoff Wilson, *American Business and Foreign Policy, 1920–1933* (1971).

2. Emily Rosenberg, *Spreading the American Dream: American Economic and Cultural Expansion, 1890–1945* (1982).

3. Wilson, *American Business and Foreign Policy*, 184–200; Mira Wilkins, *The Maturing of the Multinational Enterprise: American Business Abroad from 1914–1970* (1974), 113–22.

4. Wilkins, *Maturing of Multinational Enterprise*, 98–100; Hogan, *Informal Entente*, 193–96.

5. Wilkins, ibid., 104–6.

6. Ibid., 97–98.

7. Ibid., 135.

8. Ibid., 127.

9. Robert F. Smith, *The United States and Revolutionary Nationalism in Mexico, 1916–1932* (1972), 190–228; Karl M. Schmitt, *Mexico and the United States, 1821–1973: Conflict and Coexistence* (1974), 161–64; N. Steven Kane, "American Businessmen and Foreign Policy: The Recognition of Mexico, 1920–23," *Political Science Quarterly* 90 (1975): 293–313.

10. Smith, *U.S. and Revolutionary Nationalism in Mexico*, 229–65; Charles Chatfield, *For Peace and Justice: Pacifism in America, 1914–1941* (1971), 109; L. Ethan Ellis, *Frank B. Kellogg and American Foreign Relations, 1925–1929* (1961), 242–52.

11. Akira Iriye, *The Globalizing of America, 1913–1945*, vol. 3 of *Cambridge History of American Foreign Relations* (1993), 103–11.

12. L. Ethan Ellis, *Republican Foreign Policy, 1921–1933* (1968), 252–76; see especially Bryce Wood's *The Making of the Good Neighbor Policy* (1961), and Elting E. Morison, *Turmoil and Tradition: The Life and Times of Henry L. Stimson* (1960).

13. Iriye, *Globalizing of America*, 82–83.

14. Wilkins, *Maturing of Multinational Enterprises*, 61–74, 84–88, 106; Gordon T. Stewart, *The American Response to Canda since 1776* (1992), 127–40.

15. U.S. Department of Commerce, *Statistical Abstract of the United States, 1934* (1934), 424.

16. Warren I. Cohen, *The Chinese Connection: Roger S. Greene, Thomas W. Lamont, George E. Sokolsky, and American-East Asian Relations* (1978), 41–70, 97–119; Warren I. Cohen, "America's New Order in East Asia: The Four Power Financial Consortium and China, 1919–1946," in *Essays in the History of China and Chinese American Relations* (1982), 41–74. Wilson, *American Business and Foreign Policy*, 207–11.

17. See Wilson, *American Business and Foreign Policy*; Joseph Brandes, *Herbert Hoover and Economic Diplomacy: Department of Commerce Policy, 1921–1928*.

18. Cohen, *The Chinese Connection*, 148–60.

19. Akira Iriye, *After Imperialism: The Search for a New Order in the Far East* (1965); Thomas H. Buckley, *The United States and the Washington Conference, 1921–1922* (1970).

20. Warren I. Cohen, *America's Response to China* (1990) 3d ed., 90–93.

21. Ibid., 93–97; Dorothy Borg, *America and the Chinese Revolution, 1925–1928* (1947).

22. Borg, *America and the Chinese Revolution*, 386–431.

23. John L. Gaddis, *Russia, the Soviet Union, and the United States* (1978), 98.

24. Ibid., 99–104; Wilkins, *Maturing of Multinational Enterprises*, 107; see also Robert P. Browder, *The Origins of Soviet-American Relations* (1953).

25. Browder, *Origins of Soviet-American Relations*.

26. Warren I. Cohen, *Empire Without Tears: America's Foreign Relations, 1921–1933* (1987), 2, 15.

10

Made in the U.S.A.

Mass Culture and the Americanization of Working-Class Ethnics

in the Coolidge Era

RONALD EDSFORTH

If we refuse to travel towards Communism the only alternative
is to become Americanised.

TOM MANN[1]

I

In the years between the election of 1920, which restored Republican control of the federal government and brought Calvin Coolidge to Washington, and the election of 1936 in which a huge majority of voters endorsed
both the presidential leadership of Franklin D. Roosevelt and New Deal
reformers in Congress, national politics was transformed by a profoundly
important democratic development—the entry of massive numbers of white
working-class ethnics and black working-class migrants from the South
into the political system.[2] This mass political mobilization principally benefited the Democratic Party, helping to sweep what had been a weak and
fractionalized organization into a truly dominant national political position
during the Great Depression. Given the chronology of this development—
Democrats winning practical control of the House of Representatives in
1930, gaining overwhelming control of both Houses of Congress as well as
the White House in 1932, and expanding their majorities in 1934 and again
in 1936—it is not surprising that depression-era conditions among working people are usually viewed as the principal cause of the establishment of
a Democratic national majority that endured for fifty years.

244

Certainly, a depression-centered interpretation has much in its favor; mass unemployment and underemployment in the early 1930s undoubtedly hastened the creation of huge Democratic majorities in many urban-industrial centers. In fact, given the enormous popularity of Franklin D. Roosevelt and the New Deal among urban working-class voters and poor rural Americans, the terms "Roosevelt realignment" and "Roosevelt coalition," or variously "New Deal coalition" or even "Roosevelt revolution," are used most frequently to describe this particular political transformation.[3] Moreover, widely discussed low turnout figures for Coolidge era national elections—49.2 percent of eligible voters in 1920 and 48.9 percent in 1924—reinforce the popular contemporary impression that the depression and Roosevelt alone brought about realignment.[4]

But for a long time now, scholars have recognized that the Roosevelt realignment and formation of the New Deal coalition actually had their origins in the Coolidge era. Low overall turnout in national elections and the beginnings of the political mobilization of working-class ethnics actually occurred simultaneously. Heavier reliance on new campaign styles, particularly moral suasion and advertising, may have accounted for a large part of the long-term decline in political participation that culminated in the Coolidge era.[5] But perfection of the system of disenfranchisement of blacks and poor whites in the South, and the slowness with which women took advantage of their new voting rights in the 1920s, clearly pushed down national turnout figures (the percentage of eligible citizens actually voting) even as larger numbers of urban ethnic were politically activated.

Several years before the Great Depression, previously active working-class voters began shifting from the Republican to the Democratic Party, and significant numbers of previously nonvoting, especially younger, working-class citizens had begun to register to vote despite increasingly more complicated registration requirements.[6] Undoubtedly, as prominent scholars have long argued, the heavy urban ethnic working-class vote for New York's Irish Catholic Al Smith in the 1928 presidential election was a major step in the political transformation that still carries Roosevelt's name.[7] But this fact does not mean that Smith's Democratic campaign actually set the transformation in motion. Richard Oestreicher has shown that "an undertone of class sentiment . . . foreshadowing the class basis of the New Deal alignment" had appeared as early as the 1924 election when workers in some cities showed the same kind of strong preference for the Progressive Party's presidential candidate Robert La Follette that they would later demonstrate for Franklin Roosevelt. Oestreicher described this class sentiment as a latent force that first had appeared in pre–World War I elections and as something politicians could, and sometimes did, deliberately tap into during campaigns in the interwar period.[8] Perhaps Oestreicher is right on this last point, but his larger argument rests too heavily on a presumed link between social structure and political behavior. Fortunately, we do not have to rely on this form of interpretation for the Coolidge era. In the 1920s, the development of new political energies and new loyalties among working-class ethnics stemmed from more immediate causes. To understand these causes, we have to look at more than campaigns and election results; we have to look carefully at the variety of developments in politics, the economy, and society affecting the political culture of that time.

At first glance, it is hard to discern connections between Coolidge era political culture and the "Roosevelt realignment" that came to fruition in the 1930s. For example, the most important constitutional change of the 1920s, the implementation of universal female suffrage, appears to have benefited Republicans far more than Democrats. In fact, a careful study of the formation of the New Deal coalition in Boston suggests that this tendency persisted into the 1930s with women voters of all classes switching from the Republicans to the Democrats later than the men in their precincts.[9] Moreover, between elections, female activists generally rejected partisanship in favor of single-issue lobbying efforts in the 1920s, thereby reinforcing instead of challenging the business (and male) dominated political style of the era.[10] Hence, it seems fair to conclude that the advent of universal female suffrage had no strong causal relationship to the subsequent political realignment and reinvigoration of partisanship. Working-class women did not lead working-class men into the voting booth or the Democratic Party.

It is also difficult to connect other important well-known aspects of Coolidge era political culture to the subsequent "Roosevelt revolution." There were many strong tides running against reform and against expanded political participation by working-class ethnics and blacks in the 1920s. Business-oriented Republicans dominated national politics and lobbying efforts in Congress. Jim Crow was firmly in place in the South and in many other places outside that region, and nativism shaped political debates all over the country. Longstanding white Protestant movements to impose Prohibition and restrict immigration finally had succeeded in the Coolidge era. Moreover, other pseudo-populist forms of nativism, which had helped sweep the Republicans into power during the Red Scare, persisted. Many politicians, editors, and cartoonists continued to employ anti-immigrant political rhetoric and imagery, and many communities and corporations developed a variety of coercive Americanization programs designed to make nonnatives, in the words of the president of the Pennsylvania Railroad, "give up the languages, customs, and methods of life which they have brought with them across the ocean, and adopt instead the language, habits of this country."[11] Realignment and working-class-oriented reform were also hindered by the deteriorating condition of the labor movement. Organized labor, which had allied itself with the Democratic

Party and progressivism during the Wilson presidency, was collapsing in the Coolidge era. For all we have learned about workers in the past thirty-five years, there is still no reason to revise Irving Bernstein's assessment that the 1920s were indeed "the lean years" for American unions. Radical organizations were effectively repressed, and almost every union affiliated with the American Federation of Labor was put on the defensive. William Green, the new president of the AFL, who succeeded Samuel Gompers in December 1924, courted the approval of businessmen and the business-dominated press. During the 1920s, most unions simply did not offer immigrant and ethnic workers a way to expand their political influence. As Robert Zieger has recently written, "Everywhere, except in a few unionized enclaves, . . . the right to organize was nonexistent. . . . Everywhere, it was open season on anyone who dared to talk union." [12]

Other developments in the Coolidge era economy, society, and the emerging mass popular culture also look as if they worked against the political participation of working people. Fordism, not unionism, triumphed in the Coolidge era. A true mass-consumer economy, centered on the personal ownership of automobiles, emerged. By the time Coolidge was elected president in his own right, half the households in the country owned at least one car; by the end of Coolidge prosperity in 1929, an estimated 30 percent of all working-class households owned an automobile. [13] Workers certainly did not become affluent in the 1920s; in fact, given the uncertainties of employment, most struggled to keep up decent minimum living standards. Nonetheless, many workers, especially younger workers, did enter into the national consumer-oriented "American Dream" culture that manufacturers, advertisers, popular magazines, and movie studios disseminated. Here, the late Warren Susman's words are worth repeating.

> It is not a question of whether such abundance was a real possibility. The significant issue is the belief that it was. . . . Everywhere there was a new emphasis on buying, spending and consuming. Advertising became not only a new economic force essential in the regulation of prices but also a vision of the way the culture worked: the products of the culture became advertisements of the culture itself. [14]

And in the Coolidge era, an increasingly wide variety of those new products was developed by corporate designers and engineers, mass-produced by workers using Fordist techniques, and sold to an ever widening circle of Americans.

The publicity and hoopla that accompanied the selling of new machines designed for the everyday use and enjoyment of ordinary people undoubtedly shaped the nation's commitment to making a mass-consumer society. Everywhere things, especially the automobile and the new environment built to accommodate a nation of auto-mobile citizens, conveyed the message that America was becoming a new and better place. As Strother Mac-Minn, a designer who worked on Ford's wildly popular 1928 Model A, recalled, "it [style change] . . . says things are getting better. If they aren't changing they aren't getting better."[15] Although MacMinn was speaking specifically of the kind of surface level alterations that General Motors later turned into annual model changes (and that critics in the 1950s and 1960s rightly described as "planned obsolescence"), in the 1920s far more than the surface of things was changing. Real and dramatic improvements in everyday life underpinned corporate advertisers endlessly repeated message that America's emerging mass consumer society was the embodiment of progress.

Although historians often overlook it, remarkable improvements in life expectancy accompanied the extension of mass-consumer society. Between 1911 and 1920, life expectancy at birth in the United States averaged 51.8 years; between 1921 and 1930, the average was 58.7 years. During the 1930s, the pace of improvement slowed but did not stop, and it picked up again in the 1940s. During that latter decade, life expectancy at birth averaged 66.2 years.[16] Expanded public health programs, improvements in diet and medical care, reductions in work time and in workplace accidents, and the related expansion of white-collar work all contributed to this extremely important long-term trend.[17] The fact that people were living longer and longer as each decade passed surely had a subtle but powerful effect on the way Americans viewed their society. Increasingly, it was not just the lucky and/or the rich who could look forward to a long life. Longer lives became a birthright for most Americans in the first half of this century. But did longer lives mean richer lives?

Labor and social historians have long insisted, for good reasons, that "Coolidge prosperity" did not actually trickle down to working people.[18] Yet workers and their families were certainly aware of the direction and momentum of material changes during the 1920s. These changes were most dramatic in the metropolitan areas and small industrial cities, where most workers lived, because electric power was made rapidly available to urban homes. In the Coolidge era, electricity and all the new machines and gadgets it powered defined a key experiential difference between urban and rural America. Rural electrification proceeded at a snail's pace during the Coolidge era. Rural places, where more than two-fifths of Americans still lived in the 1920s, were far less likely to have electric power available for even the most mundane tasks such as running the pump needed for flush toilets. There was little regional variation in this pattern. In most states, fewer than 10 percent of rural homes had electric power. In the Coolidge era (and for two decades after), it was literally true that bright lights, the cinema, and the other amenities made possible by electric power drew young rural-born Americans to the cities.[19]

As a result of rapid electrification, evidence of the kinds of technological progress proclaimed in mass circulation magazine advertising and reporting was ubiquitous in urban everyday life during the 1920s. For example, at the start of the decade, only one-fifth of American households had indoor flush toilets; by 1930, more than half did. In the same ten-year period, the number of households with electric lights rose from 35 to 68 percent. Since the overwhelming majority of these homes were located in urban places, it is safe to assume that most urban workers lived in electrified apartments and houses by 1930. Workers and their families helped account for the astounding sales of radios. In 1920, home radios and radio programming did not exist, but as early as 1931, over half the households in America owned at least one radio, and despite the Great Depression, the number of owners of home radios kept on increasing during the 1930s. So did the number of households that owned vacuum cleaners, clothes washers, refrigerators, and other mundane household appliances.[20]

Working-class people, including younger working-class ethnics, were especially drawn to the more transitory and more affordable pleasures of what was often called "the New Era." The 1920s were indeed a "New Era" because the pursuit of personal pleasure, not religion or politics, seemed to characterize the public lives of more and more citizens. Hollywood stars, the most notorious pleasure seekers, were widely admired (as politicians at the time of the Teapot Dome scandal and its aftermath were not). Between 1926 and 1930, the years when "talkies" replaced silent films, weekly attendance at the movies soared from fifty to one hundred million. In addition, each month millions of Americans, including many working-class readers, followed the off-screen exploits of the stars in mass-marketed "fanzines" that offered them both the vicarious thrill of "life at the edge" and the satisfactions of feeling morally superior.[21] Celebrities like Rudolph Valentino, Fatty Arbuckle, Clara Bow, Mary Pickford, Douglas Fairbanks, and the high-living baseball star Babe Ruth expanded the boundaries of morally acceptable behavior, and in doing so, they adapted the longstanding Horatio Alger myth of individual success to a new era of mass-marketed goods and pleasures.[22]

Like the new stars of Hollywood, the increasing numbers of college and high school students of the Coolidge era were a morally troubling presence. They shocked parents, ministers, and educators with their unchaperoned dating and petting parties, but these same "youth"—a self-proclaimed new social and cultural group—helped to liberate the pursuit of pleasure from the moral constraints of the older generation.[23] Middle- and upper-class youth were not alone. Massive violations of prohibition, the proliferation of speakeasies and juke joints, and the astounding popularity of entertainments like dance halls, jazz, automobile racing, professional baseball and boxing, and college football all indicate that Americans, young and old and from *all classes and all races*, had decided paying to have "a good time" was an important part of life. Indeed, historian Robin Kelley has discovered that nothing less than "a moral panic over commercialized leisure" swept through fast-growing urban black communities in the 1920s. The same was true of white ethnic neighborhoods and middle-class communities, too.[24]

In his important book, *The Decline of Popular Politics*, Michael McGerr argued that the development of America's pleasure-oriented popular culture became an obstacle to mass political participation by the 1920s. Yet if this is true, how do we explain the beginnings of political realignment that included a significant increase in the participation of working-class ethnics and blacks in elections in those same years?[25] Clearly, we must start by abandoning any assumption that mass-consumer society and its pleasure-oriented popular culture *inevitably* generated political apathy.[26]

By registering to vote and by turning out at the polls, in the second half of the 1920s ever larger numbers of urban working-class ethnics engaged themselves in a most American activity, partisan politics. Moreover, as they first trickled and then poured into the voting booths of the nation's industrial cities and towns, these same working-class ethnics influenced candidates and elected officials and, through those officials, the policies of government. In other words, during the Coolidge era and after, at least in the political sense of the term, working-class ethnics were demonstrating that they were in fact increasingly "Americanized," that they believed in the American system of government. Using the term "Americanized" is of course a risky business, but it is necessary. For it was the Americanized working class that started to emerge during Coolidge's presidency that ultimately placed Franklin Roosevelt and the Democratic Party in command of national politics in the 1930s. And it was this same Americanized working class that greatly influenced the New Deal, leading Democrats in the White House and Congress to take two steps—the establishment of a federal welfare state and the establishment of the rights of labor—that together amounted to a revolutionary break with past political precedents. Thus, to better understand just how working-class Americans came to be able to effect such important changes in the nation's politics and government, it is necessary to reconsider the meaning of "Americanization" in the Coolidge era.[27]

II

"Americanization." The word is an evocative (as well as provocative) historical term. It is a word that lives in our present as well as the past.[28] For historians like myself who are most interested in the period between the World Wars, hearing or reading the term "Americanization" most likely triggers a flood of vivid mental images and verbal associations. These images and associations strongly color the meaning we ultimately assign to the historical term "Americanization." We historians draw many images and associations directly from the primary and secondary sources on the 1920s that we have read and studied. In this sense, our response is truly scholarly. In addition, materials drawn from other periods we have studied, and what we know of public events that have occurred during our lifetimes, also surface when we encounter the word "Americanization." Since it is created in our mental present, our response to the word "Americanization" inevitably injects present feelings into the way we use the term in our scholarly work and teaching. Our own attitudes toward today's mass immigration from Latin America and Asia and the concurrent upsurge in nativist political activity are unavoidably part of the mix. Moreover, each of us is likely to attach unique personal memory images and associations to the ostensibly historical term "Americanization." What initially coalesces then is a kind of mental collage that may violate chronology and logic but that nonetheless deeply informs the kind of history we write about the Coolidge era and its aftermath (and thus deeply influences the way the public ultimately perceives this crucial period in our history).

To illustrate, I offer the following sample of my own personal responses to this evocative word.

"Americanization." Immigrants and their children, staring out from old Lewis Hine photographs, at Ellis Island, in sweatshops, coal mines, textile mills, and heavy industry, too. Old photographs of workers in steel mills and Henry Ford's factory. Hard times. Old photographs of teeming streets on the lower Eastside, in Packingtown, and Homestead; photographs of streets crowded with pushcarts, children, and women with babies (like the opening scenes of *The Godfather*). Old photographs of people out on the stoops and row house porches; photographs of different people, so many people living in poor but vital neighborhoods—not suburbs!—neighborhoods where homes and businesses are all mixed together and the streets are full of people, not cars. Good times.

"Americanization." The word calls to mind old photographs in sepia and black-and-white, the tones that our society, now awash in color images, uses to invoke nostalgia and sentimentality. Old photographs and remembrances of times past, and stories about even earlier times told and retold, this stuff of our personal memory images: of grandparents and their homes, of weddings and family gatherings long ago, of our parents when they were young and we were even younger, their faces a reminder of our youth, as well as our current age. Hard times? No those were good times, weren't they?

"Americanization." The City Council, the Chamber of Commerce, the Employers Association, the American Legion, the PTA, the local labor council, the personnel office, the boss—solid citizens all—all working together to build the character of urban-industrial America. "The business of America is business," the president is said to have proclaimed, but this business also turns out Americans, "100% Americans." Solid citizens in suits and dresses going door-to-door, inviting, cajoling, leading the less-than-100-percent Americans down to the "Y" for classes in Citizenship and Civics. YOU WILL BEHAVE LIKE AN AMERICAN!

"Americanization." Language classes, so many different places offering classes in English, American English. Classes at the ubiquitous "Y," or at night at the public school, or maybe even at the factory as part of the employer's "American Plan." On the job "Americanization," how convenient! All these immigrant men and women, these Poles, Slavs, Czechs, Slovaks, Romanians, Hungarians, Russians, Serbs, Croats, Greeks, Jews, and Italians, these workers, gathered here at the factory; make them study English—"Yes sir, No sir. The pay is good. The work is good. I will never join a union as long as I work here, sir." Make them speak American English, the kind of English the boss likes to hear.

"Americanization." The flag—"Our Flag"—must be venerated. "And to the nation"—one nation—"for which it stands," the whole class reciting this Pledge of Allegiance, every day, month after month, year after year, generation after generation. Everyone standing, the whole stadium from box seats to bleachers, standing for the "Star Spangled Banner." Our hymn to the flag must be sung before the game can begin. We must proclaim ourselves "the home of the brave and the land of the free" before the first pitch, first basket, first face-off—before the fun can start. Over and over, season after season, year after year, the flag rituals of our national civic religion remind us, all of us, we are "one nation under God."

"Americanization." Parades, so many parades in so many towns and cities. Year after year, these parades never fail to bring out "the masses" on the appointed day; assembling the nation into crowds of people all standing, except for children crouched at curbside, all waiting for the marching bands and the flags; for Sousa and the red, white, and blue; and for the veterans in formation: veterans from the Civil War, the Indian wars, the Spanish War, the war in the Philippines, the Great War—so many wars, so many warriors, a warrior nation—all passing by under sacred flags unfurled.

"Americanization." Public rituals—pledging, parading, assembling in the Coolidge era. Some of us call it a "tribal" time. Gathering together an American tribe. The gatherings at night, the ones in the old photographs—the white robes and hoods all lit up by torches and burning crosses—those gatherings were the scariest. Ku Klux Klan-style "Americanization" flourished inside *and outside* the former Confederacy during the Coolidge era. The KKK held pep rallies for "100% Americanism." The KKK put racial nationalism on parade. White-robed white Americans out in broad daylight, marching down Main Street—in Georgia, of course—but also in Michigan, Indiana, Ohio, and New Jersey too. I've seen the pictures. The KKK marched in massed formations down Independence Avenue under "Our Flag" during the Coolidge era.

"Americanization." The Coolidge era sequel to the Red Scare. Ugly Americans, again. Close "the Golden Door." Shut down the beer gardens. Shutter the saloons. YOU WILL BEHAVE LIKE AMERICANS! A nation of sheep, treating immigrants and their children like cattle. Inspect them, indoctrinate them, persuade them, coerce them, force them into the melting pot, force them to assimilate. YOU WILL BECOME AMERICANS! "100% AMERICANS."

Although this particular collage of images of immigrant families and their communities, of native-born patriotism and coercive nativism, is my own, the incorporation of sentimental and ugly imagery into the term "Americanization" is widespread. Certainly in this form, "Americanization" is not a value-free term. Sentimentality and images of victims seem automatically to emerge from the process of envisioning "Americanization," and as they do, almost as automatically, related stories of victimization and of resistance to victimization (including efforts by working-class and middle-class ethnics to teach English and citizenship to working people) take shape linking the sentimental and ugly images into a cohesive meaningful whole.[29] Indeed, today the term "Americanization" is most often used by professional historians in the United States as a shorthand for the episodes of victimization and resistance to that victimization that extended from World War I to the Great Depression. Furthermore, these episodes are generally agreed to fit within a longer narrative, a narrative of rising and falling but ever-present tensions between "natives and strangers," between the people who see themselves as "old stock" Americans and the people who are, and who usually know they are, "new immigrants" in America. John Higham's now classic *Strangers in the Land* remains the richest, most detailed presentation of this history.[30] But its essentials are simple, like a good set of lecture notes. Indeed, I suspect that something like these essentials has been used to structure many lectures in American history.

In [pick your decade or period], mass immigration to the United States created new large ethnic communities that better established groups perceived as different and threatening; racial/ethnic pride and prejudices flourished, developing into persistent patterns of discrimination and inequality; often when [pick your cause or combination of causes: economic difficulties, or war, or the threat of war, or big strikes, or rapid social or technological changes] caused the better-off "old stock" Americans to feel uncertain about their futures, nativist organizations and nativist politicians thrived. But nearly as often, in periods of widespread optimism and confidence, nativist movements declined and nativist politics lost its mass appeal.

This simple story of conflict over the American identity is compelling. Not only does it give us a way to organize the always messy and confusing facts of ethnic group relations in any period in United States history, it also helps us makes sense of our own messy and confusing present and its relationship to the past.

Thus, as it is most commonly used among American historians, the term "Americanization" is never really just about the Coolidge era, it is also about this larger story, about the rest of American history including our own lifetime. Used in this way, the term "Americanization" is heavily colored by a necessarily negative reading of American nativism. Such usage implies that "Americanization" is always coercive because it describes the coercive efforts of "nativists" (once all native-born white Protestants, but now perhaps including most native-born Catholics as well as some Jews and blacks) who devote corporate, community, and political resources to force groups identified as "foreign" to assimilate themselves into what the native-born define as genuine American culture. Thus, in histories of the Coolidge era, education programs, run by companies like the Pennsylvania Railroad and the Ford Motor Company, are lumped with Ku Klux Klan politics, and both modern corporations and hooded Americanizers become "old stock" or "Anglo-Saxon Protestant" parts of what is variously labeled as the "mainstream," "dominant," or even "hegemonic" culture. As such, Coolidge era "Americanization" ultimately finds itself located within the centuries-long story of the repression of difference, and resistance to this repression, that is now so often presented as the essence of American history.

When American historians today employ the term "Americanization" as a shorthand to describe particular developments in the 1920s, its meaning is inevitably created and influenced by its positioning in this longer story, a narrative that runs from the Alien and Sedition Acts of the 1790s to the Know-Nothings of the 1840s, through the Coolidge era to the Cold War and McCarthyism, from the Civil Rights movement and White Citizens Councils to the ethnic revival of the 1970s and the coincidental rise of the New Right, and most recently to the demands of some of our political leaders to again restrict immigration, fortify the southern border, make English our official language, and prevent noncitizens from using public services like hospitals and clinics and public schools.

This implied, long history of "Americanization" seems almost timeless, although the details of each episode, like the rise and fall of the Ku Klux Klan in the 1920s, remain fixed in a particular historical period. Of course, as a story, the conflict over American identity always has a genesis—perhaps 1492, 1609, 1776, or some other specific date—but it has no end. Indeed, I suspect many of us believe that it is repeating itself in the 1990s. For most of this century, the idea that the United States is a nation of immigrants has retained its power no matter how far removed the vast majority of its citizens are from actual emigration from another country. And the way we argue about this nation's problems remains fundamentally the same, too. "One hundred percent Americanism" versus cultural pluralism becomes common culture versus multiculturalism; Henry Pratt Fairchild and Horace Kallen are replaced by Diane Ravitch and Molefi Kete Asante.[31]

The real persistence of these ideological divisions and the cyclical character of the rising and falling of attendant tensions that John Higham made so brilliantly clear in *Strangers in the Land* gives this version of American history a powerful myth-like appeal. Even though it highlights episodes of mass irrationality, prejudice, and repression, the story is strangely reassuring. In this view of American history, there is constancy in America. America *is* this conflict over identity no matter how much world wars, technology, the job market, family structure, the neighborhood, or the community changes. Therefore, what we confront today is essentially what earlier generations of Americans faced back then. Some "new immigrant" groups have become "old stock," but the struggle over what makes one an American goes on without end. Today, as professional historians attempt to find a unifying theme in American history, this struggle over identity gets most attention. "From the very moment of the birth of the nation, Americans had been asking themselves: 'Who are we?'" writes Alan Dawley in his recent history of the late nineteenth and early twentieth centuries. Ronald Takaki agrees in his important recent survey, *A Different Mirror: A History of Multicultural America*. "Americans have been constantly redefining their national identity from the moment of first contact on the Virginia shore," Takaki confidently proclaims.[32]

Of course, there is great truth in these statements, but is this story of the cyclical relationship of natives and strangers really history? It seems to me that more and more American historians have been slipping in the back door something that serious scholars were supposed to have thrown out the front door long ago. That something is a description of what must be called "national character." This criticism even applies to those labor historians who have recently stressed the concept of "whiteness" and the language and imagery of white racism in their descriptions of the process of "Americanization" among working people. In these accounts, embracing a "white" identity is presented as the key to entering into an American identity that is, and always has been, profoundly racist.[33] Undoubtedly, as recent case studies have reminded us, race, status, political power, and material rewards have been linked throughout our history, but we should take care not to reify racism as a fixed and always defining national characteristic. Racial thinking, racial imagery, as well as racism, all have histories that indicate their plasticity as well as their temporal (not fixed and permanent) character.[34]

To summarize, "Americanization" is, as I stated at the outset, much more than a historical term used to describe a particular aspect of the Coolidge era. It is a living word, a powerful judgmental word. And because of the negative judgment most American historians have incorporated into it, "Americanization" all too often becomes an ugly word, a word we usually scorn and denounce because we are repulsed by the national character it describes as an essential part of the past, and the present.

III

There is available in the wider world, as well as in the wider world of professional scholars, another definition of the word "Americanization" that seldom appears in the writing of American history. Although this definition of the word "Americanization" has been used variously by foreign critics to both praise and disparage economic, social, and cultural developments in the United States, it is an extremely useful definition. This "Americanization," which is sometimes spelled "Americanisation," may be defined as the process of becoming a mass-consumer society (which includes a mass popular culture). The word "Americanization" was given this meaning by foreign observers of developments in the United States around the turn of the century and has been part of unceasing political and cultural debates in Western Europe (and elsewhere) since the end of World War II. As Richard F. Kuisel explains in his recent book, *Seducing the French: The Dilemma of Americanization*:

> America and Americanization were realities that the French [and the Germans and the British among others] . . . had to face after 1945. The United States was a superpower that provided security and exerted enormous influence on postwar Western Europe. *Americanization was a process of economic modernization, and America was the first consumer society* and possibly a harbinger of Europe's future.[35]

When employed as a conceptual tool in the study of twentieth-century America, this definition of "Americanization" has much to recommend it. Most importantly, it forces American historians to recognize the twentieth-century United States as people in other nations have observed and understood it, not simply as we Americans have experienced and reflected upon it.[36] Using the word "Americanization" the way most of the rest of the world does makes us add more images and associations to our mental collage of the interwar period, makes us put together a different narrative, a history about modern American identity that certainly includes coercive nativism and resistance to it, but much else besides.

Clearly, characters in this new history have to become more complex. People in the past no longer live simply as natives and strangers. Instead, all of them become participants in a continuously unsettling process, the unceasing expansion of mass-consumer society. As such, we begin to see these Americans in the past as more than combatants, always struggling with each other. We also see that they are creators of the capitalist superpower of the twentieth century and that their struggles are part of a globally significant creative process. Conflicts between natives and strangers, as well as struggles between other groups, certainly do not disappear; instead, they find their places in what can be thought of as America's "second industrial revolution."[37] Most importantly for our purposes here, by employing "Americanization" to mean the making of the world's first mass-consumer society, we break free from dependence on the myth-like cycle of repression and resistance as the primary motive force in twentieth-century American history. And in its place, we put the phenomenal economic and popular cultural dynamism of the United States that has made, and continues to make, America a magnet to people from all over the world.[38]

Using "Americanization" as non-Americans do also helps us to avoid the assimilation trap, a scholarly quagmire that for too long has muddled our understanding of immigration and ethnic history.[39] Let me state my position on this issue plainly. In the first half of this century at least, when Americans had begun to create the world's first mass-consumer society, the whole culture was in such upheaval that it had no hegemonic core, no single group that can be said to be "the mainstream." Surely different groups (and institutions), as groups (and institutions), had more or less power. The economic power to make investment decisions was clearly concentrated in the hands of a relative few, and often this economic power was translated into power in politics and policy making. Andrew Mellon was both a private banking and a national economic policy-making colossus. Yet economic elites were not always united on political issues. And even when they were united—in their opposition to federal protection for union organizers, for example—the power of these elites could be challenged and limited as the struggles over the Wagner Act in the mid-1930s later revealed. Certainly, in the 1920s, the distribution of cultural power was much more complex than either income and wealth distribution patterns or the racial and ethnic categories that contemporaries used to simplify a very confusing reality suggest. Yes, Anglo-Saxon–dominated Harvard set quotas to exclude

Jews, but Jewish businessmen created Hollywood. It seems patently absurd to me to argue that Harvard was part of the core culture, what is often called the mainstream, but Hollywood was not. Were the Big Three automobile companies mainstream, but Tin Pan Alley peripheral? Was a Sousa march any more "American" than Louis Armstrong's "West End Blues"? In the first half of this century, the main stream of American culture was a churning, creative, destructive torrent seeking new banks. And most Americans who were contributing their own energies to this river of change were also seeking firm ground on which to stand.

This effort to find firm ground can be found everywhere in American life during the first half of the twentieth century. It infused the activities of wealthy elites who tried to insulate "high culture" from popular cultural developments they judged as beneath them.[40] And it inspired the cultural politics of black Americans' Great Migration: the Harlem Renaissance, the New Negro Movement, and the Universal Negro Improvement Association.[41] The search for firm ground also found expression in both the politics of nativists and cultural pluralists during the Coolidge era and the politics of union recognition and social security that came to fruition in the New Deal years.

In the first half of our century, nearly everyone was learning how to live in a society that was in constant flux, a society where flux was the institutionalized mainspring of economic life. As early as the Progressive Era, and certainly by the Coolidge era, living with a myriad of ongoing and seemingly unstoppable processes of "creative destruction" had become the unavoidable essence of everyday life. It still is.[42]

In mass-consumer America, the new is constantly destroying the old. Machines displace workers, new jobs replace old jobs, new production quotas replace old requirements. In the Coolidge era, a rural nation became a nation of city-dwellers, and already city-dwellers had begun a flight to the suburbs. In mass-consumer America, neighborhoods are built, change, and often disappear altogether. "New" and "improved" products are always replacing old and perfectly useful products. This year's model displaces last year's model, year after year after year. Nothing has seemed capable of stopping this dynamic process, not even the Great Depression. Alfred P. Sloan had General Motors implement the annual model change in the midst of the Great Depression. The same process of creative destruction is even more pronounced in the realms of popular culture and fashion. To use Stuart Ewen's perceptive formulation, "What will appear next is not always predictable. That *something new* will appear is entirely predictable."[43] This month's bestseller, must-see movie, most danceable tune supplants last month's. The new is always trumpeted as better than the old, so the old becomes "old-fashioned," "obsolete," "outdated," "outmoded," or simply "out of it," something no one, especially no young person, wants to be. Mass consumer America is an aggregation of all the processes and propaganda of creative destruction that have, over the last century, propelled the national economy to ever-higher levels of production and consumption.

This profoundly materialistic American culture is never fixed; its major business institutions are constantly creating new desires and aspirations that inspire new, but not always predictable, patterns of behavior. As a consequence, the dynamics of mass-consumer America are also constantly threatening, and destroying, older patterns of behavior. So it is never embraced unequivocally. Many historians recognize that the emerging mass-consumer culture of the Coolidge era was both seductive and alienating. But for the most part, scholars who find it easy to discuss the alienation and resistance to it have had difficulty describing the seduction.

We have to remember that what we call the successful development of mass-consumer society ultimately depended on millions of individual and family decisions to divert income and precious savings into discretionary expenditures on goods and services. These decisions forced both middle-class and working people to modify values learned in their ethnic enclaves and segregated neighborhoods but not necessarily to abandon them. Only if we insist that mass-consumer society is "out there" beyond the boundaries of the ethnic enclave "in here," do we have to conclude that embracing mass consumerism necessitated abandonment of ethnicity. In reality, the values of mass-consumer culture were incorporated into the lives of ethnic individuals and families as a transforming force that modified but did not necessarily obliterate the ethnic or racial sense of self. As James Grossman concluded in his study of blacks who migrated from the South to Chicago in the Coolidge era, "It seemed possible to share in the American Dream while grafting that dream onto a black consciousness."[44]

The Slovak-American novelist Thomas Bell (born Belejcak) captured the way this happened perfectly in *Out of This Furnace*, his wonderfully perceptive fictionalized memoir of the lives of three generations of ethnic working-people.[45] In one scene, two members of the second generation who would soon marry, Mary Kracha and Mike Dobrejcak, are in the home of one of the mill managers, where Mary works days as a maid. It is a Sunday, and the mill manager's family, the Dexters, are away for the day. "The Dexters' was the first private house Mike had ever set foot in which was wired for electricity," Bell writes.

> For that matter it was the first private house he'd ever been in that had a bath-room, a telephone, steam heat, and in the kitchen a magnificent icebox. . . . Mike's interest in houses, in house furnishings, was no greater than most young men's; he had used beds, chairs, and forks all his life without really noticing them. But in the Dexters' dining room, in their parlor and bed-

rooms, he saw furniture, dishes, silverware which were desirable and beautiful in themselves and not merely as articles of use. . . .

Standing in the parlor he said after a long pause, "This is the way a man
should live."

"It is beautiful, isn't it?" Mary said proudly, almost as if it were her own.

"When a man has this much what more can he want?" [Mike replies, and
then a moment later, recognizing that his life has been permanently altered
by this vision of comfort, he exclaims] "Maybe it would have been better for
me if I'd never seen it."

"Now you're talking foolishness" [Mary responds wisely].[46]

Here Thomas Bell reveals the seductive and transformative powers of
the new vision of comfort as it works on Mike. As Mike discovers that style
and comfort matter, his so-called "traditional" aspiration to be "a man"
who provides security for his family is transformed by a new desire to move
up in society. Mike and Mary subsequently struggle to save and acquire
their new American dream, but the harsh realities of a job market shaped by
fluctuating demand for steel, and prejudice against "Hunkies," doom their
efforts to failure.

The story of Mary and Mike reminds us that the powerful magnetic currents of the new mass-consumer culture were felt through all of American
society in the first decades of this century. By 1929, advertisers were spending nearly three billion dollars to reach the Americans of all classes who
were buying and reading over two hundred million magazines annually.
Those purveyors of mass-consumer culture projected versions of the vision
that Mike and Mary saw in the mill manager's house, what Warren Susman
called "a newer, more joyous vision of comfort" that almost everyone including white ethnic and black working-people found appealing.[47] In the
Coolidge era, low wages for individuals certainly prevented easy realization
of the new consumer dream. But when older workers and their employed
children pooled their resources, they could afford some of the new articles
that brought status and pleasure, new things that became conversation
pieces to be displayed proudly to relatives and friends.[48] Merchandisers of
all sorts encouraged this behavior. In the 1920s, advertising's pictorial images portrayed the comforts and luxuries of the well-to-do while advertising's words promised everyone access to these things. Roland Marchand
has called this strategy "the Democracy of Goods," and he has identified it
as "the most common advertising formula of the Coolidge era." In "the
Democracy of Goods," the acquisition of just one significant thing—one
overstuffed sofa, one fine china cabinet, etc.—could satisfy (at least temporarily) the urge to possess comfort and luxury.[49]

Younger ethnics, people born in the United States, could hardly resist
this vision even if it introduced new tensions into their lives. In her study of

various groups of immigrant women on New York's lower Eastside, Elizabeth Ewen writes, they "were torn between traditional affections and the promise of modernity."[50] She clearly demonstrates that the mere fact that immigrant women lived within the well-defined ethnic communities that John Bodnar has described as "enclaves" did not mean they were able to isolate their children (and particularly their daughters) from the seductive power of the new popular culture, no matter how hard they tried. "It was in the streets," Ewen declares. "New clothes, hair styles, street life, and dating patterns all created conflicts in the family."[51]

These new urban patterns of behavior did not require the expenditure of large sums of money, but they did require "free time." After World War I, widespread reductions in the time workers spent on the job each week encouraged this new kind of "Americanization." Unlike the steel workers in *Out of This Furnace*, most workers in the manufacturing industries worked 44–45 hours in an average work week during the Coolidge era.[52] When Thomas Bell turned to the story of Mike Dobrejcak's son, who is nicknamed Dobie, he made clear what a difference reduced hours and slightly better real wages could make among the next generation. In Part Four of *Out of This Furnace*, like many young ethnic males, Dobie temporarily leaves home in search of work and better wages. In Detroit in the late 1920s, "he made good money and he spent it almost as fast as he made it. . . . He [also] developed a collector's passion for suits, shirts, and neckties and learned to eat in good restaurants."[53] Dobie learns, in other words, what Stuart Ewen has described as "the lingua franca" of the city, "the visual vernacular of style." The pressures young working people felt to learn this new "language" were enormous. As Dobie's story and Stuart Ewen's scholarly investigations reveal, style was something that impressed (and still impresses) employers, peers, and perhaps most importantly members of the opposite sex.[54]

For young workers especially, the shorter work week of the Coolidge era had created something older generations never experienced, precious hours of "free time" on Friday and Saturday nights, and Saturday afternoons. In these hours (absolutely necessary for the creation of a true mass-consumer society) ethnic workers took advantage of the new pleasure-oriented opportunities afforded by electrified cities and towns and, along with millions of others, gave "the pursuit of happiness" a new meaning. In the process, everyone involved, "old stock" and "new immigrant," became more "Americanized." As Lizabeth Cohen is forced to admit, even as she tries to show how ethnic Chicagoans used mass-consumer culture to bolster their own ethnicity,

Ethnic, working-class parents [of the Coolidge era] were right to observe that their children craved stylish fashions, the latest motion pictures, popular tunes on the radio, and evenings at commercial dance halls. Among this first American generation, the normal process of emancipation from parental authority had taken on a larger cultural meaning. . . . Mass culture provided an ideal vehicle for expressing independence and *becoming more American*.[55]

Other studies confirm this observation. For example, in his fine history of Polish-Americans, John Bukowyczk found during the 1920s that the majority of the second and third generation born in the United States "did not object to the idea of ethnic intermarriage; and most, while retaining Polish customs had absorbed a great deal of American culture."[56] These born-in-America Poles increasingly identified themselves as "Americans." When surveyed in Buffalo between 1926 and 1928, 63 percent of the third generation and 54 percent of the second generation preferred the appellation "American" to "Polish" or even the hybrid categories "Polish-Americans" or "American-Poles."[57] Not surprisingly, this same contemporary study of Buffalo's Polonia by sociologists Niles Carpenter and Daniel Katz also found that second- and third-generation Polish-Americans showed a greater tendency to make their first big purchase an automobile, unlike the immigrant Poles, who saved to buy their own homes before acquiring cars. Carpenter and Katz concluded that the results of their extensive questioning showed that "the Poles of the second and even the third generation in the majority of cases still want to maintain their own community life and do not want to be scattered all over the city and absorbed into the American population. Yet these native-born Poles, in spite of themselves, have been shown to have acquired much of the new world culture."[58] Historian Bukowyczk's discovery that the substantial number of American Poles who tried to return to newly independent Poland in the early 1920s "received an icy welcome" lends weight to this conclusion. Indeed, Poland's people seemed to resent the returnees whom they now identified as "Americans." Bukowyczk reports that the returnees' much-discussed experience "strengthened immigrant resolve to rest content with their new lives in the United States."[59]

Looking back at the Coolidge era, Bukowyczk also sees what Poles in Poland at the time recognized as "Americanization" happening throughout Polish-America. "Developments in the American economy were integrating Poles into the larger American society and breaking down their own insular walls . . . ," he declares. "To survive as a distinct cultural community Polonia had to remain socially and economically isolated during America's prosperous 1920s—an impossibility."[60] Gary Gerstle's outstanding history of the French Canadian community in Woonsocket, Rhode Island, also shows how ethnicity could not be isolated from mass culture. Even as militants, calling themselves Les Sentinelles, led a vigorous campaign to maintain the purity of French culture in Woonsocket during the 1920s, a movie theater that featured American films prospered in the heart of the predominantly French Canadian neighborhood, French language newspapers advertised American cars and radios, and the local French Catholic church ran a parish baseball league. No wonder that by the end of the decade Les Sentinelles had been vanquished by a group of "moderates" who tolerated a controversial pan-ethnic diocesan high school and politicians who refused to go to the wall in a fight over a state law mandating the use of English in parochial school classes in American history, civics, math, and literature.[61]

Struggles over how the community should respond to such outside efforts to coerce Americanization were not restricted to French Canadians in New England. In fact, all over the United States during the Coolidge era, middle-class ethnic community leaders (typically doctors, lawyers, teachers, newspaper publishers, storekeepers, and other business owners) organized resistance to nativist city councilors and state legislators, and this increasingly involved them in electoral politics. Of course, these most successful ethnics, the ones who ultimately led the local units of the great national ethnic federations—like the Ancient Order of Hibernians, the Polish National Alliance, the Sons of Italy, and the League of United Latin American Citizens—were themselves advertisements for the "New Era." As John Bodnar has explained, "these career-oriented fraternalists adopted modern American business and investment procedures to increase the stability and efficiency of their growing ventures."[62] Such middle-class ethnics were also most likely to be the first in their communities to acquire new status symbols like cars and radios. In both these ways, ethnic leaders showed they were well integrated into the mass-consumer economy of the New Era. Therefore, they were actually expressing their identity when they conducted meetings in English, established English language instruction and citizenship classes, and set American sports programs within the local chapters of the national ethnic federations. Their embrace of a pluralist version of "Americanism" was, in fact, an extension of their own lives into the public realm.[63]

In the Coolidge era, the process of mobilizing ethnic working people to resist the coercive Americanism of nativists led increasingly well-organized ethnic Americans toward the politics of cultural pluralism and integration. Political developments among the Mexican-American population of the Southwest exemplified this trend. Historian David Gutierrez reports that in Texas, "typically attorneys, restauranteurs, teachers, printers, and small entrepreneurs" formed the local leadership of the three new organizations —El Orden Hijos de America (The Order of the Sons of America), El Orden Caballeros de America (The Order of the Knights of America), and the League of Latin American Citizens that formed in the mid-1920s and federated as the League of United Latin American Citizens (LULAC) in February 1929.[64] These groups expressed pride in their Mexican heritage, but they also believed it was time for all Mexicans in the United States to become citizens. Like other ethnic groups committed to cultural pluralism, the new Mexican-American organizations in Texas defined patriotism in terms that pointed toward increased integration in politics and society. They pledged allegiance to the flag and conducted their meetings in English, but they also worked assiduously to create political power and equal rights for all Mexican-Americans. Their main activities were citizenship and voter registration drives, get-out-the vote campaigns, and legal actions to break down discrimination against Mexican-Americans in public places and on juries. Large numbers of poorer farmers and workers joined the various local organizations, and they remained politically active even after the LULAC membership split over the issue of immigration. As a result of this political mobilization, the Mexican-American community in Texas was better prepared to resist a renewed surge of nativist activity that accompanied the onset of the Great Depression and better prepared to advance cultural pluralism during the subsequent New Deal.[65]

Only if we insist that nativist politics were in "the mainstream" or "core" of American culture in the 1920s must we conclude that the "Americanism" championed by the NAACP, the Catholic Church, Reform Jews like Rabbi Steven Wise, and LULAC and the other middle-class–dominated ethnic federations was either accommodation, or worse, a sell-out. The flaw in such a interpretation should by now be obvious. America in the Coolidge era was a society in the midst of such fundamental economic and social changes that it had no truly dominant political-cultural center.

IV

The struggle to define the political culture of mass-consumer America seemed to favor nativists in the years immediately following World War I. But the political power of Coolidge era nativists was a transitory phenomena. It rested on low voter turnouts, the erection of new barriers to political participation, and fragmentation within the party system—a fragmentation that was itself a symptom of the incoherence of the emerging mass-consumer society. After World War I, to use Alan Dawley's words, "the case for 100 percent Americanism came to rest more and more on biology."[66] Nativists of the period, who are still identified by most historians as white Protestants, relied not only on the Bible, but also on science and especially Darwin, to provide them with reasons for their politics. Their politics were thus neither "traditional" nor truly religious. Nativist politics in the United States in the 1920s was modern politics, both racist and irrational like the politics of modern reaction in contemporary Europe.

President Calvin Coolidge's response to the nativism of his day was a mixture of boldness and caution. In a speech delivered at a 1924 Washington rally organized by Catholic bishops, and in another at Howard University on the very same day the Klan marched down Pennsylvania Avenue in 1925, Coolidge condemned bigotry as a violation of constitutionally guaranteed rights. But he also rejected the appeals of the American Jewish Committee for a clear-cut denunciation of the Klan during the campaign of 1924. And he certainly never became a political champion of the ideas known as cultural pluralism.[67] That work was left for others to do.

Like the hybrid scientific/religious nativism of the Coolidge era, cultural pluralism was a response to confusion created by the amazingly rapid development of America's mass-consumer economy that led to a new mass popular culture. But unlike the nativism it challenged, cultural pluralism was a rational response to the condition of society at the time. By insisting that America was composed of people who had different cultural backgrounds and values but shared common political and economic beliefs and activities, ethnic pluralists were not trying to impose an impossible ideal on society, they were describing the actual condition of the world's first mass-consumer society.

Political elites and community leaders within ethnic communities eagerly embraced this pluralist way of talking about America, transmitting it to working-class people who themselves felt the powerful pull of what America was becoming. Pluralism was a way to be both ethnic and American, and thus it became a powerful weapon in the struggle against nativism.

The cultural pluralism that developed in the Coolidge era among politically active ethnics prepared the way for the New Deal and the transformation of progressivism into modern liberalism. In the northern industrial states, where ethnic politicians were often part of powerful urban organizations, Democratic Party leaders, including ethnics like Robert F. Wagner and Anton Cermak, and "old stock" progressives like Franklin and Eleanor Roosevelt, embraced pluralism as both an ideology and a political strategy in the 1920s. But pluralism also moved from the "bottom up." The campaigns launched within ethnic communities by secular and religious leaders to counter nativism were the primary catalysts for this mass mobilization. Not only did these Coolidge era campaigns help to launch the careers of a younger and larger generation of ethnic politicians, they also helped naturalized and native-born ethnics meet increasingly stringent voter registration requirements, thereby putting more and more of them in the position to support ethnic politicians and pluralist liberals at the polls.

Of course, working-class ethnics did not follow middle-class ethnics blindly. As two decades of work on ethnic history have shown, class tensions often expressed themselves in political differences within ethnic communities. During the 1920s, the ethnic middle-class celebration of entrepreneurial values had little appeal among workers, and middle-class attempts

to bring "high culture" from the old country into ethnic associations frequently drove working people away. Nonetheless, as Coolidge prosperity
gave way to the Great Depression, ethnic working-people were in a position to influence the Democratic Party program that was coalescing around
the governor of New York. At the individual level, two key figures in this
development, trade unionists Rose Schneiderman and Maud Swartz, developed what historian Annelise Orleck describes as a "surprisingly intimate
relationship" with Franklin Roosevelt as he recovered from polio during
the mid-1920s.[68] And nationally, Al Smith's presidential campaign enlarged the Democratic Party in the cities, bringing newly registered ethnics
to the polls. Subsequently, with their votes and through their eager embrace of unionism after 1932, ethnic workers helped to insure that a federal
commitment to provide both family security and an opportunity to participate in the economic and cultural development of mass-consumer society
would become national political priorities.

Scholars must always be on the lookout for the unintended and sometimes ironic consequences of historical developments. During the Coolidge era, corporate elites advertised the "Democracy of Goods" and urged
every citizen to partake of the pleasures offered by the new and exciting
mass popular culture. Working-class people of every ethnic background
and race did so. At the time, most business leaders believed that this New
Era—of what contemporary European observers inevitably called "Americanization"—would secure a national consensus about the benefits of free
enterprise and laissez-faire government and thus end the class conflicts that
had long afflicted the nation. Radicals like Tom Mann (who is quoted at the
beginning of this chapter) shared this conviction, but as a fear not a hope.
In retrospect, we can see that both groups of contemporaries were wrong.
Among ethnic working people, Coolidge era mass consumerism and popular culture encouraged the growth of a cultural pluralism that strengthened
what shortly became the most significant working-class challenge to the
political authority of business in American history.

NOTES

The author would like to thank Robert Zieger, Paula Fass, Lynn Dumenil, and
Elisabeth Perry, Frances Couvares, and Bruce Nelson for their comments on the
original essay.

    1. Preface to W. T. Coyler, *Americanism: Menace to the World* (London: Labour
Publishing Co., 1922), vi.
    2. Scholarly debate over the extent and duration of this political mobilization

began almost immediately in the 1930s, and it continues today. The exact dimensions and duration of it are still in dispute. Nevertheless, even the most skeptical political scientists have recognized the phenomenon and its urban, ethnic, and racial characteristics. See, for example, Paul Kleppner, *Who Voted? The Dynamics of Electoral Turnout, 1870–1980* (New York, 1982), esp. 88–96.

3. Bruce Kuklick, *The Good Ruler: From Herbert Hoover to Richard Nixon* (New Brunswick, N.J., 1988), chaps. 2–4, offers the most provocative analysis of this and other aspects of Franklin Roosevelt's enduring reputation. Also see William E. Leuchtenburg, *In the Shadow of FDR: From Harry Truman to Bill Clinton* (Ithaca, N.Y., 1993), chap. 8.

4. *The Statistical History of the United States from Colonial Times to the Present* (New York, 1976), 1071. Turnout for Congressional elections in both 1922 and 1926 was 42 percent; Michael E. McGerr, *The Decline of Popular Politics: The American North, 1865–1928* (New York, 1986), 186.

5. McGerr, *Decline of Popular Politics*, especially chap. 7, "The Vanishing Voter." McGerr's analyses of changing political styles are very acute, but his larger argument about their impact on political participation seems to falter in chapter 8 where he acknowledges the very significant increase in turnout in the North that occurred in the 1930s.

6. James L. Sundquist, *Dynamics of the Party System: Alignment and Realignment of Political Parties in the United States* (Washington, D.C., 1973), 200–4; and Kleppner, *Who Voted?*, 86–87.

7. John Allswang emphasizes this point for the groups he described in *A House for All Peoples: Ethnic Politics in Chicago, 1896–1936* (Lexington, Ky., 1971). The scholarly argument for the importance of Al Smith's campaign was first made by Samuel Lubell in chapter 3, "The Revolt of the City," of his seminal book, *The Future of American Politics* (New York, 1952). The critical character of the 1928 election was subsequently highlighted in V. O. Key, Jr.'s, important article "Secular Realignment and the Party System," *Journal of Politics* 21 (May 1959), and the work of many other historians and political scientists including Walter Dean Burnham's "The Changing Shape of the American Political Universe," *American Political Science Review* 59 (March 1965) and chapter 7, "The Brown Derby Campaign" of David Burner's *The Politics of Provincialism: The Democratic Party in Transition, 1918–1932* (New York, 1968).

8. "Urban Working-Class Political Behavior and Theories of American Electoral Politics, 1870–1940," *Journal of American History* 74 (March 1988): 1281. See Stanley Coben, *Rebellion Against Victorianism: The Impetus for Cultural Change* (New York, 1991), chap. 6, for a perceptive discussion of the uneasy role of labor in the 1924 Progressive presidential campaign.

9. Gerald H. Gamm, *The Making of New Deal Democrats: Voting Behavior and Realignment in Boston, 1920–1940* (Chicago, 1989), 162–66.

10. Michael McGerr, "Political Style and Women's Power, 1830–1930," *Journal of American History* 77 (December 1990): 880–85. Also see Nancy Cott, *The Grounding of Modern Feminism* (New Haven, 1987), 99–114 and 243–67; and Paul Kleppner, "Were Women to Blame? Woman Suffrage and Voter Turnout, 1890–1930," *Journal of Interdisciplinary History* 12 (Spring 1982).

11. Samuel Rea quoted in Howard C. Hill, "The Americanization Movement"

(1919), in Richard J. Meister, ed., *Race and Ethnicity in Modern America* (Lexington, Mass., 1974).

12. *The CIO, 1935–1955* (Chapel Hill, 1995), 10. For details see especially Bernstein's classic study, *The Lean Years: A History of the American Worker, 1920–1933* (Boston, 1960); and Craig Phelan, *William Green: Biography of a Labor Leader* (Albany, 1989), chap. 2.

13. Sue Bowden and Avner Offer, "Household Appliances and the Use of Time: The United States and Britain since the 1920s," *Economic History Review*, 47, no. 4 (1994): 729; and Frank Stricker, "Affluence for Whom?—Another Look at the Prosperity of the Working Class in the 1920s," *Labor History* 24 (Winter 1983): 32. Further discussion of the importance of the automobile may be found in chapter 2, "The Transformation of American Society in the Automobile Age," of my *Class Conflict and Cultural Consensus: The Making of Mass Consumer Society in Flint, Michigan* (New Brunswick, N.J., 1987).

14. *Culture As History: The Transformation of American Society in the Twentieth Century* (New York, 1984), xxiv.

15. Quoted in David Gartman, *Auto Opium: A Social History of American Automobile Design* (London and New York, 1994), 96.

16. *Statistical History*, 55. When the unusually low life expectancy (39.1 years) for 1918 is dropped, the average for 1911–20 is 53.2 years. This still means a remarkable 5.6-year improvement for average annual life expectancy in the 1920s.

17. Harvey Green, *The Uncertainty of Everyday Life, 1915–1945* (New York, 1992), 18–19, 155–86; and *Statistical History*, 169–72, 182.

18. See especially Stricker's "Affluence for Whom?" for an adamant presentation of this position.

19. Green, *Uncertainty of Everyday Life*, 99–102.

20. Bowden and Offer, "Household Appliances," 729; Stricker, "Affluence for Whom?" 7.

21. Green, 206; and Daniel Leab, "Growth and Impact of the Moving Picture Industry on American Society," paper presented at Calvin Coolidge and the Coolidge Era symposium, Library of Congress, October 6, 1995.

22. Michael Parrish, *Anxious Decades: America in Prosperity and Depression, 1920–1941* (New York, 1992), 159ff. Also see Susman on Ruth in *Culture as History*, 141–49.

23. Paula S. Fass, *The Beautiful and the Damned: American Youth in the 1920s* (New York, 1977), chap. 6.

24. *Race Rebels: Culture, Politics, and the Black Working Class* (New York, 1994), 45. Also James R. Grossman, *Land of Hope: Chicago, Black Southerners, and the Great Migration* (Chicago, 1989), 261–65. Also see Frederick Lewis Allen's still useful survey, *Only Yesterday* (New York, 1931), especially chaps. 5, 8, and 10; Claude S. Fischer, "Changes in Leisure Activities, 1890–1940," *Journal of Social History* 27, no. 3 (Spring 1994); and John P. Robinson, "Massification and the Democratization of the Leisure Class," *Annals of the American Academy* 435 (January 1978).

25. McGerr, *Decline of Popular Politics*, chap. 7. The recent literature on the development of a national popular culture in the 1920s is too vast to list here. For a concise overview, see Green, *The Uncertainty of Everyday Life*, 128–38, 187–230.

26. The debate about the political implications of mass popular culture has a

long history that is discussed in my essay "Popular Culture and Politics in Modern America," the introduction to Ronald Edsforth and Larry Bennett, eds., *Popular Culture and Political Change in Modern America* (Albany, 1991).

27. Russell A. Kazal's review article, "Revisiting Assimilation: The Rise, Fall, and Reappraisal of a Concept in American Ethnic History," *American Historical Review* 100, no. 2 (April 1995), presents a comprehensive overview of the ways historians and sociologists have used the terms "assimilation" and "Americanization." None of the three dominant models of "Americanization" that Kazal discusses—individual adaptation to a "core" Anglo-Saxon society, formation of new ethnic and/or class identities, and racial assimilation—incorporates the dynamism of mass-consumer society that is a fundamental fact of twentieth-century American history.

28. See, for example, Barbara Jordan, "The Americanization Ideal," *New York Times*, September 11, 1995. Michael Lind's *The Next American Nationalism: The New Nationalism and the Fourth American Revolution* (New York, 1995) is all about trying to promote a new era of progressive "Americanization."

29. James R. Barrett, "Americanization from the Bottom Up: Immigration and the Remaking of the Working Class in the United States, 1880–1930," *Journal of American History* 79, no. 3 (December 1992), details Americanization efforts among labor organizers up to 1920, but despite its title, the essay has little to say about the Coolidge era. For a discussion of Americanization programs sponsored by middle-class ethnics, see Lynn Dumenil, "The Tribal Twenties: Assimilated Catholics' Response to Anti-Catholicism in the 1920s," *Journal of American Ethnic History* 11 (Fall 1991).

30. Higham, *Strangers in the Land: Patterns of American Nativism, 1860–1925*, was originally published in 1955 by Rutgers University Press. A second paperback edition was published by Atheneum in 1963; my own copy is a dog-eared twenty-first printing of that Atheneum edition published in 1981. The most important recent challenge to Higham's paradigm is David H. Bennett's *The Party of Fear: From Nativist Movements to the New Right in American History* (New York, 1990). Bennett does not break significantly with Higham in the first twelve chapters of his book, which trace the history of anti-alien politics to the 1920s. But in the final three chapters, which include discussion of the Great Depression, McCarthyism and the rise of the New Right, Bennett insists that what he calls "traditional nativism" lost its viability and thus has no real political significance. This is a questionable thesis. Indeed, in light of political developments such as the Pat Buchanan campaigns for the Republican presidential nominations in 1992 and 1996, Bennett's judgment that "the growth of the religious Right and the political hard Right suggests that in the future important right-wing movements will find their energizing themes in very different threats to the American way than had their predecessors on the old anti-alien Right"(14) seems very much off the mark.

31. For the earlier period, see various documents in Benjamin Munn Ziegler, ed., *Immigration: An American Dilemma* (Boston, 1953); and Meister, ed., *Race and Ethnicity in Modern America*. For more recent evidence, consult Paul Berman, ed., *Debating P.C.: The Controversy over Political Correctness on College Campuses* (New York, 1992).

32. Dawley, *Struggles for Justice: Social Responsibility and the Liberal State* (Cam-

bridge, Mass., 1991), 254. *A Different Mirror* (Boston: Little, Brown and Company, 1993), 17.

33. David R. Roediger, *The Wages of Whiteness and the Making of the American Working Class* (London, 1991) has been especially influential. Kelley, *Race Rebels*, 4–34, discusses the implications of Roediger's analysis for the definition and study of a black working class. Recent case studies that employ Roediger's approach include chaps. 2–5 of *Race Rebels*; Eric Arnesen, "'Like Banquo's Ghost, It will not Drown': The Race Question and the American Railroad Brotherhoods, 1880–1920," *American Historical Review* 99, no. 5 (December 1994); and Bruce Nelson, "Organized Labor and the Struggle for Black Equality in Mobile During World War II," *Journal of American History* 80, no. 3 (December 1993).

34. See especially Kwame Anthony Appiah, *In My Father's House: Africa in the Philosophy of Culture* (Oxford, 1992), chaps. 1–3 on historical plasticity of racial categories.

35. *Seducing the French* (Berkeley, 1993), xi–xii; emphasis added.

36. The history of this definition of "Americanization" is nicely summarized in Dominic Strinati, *An Introduction to Theories of Popular Culture* (London, 1995), 21–31. Also see Ralph Willett, *The Americanization of Germany, 1945–1949* (New York, 1989); Roger Rollin, ed., *The Americanization of the Global Village: Essays in Comparative Popular Culture* (Bowling Green, Ohio, 1989); Edward McCreary, *The Americanization of Europe: The Impact of Americans and American Business on the Uncommon Market* (Garden City, N.Y., 1964); the essays collected in "America Through Foreign Eyes," a special edition of *The Annals of the American Academy of Political and Social Science* (hereafter cited as *Annals*), 295 (September 1954); and the still valuable collection edited by Henry Steele Commager, *America in Perspective: The United States Through Foreign Eyes* (New York, 1947). Anti-Americanism has often taken the form of an attack on the materialism and inequality of the mass-consumer society that developed in the United States. In chapter 6 of his massive survey *Anti-Americanism: Critiques at Home and Abroad, 1965–1990* (New York, 1992), Paul Hollander presents Western European anti-Americanism as nothing less than a strategy for attacking modernity itself. Also see the essays collected in "Anti-Americanism: Origins and Context," a special edition of *Annals* 432 (December 1988); and Ian Lumsden, ed., *Close the 49th Parallel: The Americanization of Canada* (Toronto, 1970).

37. For a detailed definition of this term, see my *Class Conflict and Cultural Consensus*, 1–9.

38. British historian Philip Taylor highlighted this view of America when he titled his magnificent book, *The Distant Magnet: European Emigration to the U.S.A.* (New York, 1971). I also use the term because I agree with John Higham's recent statement "That at the center of American society there is not just an arena, but a magnet." ("The Future of American History," *Journal of American History* 80 [March 1994]: 1305).

39. The seminal postwar study remains Milton M. Gordon, *Assimilation in American Life: The Role of Race, Religion, and National Origins* (New York, 1964). Stephen Steinberg presented a vigorous defense of Robert Park's early-twentieth-century model of assimilation and "amalgamation" through intermarriage and interbreeding in *The Ethnic Myth: Race, Ethnicity, and Class in America* (Boston, 1981). Elliot R.

Made in the U.S.A. 271

Barkan's has recently tried to revise Gordon's model of assimilation, "Race, Religion, and Nationality in American Society: A Model of Ethnicity—From Contact to Assimilation," *Journal of American Ethnic History*, 14 (Winter 1995). Critical comments by Rudolph J. Vecoli, Richard D. Alba, and Olivier Zunz in the same issue, as well as Kazal's essay "Revisiting Assimilation" (note 27 above) make it clear that Barkan's new six-stage model will not end the debate.

40. See especially, Lawrence Levine, *Highbrow/Lowbrow: The Emergence of Cultural Hierarchy in America* (Cambridge, Mass., 1988).

41. David Levering Lewis, *When Harlem Was in Vogue* (New York, 1982); and Lynn Dumenil, *Modern Temper: American Culture and Society in the 1920s* (New York, 1995), 283–302.

42. The meaning of the term "creative destruction" is best elaborated in Marshall Berman's magnificent book, *All That's Solid Melts into Air* (New York, 1982). Critical readers of this essay will notice that the definition of Americanization I use in this section does not depend on repeated cycles of conflict and resistance, but it does presume current as well as past relevance. This presentism seems to me unavoidable since the United States remains the world's foremost mass-consumer society.

43. *All Consuming Images: The Politics of Style in Contemporary Culture* (New York, 1988), 51.

44. *Land of Hope*, 265.

45. Belejcak had changed his name to Thomas Bell before Little, Brown and Company published the novel in 1941. It was brought out in a new edition as *Out of This Furnace: A Novel of Immigrant Labor in America* in 1976 by Pittsburgh University Press. All quotations in this essay are from that later edition. Oral historians seem to have seldom been interested in the consumer behavior of early-twentieth-century Americans. Therefore, collections of family photographs and this type of autobiographical fiction written by authors from working-class backgrounds are among the best sources we have on how mass-consumer culture penetrated ethnic enclaves.

46. *Out of this Furnace*, 136–37.

47. Susman, *Culture as History*, xv; and Dumenil, *The Modern Temper*, 88–89.

48. See, for example, the photograph titled "The Living Room of a Coal Miner's House in Pennsylvania," which shows three generations of a family gathered in a well-furnished living room with a young man standing proudly next to a large cabinet-style radio in John Bodnar, *Workers' World: Kinship, Community, and Protest in an Industrial Society, 1900–1940* (Baltimore, 1982), 12.

49. *Advertising the American Dream: Making Way for Modernity, 1920–1940* (Berkeley, 1985), 217–22.

50. *Immigrant Women in the Land of Dollars: Life and Culture on the Lower East Side, 1890–1925* (New York, 1985), 266.

51. *Immigrant Women*, 197. In *Workers' World*, Bodnar uses the term "enclave" extensively. Although he also employs other terms like "ethnic community" and "ethnic cluster" in his important subsequent work on immigrants and ethnicity, *Lives of Their Own: Blacks, Italians, and Poles in Pittsburgh, 1900–1960* (Urbana, Ill., 1982), and *The Transplanted: A History of Immigrants in Urban America* (Bloomington, Ind., 1985), Bodnar has insisted the places where ethnic working-people lived were essentially inward-looking, self-enclosed enclaves.

52. *Statistical History*, 172.

53. *Out of This Furnace*, 263–64. My own investigation of workers' behavior in Flint, Michigan, in the 1920s confirms the conclusion that Dobie's experience was quite common. See *Class Conflict and Cultural Consensus*, 87–96.

54. *All Consuming Images*, 73ff.

55. *Making a New Deal: Industrial Workers in Chicago, 1919–1939* (Cambridge and New York, 1990), 144 (emphasis added).

56. *And My Children Did Not Know Me: A History of the Polish-Americans* (Bloomington, Ind., 1987), 71.

57. Niles Carpenter and Daniel Katz, "A Study of Acculturization in the Polish Group in Buffalo, 1926–1928," *Monographs in Sociology, No. 3, The University of Buffalo Studies* 7 (June 1929): 126–27.

58. "A Study of Acculturization," 123.

59. *My Children Did Not Know Me*, 66–67.

60. *My Children Did Not Know Me*, 75.

61. *Working Class Americanism: The Politics of Labor in a Textile City, 1914–1960* (New York, 1989), 49–53.

62. *The Transplanted*, 128.

63. Dumenil, *The Modern Temper*, 257–83; and Bodnar, *The Transplanted*, 138–41.

64. *Walls and Mirrors: Mexican Americans, Mexican Immigrants, and the Politics of Ethnicity* (Berkeley, 1995), 75. Also see Richard A. Garcia, *Rise of the Mexican American Middle Class: San Antonio, 1929–1941* (College Station, Tex., 1991), 3–5.

65. *Walls and Mirrors*, 76–82.

66. *Struggles of Liberty*, 263.

67. Dumenil, *Modern Temper*, 250–51, 276–79.

68. *Common Sense and a Little Fire: Women and Working Class Politics in the United States, 1900–1965* (Chapel Hill, 1995), 147–50.

11

"Now at Last We Can Begin!"

The Impact of Woman Suffrage in New York

ELISABETH I. PERRY

In an article written in 1920, feminist Crystal Eastman surmised that on the day the Tennessee legislature ratified the woman suffrage amendment, men would say, "Thank God, this everlasting woman's fight is over!" In contrast, she continued, women would say, "Now at last we can begin!"[1] But *how*? Eastman took for granted the existence of a clear, well-marked path toward women's political empowerment. In reality, the path was strewn with perilous traps and agonizing choices.

Women were unsure how to proceed. Some thought they should join political parties. Others said women should wait until they knew more about partisan politics, meanwhile continuing to associate primarily with women's voluntary organizations and pursuing their traditional, nonpartisan goals. Yet others warned that as long as women held aloof from partisanship, they would remain politically inconsequential. Women, these analysts argued, must enter the arena on the same terms as men, terms that included competing with men for political office. Traditionalists countered that such a course would expose women to the temptations of the spoils systems and thus taint women's historic claim to moral superiority.

Men were perhaps less conflicted over the issue. In the early 1920s, politician Cornelia Bryce Pinchot used to tell the story about how one man said to another, "see what happens if the women get the vote." The other replied, "No Sam, the vote's alright. Just don't let them get into politics."[2] Indeed, most political men managed to keep women out. In the early 1920s, when men feared that women might vote as a bloc, political men made some concessions to them, setting up women's divisions in their party structures and electing or appointing women committee chairs in numbers equal to men committee chairs. But they rarely allowed women into their party "war rooms" and hardly ever put them up for office.[3]

In this chapter, I examine the consequences of this two-sided situation: women's initial confusion, after winning the vote, over their future political role and men's resistance to women entering their political space. To elucidate this situation, I focus on post-suffrage New York State, where the political ideals of a group of former suffragists, members of the League of Women Voters but also active Republican Party members, clashed with their partisan loyalties and thus compromised their ability to function effectively in politics. While this group represents only the state's elite— white, middle-class, and native-born citizens—their experience was typical of many politically active women of the period. Thus, they can provide insight into the question of why woman suffrage failed to fulfill the promise to women of full political equality with men.

Mary Garrett Hay and James W. Wadsworth, Jr.

On June 10, 1920, an article in the *Chicago Evening Mail* entitled "Morsels of Favor Passed out by G.O.P. Dissatisfying Women" reported the following exchange in the corridor of a hotel near the Republican Party convention. An unidentified man caught sight of Miss Mary (Molly) Garrett Hay, former head of the New York City Woman Suffrage Party. He congratulated her. "What for?" she asked. He replied, "For placing your sex on an equal footing." "Humph," she sniffed. "I haven't. They aren't." And off she went.[4]

Indeed, by the summer of 1920, women were *not* "on an equal footing" with men in the national Republican Party. Although Mary Garrett Hay had tried to put them there, she had failed to do so. Even though ratification of the federal woman suffrage amendment would occur later that summer, by summer's end Republican women's status in the party had declined even further. Why did Hay's unidentified interlocutor *think* she had made women equal to men in the party, and how did Hay already know that she had not? What had she done wrong, if anything, and could the decline of women's power that followed the ratification of woman suffrage have been avoided?

To answer these questions, we must move from Chicago and the Republican national convention of 1920 to New York State Republican Party politics in the previous year. New York women had won the vote in November 1917. This event culminated a long struggle begun at the 1848 woman's rights meeting in Seneca Falls, New York. It capped a long tradition of nonpartisan political activism on the part of New York women.[5] Before they won the vote, some New York suffragists had joined political parties, most notably the Progressive Party in 1912, or had campaigned actively for and against political party candidates. But most suffragists had given priority to their nonpartisan causes, such as winning votes for women or changing liquor laws. When they finally won the vote, new opportunities for activism opened before them, but also a great deal of uncertainty.

The 1919–20 reelection campaign of U.S. Senator James W. Wadsworth, Jr., provides the political stage on which this uncertainty played itself out. Two personalities dominated the scene—Wadsworth, the upstate New York Republican who had won election to the Senate in 1914, and Mary Garrett Hay.

Wadsworth came from a wealthy, politically powerful farm family in the Genesee Valley. His father, James Wadsworth, Sr., was a congressman who had opposed the progressive legislation of President Theodore Roosevelt. Although Wadsworth, Sr., lost his congressional seat in 1906, he continued to dominate state politics as the head of what was called the "Wadsworth group." James Wadsworth, Jr., his son, started his political career in the New York State Assembly, of which he became Speaker in 1906 at the age of twenty-nine. According to Buffalo lawyer John Lord O'Brian, Wadsworth, Jr., was a "*very* powerful figure politically." Like his father, O'Brian said, James, Jr., was a strong conservative who often found himself at loggerheads with the more progressive wing of the state party, then headed by Charles Evans Hughes.

As a U.S. senator after 1914, Wadsworth, Jr., gained notoriety for taking a states' rights position against national prohibition, a cause then favored by most suffragists. Appealing again to states' rights, Wadsworth also opposed woman suffrage, even when suffrage was failing in the Senate by only one or two votes. In mid-1917, his wife, Alice Hay Wadsworth, became head of the National Association Opposed to Woman Suffrage, a group that identified woman suffrage and other feminist causes with "Bolshevism."[6] By the time Senator Wadsworth announced in 1919 that he would run for reelection the following year, New York suffragists had amassed a slew of reasons to work for his defeat.

Mary Garrett Hay, the second major figure in this drama, had led the middle-class, political wing of New York City suffragists since 1912. Born in 1857, Hay had grown up in an Indiana doctor's family that had been active in Republican politics. Her great uncle, Indiana's first governor, Jonathan Jennings, had opposed the introduction of slavery into the state. Like many midwestern women activists, Hay moved into suffrage through temperance work. In the suffrage movement, she became great friends with Carrie Chapman Catt, later the "generalissimo" of the final triumphant stages of the national woman suffrage movement. After moving to New York in 1895, Hay made common household with Catt after Catt's second husband died. This living arrangement lasted until Hay's death in 1928; the two women were buried together in New Rochelle.

In New York, Miss Hay became active first in women's clubs. After serving as president of the New York State Federation of Women's Clubs from 1910 to 1912, she became head of the New York City Woman Suffrage Party. In this role, she worked closely with Mrs. Catt on one of the final battlegrounds of the woman's vote campaign, New York State. They came close to victory in 1915 but did not succeed until 1917. Afterward, Hay continued to hold leadership roles in women's nonpartisan politics. She served as president of the two New York City organizations around which much of white middle-class women's nonpartisan activism gravitated, the New York City League of Women Voters from 1917 to 1923 and the Women's City Club of New York from 1918 to 1924.

Many political women and men held Hay in high esteem. Seen as an able leader of women, she was also thought to be one who could "cooperate with men in politics." Some observers even predicted a partisan political future for her. Ever since moving to New York, she had been attending state Republican conventions, year after year asking the party platform committee to approve the woman suffrage amendment. She succeeded only the year after New York State women got the vote. In 1918, a secret conference of party leaders chose her over Columbia University President Nicholas Murray Butler to chair the platform committee. This position enabled her to get the committee to do as she had wished for some twenty years: it finally endorsed the federal woman suffrage amendment.

The same year that she relished this triumph—1918—she also began to rise in Republican national politics. Thanks to a long friendship with fellow Indianan Will H. Hays, then chair of the Republican national committee and longtime supporter of woman suffrage, she won a seat on the Republican Women's National Executive Committee. This was a separate entity through which Republican women hoped, "temporarily," until they were fully "amalgamated" into the party, to pursue women's political interests. In 1919, after becoming the executive committee's chair, Miss Hay began to work closely with Will Hays to equalize women's roles with men's in the national party.[7]

In the immediate post-suffrage era, then, Miss Hay seemed to be carving out a constructive political role for herself. Remaining active in nonpartisan, women's voluntary groups, she was making significant inroads into state and national partisan politics. Where this two-pronged approach toward post-suffrage women's political empowerment might have led is impossible to know, for by 1920 Senator James W. Wadsworth, Jr.'s, announcement of his reelection campaign had derailed it.

As soon as New York suffragists heard Wadsworth's announcement, they declared their opposition to him. Mary Hay took the lead. That she would do so was hardly surprising. She despised him, and no wonder, given his political opposition to positions she had espoused. She had also been public about her feelings. According to one newspaper report, at a Republican party luncheon for Wadsworth, Hay "created a sensation" by refusing to sit at the same table with him.[8] Moreover, in the first days after woman suffrage passed in New York State, she had made it clear that she would change little in the way she would engage in politics. Nonpartisan issues would always take priority for her over party issues.

When she delivered a suffrage victory speech to the New York State Federation of Women's Clubs in November 1917, for example, she begged former suffragists to remain nonpartisan until they had learned how to be voters. "Oh, women [she said], let me urge you[,] while you may believe in this party or that party, . . . first get on your feet, grasp the situation, study the condition, study what parties stand for, study what candidates stand for and let us as women not be partisan but stand for the man or the woman that stands for the *right* (applause) [emphasis mine]." She not only urged her followers to go slow on party membership but discouraged them from even thinking about running for office. "Don't let us have our heads turned," she warned. She told the story of how, after the November 6 vote on woman suffrage in the state, she had gone to Albany to consult the secretary of state on how the count of soldiers' ballots would proceed. While she was in Albany, New York City papers ran the story that three woman suffragists were going to run for Congress. All three of these women then wired her, she told her audience, pleading, "Don't believe it, Miss Hay, we are going to be non-partisan, so don't believe all you see in the papers! . . . the reason we wanted the ballot was to do something constructive and worth while in this glorious old state" (applause). To Mary Hay's mind, "politics," defined as running for office, was neither "constructive" nor "worth while."[9]

The following summer (1918), Mary Hay triumphed over Nicholas Murray Butler by winning the headship of the Republican state party platform committee. Even so, when friends of the Republican governor Charles S. Whitman asked her whether women "wanted representation on the state ticket," she had said that, as far as she knew, "they did not."[10] Finally, after Warren Harding's victory in 1920, there was talk that Harding might establish a Welfare Department with a woman at its head. Mary Hay warned women against taking such an offer, as it would be a political "plum" accepted in return for having supported Harding. Moreover (and here she was prescient), it would put an enormous burden on the woman who accepted it, for such a woman would inevitably be judged as representing *all* women.[11]

Following Mary Hay's lead, state suffrage party headquarters also asked their members not to leap into party politics. Early in 1918, an upstate suffragist wrote to suffrage headquarters in Utica reporting that some of the "newly enfranchised women here are worried because, if they refrain from

joining any of the political parties (the advice given from suffrage headquarters), they will not be able to take any part in the party caucus." She
then asked, "Could you supply me with arguments to uphold the Head-
quarter instructions?"[12] By April 1918, headquarters had revoked these
"instructions," but there was still hesitation, if not confusion, about the
right path to take. At the end of May, less than 50 percent of New York's
registered women had enrolled in a political party, a situation that some
critics later blamed on Miss Hay.[13]

In the early months after New York State suffrage, Molly Hay had not
only opposed women running for office and rushing into political parties
but hesitated to endorse the direct exercise of political power even by
women knowledgeable in party affairs, such as herself. Late in 1919, after
Wadsworth announced his reelection campaign, she predicted that a
women's voting bloc would defeat him. But when asked if she planned to
come up with an alternative candidate, she said it was not the "business of
women voters to select the Republican candidate. The task is for the *men in
charge* [emphasis mine] of Republican affairs. They should see to it at an
early day."[14]

These and other statements of Mary Hay indicate her continuing adherence to old traditions in American women's political activism. They also
reveal her ambivalence about suffrage's potential for major change in gender relations. She wanted the "men in charge" to heed her warnings about
woman's power at the ballot box but also wanted to leave the major power
decisions to them. She wanted an equal role for women on the party's executive committee but would not, perhaps could not, give up her nonpartisan
approach to politics. If one of the strongest suffrage leaders in the country
displayed such ambivalence, the confusion among rank-and-file political
women can only be imagined.

As soon as Miss Hay announced her opposition to Wadsworth, relations
between Republican women and the party hierarchy soured. In the backlash that ensued, Miss Hay bore the brunt. It came at her from three sources:
national Republican Party men, state Republican Party men, and some
state Republican Party women anxious to rise in party ranks. The first sign
of trouble came in May 1920, when Mary Hay received word that if she
continued to oppose Wadsworth she would lose her "delegate-at-large"
status to the Republican national convention in June. "Being a new voter,"
she said ingenuously, "I can not see how my opposition to the candidacy or
election of a United States Senator can have anything to do with being a
delegate to the Republican National Convention."[15] How her party con-
freres responded to this remark was not recorded.

In June 1920, Hay presented herself at Chicago. Despite sensing that
party leaders were marginalizing her, she went ahead with a revolutionary
request. She asked that the size of the party's executive committee be dou-

bled and that only women be appointed to the newly opened seats. Failure to do this, she said, doomed women to playing merely "decorative" roles in the party. Will Hays, her friend and party chair, tried to push her request along, but it came to little. Republican men charged that Hay's plan would create a "sex division" in the party. Some joked that the nation might as well elect two presidents, one for the men and one for the women. In the end, twelve men on the committee gallantly ceded their seats to women, but Hay would not settle for less than a fifty-fifty solution. "Men should be ashamed of the representation given women from any state," she said. "They will learn, however, that they can not toss a few crumbs to the women and then sit down to the feast table." This threat would soon prove idle.[16]

By the end of the convention, the executive committee had forced Mary Garrett Hay to step down from her post as chair of the Women's Executive Committee. In her public statements explaining her resignation, she put a positive construction upon it, saying that Will Hays had given her the post only as a "temporary" measure in order to work out a "permanent model of organization by means of which to relate the woman voter to the Republican Party." She also said that her top priorities were to work for the ratification of the federal suffrage amendment and the defeat of Senator Wadsworth. In her statements, she took care not to attack men *qua* men. In an interview given to a reporter later that month, she insisted generously that "The men don't mean to shut us out. They just do not think about us."[17] Mary Hay returned to New York only to find that her base in the state Republican Party had eroded, too. She had been dropped from the state executive committee. It was at this point that her attitudes toward women running for office began to change. In statements bordering on the militant, she began to decry the continued male control of political parties. Although she did not believe in a "Woman's Party," she urged women to help younger women "take their right places in politics." She hoped the League of Women Voters would assist women running for public office, supporting "good" ones, regardless of party affiliation.[18]

Less than three years after New York State woman suffrage, the Molly Hay who knew how to "cooperate with men in politics" had become much less cooperative. "I rebel," she said in one of her stronger statements, against the "crack of the party whip." How dare her party tell her she could not oppose a man who was working to delay the ratification of woman suffrage! The *women* aren't making a "sex war," she riposted; the *men* are, by keeping the party a "man's party." In Saratoga for the state Republican party convention, she complained that the men were holding scores of secret conferences without inviting any women, or they were calling a meeting for a certain time but then not showing up until half an hour later and then only to tell the women what they were to do. She would not stand for it![19]

Again, the backlash against her in her home state was severe. Newspaper editors attacked her, pointing out that suffragists themselves had said there should be "no sex in politics" and that men and women should participate equally "on the basis of worth and merit." Miss Hay and millions of other men, the *Knickerbocker Press* observed, are excluded from the inner councils because they had not worked their way up from the bottom or proved their abilities.[20]

Then, "stand-pat Republican women" (as one journalist phrased it) went "after her head."[21] Grace Vanamee and Rosalie Loew Whitney, both members of the Republican Women's State Executive Committee, led the attack. They made three major points. First, they observed that a secret conference is not necessarily corrupt. Miss Hay may have been excluded, they noted, but so were many men. Referring to the designation of Wadsworth as the party's candidate, they claimed that Hay could have fought that endorsement from the floor. As for the party platform, the women pointed out that *they* had been on the resolutions committee and had worked with the men as equals. Their final, most telling hit was to remind party women that, in 1918, a secret conference had chosen Mary Hay rather than Nicholas Butler as chair of the state party platform committee. They recalled "no animadversions by Miss Hay following that occasion."[22]

James Wadsworth, Jr., won his renomination for the Senate. In response, the head of the New York State League of Women Voters, Caroline Slade, a Molly Hay supporter, took action along traditional pre-suffrage lines. Calling upon her network of former suffragists, she organized a meeting of a thousand women to raise money for a "Non-Partisan Senatorial Committee."[23] Mary Hay also persuaded Ella Boole, then president of the New York State Woman's Christian Temperance Union, to run against Wadsworth in the primary. Boole lost but went on to run in the main contest on the Prohibition ticket. She won four counties, amassing 153,000 votes, an impressive total for a novice woman candidate running against a male incumbent, but still insufficient to defeat Wadsworth.[24] On the other hand, his winning total was 600,000 votes short of Warren Harding's total New York State vote.

The Political Consequences for New York Women

What did New York suffragists learn from this experience? In *local* elections the following year, the New York City League of Women Voters partially abandoned strict nonpartisanship and endorsed some individuals running for office. This effort on behalf of a few New York City candidates changed little in the larger picture, however. By 1921, neither the Republican nor Democratic state party had advanced any female candidates for office, and when a measure came up in the legislature to get equal representation of women on all state political committees, the men in both parties killed it.[25]

Mary Garrett Hay pretty much retired from politics, her approach toward realizing women's political dreams after suffrage discredited. She was still a revered figure, rarely openly attacked, but the New York City League of Women Voters eased her out of the presidency in 1923, and some political women of the era indicted her behind the scenes. In a circulated but unpublished and powerful essay, Frances Kellor, sociologist, author, and Progressive Party activist, condemned former suffrage leaders for having "disinherited women by regulations forbidding them to engage in political activities and discouraging their participation in public affairs. 'Get the vote first' was the order." By the time they had gotten the vote, Kellor observed, they had neither training nor experience in public affairs. Their leaders, tired, disillusioned, "egotistical through use of power, had no enthusiasm to lead a new cause. Embittered by many humiliating experiences, thirsting for revenge against those who had so long delayed victory, they did not find it easy to subordinate their point of view, or to make the adjustments which the new situation required. In the nature of things they could be of little consequence. To see their child adopted by the political organization was a little more than they could bear."

Kellor went on to accuse the former suffragists of having misjudged the situation. In her words, they clung to a "non-partisan doctrine in the face of a victory in which the only fruit could be partisanship." They urged members to join political parties as "rebels" to destroy them and then ridiculed potential allies, such as the "antis," who were then taking up the duties they had once opposed. Kellor noted further that many of them were "distinguished members of society with influence in high political places," but "they closed, rather than opened, some avenues essential to the orderly recognition of women in political affairs," receiving only those posts that were circumscribed by "women's concerns." Finally, they put the "highly sensitized masculine organization called the political machine" on the defensive, ready to guard its sacred ground against the threatened female domination.[26] This indictment, while never once naming Mary Garrett Hay, so accurately depicted what Hay had done as to leave little doubt that she was at least one of its targets.

For his part, James Wadsworth, Jr., continued to oppose woman suffrage, even after the federal amendment was ratified. He supported a challenge in the U.S. Supreme Court to the legality of the ratification and in 1921 joined with Finis J. Garrett, Democratic congressman and minority leader from Tennessee, to propose a constitutional amendment that would make amending the constitution virtually impossible. As soon as women and union political activists heard of this plan (deliberations about it were held in secret), they teamed up to stall it. By 1925, the Wadsworth-Garrett amendment to end all amendments was dead.[27]

Wadsworth ran again for the Senate in 1926. By then, his chances for re-election had diminished. After twelve years in Washington, D.C., he had become aloof from his home political base. Many of his old cohorts had died, and he had failed to build new, younger support. Women prohibitionists, eager to preserve the faltering Volstead Act, decided to back State Senator Franklin Cristman, an independent "dry" who drew Republican votes away from Wadsworth. Finally, 1926 was a Democratic year in New York. Alfred E. Smith won an unprecedented fourth gubernatorial term, and, taking advantage of rising ethnic support from the cities, his friend Robert F. Wagner, Sr., another "wet," won Wadsworth's seat in the Senate. Male Republican Party regulars blamed Wadsworth's defeat exclusively on the "fanatics," by which they meant the "drys." They never explained just how another "wet" had won.[28]

Other questions remain from this clash between New York's male and female Republicans. Had the Wadsworth renomination not been an issue, would Hay's demands for equal political space with men have been met? Probably not. The "men in charge" were just as unable to visualize new ways for women to function in politics as were the suffragists of Hay's generation. Men like Will Hays and the gallant twelve on the national Republican executive committee were sympathetic but in the end unable or unwilling to do much. As for the rest of the party men, they did not like it when Miss Hay "bullied" them, and they could not understand what motivated her when she did so.

A letter from Nicholas Murray Butler, Molly Hay's rival for chair of the state Republican platform committee in 1918, to James Wadsworth, Jr., is instructive on this point. Written in January 1920, after Miss Hay had announced her opposition to Wadsworth but before she had lost her party posts, the letter expresses Butler's total commitment to Wadsworth's re-election. He predicted that "the opposition of a certain group here [the former suffragists], however bitter and well organized, will prove ineffective," as voters will not "punish a public officer for a standing on a question that has been settled, not to his liking, but to theirs." He went on to say, "If these people had been disappointed in their hopes, the situation would be quite different, but they have had their way, and you did not get yours." He followed this observation with the advice that Wadsworth counter his opponents by making "substantially the same convincing speech on the duties of the United States Senate which you made before the Committee on Resolutions at the time of the Republican State Convention at Saratoga in July, 1918."[29]

This letter illustrates how well Crystal Eastman had constructed the divergent reactions of men and women to winning the vote for women. For Butler, the "everlasting fight" was over. In his view, since the state woman suffrage campaign had succeeded, suffragists had no reason to continue opposing a man who had lost that battle. That Wadsworth was, at that very moment, continuing to fight the federal woman suffrage amendment bore no weight with him. He even advised Wadsworth to make the same speech he had made before the very committee whose headship Mary Garrett Hay had won *only* because woman suffrage had passed in the state. Butler's lack of awareness of the ironies embedded in his advice to Wadsworth reveals how deep a chasm remained to be crossed between the male and female political cultures of the early post-suffrage era.

New York women would experience few political triumphs in the immediate years after suffrage. Even Wadsworth's defeat in 1926 could not be attributed to them. Still, at least one unknown person believed women had played an important role. The day after his defeat, this person sent him an anonymous telegram boasting, "THE WOMEN OF NEW YORK STATE DID NOT FORGET."[30] The telegram, carefully preserved in Wadsworth's otherwise well-pruned papers at the Library of Congress, reveals that, although consigned to the political margins in the 1920s, some women still believed in the power of their ballot.

A Research Agenda

Two generalizations have dominated historians' views of the woman suffrage amendment: that women voters tended to vote as men did and that fewer women voted than expected. Some scholars have questioned these generalizations. They argue that it is impossible to determine whether regional or local vote totals may have been based on gendered issues, since only Illinois kept sex-segregated voting records.[31] In regard to the second generalization, other scholars point out that the low incidence of women voters merely reflects a larger decline in voter turnouts that occurred after the turn of the twentieth century and that centuries of disfranchisement meant that women would need time and experience to learn how to exercise their new citizenship rights.[32]

Yet other scholars—especially those who have written on the rise and fall of the movement to pass an Equal Rights Amendment—have focused on how women's ideological differences after suffrage prevented women from voting or acting politically as a bloc or "third force" in politics and how older generations of suffragists failed to inspire feminist sensibilities among younger women. Historian Nancy Cott has also argued that the paradoxes unavoidably inherent within feminist ideologies placed the movement on the defensive, making it easy prey to the conservative political backlash of the twenties and the economic crisis of the thirties.[33]

To clarify these issues further, future researchers might look more closely at the struggles of women, as individuals and in groups, to work out and refine their political roles after suffrage. Local activism needs special attention, because that is where women were most apt to be politically engaged and to have the most clout. Researchers should also examine some of the generational clashes among the suffragists themselves. In Mary Garrett Hay's time, the power of the nonpartisan pull on women's loyalties was still strong. By mid-decade, it had waned somewhat. How did that development play itself out, especially among women in their thirties and forties whose careers were just beginning to bloom? How did the Great Depression alter their ambitions?[34] I think we will find that, starting in the late twenties and continuing into the thirties and forties, more women were balancing partisan *and* nonpartisan activism, and protesting—politely, at first, but after World War II with increasing vehemence—when the doors to party opportunities were shut in their faces.

Other research agendas include finding out more about the women who ran for office in those first decades after suffrage, why they ran, and what happened to them and their political ambitions. How many of them had to run against incumbents? How many women with families even contemplated holding office? If an unmarried woman ran, was she seen as an interesting novelty but not expected to win, as was Mississippi's Belle Kearney? Or was she dismissed as a "hussy," as was Florida's Myrtice McCaskill?[35] We must also look increasingly closely at what ethnic women and women of color were doing—in their own communities and in their efforts to gain entry among the country's power elites. Moreover, instead of assuming that the women who opposed one another over feminist issues never worked together effectively on anything, we might look more closely at the political areas in which they actually cooperated, on issues of common concern, such as jury service for women, the rights of women criminals, consumer issues, and the like. We may find evidence of much more political effectiveness based in a commonality of gender identity than we hitherto have thought was possible. Finally, we must look at both genders—at what men did and did not do, how they took advantage of women's inexperience and lack of incumbency, and how they held on to the power they were accustomed to wielding.

There are hundreds of political women to study—women holding appointive offices at all government levels, women acting as citizen lobbyists, women attorneys and judges who influenced the law. Without the vote, these women would have had no careers at all. To develop a full picture of women's political history after suffrage, we must analyze what actually went on rather than set up an ideal of what should have happened. We need to dig beyond the dismissive generalizations about the impact of suffrage and study the political choices, accomplishments, and failures of these political women. Their lives will show us the links between the women of the immediate post-suffrage era and the rise of modern feminism in the sixties and seventies. They will also help us understand why, in one of the most modernized nations of the world, women still have not achieved political equity with men.

NOTES

1. From "Now We Can Begin," published in *The Liberator*, December 1920, in Blanche Cook, ed., *Crystal Eastman on Women and Revolution* (New York: Oxford University Press, 1978), 53.

2. From a memo dated July 1923, quoted in John W. Furlow, Jr., "Cornelia Bryce Pinchot: Feminism in the Post-Suffrage Era," *Pennsylvania History* 10, no. 76: 337.

3. On these issues, see J. Stanley Lemons, *The Woman Citizen: Social Feminism in the 1920s* (1975), Felice D. Gordon, *After Winning: The Legacy of the New Jersey Suffragists, 1920–1947* (1986), and Nancy F. Cott, *The Grounding of Modern Feminism* (1987), all of which make close study of the aftermath of suffrage. Other studies of the period include William H. Chafe, *The American Woman: Her Changing Social, Economic, and Political Roles, 1920–1970* (1972), Louise M. Young, *In the Public Interest: The League of Women Voters, 1920–1970* (1989), and my own *Belle Moskowitz: Feminine Politics and the Exercise of Power in the Age of Alfred E. Smith* (1987).

4. "Morsels of Favor Passed Out by G.O.P. Dissatisfying Women," *Chicago Evening Mail*, June 10, 1920.

5. For a discussion of women's nonpartisan political activism in New York before suffrage, see S. Sara Monoson, "The Lady and the Tiger: Women's Electoral Activism in New York City Before Suffrage," *Journal of Women's History* 2, no. 2 (Fall 1990): 100–135. Several historians of women are now working on women's *partisan* political activism in the premodern era: see, for example, Mary Ryan, *Women in Public: Between Banners and Ballots, 1825–80* (1990), Elizabeth Varon, "Tippecanoe and the Ladies, Too: White Women and Party Politics in Antebellum Virginia," *Journal of American History* 82, no. 2 (Sept. 1995): 494–521, and Melanie Gustafson, "Partisan Women in the Progressive Era: The Struggle for Inclusion in American Political Parties," *Journal of Women's History* 9, no. 2, (Summer 1997): 8–30.

6. To construct this portrait of James W. Wadsworth, Jr. [hereafter referred to as JWW], I consulted the following oral histories, all collected by the Columbia University Oral History Office: that of JWW himself, 344–56; William A. Prendergast, 236–37; John Lord O'Brian, 65–66, 112–13, 325–27; Paul Windels, 174–78; Alice Paul, 135–37, 443; Robert F. Wagner, Jr., 45–46; and Ella A. Boole, 22–24. For JWW's views on prohibition, see his letter to Nicholas Murray Butler, February 14, 1926 (Butler Papers, Columbia University). I also consulted JWW's papers at the Library of Congress.

7. Biographical information on Mary Garrett Hay comes from James P. Louis's article in *Notable American Women*, ed. Edward T. James et al., 3 vols. (1971), and

newspaper interviews (especially, Grace Julian Clarke, "Says Club Women Are Equal to All Demands," *Indianapolis Star*, September 19, 1920; Fay Stevenson, "New York League of Women Voters Pays High Tribute to Old Leader, Mary Garrett Hay, Who Retires," *New York Evening World*, March 13, 1923; and "Miss Hay Tells of Experiences in Long Career," *Indianapolis Star*, June 2, 1925), all preserved in the Mary Garrett Hay [MGH] Scrapbook. This scrapbook is wonderfully entitled, "SOME INCIDENTS IN THE LIFE OF MARY GARRETT HAY, A WONDERFUL BOSS AND A GALLANT FIGHTER" (Rare Books and Manuscripts Division, New York Public Library [NYPL]). The state Republican Party platform committee consisted of fifty-one members, only two of whom besides Hay were women: Mary Wood and Mary Weitmer Schmiedendorf. See also Will Hays's autobiography, *The Memoirs of Will H. Hays* (New York: Doubleday, 1955), 257–61.

8. Emma H. De Zouche, "Fight to Defeat Wadsworth: A Cause of Angry Strife in Feminine Electorate" [n.p., n.d.], clipping in "Women in Politics" fol., Box 3, Ethel Eyre Dreier Papers, Sophia Smith Collection, Smith College.

9. A typescript of this speech, which she delivered in Albany, is in the MGH Scrapbook.

10. "She Wins Place, Beating Butler," *New York Globe*, July 18, 1918.

11. "Harding Wants Woman in Cabinet; Mary Garrett Hay Makes Conditions," *New York Evening Mail*, December 16, 1920.

12. Frances E. (Mrs. A. E.) Rhodes (of Clark Mills, N.Y.), to Glendolen (Mrs. Samuel J.) Bens, New York State Suffrage Party leader in Utica, N.Y., January 17, 1918 (New York Woman Suffrage Collection, NYPL).

13. The lifting of the ban against women joining parties was announced in the *New York Times*, April 2, 1918.

14. "Republican Chief Shy at Wadsworth," *New York Sun*, November 23, 1919.

15. "Republican State Convention May 1920, Statement of Mary Garrett Hay," MGH Scrapbook. She also protested that her own state Republican Party was sending women to Chicago "merely as alternates" and not as delegates. Such action showed scant recognition in "the Empire State" to "the new electorate," she complained, but nothing was done.

16. See "Miss Hay Confers on Women Voters," *Chicago Tribune*, June 3, 1920; and "Leader of GOP Women's Division to Leave Office After Convention," June 5, 1920, and "Morsels of Favor Passed Out by G.O.P. Dissatisfying Women," June 10, 1920, both from the *Chicago Evening Mail*, all in the MGH Scrapbook. The Republican national committee finally acceded to Hay's original demand for 50 percent representation in 1924, copying the Democratic national committee, which had made that change in 1920.

17. MGH public statement (no title), dated June 1, 1920, and articles from early June, 1920, in the *Chicago News*, *New York Sun*, and *New York Herald*, and Gladys Denny Shultz article, *Des Moines Register*, July 16, 1920, all in the MGH Scrapbook.

18. MGH Statement, "Present Responsibility of Women as Citizens," August 1920, MGH Scrapbook. In the national elections of 1920, Carrie Chapman Catt also endorsed individual candidates. Local Leagues found themselves doing the same, arguing that they were not endorsing parties but individuals.

19. Numerous newspaper articles commented on these events in the *New York Tribune*, *New York Times*, and *New York World* of July 24 and 27, 1920.

20. "Miss Hay's Position," *Knickerbocker Press*, July 29, 1920.

21. Emma H. De Zouche, "Fight to Defeat Wadsworth . . . ," Ethel Eyre Dreier Papers, Sophia Smith Collection, Smith College.

22. "Women Delegates at Saratoga," *Evening Post*, August 26, 1920. A third group that took out its animus upon Miss Hay was the Women Voters Anti-Suffrage Party. Entering the fray with a flyer, entitled "Watch the Woman Boss in Action!", it charged that Mary Hay had started "sex warfare" in the state. See flyer, "Women Voters Anti-Suffrage Party," MGH Scrapbook.

23. It raised $5,000.

24. Boole claimed this was the largest vote any woman had yet received running for public office. She would never run for office again but went on to become national and then world WCTU president. Ella Boole, Oral History, Columbia University Oral History Office, 22–24.

25. *New York Telegram*, September 5, 1921.

26. Frances Kellor, "Cloisters in American Politics," carbon copy of a rough draft, in "Women in Politics" folder, Box 3, Ethel Eyre Dreier Papers, Sophia Smith Collection, Smith College. Dreier, a nonpartisan activist herself and the sister-in-law of Mary Dreier, Kellor's lifelong companion, underlined and queried many sections of this article. On Kellor and the Dreiers, see Ellen Fitzpatrick, *Endless Crusade: Women Social Scientists and Progressive Reform* (New York: Oxford University Press, 1990).

27. J. Stanley Lemons relates this episode in *The Woman Citizen*, 241–43; see also, Hilda R. Watrous, "Narcissa Cox Vanderlip: Chairman, New York State League of Women Voters, 1919–1923" (New York State League of Women Voters pamphlet), 6.

28. Buffalo lawyer John Lord O'Brian pointed out in his Oral History that Wadsworth had alienated not one but two groups of voters, suffragists and prohibitionists. Wadsworth's career was far from over in 1926. He returned to Washington as a congressman, serving in the House for more than two decades. After World War II, he worked amicably with a younger generation of League of Women Voters leaders on an Equal Rights Amendment, albeit one that preserved a recognition of the social importance of female and male biological differences. In the early 1950s, when Wadsworth recorded his oral memoirs for Columbia University, he blamed his 1926 defeat only on the "drys."

29. Butler to Wadsworth, Jr., January 15, 1920, Butler Papers, Columbia University Rare Books and Manuscripts Library. At the end of the letter, Butler advised Wadsworth, as a "practical matter," to form a "Woman's Committee" on his behalf, made up "not wholly of women who opposed the Suffrage Amendment, but of women drawn from all types and classes of thought." This plan would, he thought, "to some extent blanket the fire on the other side." Unfortunately, there was no reply preserved in Butler's collection.

30. Fol., "Senate Campaign of 1926," James W. Wadsworth, Jr., Papers, Library of Congress. Although when Wadsworth organized his papers for the Library of Congress, he threw away many things—the collection has a distinctly cleaned-up look—he, or someone, kept this telegram. There is little else in the folder.

31. See, for example, Sara Alpern and Dale Baum, "Female Ballots: The Impact of the Nineteenth Amendment," *Journal of Interdisciplinary History* 16, no. 1 (Sum-

mer 1985): 43–67; the authors conclude that, while there was "no uniform sex difference in voting in the North in the 1920 election," regional differences did exist,
and that historians should be more cautious about assuming that women everywhere voted as their husbands, fathers, or brothers did.

32. See Paul Kleppner's "Were Women to Blame? Female Suffrage and Voter
Turnout," *Journal of Interdisciplinary History* 12, no. 4 (1982): 621–43, and Kristi
Andersen, *After Suffrage: Women in Partisan and Electoral Politics before the New Deal*
(Chicago, Ill., 1996), especially ch. 3.

33. See Susan D. Becker, *The Origins of the Equal Rights Amendment: American
Feminism Between the Wars* (Westport, Conn., 1981); Joan Hoff-Wilson, ed., *Rights
of Passage: The Past and Future of the ERA* (Bloomington, Ind., 1986); and Nancy
Cott, *The Grounding of Modern Feminism* (New Haven, Conn., 1987).

34. Susan Ware's book *Beyond Suffrage: Women in the New Deal* (Cambridge,
Mass., 1981) is the best study to date of this topic.

35. See Vinton M. Prince, Jr., "The Woman Voter and Mississippi Elections in
the Early Twenties," *The Journal of Mississippi History* 49, no. 2 (May 1987): 105–14,
and Allen Morris, "Florida's First Women Candidates," *Florida Historical Quarterly*
63, no. 4: 406–22.

12

American Foreign Policy

The European Dimension, 1921–1929

STEPHEN A. SCHUKER

In August 1923, President Harding suffered a cardiac collapse and died. His death left the country anxious and distressed.[1] Calvin Coolidge, a fortuitous vice president, who like most of his predecessors had played a mere walk-on role in the great dramas of state, suddenly faced the manifold responsibilities of the Oval Office. The incoming chief executive had no public track record in foreign affairs. Nevertheless, financier Thomas Lamont, the senior partner of J. P. Morgan and Co., sought to reassure his European friends. Coolidge figured personally as an "enigma," he conceded. But the new president's intimates predicted a "bold stroke" toward greater participation in the councils of the world. The country, Lamont interpolated, was "ripe for such new policy." It was tired of hanging back and "seeing its markets go to ruin."[2]

The prophesied bold stroke never came. Coolidge issued no clarion call for tariff reduction or debt forgiveness; American foreign economic policy remained prudent, pragmatic, and mindful of Congressional constraints for the rest of the decade. All the same, the United States played a larger role in shaping international politics and economics than ever before. The country assumed pride of place as the engine of technological progress, the leading source of investment capital, the second greatest exporter, and a pillar of the world monetary system. If the advanced industrial nations had recovered from war and attained relative stability by 1929, the steady and quiet efforts of public and private U.S. diplomacy contributed much to the result.

Calvin Coolidge rated as a modest man with much to be modest about. In Massachusetts politics, he had slowly ascended the greasy pole. He had put in a decade on Beacon Hill defending the parochial concerns of his

Northampton constituency while living in a dingy bed-sitter with one wash-stand. He had served as lieutenant-governor and then as governor without moral blemish in the most politically corrupt of states. In 1919 he won fleeting fame by putting down the Boston police strike. Never a phrase-maker and by no means a visceral opponent of labor, he serendipitously coined the slogan that rallied the forces of order and sold the yellower tab-loids: "There is no right to strike against the public by anybody, anywhere, any time."[3] Nothing suggests that Calvin Coolidge had devoted a mo-ment's thought to foreign economic policy before he arrived in Washing-ton in 1921. Nothing indicates that he labored assiduously to remedy that deficiency thereafter.

Warren Harding, though by no means an original thinker, had come to the White House in 1921 with far more foreign-policy experience. In six years in the Senate, Harding had valiantly supported intervention in World War I and diligently worked on committee assignments dealing with the Philippines, other territories, and naval affairs. He had served as a faithful second to Henry Cabot Lodge on the Senate Foreign Relations Commit-tee in the fight over the League. In his genial midwestern way, he embraced the Republican "realist" approach to American responsibilities abroad em-bodied by Lodge, Theodore Roosevelt, Elihu Root, and William Howard Taft.[4] Harding also boasted a reasonable acquaintance with prominent busi-ness and banking leaders and the foreign-policy elite. He had no fear of sur-rounding himself with finer minds than his own; he naturally chose sophis-ticated internationalists of impeccable credentials—Charles Evans Hughes at State, Andrew Mellon at Treasury, and Herbert Hoover at Commerce—for the top cabinet posts involved with foreign affairs.

From his preferred vantage point on the Foreign Relations Committee, Senator Lodge welcomed the advent of the Harding administration. He deemed it a narrow escape from disaster. Most nonpartisan Washington insiders echoed that view. In the year and a half following Wilson's stroke, able men had drifted away from government and simply were not replaced. The State Department had fallen into a state of paralysis mirroring Wil-son's own condition. Nearly every other agency experienced similar deteri-oration. The chaos had become indescribable.[5] Harding had taken hold and named "the best cabinet" that Lodge had known in his time. The ap-pointments at the undersecretary and assistant secretary level proved a wel-come relief, in Lodge's judgment, from the "obscurities and subservient time-servers" who had filled out the supporting cast of government under Wilson. Admittedly, Harding had an embarrassing weakness for malaprop-isms. Lodge reminded his Somerset Club friends that proper Bostonians had once supported Bell and Everett over Lincoln on such social grounds. He cautioned them not to repeat the error. Harding figured as "a thoroughly upright, patriotic, and honest man, a man of genuine ability and of very admirable intentions."[6] Those who worked with Harding in the foreign-policy realm continued to take that view, whatever the later revelations about the pecadillos of his friends.

Coolidge, by contrast, inspired less personal warmth. The adventitious successor felt closer to Main Street than to Wall Street. Aside from a few old Amherst cronies like the dry-goods merchant Frank Stearns, Coolidge could boast few intimates in the East Coast circles that habitually concerned themselves with foreign affairs. The distinction lay in the realm of social class rather than policy preference. Senator Lodge, acknowledged as the senior Massachusetts Republican, praised Governor Coolidge publicly in 1920 as a "first-rate" man who had a "long and distinguished career" in front of him. All the same, Lodge did not feel impelled to step down as keynote speaker at the Republican National Convention in order to place the governor's name in nomination. Such a corvée he left to others.[7] In short, the class rigidities of Yankee Boston remained. Nor did Coolidge make an effort to overcome them. For example, Coolidge had never traveled abroad and evinced no curiosity to do so either before or during his presidency. "I always tell people," he artlessly declared at one of his valedictory press conferences, "that I have so many places still to go in the United States that I don't know when those will be so much exhausted that I will arrive at a time when I can visit other countries."[8] This was not the sort of chap to invite to the Somerset Club or the Myopia Hunt.

Unsurprisingly, Coolidge's quiet self-confidence masked a touch of jealousy of urbane and polished intellects. Shortly after assuming the presidency, Coolidge lauded the forbidding Charles Evans Hughes as "the greatest secretary of state this country had ever had" and "the backbone of his administration."[9] Yet in his second term he let Hughes depart unmourned and replaced him with the competent but unassuming Minnesotan Frank Kellogg.[10] Similarly, in the early part of his presidency, Coolidge listened respectfully to Herbert Hoover.[11] But shortly he tired of Hoover's ill-disguised and restless ambition, and he privately derided the Great Humanitarian, with his pretentious aspirations for scientific government, as a "wonder boy" or "miracle worker."[12]

Whatever his personal sensibilities, Coolidge, like Harding, almost always appointed sober-minded people to handle foreign-policy concerns. He listened dispassionately to their recommendations and sought to find sensible solutions to the problems that crossed the presidential desk. Admittedly, Coolidge did not often speak out in detail on foreign affairs. Yet behind the scenes, he rated as a more activist president than outsiders generally realized. He took a lively interest in diplomatic appointments. He periodically sent his friend Frank Stearns around to the State Department to take informal soundings. And he supervised the day-to-day development of Kellogg's policy initiatives more closely than the secretary would have preferred.[13]

At the same time, Coolidge ran interference for Kellogg when outsiders talked him down. Early in the second term, Alanson Houghton, ambassador to England, elaborated a scheme for a solemn contract among the great powers not to make war for fifty years. Coolidge, he thought, should "make a really big gesture" and "put himself prominently before the public in a way that cannot be ignored." If the president squandered the opportunity, he feared, the isolationist Senator William Borah, new head of the Senate Foreign Relations Committee, would thrust himself forward as the sponsor of humanitarian ideas; Republican chances at the polls would go glimmering. When Kellogg failed to act, Houghton began to complain that the State Department merely managed the paper flow but possessed no "world point of view." The diplomatic machine, he charged, stood "on the verge of collapse."[14] Coolidge stolidly backed his secretary on this and other occasions. The Houghton idea would eventually metamorphose into the Kellogg-Briand pact. But Coolidge prized orderly administration and disdained a premature bid to the gallery. When overwrought staffers called the State Department "a mad house" and lamented that their chief lived in a "state of continual grouch," Coolidge stepped in tactfully to dispatch Kellogg on holiday.[15] Nonetheless, the president vigorously defended the secretary's ultimate prerogatives. As Treasury Secretary Mellon prepared a European junket in 1927, Coolidge took care to remind him of the ground rules: "If foreign interests approach you . . . , you will of course listen to them if you desire, but suggest to them that such relationships are entirely in the hands of the State Department and their problems should properly be taken up through regular diplomatic channels."[16]

Throughout his presidency, Coolidge took a keen interest in the orderly workings of the bureaucracy. He would have liked to see permanent undersecretaries assuring continuity in all major executive departments.[17] The drive for efficient government had figured as a staple of American political thought since the Progressive Era; it did not derive from the impetus of a single individual. All the same, the key administrative agencies made notable strides toward professionalization in the 1920s. Generally they offered sound if unadventurous advice. The Foreign Service broadened the base of its recruitment, established entrance examinations for the first time, and slowly moved toward a merit system of promotions. While the public image of diplomats as feckless cookie-pushers in black tie and spats reflected one part of the truth, the higher officials recognized those weaknesses and earnestly pursued improvement.[18] The most talented foreign service officers sought to serve in the high-prestige European division, and, though ministerial appointments varied in quality, Harding and Coolidge avoided the capriciousness that later marked some of Franklin Roosevelt's more bizarre selections.[19]

At the Commerce Department, Herbert Hoover attracted superbly qualified academics and other experts as his division chiefs, vastly improved the performance of the foreign commercial attachés, and offered a range of trade information and statistical services that facilitated the expansion of American business abroad.[20] At the Treasury, the avuncular septuagenarian Andrew Mellon restricted his personal activity to the highest reaches of policy. Yet he successfully delegated day-to-day management to a succession of brilliant undersecretaries—S. Parker Gilbert, Garrard Winston, and Ogden Mills. This farsighted team fashioned three successive supply-side tax-cuts that did much to facilitate economic growth over the decade. Other governmental agencies operating in the international arena also performed at a level of efficiency rarely equaled previously. The Federal Reserve Board remained a backwater dominated by small-town bankers. But the Federal Reserve Bank of New York, under the sagacious leadership of Benjamin Strong and George L. Harrison, provided the indispensable leadership and expertise that led to the reestablishment of stable currencies abroad.[21] And while the Tariff Commission fell into protectionist hands after the resignation of William S. Culbertson, the technical studies produced by the commission met a high standard.[22]

Committed Wilsonians longed to see the United States seize high moral ground in the 1920s at the League of Nations and the World Court. Many bemoaned, in the journals of opinion, a lack of presidential leadership in foreign affairs. Promoters of the "imperial presidency," especially those who consider the growth of executive authority after World War II an unalloyed blessing, frequently echo those views.[23] Yet most Republican politicians—and evidently the voters who elected them as well—took a less benign view of expanding presidential power during World War I and of the uses to which President Wilson had put that power. They actively sought to redress the balance.

A pointed joke went the rounds at the Paris Peace Conference in early 1919. Someone asked Wilson when he would return to America. He replied, "as soon as possible." "But there is no hurry," suggested his interlocutor. "Oh, yes, there is," the president answered, "they may establish a Republic in my absence."[24] Henry Cabot Lodge characteristically portrayed the debate over ratification of the Versailles treaty as a contest between the old freedom and the so-called New Freedom. "Underlying the whole question of the treaty is the determination to put an end to executive encroachments and to reestablish the legislative branch of the government and its proper Constitutional power. Mr. Wilson's comprehension of government is that of the third Napoleon, an autocrat to be elected by the people through a plebiscite and no representative bodies of any consequence in between."[25]

Following the unambiguous repudiation of Wilson in the election of
1920, leaders of the Republican administration maintained a healthy respect for Congressional prerogative. The story that Coolidge asked Senator William E. Borah to become his running mate in 1924 may well be
apocryphal, but State Department staffers shivered in fear when that self-
promoting buffoon succeeded Lodge as chairman of the Foreign Relations
Committee.[26] The broad public lagged well behind Wall Street and Washington in understanding America's altered place in the world, and the Congressional majority in both parties remained inward-looking and proudly
provincial. Cabinet officers and the bureaucracies supporting them habitually looked over their shoulders twice, ever mindful of what the Congress
would or would not approve.

Although internationalist Republicans held the presidency, the balance
of power in Congress fell to a group of radical Progressives, often Republican only in name, from the Plains States and the Far West. Some scholars
have attributed a coherent worldview to that group and denominated them
the "peace progressives."[27] But the leading radical Senators—among them
William Borah, Hiram Johnson, Robert M. La Follette, Sr., Joseph France,
and later Gerald Nye—had scant use for each other. Indeed, although they
all nourished a conspiratorial fear of international bankers and a visceral
aversion to the wily statesmen of Europe, they agreed on little positive.
Johnson, as typical of the group as any, considered Hughes a man of "dia-
bolical cunning," Hoover an "intellectual crook," and Kellogg a courtier
and a sycophant "absolutely subject to the influences of great financial
power and big business."[28]

The radicals feared that such Harding-Coolidge initiatives as the Washington Naval Conference, the movement to join the World Court, and
participation in the Dawes Committee on German reparations were recidi-
vist steps down the slippery slope of Wilsonianism.[29] Coolidge, always a
strong party man, at first sought to placate the isolationist wing. In 1922, he
campaigned in California and lauded Johnson with a straight face as "a
credit to his state and to the nation." On the principle that no good deed
goes unpunished, Johnson turned around and challenged Coolidge for the
presidential nomination in 1924. Of course, the fundamental divisions of
American politics derived at the time from agricultural distress, ethnic resentment, and liquor. All the same, Johnson sought to focus the Republican
primaries in part on foreign policy. He flayed Coolidge's putative weakness
in allowing Americans to sit on the Dawes Committee.

The president, championing free markets, economy in government, and
limited involvement in world affairs, fought off the challenge from Johnson
within Republican ranks and subsequently the threat from the third-party
candidacy of La Follette. In the 1925 Congress, several dissenters lost their
committee chairmanships. At the next off-year elections, however, the in-

surgents took advantage of farm-state discontent to replace several regular Republicans, while the overall Republican margin in the Senate dwindled from sixteen to two.[30] Privately, State Department officials derided their Congressional critics as "crazy." "When one reads what goes on in Congress," William R. Castle minuted in frustration on one occasion, "it is difficult not to agree with Mussolini that representative government has proved a failure."[31] But no one who drew a public paycheck cared to voice such sentiments openly. Coolidge and his supporting team maneuvered always within the limits of the practicable and the possible.

Charles Evans Hughes, who set the foreign-policy tone during the first Republican administration, drew the lesson from the Versailles treaty fiasco that it was idle to challenge the dominant public mood. Hughes felt a strong commitment to public service. He displayed a refined sense of ethics. Still, he did not consider it his obligation to mount the bully pulpit. The secretary knew Europe relatively well and spoke passable French and German. But in contrast to the Wilsonians, he declined to philosophize in grand terms about America's mission in the world. As a highly resourceful lawyer, he took pride in mastering the details of his assigned brief; he likewise believed that intellectual efficiency and juridical craft mandated the solution of each consecutive problem on the narrowest possible lines.[32] Characteristically, Hughes appealed to A. Lawrence Lowell of the World Peace Foundation in 1922 not to renew the "barren controversy" over American participation in the League of Nations. "What is needed at this time is not an academic discussion, or a debate about international organization. . . . With the present lack of stability there are certain fundamental problems that must be solved. It is not lack of machinery which stands in our way, but the attitude and opinion of peoples." He and the president therefore preferred "doing the day's work and gradually extending the range of our helpful influence."[33]

Hughes spoke the language of "helpful influence" and not of "national interest." He did so for good reason. The United States had emerged unscathed from World War I and by every conventional measure richer than before. As the secretary of the treasury had observed flatulently, "the impious hand of the enemy has not touched any part of her fair land and there are no waste places here to restore."[34] Despite the radical changes wrought elsewhere in the international economy, America remained basically self-sufficient. Commerce Department analysts reiterated throughout the 1920s that "the United States is self-contained to an exceptional degree."[35] The country required certain essential imports—rubber, wood pulp, silk and wool, nitrates, coffee, and tin—but these could be drawn, with some exceptions, from underdeveloped countries where the North American colossus determined the terms of trade. Exports played a less vital role in the workings of the U.S. economy. Overseas sales grew from 10 percent of manufactured goods produced in 1914 to 14 percent of such goods at the postwar peak in 1919, but declined again to under 8 percent of manufactures in 1929. Similarly, only 15 percent of farm income derived from foreign sales in 1929, compared with 16.5 percent in 1914.[36] The absolute value and volume of exports increased steadily over this fifteen-year period, of course. The domestic economy, however, grew still faster.

Certain sectors admittedly ran counter to the trend. The automobile companies depended heavily on foreign markets. So did producers of cotton, copper, rice, tobacco, and a few other commodities. Representatives of those industries manned the busy mimeograph machines at the National Foreign Trade Council and similar pressure groups.[37] The prosperity of the country as a whole, however, emanated first and foremost from an explosion of domestic demand on a scale that had few precedents in history. Coolidge's much-derided aphorism—"the business of America is business" —rested on a fundament of truth.[38]

American economic growth in the generation before World War I benefited from a vast, homogeneous, and accessible domestic market—the largest free-trade area in the world. The country had pulled ahead of other industrial nations in part through the application of advanced science and engineering knowledge to processes at the cutting edge of the ongoing industrial revolution, especially in the electrical, chemical, and motor-car industries. America had also prospered through the application of innovative management techniques to capital-intensive, energy-consuming industries using continuous-batch technology (for example, primary metals, packaged foods, petroleum, transportation equipment, and machinery manufacture). Despite the strictures of antitrust, that peculiar emanation of Progressive culture, giant integrated firms achieved unparalleled efficiencies of scale and scope through mass production, mass distribution, and mass marketing.[39] Finally, wages and working conditions compared favorably with those elsewhere, thus sustaining consumer demand, even though improvements in pay, despite pressures from Marxist-oriented industrial unions, rarely outstripped productivity gains.[40] In these factors lay the wellsprings of American well-being. Involvement in the world economy appeared a matter of secondary importance.

To be sure, some of the largest firms, particularly in the extractive industries, relied on raw materials from abroad; others sold their surplus production overseas.[41] Since the McKinley era, the American government had fought to protect the interests of those engaged in foreign trade by promoting the principle of the "Open Door." Government officials and business publicists elaborated increasingly sophisticated justifications for foreign-trade expansion.[42] Yet rhetoric changed more rapidly than the configuration of trade itself. Exports and imports together amounted to scarcely 10 percent of U.S. gross national product before the war, compared with a third or more for the leading European nations. After the temporary dislocations of the war and immediate postwar period had subsided, old commercial patterns reasserted themselves.

In other words, while American economic and foreign policies decisively affected Europe, European nations lacked a balancing reciprocal importance for the welfare of the United States. The sheer size of the respective economies underscores the point. Already in 1913, the United States produced 35.8 percent of world manufactures, roughly equal to the output of Germany, Britain, and France combined. By 1926–29, U.S. manufacturing output had risen to 42.2 percent of the world figure, exceeding the total production of all eight competitive industrial economies (Germany, Britain, France, Italy, Canada, Belgium, Japan, and the Soviet Union).[43] The advanced European countries, meanwhile, took a sharply declining share in international trade.[44] While the European belligerents fought their fratricidal war, the United States had managed to undermine their banking monopolies and to penetrate heretofore closed third markets. Hence, while 60 percent of American exports had still gone to Europe in 1913, Asian and Latin American markets flourished over the next decade. By the late 1920s, the United States drew only 30 percent of its imports from Europe and directed no more than 47 percent of its exports to the old continent.[45]

A similar imbalance obtained in the field of foreign investment. Europeans desperately needed American capital for postwar reconstruction, particularly since Britain redirected its own holdings away from the Continent and toward the Empire. Americans, however, found many profitable places to invest. The country's direct and portfolio investments overseas rose from $7 billion to $17 billion over the course of the postwar decade, with approximately 30 percent of the loans going to Europe.[46] But those figures were dwarfed by the explosion of opportunities for lucrative placements on domestic stock and bond markets.[47] In short, those who examined the various economic indices might reasonably conclude that the United States should lend its influence for the construction of a peaceful world order in which stability would promote beneficent trade and capital flows. They might equally well reason that the details of diplomacy outside the Western Hemisphere did not often engage vital national interests.

Critics of U.S. policy toward Europe in the 1920s fault the Harding and Coolidge administrations for four interrelated errors of omission. They claim, first, that Washington should have played a larger political role in European affairs by joining the League of Nations and other international institutions. They hold, second, that the United States should have reduced tariff barriers and facilitated European recovery by making it easier for Europeans to sell their goods on this side of the ocean. They assert, third, that the United States missed an opportunity to make a generous gesture regarding war debts. A marginal sacrifice for the American bondholder and taxpayer, so goes the argument, would have granted decisive breathing room to hard-pressed European governments and thus promoted domestic stability in debtor countries and fostered international comity. Last but not least, the critics suggest, the United States could and should have managed capital flows in order to minimize improvident investments before 1928 and to slow the repatriation of funds from abroad once the depression had struck.

Charles Kindleberger has encapsulated the theoretical expression of this view with unusual elegance. Every successful international economic system needs a beneficent hegemon: a country that is willing to set standards of international conduct and to make sacrifices to maintain them. Such a country should stand prepared to accept redundant goods, to maintain a flow of investment capital, and to discount foreign paper during a period of adversity. Great Britain performed that role in the international system before World War I; the United States did so after World War II.[48] American policymakers should have understood the vital importance of shouldering the burden earlier. Their failure to do so accounts in part for the breakdown of the global economic order in 1930–33, the unusual length and severity of the world depression, and the political and social conflicts that led to World War II.

Kindleberger has handed up a grave indictment. The generation of policymakers who came of age in World War II generally accepted that outlook on the past. Leaders of the World War II generation not only felt their responsibilities keenly, they also created the institutions and moulded the attitudes that shaped a more interdependent world. They have earned both acknowledgment and gratitude. The question remains whether the charges they framed about the 1920s make sense in terms of the vital national interests and actual constraints on policymakers at the time. To adopt a phrase that has recently made its fortune, if the facts don't fit, we must acquit. When one examines the evidence closely, the version of the past that internationalists constructed for themselves in the 1940s—with largely beneficent effects in their own era—does not correspond closely to the real policy options open to their predecessors in the 1920s.

For practical purposes, the League of Nations had become a dead issue by the time a Republican administration took power in March 1921. The protracted debate that raged in the Senate and the country in 1919–20 over America's potential obligations under Article X of the Covenant did not take place in a vacuum. During that period, it became obvious that any attempt to reform the League would split the Republican Party. At the same time, the League showed itself impotent to settle the Russo-Polish war or to protect the small peoples of Asia Minor from the competitive depredations of the Bolsheviks and the Turks. The League, wrote Senator Lodge, presented "the most melancholy spectacle"; its Council hid itself away "somewhere in a corner." Practical experience had wrought a great change in public opinion and promoted the constantly growing feeling "against the United States involving itself in the quarrels of Europe at all."

During the next few years, League enthusiasts attempted several times to create a workable scheme for collective security. The three principal efforts to do so—the Draft Treaty of Mutual Assistance, the Draft Treaty of Mutual Guarantee, and the Geneva Protocol—all failed ignominiously. When push came to shove, self-proclaimed internationalists in Great Britain proved no more willing to embrace such schemes than politicians in more cautious powers.[49] Coolidge voiced the common view that the United States should not get mixed up with "the terrible political intrigues of Geneva." He dreaded commitments raising the possibility that "Americans would have to go abroad to fight." Uppermost in his mind, however, lay a shrewd political calculus. Behind all the flag waving, the war had exposed the ugly fissures dividing American ethnic groups. If the United States joined the League, he feared, each hyphenate group would lobby for support of its former homeland. The result would be that "the country would be more than ever divided into un-American nationalistic groups."[50]

No wonder that Coolidge, like Harding, preferred to foster international appeasement through the less divisive method of naval disarmament. Numerous self-proclaimed leaders of "women's" and "peace" groups in the 1920s exhibited sufficient credulity to believe that disarmament actually leads to peace. The same sort of people later accepted the Kellogg-Briand pact as a serious barrier against war. Most administration officials did not share those illusions. Hughes did a brilliant job at the Washington Naval Conference of 1921–22 by focusing on the limits of the possible. By the adept exploitation of secret intelligence, the secretary avoided an expensive capital-ship naval race that no one wanted for the moment while preventing renewal of the Anglo-Japanese alliance with least embarrassment to the respective parties.[51] Coolidge left no illusions about his reaction when the British cynically declined to go along with cruiser limitation in 1927. In calling for a new cruiser-building program, he spoke the plain and painful truth about arms limitation: "Foreign governments made agreements limiting that class of combat vessels in which we were superior, but refused limitation in the class in which they were superior."[52]

It is true enough that the Congress imposed an Emergency Tariff in 1921 to prevent dumping by nations that had depreciated their currencies. The legislators followed with higher general rates in the Fordney-McCumber Tariff of 1922. Protectionist winds blew at gale force on Capitol Hill, and rates on dutiable items were raised substantially. However, scholars have tended to exaggerate the macroeconomic effects of the tariff. Some have argued that policymakers failed to comprehend the significance of the country's shift to creditor status and therefore formulated tariff policy in a "nineteenth-century frame of reference."[53] In fact, under Fordney-McCumber a large free list remained. The overall level of protection rose only a few percentage points over that obtaining by virtue of the "low" Underwood tariff of 1913.[54]

William Culbertson and other tariff reformers who advised the State Department hoped to work against high rates over a period of years through two instrumentalities. The first was application of the unconditional most-favored-nation clause, which would generalize bilateral reductions to all. The second was a provision authorizing the president to reduce applicable levies by half through negotiation. In the event, the reformers met disappointment. Coolidge came under pressure to displace the high-minded but politically unresponsive Culbertson, and the State Department obediently packed him off to gilded exile as minister to Roumania. The Tariff Commission fell into the hands of arch-protectionists.[55] The cost-of-production standard almost invariably provided an excuse for the commission to raise duties rather than to lower them.[56] Yet the fault did not lie all on one side. European nations showed mixed interest in mutual reductions that would apply to all. The Germans compliantly swallowed the most-favored-nation principle as well as some unilateral advantages for American shipping in order to win reacceptance into the American market. But the French sought to preserve their two-column tariff and fought an off-and-on tariff war with their former allies for the balance of the decade.[57] While the data are not wholly unambiguous, tariffs probably did not matter very much in the end, except in specialized market segments like optics or specialty steels. Imports continued to rise smartly under the Fordney-McCumber regime. The United States actually ran an average $216 million deficit on commodity trade and invisibles from 1922 to 1930. In other words, the boom in U.S. tourist travel and the high level of immigrant remittances to Europe more than compensated for the modestly rising trend in U.S. exports.[58]

The third element in the internationalist catechism holds that the United States should have treated Europeans more generously on their war debts. No issue led to more misunderstanding during the interwar period; none remains subject to such grave misconceptions today. The European governments kept up a steady barrage of cancellationist propaganda right through the 1920s.[59] The British government repeatedly proposed what it called the writing down of the world balance sheet, as if the perfectly good claim that Washington had on the British treasury could be equated with the phantom British claim on the defunct czarist government. French publicists dwelt with notable indiscretion on the blood debt owed by the United States for its late entrance into the war rather than on the real financial claims. The fact is that, by any reasonable standard, Washington treated all the Europeans generously.

The American authorities could not flout public opinion, which demanded a show of debt collection. They remained mindful that they had to service the underlying Liberty Bonds from which the money for overseas loans had come. Nevertheless, the World War Foreign Debt Commission ignored the limitations imposed on it by Congress. It offered a series of negotiated settlements stretching over sixty-two years and with magnanimous interest concessions based on capacity to pay. The present value of the British settlement implied a 35.1 percent cancellation of prior obligations. France received 64.8 percent forgiveness, and Italy and Belgium obtained respectively 81.5 percent and 63.3 percent off the bill.[60] Moreover, Secretary of the Treasury Andrew Mellon hinted to foreign diplomats that his department would take a new look at collection in 1942, once it had retired the Liberty Bonds; hence the effective reduction exceeded what those figures imply.[61]

No one knows whether Coolidge ever said, "They hired the money, didn't they?" Grace Coolidge could not remember the remark, although she said it sounded like her husband.[62] Certainly Coolidge shared the distaste so volubly expressed in Congress for the tone in which Europeans discussed the matter. He did not feel an inclination to make the private loans of international bankers more secure by canceling those owed to the American people.[63] On the other hand, he did not wish to worsen relations among the former Allies by quarreling. When in 1927 Mellon stumbled into an acrimonious dispute with Whitehall over the morality of debt collection, the president did everything he could to damp the controversy down.[64] The main point, as administration officials knew full well, was that war debts never figured as a major item in the balance of payments. Debt payments averaged only $185 million annually from 1919 through 1930, while new foreign capital issues floated in the United States averaged $925 million over the same period. Great Britain made the lion's share of payments, and such payments never amounted to more than a modest fraction of the new capital issues floated on the London market for overseas account.[65] War debts festered as a political sore but never posed an economic problem.

Finally, critics argue that the United States should have managed capital flows to Europe better. Because Congress would not allow direct political involvement, Harding and Coolidge preferred to act through the private sector or through the intermediation of nominally independent experts. The public believed in business expertise and more easily accepted intervention in that form. Thus the experts who represented the United States on the two committees that reviewed German capacity to pay reparations —the Dawes Committee in 1924 and the Young Committee in 1929—held no official mandate. Similarly, the bankers called upon to float the loans to put those plans into effect operated largely on their own. This inevitably led to potential conflicts of interest. The leading firm on Wall Street, J. P. Morgan and Co., believed that it exercised a type of public trust. Morgan partners brooded about the problem of public accountability and control. "The Morgan firm is an anachronism," Dwight Morrow once admitted; "it is accountable to nobody but its own sense of responsibility." [66] The leading figures at Morgan corner felt their moral obligations keenly. They were the finest types of engaged internationalists and evinced a genuine commitment to foster European recovery. Nevertheless, they always had to reconcile wider aspirations with specific business obligations. Whatever their convictions on the proper role of the United States in the world, their primary job remained to market securities and to ensure the safety of those securities.

Moreover, investment banking became more competitive over the course of the decade. Many of the new firms crowding into the field did not share the ethics of Morgans. This led after 1925 to the overpromotion of German bonds without attention to the proper relation of risk and return. The administration found itself caught in a conundrum. Herbert Hoover's Commerce Department favored imposing strict government supervision over foreign lending. Coolidge, thinking that such supervision would prove practicable and effective, initially backed Hoover. [67] State and Treasury experts concluded, however, that the United States government dared not interfere. Washington officials fully understood the perils inherent in the loosening of underwriting standards on domestic security markets. They also grasped the political implications of improvident borrowing by German public authorities. They realized that Germany might well seek to produce a crisis for the Dawes Plan. When that crisis came, the Weimar regime might well claim that repayment of commercial debts ought to rank ahead of reparations. That would exacerbate the latent conflict of interest between Allied reparations creditors and American private lenders, increase the resentment of the Allies toward war debts, and generally stir dissension among all those on the American-Allied side. Nevertheless, for the U.S. government, a more immediate danger loomed. If the Treasury once began evaluating the business risk involved in German (and Latin American) loans, it would open itself to litigation on the charge of having implicitly endorsed loans that it did not forbid. [68]

The American government sought to escape the problem by inducing Germany to supervise the quality and volume of borrowing directly. The German government promised to do so but did not follow through. Toward the end of 1927, Agent-General for Reparations S. Parker Gilbert began negotiations for a general settlement that he hoped would square the circle. Gilbert suspected the Reichsbank president of attracting excess loans from the United States with a view to preparing a "transfer crisis." He hoped that a new reparations plan that fixed German obligations and abolished transfer protection would help investors assess risk more accurately, as well as facilitate the commercialization of a part of the reparations bonds. With luck, he might also induce the French to use the commercialized loans to prepay the last forty years of the war debt at a discount, thus removing the chief focus of Franco-American discord.[69]

Was that scheme realistic? Although Gilbert expected at one time to win assent from moderates in both Britain and Germany, powerful forces in both countries sought to blow up the existing reparations and war-debts arrangements. Gilbert pursued his tortuous discussions with the consent and encouragement of backers at the Federal Reserve Bank of New York and the Treasury, including Andrew Mellon. The scheme would have required sacrifices by Congress, but Mellon evidently did not despair of securing Coolidge's approval.

Close observers perceived Coolidge as moving in an isolationist direction during his final year in office. The president expressed white-hot fury at the Anglo-French naval agreement of 1928, curtly refused to receive the British ambassador, and forbade the secretary of state from setting foot in England when he traveled to Europe to sign the Kellogg-Briand Pact. Assistant Secretary William R. Castle feared that Coolidge was becoming "blindly anti-foreign."[70] Certainly the president won no friends on the other side of the water with his carefully scripted 1928 Armistice Day address. Striking a nationalist note, Coolidge proclaimed, "Europe on the whole has arrived at a state of financial stability and prosperity where it cannot be said we are called on to help or act much beyond a strict business basis. The needs of our own people require that any further advances by us must have most careful consideration."[71] With Ramsay MacDonald looking on in embarrassment, the voluble Lady Astor denounced the president in London as "a narrow-minded little beast." Even the preternaturally discreet representatives of the Foreign Office voiced alarm about the future course of Anglo-American relations.[72] Yet however plainspoken his rhetoric, Coolidge habitually played close attention to the views of his advisers. It was not foreordained that he would refuse to give careful consideration to Parker Gilbert's scheme for a final settlement of reparations and debts, if Secretary Mellon commended it to him. Under Herbert Hoover, who kept his own counsel and had unlimited confidence in his own judgment, matters would take a different course.

When President Coolidge announced in August 1927 that he would not stand for another term, his admirers did not give up. Frank Stearns, who many people thought spoke implicitly for his White House patron, expressed the hope that the Republican National Convention would deadlock; Coolidge would then accept a draft to head the bumptious Hoover off. And Hoover himself nurtured the suspicion that Coolidge, at the last minute, might throw his weight behind Dwight Morrow, the former Morgan banker who now served as ambassador to Mexico.[73]

The eastern internationalist wing of the party had little use for Hoover. In early May 1928, Parker Gilbert warned Secretary Mellon that Hoover's nomination might ruin their plans for an accommodation with Europe. "He will be more subject than almost any other important candidate to being moved by his own personal prejudices and his own preconceived ideas," observed Gilbert. "The fact is . . . that he would be about the *worst* possible president from the standpoint of foreign affairs, and that there would be real danger to our foreign policy if he should be elected."[74] Mellon largely agreed. He would never appoint an engineer who lacked an understanding of the "human element" to run one of his businesses. And yet, he replied, Coolidge would not reconsider his decision; Hughes declined to run; and Vice President Dawes had effectively spoiled his chances by supporting the McNary-Haugen bill for dumping farm surpluses abroad. And so, concluded Mellon, it looked "as though we had no other place to go to but to Hoover."[75]

In the event, Gilbert's prognostications proved all too accurate. Coolidge had expressed misgivings about allowing an American citizen to serve as chairman of the new Expert Committee on German reparations in 1929. After urging by the State Department, he nevertheless listened dispassionately to Owen Young's presentation of the case, and eventually he agreed to let him serve.[76] By contrast, Hoover's personal emissary, Henry M. Robinson, laid down the law apodictically to Young and his colleagues shortly before the new president's inauguration. The American members of the new committee should under no circumstances agree to discuss Allied indebtedness. If the Europeans attempted to do so, they should simply withdraw.[77] Coolidge, in his Armistice Day address, had given a verbal justification of isolation. "We are not the only people . . . who desire to give their attention to their own affairs." But he remained cautious and prudent, respectful of the constraints of office.[78] His more brilliant successors did not.

NOTES

1. Robert H. Ferrell, *The Strange Deaths of President Harding* (Columbia, Mo., 1996).

2. Thomas W. Lamont to Lord Robert Cecil, August 12, 1923, Cecil Papers, Add. Mss. 51144, British Library.

3. Donald R. McCoy, *Calvin Coolidge* (New York, 1967), 94; William Allen White, *A Puritan in Babylon* (New York, 1938), 164–67.

4. Robert K. Murray, *The Harding Era* (Minneapolis, 1969), esp. 16–18. For an

excellent elucidation of the Republican realist approach, see also Robert E. Osgood, *Ideals and Self-Interest in America's Foreign Relations* (Chicago, 1953).

5. Lodge to William C. Endicott, March 28, 1921, Box 69, Henry Cabot Lodge Papers, Massachusetts Historical Society.

6. Lodge to John T. Morse, April 7, 1921, Box 70, Lodge Papers.

7. Lodge to L. A. Coolidge, April 17, 1920; Lodge to Calvin Coolidge, May 15, 1920; Lodge to Medill McCormick, June 25, 1920, Box 62, Lodge Papers.

8. Howard H. Quint and Robert Ferrell, eds., *The Talkative President: The Off-the-Record Press Conferences of Calvin Coolidge* (Amherst, Mass., 1964), 253.

9. William R. Castle Diary, February 11, 1924, Houghton Library, Harvard University.

10. Hughes never learned why a call inviting him to reconsider his proposed resignation never came (interview with grandson H. Stuart Hughes, December 6, 1965).

11. Castle Diary, April 15 and 20, 1925.

12. Coolidge became increasingly open in his criticisms of Hoover after the latter began to interfere in the work of the State and Treasury departments and to propose himself as head of those departments as well as the logical successor to the president himself. Assistant Secretary William R. Castle, who frequently served as a back-channel informant to the president on foreign affairs, emphasized that "all the Jews who surround [Hoover] tell him what a great man he is every day of his life." See White, *A Puritan in Babylon*, 353; also Castle Diary, April 15, 1925; January 4, 7, and 11, 1926; October 4, December 9–10, 1927; comment about Jews, July 28, 1926.

13. Castle Diary, November 16, 1928.

14. Castle Diary, April 8, 1925; March 30, 1926.

15. Castle Diary, January 25, 1926; February 13, 1928.

16. Coolidge to Andrew Mellon, June 28, 1927, Mss. in private hands.

17. Frank Stearns explanation, in Castle Diary, December 30, 1924.

18. On the Foreign Service, see Warren F. Ilchman, *Professional Diplomacy in the United States, 1779–1939* (Chicago, 1961); and Waldo Heinrichs, *American Ambassador: Joseph Grew and the Development of the United States Diplomatic Tradition* (Boston, 1966); for a more critical appreciation, cf. Martin Weil, *A Pretty Good Club: The Founding Fathers of the U.S. Foreign Service* (New York, 1978).

19. I base these judgments in part on treatments of personnel matters in the Diary of William R. Castle (who rose from head of the Western European Division to undersecretary, 1920–33); as well as the Papers of Joseph Grew, who handled personnel matters as undersecretary, 1924–27, also in Houghton Library, Harvard University.

20. Joseph Brandes, *Herbert Hoover and Economic Diplomacy: Department of Commerce Policy, 1921–1928* (Pittsburgh, 1962); Ellis W. Hawley, ed., *Herbert Hoover as Secretary of Commerce* (Iowa City, 1981).

21. Lester Chandler, *Benjamin Strong: Central Banker* (Washington, D.C., 1958); Steven V. O. Clarke, *Central Bank Cooperation, 1924–1931* (New York, 1967).

22. William B. Kelly, Jr., "Antecedents of Present Commercial Policy, 1922–1934," in *Studies in United States Commercial Policy* (Chapel Hill, 1963); J. Richard Snyder, "Coolidge, Costigan, and the Tariff Commission," *Mid-America* 50 (April 1968): 131–48; ibid., "William S. Culbertson and the Formation of Modern Com-

mercial Policy, 1917–1925," *Kansas Historical Quarterly* 35 (Winter 1969): 396–410.

23. See, e.g., D. F. Fleming, *The United States and World Organization, 1920–1933* (New York, 1938); Arthur M. Schlesinger, Jr., *The Imperial Presidency* (New York, 1974).

24. Charles Prince to Henry Cabot Lodge, January 16, 1919, Box 54, Lodge Papers.

25. Lodge to Lord Charnwood, January 24, 1920, Box 66, Lodge Papers; also Lodge to James M. Beck, September 30, 1920, ibid.; cf. James M. Beck, *The Passing of the New Freedom* (New York, 1920).

26. When at the 1924 convention the chairman of the Republican National Committee asked Mellon what he thought of Borah, the secretary quipped: "I never think of him unless somebody mentions his name" (White, *A Puritan in Babylon*, 302n). But few had Mellon's courage—or his private income.

27. See the much-praised book by Robert David Johnson, *The Peace Progressives and American Foreign Relations* (Cambridge, Mass., 1995).

28. Richard Coke Lower, *A Bloc of One: The Political Career of Hiram Johnson* (Stanford, 1993), 169, 179–80.

29. John Maurer and Erik Goldstein, eds., *The Washington Confererence, 1921–1922* (London, 1994); Michael Dunne, *The United States and the World Court, 1920–1935* (New York, 1988); Karen A. J. Miller, "The Formulation of the Dawes Plan: The Impact of Domestic Politics on Foreign Policy Making," paper presented at the American Historical Association, 1996.

30. Lower, *A Bloc of One*, 212–30.

31. Castle Diary, January 14, 1926. The immediate impetus for the observation derived from Congressional objections to the Italian debt settlement.

32. Merlo J. Pusey, *Charles Evans Hughes*, 2 vols. (New York, 1951); also interview with H. Stuart Hughes, December 6, 1965.

33. Hughes to A. Lawrence Lowell, July 20, 1922, Box 4B, Hughes Papers, Library of Congress.

34. U.S. Treasury, *Annual Report, 1919* (Washington, D.C., 1920), 1901; quoted by Vincent Carosso, *Investment Banking in America* (Cambridge, Mass., 1970), 240.

35. Quoted in Melvyn Leffler, "Expansionist Impulses and Domestic Constraints, 1921–1932," in William H. Becker and Samuel F. Wells, Jr., *Economics and World Power* (New York, 1984), 259. The argument that follows draws heavily on Leffler's figures as well as his brilliant analysis.

36. Leffler, ibid., 228, 231, 258.

37. See the helpful discussion of the export lobby in Joan Hoff Wilson, *American Business and Foreign Policy, 1920–1933* (Lexington, Ky., 1971).

38. For the quotation, see Quint and Ferrell, *The Talkative President*, 113.

39. Alfred D. Chandler, Jr., *The Visible Hand: The Managerial Revolution in American Business* (Cambridge, Mass., 1977), 285–376; David Landes, *The Unbound Prometheus: Technological Change and Industrial Development in Western Europe from 1750 to the Present* (Cambridge, 1969), 231–358.

40. John W. Kendrick with Maude R. Pech, *Productivity Trends in the United States* (Princeton, N.J., 1961). In the 1920s, labor claimed only 81.2 percent of total

productivity gain, increasing the competitive advantage of U.S. industry (ibid., 128–30).

41. Mira Wilkins, *The Maturing of Multinational Enterprise: American Business Abroad from 1914 to 1970* (Cambridge, Mass., 1974).

42. Burton I. Kaufman, *Efficiency and Expansion: Foreign Trade Organization in the Wilson Administration, 1913–1921* (Westport, Conn., 1974).

43. League of Nations, *Industrialization and Foreign Trade* (Geneva, 1945), 13.

44. P. L. Yates, *Forty Years of Foreign Trade* (London, 1959), 32–33, 49–50; good analysis in Derek H. Aldcroft, *From Versailles to Wall Street* (Berkeley, 1977), 305–13.

45. Gerd Hardach, *The First World War* (Berkeley, 1977), 8; Leffler, "Expansionist Impulses and Domestic Constraints," 248.

46. Hoff Wilson, *American Business and Foreign Policy*, 103; Leffler, "Expansionist Impulses," 248.

47. Vincent Carosso, *Investment Banking in America*, 240–55.

48. Charles Kindleberger, *The World in Depression, 1929–1939* (Berkeley, 1986), 10–12.

49. Stephen A. Schuker, *The End of French Predominance in Europe* (Chapel Hill, 1976), 242–43, 355–56; Jon Jacobson, *Locarno Diplomacy* (Princeton, N.J., 1972), 14–26; Melvyn Leffler, *The Elusive Quest* (Chapel Hill, 1979), 114–15.

50. Coolidge conversation with William R. Castle, September 23, 1923, Castle Diary.

51. Thomas H. Buckley, *The United States and the Washington Conference, 1921–1922* (Knoxville, 1970).

52. Armistice Day Speech, in *New York Times*, November 12, 1928. Coolidge had ample reason to express annoyance. Lord Robert Cecil, who quit the British government in protest, charged that Winston Churchill and his other cabinet colleagues had torpedoed the Geneva Naval Conference largely out of pique at the growth of American power. British policy was "much more directed to the amour propre of the two countries than to any strategical considerations" (Cecil to 4th Marquess of Salisbury, July 18 and 31, 1927, Lord Robert Cecil Papers, Add. Mss. 51086, British Library). For full treatment of the Geneva Conference, see also Richard W. Fanning, *Peace and Disarmament: Naval Rivalry and Arms Control, 1922–1933* (Lexington, Ky., 1995).

53. Benjamin Rhodes, "Reassessing Uncle Shylock," *Journal of American History* 55 (March 1969): 389.

54. Robert Pastor, *Congress and the Politics of U.S. Foreign Economic Policy, 1929–1976* (Berkeley, 1980), 78.

55. For evidence that the president himself ordered the replacement of Culbertson, see Castle Diary, March 16 and May 21, 1925; for indications that Culbertson bitterly resented the policy changes that his successor carried through at the Tariff Commission, see ibid., May 20, 1926.

56. Stephen A. Schuker, *American "Reparations" to Germany, 1919–1933* (Princeton, N.J., 1988), 97–101.

57. Elisabeth Glaser-Schmidt, "German and American Concepts to Restore a Liberal World Trading System after World War I," in Hans-Jürgen Schröder, ed., *Confrontation and Cooperation: Germany and the United States, 1900–1924* (Providence and Oxford, 1993), 353–76; Werner Link, *Die amerikanische Stabilisierungs-*

politik in Deutschland, 1921–32 (Düsseldorf, 1970), 190–99, 324–37; Leffler, *Elusive Quest*, 51–53, 165–73, 295–300.

58. Hal B. Lary et al., *The United States in the World Economy* (Washington, D.C., 1943), 54–79. For a spirited defense of the high-tariff position, see also Alfred E. Eckes, *Opening America's Markets: U.S. Foreign Trade Policy since 1776* (Chapel Hill, 1995).

59. See Denise Artaud, *La question des dettes interalliées et la reconstruction de l'Europe (1917–1929)*, 2 vols. (Lille, France, 1978); also Ellen Schrecker, *The Hired Money: The French Debt to the United States, 1917–1929* (New York, 1978).

60. Commerce Department "Memorandum on War Debt Settlement," June 1926, State Department Record Group 59, 800.51W89/283, National Archives.

61. Frank Costigliola, *Awkward Dominion, 1919–1933* (Ithaca, 1984), 339.

62. Quint and Ferrell, *The Talkative President*, 176.

63. For some of his flat and maddeningly discreet statements at press conferences, see ibid., 174–200.

64. Castle Diary, May 3, 1927.

65. For figures, see Schuker, *American "Reparations" to Germany*, 90–97.

66. Schuker, *The End of French Predominance in Europe*, 277.

67. Kellogg report on cabinet meeting, in Castle Diary, April 20, 1925.

68. Schuker, *American "Reparations" to Germany*, 35–46; see also the discussion in William McNeil, *American Money and the Weimar Republic* (New York, 1986), 135–96.

69. Stephen A. Schuker, "American Foreign Policy and the Young Plan, 1929," in Gustav Schmidt, ed., *Konstellationen internationaler Politik, 1924–1932* (Bochum, Germany, 1983), 122–29.

70. Castle Diary, August 7 and 27, September 26, October 22, 1928.

71. *New York Times*, November 12, 1928.

72. Castle Diary, November 15, 1928, reporting conversations with Lady Astor, Sir Robert Craigie and Sir Robert Vansittart of the Foreign Office, and Sir Warren Fisher of the Treasury.

73. Castle Diary, August 3, September 27, December 9–10, 1927, March 10, May 1, 1928.

74. Gilbert to Mellon, May 7, 1928, Box 6, David I. Finley Papers, Library of Congress.

75. Mellon to S. Parker Gilbert, May 24, 1928, copy in private hands; Mellon comment about engineers recalled in Garrard B. Winston interview, April 7, 1942, same collection.

76. Castle Diary, January 10–11, 1929.

77. Robinson to Hoover, January 13, 1929, Robinson individual file 1059, Herbert Hoover Presidential Papers, Herbert Hoover Presidential Library.

78. Note Coolidge's characteristic complaint in 1928 that as president he found his "privileges of free speech are a good deal curtailed, because I am president" (Quint and Ferrell, *The Talkative President*, 169). Neither Hoover nor Franklin Roosevelt would have imposed such a self-denying ordinance.

Contributors

MICHAEL A. BERNSTEIN, associate professor in the Department of History and associate faculty member in the Department of Economics at the University of California, San Diego, is the author of *The Great Depression: Delayed Recovery and Economic Change in America, 1929–1939* (1987), and *Understanding American Economic Decline* (1994).

JOHN BRAEMAN, professor of history at the University of Nebraska, is the author or editor of *Before the Civil Rights Revolution: The Old Court and Individual Rights* (1988), *American Foreign Policy in the Twentieth Century* (1971, with Robert Bremner and David Brody), *American Politics in the Twentieth Century* (1969), *Change and Continuity in Twentieth-Century America: The 1920's* (1968, with Robert Bremner and David Brody), *Wilson: Great Lives Observed* (1972), *The New Deal: The National Level* (1975), *The New Deal: The State and Local Levels* (1975, with Robert Bremner and David Brody), and *Albert J. Beveridge: American Nationalist* (1971).

WARREN I. COHEN, Distinguished University Professor, University of Maryland, Baltimore County, has authored *Empire Without Tears: American Foreign Relations, 1921–1933* (1987), *Lyndon Johnson Confronts the World: American Foreign Policy, 1963–1968* (1994, with Nancy Bernkopf Tucker), *America in the Age of Soviet Power, 1945–1991* (1993), *East Asian Art and American Culture: A Study in International Relations* (1992), *America, China, and Japan in Wartime, 1931–1949* (1990, with Akira Iriye), *The Great Powers in East Asia, 1953–1960* (1990, with Akira Iriye), *America's Response to China: A History of Sino American Relations* (1971), *America and Japan in the Postwar World* (1989, with Akira Iriye), *New Frontiers in American East-Asian Relations* (1982), *Dean Rusk* (1980), *The Chinese Connection: Roger S. Greene, Thomas W. Lamont, George E. Sokolsky, and American-East Asian Relations* (1978), *The American Revisionists: The Lessons of Intervention in World War I* (1967).

LYNN DUMENIL, professor of history at Occidental College, is the author of *The Modern Temper: American Culture and Society in the 1920s* (1995) and *Freemasonry and American Culture, 1880–1930* (1984).

RONALD EDSFORTH, associate professor of history at Dartmouth College, is the author or editor of *Popular Culture and Political Change in Modern America* (1991, with Larry Bennett), *Class Conflict and Cultural*

Consensus: The Making of a Mass Consumer Society in Flint, Michigan (1987), and *Auto Work* (1995, with Robert Asher).

ROBERT H. FERRELL, professor emeritus at Indiana University in Bloomington, has edited or authored *The Talkative President: The Off-the-Record Press Conferences of Calvin Coolidge* (1979, with Howard H. Quint), *Off the Record: The Private Papers of Harry S. Truman* (1980), *The Eisenhower Diaries* (1981), *The Diary of James C. Hagerty: Eisenhower in Mid-Course, 1954–1955* (1983), *Dear Bess: The Letters from Harry to Bess Truman, 1910–1959* (1983), *American Diplomacy in the Great Depression: Hoover-Stimson Foreign Policy, 1929–1933* (1957), *American Diplomacy* (1959), *The American Secretaries of State and Their Diplomacy: Frank B. Kellogg and Henry L. Stimson* (1963), *The American Secretaries of State and Their Diplomacy: George C. Marshall* (1966), *Foundations of American Diplomacy: 1775–1972* (1968), *America as a World Power, 1872–1945* (1971), *America in a Divided World, 1945–1972* (1975), *The Ordeal of World Power* (1975), *Peace in Their Time: The Origins of the Kellogg-Briand Pact* (1952), *Woodrow Wilson and World War I* (1985), *Ill-Advised: Presidential Health and Public Trust* (1992), *Harry S. Truman: His Life on the Family Farms* (1991), *Harry S. Truman and the Modern American Presidency* (1983), *Choosing Truman: The Democratic Convention of 1944* (1994), *Harry S. Truman: A Life* (1994), *FDR's Quiet Confidant: The Autobiography of Frank C. Walker* (1997), and *The Presidency of Calvin Coolidge* (1998).

JOHN EARL HAYNES, twentieth century political historian, Manuscript Division, Library of Congress, is the author of *The Soviet World of American Communism* (1998 with Harvey Klehr and Kiril Anderson), *Red Scare or Red Menace? American Communism and Anticommunism in the Cold War Era* (1996), *The Secret World of American Communism* (1995, with Harvey Klehr and Fridrikh Firsov), *The American Communist Movement: Storming Heaven Itself* (1992, with Harvey Klehr), *Communism and Anti-Communism in the United States: An Annotated Guide to Historical Writings* (1987), and *Dubious Alliance: The Making of Minnesota's DFL Party* (1984).

PAUL JOHNSON has authored *The Suez War* (1957), *Journey into Chaos* (1958), *Merrie England* (1964), *The Offshore Islanders: England's People from Roman Occupation to the Present* (1972), *The Highland Jaunt* (1973), *Elizabeth I: A Biography* (1974), *Pope John XXIII* (1974), *A Place in History* (1975), *The Life and Time of Edward III* (1973), *Statesmen and Nations* (1971), *A History of Christianity* (1976), *Enemies of Society* (1977), *The Civilization of Ancient Egypt* (1978), *Civilizations of the Holy Land* (1979), *British Cathedrals* (1980), *Ireland, Land of Troubles: A History from the Twelfth Century to the Present Day* (1980), *The Recovery of Freedom* (1980), *Modern Times: The World from the Twenties to the Eighties* (1983), *A His-*

tory of the English People (1985), *A History of the Jews* (1987), *Unsecular America* (1986), *Intellectuals* (1988), *The Birth of the Modern: World Society, 1815–1830* (1991), and *The Quest for God: A Personal Pilgrimage* (1996).

DANIEL J. LEAB, professor of history at Seton Hall University, is editor of *Labor History*, and author or editor of *American Working Class History* (1983), *A Union of Individuals: The Formation of the American Newspaper Guild* (1970), *From Sambo to Superspade: The Black Experience in Motion Pictures* (1975), *Federal Bureau of Investigation Confidential Files: Communist Activity in the Entertainment Industry* (1991), *Labor History Archives in the United States: A Guide for Researching and Teaching* (1992), and *The Labor History Reader* (1985).

GEORGE NASH is the author of *The Conservative Intellectual Movement in America Since 1945* (1976), *Herbert Hoover and Stanford University* (1988), *Herbert Hoover: Political Orphan* (1989), and *The Life of Herbert Hoover*, vol. 1: *The Engineer, 1874–1914* (1983), vol. 2: *The Humanitarian, 1914–1917* (1988), and vol. 3: *Master of Emergencies, 1917–1918* (1996).

ELISABETH I. PERRY, president of the Society for Historians of the Gilded Age and Progressive Era, has authored or edited *From Theology to History: French Religious Controversy and the Revocation of the Edict of Nantes* (1973), *Belle Moskowitz: Feminine Politics and the Exercise of Power in the Age of Alfred E. Smith* (1987), and *The Challenge of Feminist Biography: Writing the Lives of Modern American Women* (1992).

STEPHEN A. SCHUKER, William W. Corcoran Professor of History at the University of Virginia, is the author of *The End of French Predominance in Europe: The Financial Crisis of 1924 and the Adoption of the Dawes Plan* (1976) and *American "Reparations" to Germany, 1919–1933: Implications for the Third-World Debt Crisis* (1988).

GENE SMILEY, professor of economics at Marquette University, is the author of *The American Economy in the Twentieth Century* (1994).

Index

Page numbers appearing in **bold** type indicate tables.

313

University Press of New England publishes books under its own imprint and is the publisher for Brandeis University Press, Dartmouth College, Middlebury College Press, University of New Hampshire, Tufts University, and Wesleyan University Press.

Library of Congress Cataloging-in-Publication Data
Calvin Coolidge and the Coolidge era : essays on the history of the
   1920s / edited by John Earl Haynes.
        p.   cm.
   Based on papers presented at a Library of Congress symposium held
in 1995.
   Includes index.
   ISBN 0–8444–0922–7
   1. United States—Politics and government—1923–1929—Congresses.
2. Coolidge, Calvin. 1872–1933—Congresses. 3. United States—
History—1919–1933—Congresses. I. Haynes, John Earl.
II. Library of Congress.
E791.C67   1998
973.91'5'092—dc21   98–13224